# THE IMPACT
# OF THE CIVIL WAR AND
# RECONSTRUCTION ON
# ARKANSAS

# THE IMPACT
# OF THE
# CIVIL WAR AND
# RECONSTRUCTION
# ON ARKANSAS

## PERSISTENCE IN THE MIDST OF RUIN

# Carl H. Moneyhon

The University of Arkansas Press
Fayetteville
2002

06   05   04   03   02      5   4   3   2   1

Designer: Amanda McDonald Key

☯ The paper used in this publication meets the minimum requirements
of the American National Standard for Permanence of Paper for Printed
Library Materials Z39.48-1984.

*Library of Congress Cataloging-in-Publication Data*
Moneyhon, Carl H., 1944–
   The impact of the Civil War and reconstruction on Arkansas :
persistence in the midst of ruin / Carl H. Moneyhon.
      p. cm.
   Originally published: Baton Rouge : Louisiana State University
Press, c1994.
   Includes bibliographical references (p. ) and index.
   ISBN 1-55728-735-X (pbk. : alk. paper)
      1. Arkansas—History—Civil War, 1861–1865. 2. Reconstruction—
Arkansas. 3. Arkansas—History—1865– I. Title.
E553 .M66 2002
976.7'04—dc21

                                                            2002026796

This project is supported in part through a grant from the Arkansas
Humanities Council and the National Endowment for the Humanities.

*To Patricia, for the usual reasons, and
for Desmond Allen and Kirsten Elizabeth Rose Walloch,
grandchildren who have given
me new joy and purpose*

# CONTENTS

# TABLES AND MAPS

## TABLES

# ACKNOWLEDGMENTS

THIS HISTORY OF ARKANSAS DURING THE CRITICAL YEARS of 1850 through 1874 began in the summer of 1977 during an NEH Summer Teaching Seminar with the late Bell I. Wiley at Emory University. That seminar provided me with the opportunity to explore the literature on the interaction of war and society and first work with some of the ideas that are a part of this book. In the intervening years I have incurred many debts to individuals who encouraged and supported this study, and I wish to thank many of them here.

Two of my greatest debts are owed to the National Endowment for the Humanities and the Arkansas Humanities Council. The NEH summer seminar in 1977 not only gave me the time to start this work but also offered an intellectually stimulating climate with the participation of many wonderful scholars, particularly Melton McLaurin and Robert B. Toplin, who are both now at the University of North Carolina at Wilmington. An NEH Research Award during the 1981–82 academic year allowed me to carry out basic research involved in this project. The Arkansas Humanities Council offered assistance in 1980 that allowed me to transcribe tax rolls from manuscript form to computer format with the help of two excellent assistants—Eric Melvin, now teaching philosophy in Chicago, and Todd Kersten, who is currently working to develop banks in Warsaw, Poland.

The University of Arkansas at Little Rock also encouraged this project, particularly in providing support with travel funds. Most of all, however, the university provided a congenial atmosphere, despite the teaching load, for research and writing. The university created and developed special collections and archives with excellent manuscript holdings in nineteenth-century Arkansas history. It has also worked to develop a history faculty that gave me colleagues who always have been supportive and at the same time critical and stimulating. I appreciate particularly T. Harri Baker for his numerous readings of this entire manuscript. I also thank Edward Anson, S. Charles Bolton, Thomas Kaiser, Pat Melvin (now at Loyola University of Chicago), and C. Fred Williams for reading portions of the manuscript or putting up with all too many hallway discussions as my ideas took shape.

The manuscript was read in various stages by a number of individuals whose assistance was valued and whose comments played roles in its development. I especially appreciate the time devoted to it by Randolph B. Campbell of the University of North Texas, Fred Bailey of Abiline Christian University, Harold Woodman of Purdue University, and Tom Dillard of the University of Central Arkansas.

Libraries and archives were essential to this work. I especially want to thank Bobby Roberts, coauthor of another series of books with me and now director of the Central Arkansas Library System, who began the special collections at UALR for his support. His successor, Linda Pine, has been of equal help. Staff members such as Joy Geisler and Paula Kaiser have done more than their share of telephone research and note checking for me. Director John Ferguson and Russell Baker of the Arkansas History Commission were generous with their time and support. I appreciate the help of Michael Dabrishius, director of special collections at the University of Arkansas at Fayetteville, and Faye Phillips, head of the Louisiana and Lower Mississippi Valley Collections at Louisiana State University, Baton Rouge. Many staff members at the Library of Congress, the National Archives, the Amistad Research Center at Tulane University, the Duke University Library, the Southern History Collection at the University of North Carolina at Chapel Hill Library, and the Tennessee State Library also provided useful assistance.

I am also under obligation to the staff at Louisiana State University Press for all of their help. I would like to thank editor-in-chief Margaret Dalrymple for her early encouragement. Senior editor John Easterly and managing editor Catherine Landry have provided thoroughly professional guidance throughout. Gerry Anders' capable copy editing pointed up many problems in the manuscript and added greatly to the bettering of the final version. They and others have made the sometimes painful experience of publishing a pleasure.

Lastly, I wish to acknowledge two personal debts. The first is to Patricia Moneyhon, who has been supportive through what sometimes seems like too many of these projects. She is a critic whose opinion I value, even when I do not take her advice. I am not sure she realized fully what marrying a historian entailed, but she has never failed to give what she could to support my efforts.

The second is to John Hope Franklin for what he gave me as a graduate student and what he continues to provide. This book moves away from some of the topical research interests that motivated me to work with him at the University of Chicago, but he remains daily an inspiration to me in my work. A model scholar and teacher, he serves as an example of the finest characteristics that our profession can achieve. I hope to achieve only a degree of his excellence in my work.

Ultimately every author must be responsible for a work, and I hope that those who have supported me will consider this work to have been worth their time and aid.

# ABBREVIATIONS

| | |
|---|---|
| *Acts of Arkansas* | *Acts Passed by the General Assembly of the State of Arkanas.* Various publication places and dates. |
| AHC | Arkansas History Commission. |
| *AHQ* | *Arkansas Historical Quarterly.* |
| *Arkansas House Journal* | *Journal of the House of Representatives of the General Assembly of the State of Arkansas.* Various publication places and dates. |
| *Arkansas Reports* | *Reports of Cases at Law and in Equity Argued and Determined in the Supreme Court of Arkansas.* Various publication places and dates. |
| *Arkansas Senate Journal* | *Journal of the Senate of the General Assembly of the State of Arkansas.* Various publication places and dates. |
| ARC | Amistad Research Center, Tulane University. |
| *AS/AN* | George P. Rawick, ed. *The American Slave: A Composite Autobiography.* 24 vols. Westport, Conn., 1972–. *Arkansas Narratives,* Vols. 8–10. |
| *AS/ON* | George P. Rawick, ed. *The American Slave: A Composite Autobiography: Supplement, Series 1.* 12 vols. Westport, Conn., 1977. *Oklahoma Narratives,* Vol. 12. |
| BRFAL | Bureau of Refugees, Freedmen, and Abandoned Lands. |
| DU | Special Collections, William Perkins Library, Duke University. |
| *JSH* | *Journal of Southern History.* |
| *G/CA* | *Biographical and Historical Memoirs of Pulaski, Jefferson, Lonoke, Faulkner, Grant, Saline, Perry, Garland, and Hot Spring Counties, Arkansas.* Chicago, 1889. |
| *G/EA* | *Biographical and Historical Memoirs of Eastern Arkansas.* Chicago, 1890. |
| *G/NEA* | *Biographical and Historical Memoirs of Northeast Arkansas.* Chicago 1889. |
| *G/NWA* | *History of Benton, Washington, Carroll, Madison, Crawford, Franklin, and Sebastian Counties, Arkansas.* Chicago, 1889. |

| | |
|---|---|
| *G/SA* | *Biographical and Historical Memoirs of Southern Arkansas.* Chicago, 1890. |
| ISHL | Illinois State Historical Library. |
| LC | Library of Congress. |
| LSU | Louisiana and Lower Mississippi Valley Collections, Hill Memorial Library, Louisiana State University at Baton Rouge. |
| LSUS | Special Collections, Louisiana State University at Shreveport. |
| NA | National Archives |
| OR | *The War of the Rebellion: A Compilation of the Official Records of the Union and Confederate Armies.* 128 vols. Washington, D.C., 1880–1901. |
| TSLA | Tennessee State Library and Archives. |
| UAF | Special Collections, University of Arkansas at Fayetteville. |
| UALR | Special Collections, University of Arkansas at Little Rock. |
| UNC | Southern History Collection, University of North Carolina at Chapel Hill. |
| UT | American History Center, University of Texas at Austin. |

# The Impact

## of the

## Civil War and

## Reconstruction

## on Arkansas

# INTRODUCTION

IN 1875 CHARLES NORDHOFF TOURED THE COTTON STATES of the South as a reporter for the New York *Herald*. The Civil War had been over for ten years, and Nordhoff wanted to know the extent of change brought about by the war and Reconstruction. One of the states that he visited was Arkansas, where he encountered difficulties in finding a simple answer to his problem. Obvious and dramatic changes had occurred, yet many things appeared to be much as they had been before the war.

The most apparent difference between pre- and postwar Arkansas was the position of blacks. Slavery was gone. Black workers had made the transition to free labor, and in some cases they seemed to have achieved the status of yeoman farmers. The freedmen still held political rights in 1875. The white community, which had fought in part to maintain slavery, appeared to have accepted the freedom of the former slaves.

There were also signs of suffering resulting—at least according to the local Democrats—from the misrule of the Republican state and local Reconstruction governments. Nordhoff reported a state debt of more than fifteen million dollars, run up on a people "singularly innocent of political wiles" by "young and enterprising men" to support railroads, build levees, and construct other public works. Although taxes were higher than they had been before the war, few of the proposed projects were ever built. Despite increased state budgets, Nordhoff found that "the old State-house looks as dilapidated as when the reconstruction began, and has been changed in nothing except having its door-lintels mutilated that a Brooks cannon might be squeezed into the hall."[1]

Other than the changes brought about by emancipation and during Reconstruction, Nordhoff found that much remained unaltered in Arkansas. The source of this continuity, he perceived, was the persistence of the antebellum planter elite. Relationships between the planters and the rest of society were no longer the same, but the position of this elite group economically, socially, and politically remained the same. They retained ownership of their land. Their former slaves were free, but most continued to work for them as tenants. The planter might rent out his lands and keep a store with a cotton gin and gristmill, but he managed his lands in much the same way planters had overseen their properties for decades. "In practice," Nordhoff wrote, "the planter finds it necessary to ride daily through his fields to see that the renters are at work, and aid them with his advice. During the winter, he hires them to chop wood for his own use, and to

---

1. Charles Nordhoff, *The Cotton States in the Spring and Summer of 1875* (New York, 1876), 29, 37–40.

split rails and keep up the fences." In addition, black workers often voted with their former masters, ensuring planter domination of state and local government.[2]

Nordhoff also found a sense of optimism about the future of the state's agricultural interests similar to that held in the antebellum years. Despite losses during the war and the problems of Reconstruction, leaders of all political parties informed the newspaperman that economic activity was reviving rapidly throughout the state. In March, 1875, they assured Nordhoff that if the season were favorable the state would produce more corn, wheat, and cotton than ever before. The statement of a black supporter of Governor Joseph Brooks could have been the words of an antebellum planter when he said: "What we need now is men and capital; . . . we are done with politics for a while, and will all go to work in earnest to recover our losses and make the State rich. Give us only a good crop this year, and we'll be out of the woods."[3]

Nordhoff's portrait suggests that the Civil War and Reconstruction had ended slavery without revolutionizing society. For many contemporary Arkansans this conclusion must have seemed absurd. Their worlds had been turned upside down and their futures destroyed. The society they had known was obliterated. W. E. Bevens, who had left Jackson County in 1861 with the Jackson Guards and had fought at First Bull Run and in battles in Tennessee and Georgia, returned home in 1865 to find everything changed. He remembered that "those of us who returned at all, returned to find our (personal) properties destroyed, ourselves with no money and no jobs, and all our friends in the same condition. Everyone had to start at the bottom."[4]

Nordhoff's suggestion that by 1874 prosperity had returned would also have appeared a gross misstatement. Many Arkansans did not see prosperity but instead perceived a once-wealthy world that had been deprived of its resources. Its people were not on the verge of new wealth but were impoverished, and anything they accomplished was through suffering and hardship. Elmira Snodgrass of Little Rock concluded: "The Federal army robbed my children of their rights before they were born. The Old South with all its resources was theirs by inheritance, but in lieu of its advantages, they have been made a part of the brick and mortar worked into the building of a New South."[5]

2. *Ibid.*, 37–40.
3. *Ibid.*, 29–34.
4. Lady Elizabeth Luker, "Post Civil War Period in Jackson County," *Stream of History,* IV (1966), 31.
5. *Confederate Women of Arkansas in the Civil War, 1861–'65: Memorial Reminiscences* (Little Rock, 1907), 130.

The conflicting views of contemporary observers help explain the continuing historical interest in and disagreements over the impact of the Civil War and Reconstruction in the South. Although showing how the South changed in these years has proved difficult, historians have continued to wrestle with the problem because an answer has been seen as critical to explaining the subsequent history of the region—its poverty, its racial institutions, its society and politics. This study examines Arkansas during the period 1850 to 1874 in an effort to show the war's impact. It tries to reconcile the contemporary evidence into a comprehensive account and to produce a historical model that resolves some of the difficulties within the extensive existing literature on the topic.

The historical work on the question of the continuity or discontinuity of the antebellum South is large, and consequently any study must begin with a review of the discussion that has taken place. The most important modern comprehensive analysis is that advanced by C. Vann Woodward in his 1951 study *Origins of the New South*. Although not writing specifically about the war or Reconstruction, Woodward explained the origins of a community that languished, afflicted with poverty and racism, while the rest of the United States moved toward modernity and economic prosperity. He radically altered the way historians looked at the South and at previous histories of it. His dominant theme was that the South had experienced revolutionary change.

The heart of change, in Woodward's view, was economic and war-related. The devastation and pillage caused by invading armies destroyed basic material resources, particularly the wealth of the antebellum planter and farmer. Economic recovery consequently fell into the hands of a new class, composed of merchants, industrialists, and a few planters. They monopolized the means of production in the South, particularly the land. As a result, most postwar farmers worked land that they did not own, thus missing out on what Woodward called the "economic virtues associated with proprietorship." To obtain the credit necessary for them to operate, they were forced to mortgage their crops, the only thing that they had for use as collateral. The crop-lien system—called by Woodward "financial baling wire"—made the farmer an agent of the merchant, who refinanced only for the production of more cotton, the principal cash crop, and pushed the South into a one-crop system.[6]

The new system of agriculture proved to be inefficient. Land monopoly, the one-crop system, absentee ownership, and soil mining combined to prevent the South from successfully rebuilding its antebellum wealth. The

6. C. Vann Woodward, *Origins of the New South, 1877–1913* (Baton Rouge, 1951), 177–84.

resulting grim poverty of the postwar South caused rural and urban life to languish before 1880. Once the wealthiest section in the country, the South was now the poorest. By 1880 the per capita wealth of the South was $376, compared with a per capita wealth of $1,086 in the rest of the nation.[7]

According to Woodward, the economic revolution produced changes in basic social structure. As the planter class gave way to the new elite of merchants and industrialists, the middle class of independent landowners that had numerically dominated prewar society diminished in numbers and status as its members lost land and economic power. A new class of poor whites, who had not been present in large numbers before the war, emerged at the bottom of society. Landless, caught up along with the freedmen in the crop-lien system, they drifted across the South looking for new opportunities in places such as Arkansas and Texas.[8]

Economic depression also thwarted efforts by the former slaves to improve their situation, crushing their aspirations for economic independence. They would remain on the plantation lands, farming as tenants rather than slaves. They would be like the poor whites, farmers without lands, distinguished by being even more impoverished and by their color. The discrimination of slavery was replaced by the discrimination of caste. Blacks were forced to live their lives separately, initially in social practice, eventually in legal segregation. Their labor was needed, but white society refused to accept them as anything other than people of a second class.[9]

Changes in the economic and in the social order affected the ideas and attitudes of Southerners. The values of the new elite were espoused rather than those of the antebellum elite. The aristocrat was no longer the ideal model; the businessman was. The virtues traditionally associated with Yankees became the ideal; the worship of money was commonplace. The individual who could make money was put on the same level as the person with a heritage of family wealth and culture. Woodward maintained that bourgeois values triumphed even in religion, where the new elite imposed its Puritan world view on the faith of the region.[10]

Woodward saw the final proof of the South's change in the emergence of new political leadership. "Redemption"—the political triumph of the Democratic party following Reconstruction—marked the final stage in the revolutionary process begun in 1865. A new political elite triumphed that represented the interests of industrialists and capitalists and that had minimal ties to the old planter regime. Planters allied themselves to the new leaders

7. *Ibid.*, 111–13, 140.
8. *Ibid.*, 110, 151–52, 179–80, 184.
9. *Ibid.*, 205–12.
10. *Ibid.*, 150–53, 171.

to protect themselves, but they no longer controlled government. Whig ideas of state-backed economic development, rather than the states'-rights ideas of the antebellum Democracy, dominated the language of the new leaders.[11]

Among scholars, Woodward's revisionist work remains the most widely accepted interpretation of the southern experience. Critics have emerged, however, who question Woodward's analysis and who have created two major postrevisionist schools. The first group to develop examined Woodward's explanation for the relative impoverishment of the postwar South. Instead of exploitation, they emphasized the role of market forces in producing New South economic conditions. The second school of critics attacked Woodward's emphasis upon change, arguing instead for continuity as the central theme of southern history from the pre- to postwar years.

The earliest critics, who emphasized the importance of market forces, were chiefly economic historians. They accepted Woodward's conclusion that the New South was different from the Old South, but not his idea that exploitation produced impoverishment. They concluded that the Civil War caused losses of capital, reducing the economic base of the South, and disorganized the labor force. The collapse of prices for important southern commodities, particularly cotton, compounded regional problems. The war and the market, then, produced postwar economic characteristics. The similarity of postwar growth rates in the South and North convinced these critics that postwar economic institutions were not responsible for regional conditions. The one-crop economy, the crop-lien system, and sharecropping and tenancy were seen as rational and understandable responses of capital, landowners, merchants, and labor to given conditions—responses productive of the best possible benefits for all parties.[12]

11. *Ibid.*, 1, 20–21.

12. For a discussion of this interpretation, see Robert Higgs, *The Transformation of the American Economy, 1865–1914: An Essay in Interpretation* (New York, 1971), 80–81, 108–109, 111, 112, 114; Higgs, *Competition and Coercion: Blacks in the American Economy, 1865–1914* (Cambridge, Mass., 1977); Stanley Engerman, "Some Economic Factors in Southern Backwardness in the Nineteenth Century," in *Essays in Regional Economics*, ed. John F. Kain and John R. Meyers (Cambridge, Mass., 1971), 300–302; Stephen DeCanio, *Agriculture in the Postbellum South: The Economics of Production and Supply* (Cambridge, Mass., 1974), 12–14; and Eugene Lerner, "Southern Output and Agricultural Income, 1860–1880," *Agricultural History*, XXXIII (1959), 117, 121.

On tenancy, see Marjorie Stratford Mendenhall, "The Rise of Southern Tenancy," *Yale Review*, n.s., XXVII (1937), 110–29; Robert Higgs, "Race, Tenure, and Resource Allocation in Southern Agriculture, 1910," *Journal of Economic History*, XXXIII (March, 1973), 149–69; Higgs, "Patterns of Farm Rental in the Georgia Cotton Belt, 1880–1900," *Journal of Economic History*, XXXIV (1974), 468–82; Higgs, "Did Southern Farmers Discriminate?" *Agricultural History*, XLVI (1972), 325–28; Higgs, "Did Southern Farmers Discriminate? Interpretive

By the 1970s and 1980s Woodward's interpretation faced a further challenge, by historians who emphasized continuity of the southern experience. They argued that despite physical destruction and the end of slavery, the basic institutions of the prewar South remained intact. No revolution occurred. This new interpretation rested primarily on new studies of the war's impact on the region's planter elite, and was enlarged subsequently to include reanalysis of how the war affected economic structures and political power.

Social historians of this school used new tools, particularly the computer and statistical analysis, to examine census and tax data, and their examinations of communities in Alabama, North Carolina, Texas, and Virginia produced a new model of southern society. They concluded, first, that the war did not destroy the antebellum planter elite, who either individually or as families persisted through the war years; second, that this elite maintained its control over the local economy despite wartime losses. Relying on more traditional methods, the same historians also concluded that the South's elite was able to retain its basic ideology—paternalism and an antibourgeois spirit—despite the end of slavery. Survival of the elite presented a continuing barrier to change in the South.[13]

Political historians reexamining state and county politics in South Carolina, North Carolina, and Virginia also advanced the idea of continuity. Their reevaluations showed continuity between antebellum and postbel-

Problems and Further Evidence," *Agricultural History*, XLIX (1975), 445–47; Joseph D. Reid, Jr., "Sharecropping as an Understandable Market Response: The Post-Bellum South," *Journal of Economic History*, XXXIII (1973), 106–30; Reid, "Antebellum Southern Rental Contracts," *Explorations in Economic History*, XIII (1976), 69–83; Reid, "Sharecropping and Agricultural Uncertainty," *Economic Development and Cultural Change*, XXIV (1976), 549–76; Reid, "Sharecropping in History and Theory," *Agricultural History*, XLIX (1975), 426–40; Reid, "Progress on Credit: Comment," *Agricultural History*, L (January), 117–24; and William Cohen, "Negro Involuntary Servitude in the South, 1865–1940," *JSH*, XLII (1976), 31–60.

A discussion of black labor in the immediate postwar era is in Ralph Schlomowitz, " 'Bound' or 'Free'? Black Labor in Cotton and Sugarcane Farming, 1865–1880," *JSH* , L (1984), 569–96.

13. Jonathan M. Wiener, *Social Origins of the New South: Alabama, 1860–1885* (Baton Rouge, 1978); Wiener, "Planter Persistence and Social Change, 1850–1870," *Journal of Interdisciplinary History*, VIII (1976), 235–60; Wiener, "Class Structure and Economic Development in the American South, 1865–1955," *American Historical Review*, LXXXIV (1979), 970–1006; Dwight B. Billings, Jr., *Planters and the Making of a 'New South': Class, Politics, and Development in North Carolina, 1865–1900* (Chapel Hill, 1979); Lee W. Formwalt, "Antebellum Planter Persistence: Southwest Georgia—A Case Study," *Plantation Society*, I (1981), 410–29; Randolph B. Campbell, *A Southern Community in Crisis: Harrison County, Texas, 1850–1880* (Austin, 1983); Kenneth S. Greenberg, "The Civil War and the Redistribution of Land: Adams County, Mississippi, 1860–1870," *Agricultural History*, LII (1978), 292–307.

lum local political leadership and in governmental operations. Individual politicians from the prewar years may not have reemerged afterward, but the same type of men held power. More important, the political ideas of the postwar leaders differed little from those of their prewar predecessors. A study of South Carolina, the only statewide political study within the continuity school, observed that the postwar Conservatives of that state to a man had been antebellum Democrats and that the world they tried to build after the war was based on the idea that antebellum and Confederate society represented the best possible model.[14]

Economic historians added to the argument for continuity. Critical of those scholars who emphasized a simple economic interpretation of the South's problems, they stressed the role played by social groups and ideas in restricting economic opportunities. Merchant monopoly and racism, outgrowths of prewar institutions, were seen as critical to the development of the crop-lien and labor systems. These systems in turn constrained freedom of action and autonomy in the southern economy and resulted in an emphasis on commodity production, a loss of agricultural self-sufficiency, low wages, and the neglect of meaningful economic diversification. The continuing concentration of the means of production among a small group burdened with antebellum ideas minimized disruption of the status quo.[15]

The work of scholars emphasizing market forces in the creation of postwar conditions has to some degree been integrated into Woodward's overall interpretation, but the continuity school has not. Recently it has faced its own challenges, with critics raising several major questions about it. One concerns the validity of the samples chosen to prove the persistence of elites and, thus, the universal applicability of the idea. A second question is whether the persistence of antebellum elites is pertinent to the issue of continuity at all, since even if elites did survive, their prewar social ideology did not. A third, although accepting the survival of the antebellum leaders, asks whether changes among other classes constituted the real revolution in antebellum society.

The methodological question was the earliest to emerge. The critics suggested that samples upon which continuity was based particularly over-

14. William J. Cooper, Jr., *The Conservative Regime: South Carolina, 1877–1890* (Baltimore, 1968), 13–25; Gail W. O'Brien, "Power and Influence in Mecklenburg County, 1850–1880," *North Carolina Historical Review*, LIV (1977), 121–44.

15. Gavin Wright, *The Political Economy of the Cotton South: Households, Markets, and Wealth in the Nineteenth Century* (New York, 1978), 183–84, ch. 6; Roger L. Ransom and Richard Sutch, *One Kind of Freedom: The Economic Consequences of Emancipation* (Cambridge, Mass., 1977), 7, 12–13, 88, 94, 177; Jay R. Mandle, *The Roots of Black Poverty: The Southern Plantation Economy After the Civil War* (Durham, N.C., 1978), 21, 23, 38.

looked two crucial variables—whether a community was urban or rural, and whether or not it was actually subjected to the destruction of the war— each of which could have produced different results. The critics produced their own studies, demonstrating that in some cases there was considerable prewar-to-postwar change. Although they have not disproved the continuity thesis, these scholars have shown that elite persistence was not universal, that we have much to learn about local social dynamics during the war, and that more local studies will be necessary before satisfactory generalizations can be made for the South as a whole.[16]

The argument that antebellum social ideology died during the war has been less convincingly tested. Its basic assumptions are that the ideology of the antebellum elite was paternalistic in nature and that paternalism could not survive in a world without slaves. Paternalism as the determining factor in labor relationships was replaced by the cash nexus. If ideology changed, the mere physical persistence of the planter elite is irrelevant. It does not matter if they survived if their world view did not. Unfortunately, historians disagree about what actually constituted antebellum planter ideology, leaving the issue of how it might have changed unresolved.[17]

Critics of postrevisionism desiring a broader picture of the war and southern society have produced studies suggesting that beneath the white elite the southern world was in considerable turmoil, a view that raises another challenge to the idea of continuity. Of these studies, one shows blacks in middle Tennessee migrating to towns, where they completely rejected the institutions of antebellum society that had relegated them to servile status and asserted a new role as free laborers and citizens. The same study, however, suggests that lower-class whites refused to take advantage of the destruction of antebellum society to create a new order and opted for a reconstruction of the old society that was even more inflexible than that which had existed. Such studies do not completely disprove the persistence thesis, but they do suggest the complexity of determining the war's impact on the South and indicate the need to take into account more than the elite in examining the issue.[18]

Going back to the problem raised at the beginning of this Introduction—

16. James Roark, *Masters Without Slaves* (New York, 1977), 151–269; Frank J. Huffman, Jr., "Town and Country in the South, 1850–1880: A Comparison of Urban and Rural Social Structures," *South Atlantic Quarterly*, LXXVI (1977), 366–81.

17. Michael Wayne, *The Reshaping of Plantation Society: The Natchez District, 1860 1880* (Baton Rouge, 1983), chaps. 5–6, pp. 202–204.

18. Steven Hahn, *The Roots of Southern Populism: Yeoman Farmers and the Transformation of the Georgia Upcountry, 1850–1890* (New York, 1983); Stephen V. Ash, *Middle Tennessee Society Transformed, 1860–1870: War and Peace in the Upper South* (Baton Rouge, 1988).

namely, whether Charles Nordhoff, W. E. Bevens, or Elmira Snodgrass best characterized what took place in Arkansas as a result of the Civil War and Reconstruction—this review of the general literature offers no answers. With a few notable exceptions, Arkansas' past has been overlooked by historians concerned with the Old South, the impact of the Civil War, and the emergence of the postwar South. The one conclusion that can be drawn from all of the work done through the last several years is that it is dangerous to draw conclusions at all concerning the basic issues connected with the war's impact without a serious examination of the evidence for local communities.[19]

This study attempts such an examination for Arkansas. The first four chapters describe the community that would encounter the forces unleashed by Civil War—its economic life and ideas, its society, and its politics. The next four chapters examine the interactions of the state, its people, and its institutions with the events of the war, determining what happened to the state's people during the years of conflict. The final chapters look at Arkansas between 1865 and 1875, assessing the war's impact over a longer range of time. The existing literature raises numerous questions about each of the topics addressed in this study. I have attempted wherever possible to be instructed by previous works regarding basic issues and problems. The relationship of my own conclusions to the findings of other scholars will be addressed where appropriate.

Although this study examines an important problem that concerns professional historians, I hope that the general reader will discover that it does more than just address academic issues. Arkansans faced a life-and-death struggle during the years of the Civil War, a struggle not only for personal survival but for that of their community. I believe that readers will recognize in the tale something about their own nature. The story of these Arkansans acting amidst the chaos of war seems to me to be worth retelling above and beyond any academic purpose that might be achieved in so doing. My hope is that I do justice to their experiences.

19. Michael B. Dougan, *Confederate Arkansas: The People and Policies of a Frontier State in Wartime* (University, Ala., 1976); Thomas S. Staples, *Reconstruction in Arkansas, 1862–1874* (New York, 1923); George H. Thompson, *Arkansas and Reconstruction: The Influence of Geography, Economics, and Personality* (Port Washington, N.Y., 1976).

# Part I

## Antebellum Arkansas

# 1

## ECONOMIC LIFE

IN 1857, THE EDITOR OF *DE BOW'S REVIEW* OBSERVED THAT the economy of Arkansas was experiencing a rapid expansion and that the state possessed advantages that ensured continued growth. Other accounts of conditions in Arkansas agreed with this assessment. Jesse Everett had informed relatives in the North ten years earlier, "I would advise any man who has no home of his own to come to the South where it is in the power of every one that wishes to make himself an independent farmer in one of the most fertile countries on the face of the earth." Joseph Morris, another Arkansan, predicted: "Arkansas will be a pleasant place to dwell. . . . Arkansas is destined at no distant day to be the *Banner* state of the South."[1]

Statistics affirm the existence of an economic boom during the 1850s. The value of the average farm in the state increased from $859 in 1850 to $2,712 in 1860. The per capita value of real estate (based on white population) grew in the same period from $107 to $195, while the per capita value of personal property rose from $117 to $361. Although Arkansas was hardly a manufacturing center, even that sector of the economy grew during these years as the number of manufacturing concerns increased from 261 to 518 and the capital invested in them from $305,015 to $1,316,610.[2]

The prosperity of the 1850s touched every part of the economy, but agriculture was the driving force. In 1860 investments in land, farm implements, and farm improvements, a total of $103,000,425, represented 98 percent of the capital invested in the state. The value of the goods produced on the farms, $33,251,334, represented about 95 percent of the total goods produced in the agricultural and manufacturing sectors in that year. Labor

1. *De Bow's Review*, XXIII (1857), 209–10; J. Everett to Dear Brother, December 1, 1844, in Sandford-Everett Family File, UALR; J. R. Montgomery to A. Haines, August 16, 1858, in Montgomery Family Papers, AHC; Tommy R. Thompson, ed., "Searching for the American Dream in Arkansas: Letters of a Pioneer Family," *AHQ*, XXXVIII (1979), 176.

2. *Ninth Census, 1870: Compendium*, Table VIII, p. 26; *Eighth Census, 1860: Agriculture*, 6; *Seventh Census, 1850: Statistics of Manufacturers*, Table IV, p. 43; *Eighth Census, 1860: Manufactures*, Table II, p. 21; *Seventh Census, 1850*: States and Territories, Table X, p. 553; *Eighth Census, 1860: Population*, Table VI, p. 21; *Seventh Census, 1850: Compendium*, Table CLXXXIII, p. 169, Table CCXIV, p. 190; *Eighth Census, 1860: Statistics*, 296, 333.

statistics provide further evidence of the importance of farming: in 1860 nearly 70 percent of the white labor force, and of course the vast majority of the black population, were tied to farming.[3]

Among farm goods, cotton was the most important product throughout the antebellum years. In 1860 the value of the state's 367,393 bales of ginned cotton, based on the average price for the commodity that year, was $16,165,292. No other crop compared with it in commercial worth. The corn produced that year, had it been marketed at the average price of $.65 per bushel, would have sold for $11,585,332, but corn planters and farmers generally used this crop to sustain their own operations. The wheat crop was worth $1,431,613, based on an average price of $1.50 per bushel. The estimated value of livestock slaughtered was $3,878,990. Individual operators might successfully specialize in the production of something other than cotton, but cotton was undisputably the most important factor in the state's economy.[4]

Contemporaries were aware of the relative importance of crops that could be grown in Arkansas, and they believed that planting cotton was the best way to become wealthy. Cotton captured the imagination of planter and farmer alike. One small farmer wrote to his uncle: "Cotton growing is more profitable than wool growing or any other branch of farming pursued in the north. Men accumulate large fortunes in a few years raising cotton." Another farmer indicated the relative importance of cotton when he wrote that although he tried to produce a variety of goods, "cotton is the principle staple of our country and is the only article we can obtain ready money for."[5]

During the 1850s cotton became more and more important for the state, and this increasing domination was reflected in the shift from general

3. *Eighth Census, 1860: Manufactures,* Table II, p. 21; *Eighth Census, 1860: Population,* Table VI, p. 21, Table III, p. 19.

4. *Eighth Census, 1860: Agriculture,* 6–9; E. H. Fletcher, Jr., to My Dear Father, January 18, 1860, in Elliott H. Fletcher Papers, AHC; C. C. Scott to D. Walker, August 30, 1852, in David Walker Papers, UAF; J. E. Hudson to S. McCollom, February 15, 1849, in A. O. McCollom Papers, AHC; W. S. Davis to W. E. Woodruff, May 15, 1860, in William E. Woodruff Papers, AHC; E. Benson to Dear Brother, April 1, 1857, in Burwell Benson Papers, DU; Little Rock *Arkansas Gazette,* February 10, 1854, March 2, 1855, January 9, 1852; J. Martin to Dear Brother and Sister, January 16, 1855, in Booker and Martin Family Papers, LSUS; G/NWA, 1043; G/NEA, 692; John Solomon Otto and Ben Wayne Banks, "The Banks Family of Yell County, Arkansas: A 'Plain Folk' Family of the Highland South," *AHQ,* XLV (1982), 157, 159.

5. E. Sherman to My Dear Uncle, February 25, 1858, in Sandford-Everett Family File; E. F. Strong to Dear Sister, March 28, 1854, in Strong-McColloch Family Papers, AHC.

farming to plantation agriculture. The spread of the plantation involved several major changes in how farming was pursued. Plantations, as opposed to general farms, specialized in the production of a cash crop and deemphasized cultivation of alternative crops. In addition, plantations were larger than general farms and relied on slave labor. The anticipated profits from producing large amounts of cotton encouraged this abandonment of self-sufficiency and the investment of capital in land and slaves. The rise of the plantation during the 1850s can be seen in the expansion of large slaveholdings, the concentration of lands into large holdings, and the increasing importance of cotton relative to other crops produced on the state's farms.

The expansion of large slaveholdings provides one measure of the development of the plantation. Quantifying the differences between general farms and plantations is a topic of considerable historical discussion, but the size of the work force has been one means of defining plantation versus general-farm operations. The ownership of slaves did not necessarily mean a landowner was operating a plantation, but with the acquisition of twenty or more slaves a farmer generally had to be producing a large cash crop in order to justify an investment in this number of workers. Not all slaveholders with twenty or more slaves were necessarily planters, but most probably were, and an examination of such owners provides a rough view of the spread of the plantation.[6]

6. Lewis Cecil Gray, *History of Agriculture in the Southern United States to 1860* (2 vols.; Gloucester, Mass., 1958), I, 302, provides a useful definition of a plantation: "The plantation was a capitalistic type of agricultural organization in which a considerable number of unfree laborers were employed under unified direction and control in the production of a staple crop." Scholars disagree on the number of laborers, the amount of land, or the crop size that define a plantation.

The labor force is the usual criterion used to define a plantation quantitatively. Gray, *ibid.*, 481–82, 498–500, defined "large planters" as having fifty or more slaves, "middle-class planters" as having ten to forty-nine, and "small planters" as having five to nine. Roger L. Ransom and Richard Sutch, *One Kind of Freedom: The Economic Consequences of Emancipation* (Cambridge, Mass., 1977), 73, use fifty slaves to define a plantation. Gavin Wright, *The Political Economy of the Cotton South: Households, Markets, and Wealth in the Nineteenth Century* (New York, 1978), 31, broke the slaveholding class into those with fifty-one or more slaves, those with sixteen to fifty, and those with one to fifteen. Kenneth M. Stampp, *The Peculiar Institution: Slavery in the Antebellum South* (New York, 1956), 30–38, defined "planters" as owning twenty or more slaves. This figure was also used by Eugene D. Genovese, *Roll, Jordan, Roll: The World the Slaves Made* (New York, 1974), 7–9, and Randolph B. Campbell, *A Southern Community in Crisis: Harrison County, Texas, 1850–1880* (Austin, 1983), 31–39. James Oakes, *The Ruling Race: A History of American Slaveholders* (New York, 1982), 52, warns that all such categories must be considered arbitrary, although they are necessary to examine plantation dynamics.

This study defines a plantation labor force as twenty or more slaves, in part because the

If a slaveholding of twenty or more slaves is one criterion for a plantation holding, most farms in Arkansas were not plantations in 1860. Only 1,363 slaveholders in the state at that time owned the necessary number of slaves. At the same time there were 39,004 farms reported overall. Based on these figures, no more than 3.5 percent of the state's farms had the labor force necessary to be considered plantations. Even so, such units increased dramatically in number during the 1850s, gained a greater share of the overall slave-labor force, and expanded in their average size. Besides becoming more important over the decade, plantation agriculture spread geographically.[7]

The general growth of the number of plantation slaveholdings in the 1850s is apparent in the data from eight sample counties—Chicot, Independence, Montgomery, Phillips, Pulaski, Union, Van Buren, and Washington (see Map 1). Except for one instance in Washington County, there were no slaveholdings of twenty or more slaves in the samples drawn from the western and northwestern parts of the state in 1850 (Table 1). In all of the other counties, however, the number of units increased, at rates ranging from 35 percent in Union County to 420 percent in Pulaski County. In the two primary cotton-growing counties in the sample, Chicot and Phillips, holdings of twenty or more slaves expanded by 60 and 304 percent respectively.[8]

The figures also show the increasing importance of plantation-sized holdings relative to the total number of slaveowners and landowners in parts of the state. Again excluding the nonplantation counties in the west, plantation slaveholdings came to represent a larger proportion of total slaveholdings in all the remaining sample counties during the 1850s; in Phillips County, a rapidly expanding agricultural area, the percentage jumped threefold. In Chicot, Phillips, and Pulaski over the decade, planters with twenty or more slaves came to represent a greater percentage not only of slaveowners, but of all landowners. The greatest relative gain occurred

---

number makes possible comparisons with other works. I also use a landholding of six hundred acres or more as a definition of a plantation-sized holding. This approach has drawbacks because it does not assess the actual use of land, but it allows a comparison of antebellum and postemancipation holdings. Six hundred acres was the average for a twenty-slave work force.

7. *Eighth Census, 1860: Agriculture,* 222, 224.

8. I chose these eight counties because they represented different types of economic communities. Chicot, Phillips, and Union were cotton plantation areas. Independence, Pulaski, and Washington had mixed economies. Montgomery and Van Buren counties produced little cotton; agriculture there was of a subsistence nature. In addition, their boundaries changed little between 1850 and 1874.

Tax rolls for 1850, 1860, and 1866 were used for analysis. The data base used was the entire taxpaying population.

TABLE 1

INCREASE OF PLANTATION-SIZED UNITS (20 OR MORE SLAVES) IN SAMPLE
COUNTIES, 1850–1860

| County | Number of Units | | Percent of Slaveowners | | Percent of Landowners | |
|---|---|---|---|---|---|---|
| | 1850 | 1860 | 1850 | 1860 | 1850 | 1860 |
| Chicot | 52 | 83 | 34.7 | 40.5 | 29.4 | 38.8 |
| Independence | 3 | 7 | 2.1 | 3.2 | .6 | .2 |
| Montgomery | 0 | 0 | 0.0 | 0.0 | 0.0 | 0.0 |
| Phillips | 28 | 113 | 12.1 | 36.2 | 6.4 | 16.3 |
| Pulaski | 5 | 26 | 3.0 | 8.1 | 1.5 | 3.5 |
| Union | 31 | 42 | 6.1 | 7.5 | 5.4 | 5.1 |
| Van Buren | 0 | 0 | 0.0 | 0.0 | 0.0 | 0.0 |
| Washington | 1 | 0 | .4 | 0.0 | .1 | 0.0 |

in Phillips, although this increase still did not bring that county near the
level of Chicot, one of the oldest plantation areas in the state: on the eve of
the war, nearly four of every ten landowners in Chicot had plantation-sized
slaveholdings.

Overall, plantation slaveholders remained a minority of slaveowners and
landowners in the state in 1860, but they had increased their control over
the work force and the land. During the 1850s this group made large gains
in the numbers of the slaves held and the share of the work force that their
holdings represented. In all of the counties with plantation-sized operators,
the average number of slaves held by such operators increased (Table 2).
Chicot County came to resemble counties with large-scale farming across
the Mississippi River in the area of Natchez. The average slave population
on the plantation-sized units increased from 48 to 81.1, and individual
slaveowners put together very large holdings. Tax rolls showed eight individuals in Chicot County in 1860 with more than 100 slaves. Elisha
Worthington became the largest slaveowner in the entire state, with 320
slaves on his Sunnyside and Redleaf plantations.

The proportion of the total slave-labor force also grew on the

# Map 1

## Arkansas 1860—Sample Counties

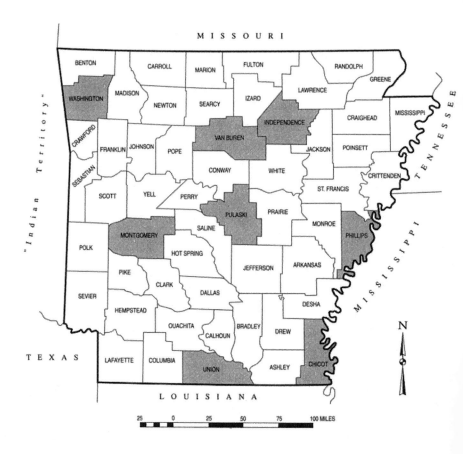

TABLE 2

INCREASE OF SLAVES ON PLANTATION-SIZED UNITS (20 OR MORE SLAVES) IN
SAMPLE COUNTIES, 1850–1860

| County | Number of Slaves on Plantation | | Plantation Slaves as % of Total Slaves | | Average Size of Plantation Force | |
|---|---|---|---|---|---|---|
| | 1850 | 1860 | 1850 | 1860 | 1850 | 1860 |
| Chicot | 2,498 | 4,621 | 84.1 | 84.8 | 48.0 | 81.1 |
| Independence | 77 | 188 | 15.9 | 20.5 | 25.7 | 26.9 |
| Montgomery | 0 | 0 | 0.0 | 0.0 | 0.0 | 0.0 |
| Phillips | 946 | 4,655 | 52.8 | 71.3 | 33.8 | 41.2 |
| Pulaski | 129 | 1,967 | 16.9 | 49.4 | 24.0 | 41.5 |
| Union | 975 | 1,372 | 25.8 | 33.0 | 31.5 | 32.7 |
| Van Buren | 0 | 0 | 0.0 | 0.0 | 0.0 | 0.0 |
| Washington | 21 | 0 | 2.6 | 0.0 | 21.0 | 0.0 |

plantation-sized units—that is, planters increased their share of the total
slave population. In Chicot County the proportion of slaves on these units
rose by only seven-tenths of a percent, but that was because, at more
than 84 percent to begin with, the proportion was probably reaching the
practical maximum. In Union County the share increased from 26 percent
to 33 percent, in Independence County from 16 percent to more than 20
percent, and in Phillips County from 53 percent to more than 71 percent.
The greatest change took place in Pulaski County, where the proportion
of large holdings increased from only 17 percent to nearly 50 percent. In
1860 in Chicot and Phillips counties, heavy majorities of the total slave
populations were owned by planters. Close to a majority were owned by
planters in Pulaski County, and sizable minorities were part of plantation
holdings in Union and Independence counties.

Plantation operators also increased their control over the land in the
sample counties (Table 3). They expanded the average number of acres
that they held in all of the counties except Pulaski and, despite the opening

TABLE 3

INCREASED REAL-ESTATE HOLDINGS BY PLANTATIONS (UNITS OF 20 OR MORE
SLAVES) IN SAMPLE COUNTIES, 1850–1860

| County | Number of Units | | Average Acres/Unit | | % of Total Land | |
|---|---|---|---|---|---|---|
| | 1850 | 1860 | 1850 | 1860 | 1850 | 1860 |
| Chicot | 52 | 83 | 1,611.5 | 2,251.1 | 68.6 | 70.4 |
| Independence | 3 | 7 | 1,045.3 | 1,623.7 | 3.1 | 3.3 |
| Montgomery | 0 | 0 | 0.0 | 0.0 | 0.0 | 0.0 |
| Phillips | 28 | 113 | 1,120.8 | 1,315.5 | 20.4 | 47.4 |
| Pulaski | 5 | 26 | 1,502.8 | 1,295.8 | 6.0 | 13.2 |
| Union | 31 | 42 | 1,066.6 | 2.018.9 | 20.9 | 22.8 |
| Van Buren | 0 | 0 | 0.0 | 0.0 | 0.0 | 0.0 |
| Washington | 1 | 0 | 340.0 | 0.0 | 2.4 | 0.0 |

up of more land to farming, increased their share of the total acreage in all
except the nonplantation counties.

The actual concentration of land into large holdings provides another
indicator of the increasing importance of large-scale farm operations. A
large landholding was not necessarily a plantation, but it was usually a first
step in that direction as farmers bought up land that could be cultivated
after acquiring the necessary laborers. Establishing the nature of this particular trend is historically valuable because it provides the only quantitative
basis for comparing the importance of the plantation in the antebellum and
postbellum world.

Concentration was evident in all of the sample counties, including those
without plantation-sized slaveholdings. The opening of more land to settlement through the building of levees and the clearing of forests meant that
the large landowners did not monopolize the land, but the pattern is clear.
An examination of land held in units of six hundred acres or more demon-
strates what was taking place. This particular acreage was chosen because
it was the area necessary to justify a holding of twenty slaves. Six hundred
acres is, thus, the rough equivalent of twenty slaves in defining a plantation.

TABLE 4

LANDHOLDINGS OF MORE THAN 600 ACRES, 1850 AND 1860

| | 1850 | | | | 1860 | | | |
|---|---|---|---|---|---|---|---|---|
| | Landowners | | Land | | Landowners | | Land | |
| County | No. | (%) | Acres | (%) | No. | (%) | Acres | (%) |
| Chicot | 64 | (30) | 101,577 | (56) | 87 | (42) | 152,167 | (84) |
| Independence | 25 | (5) | 28,270 | (28) | 58 | (4) | 88,988 | (26) |
| Montgomery | 0 | (0) | 0 | (0) | 1 | (1) | 620 | (2) |
| Phillips | 54 | (12) | 78,666 | (51) | 148 | (21) | 195,639 | (63) |
| Pulaski | 49 | (14) | 62,384 | (57) | 99 | (13) | 138,297 | (54) |
| Union | 50 | (9) | 52,415 | (33) | 168 | (21) | 211,885 | (57) |
| Van Buren | 0 | (0) | 0 | (0) | 0 | (0) | 0 | (0) |
| Washington | 19 | (2) | 18,682 | (13) | 32 | (3) | 33,353 | (15) |

The tendency toward concentration of land in units of six hundred acres or more paralleled that in plantation-sized slaveholdings, with a larger percentage of landholders owning such units in all of the counties except Independence, Pulaski, and Van Buren (Table 4). The proportion of land in such units also increased in every county except those three. These comparisons do not provide an absolute picture of the growing importance of the plantation, but they do show that the concentration of land necessary for plantation agriculture was taking place.[9]

A measure of the geographic advance of plantation agriculture across the state is the shift of farmers from self-sufficiency to specialization in cotton. The ratio of corn production to cotton provides an indicator of this trend. Self-sufficient farmers concentrated on producing corn more than did planters, who devoted more of their resources to cotton. Thus, a decrease in the ratio of corn to cotton indicates a shift from self-sufficiency to specialization. This trend took place statewide during the 1850s as the

9. Ownership of six hundred acres or more does not necessarily indicate actual plantation operations, but it does allow a comparison of concentration of landholding (see note 6 to this chapter).

# Map 2

## Corn-to-Cotton Ratios, 1850

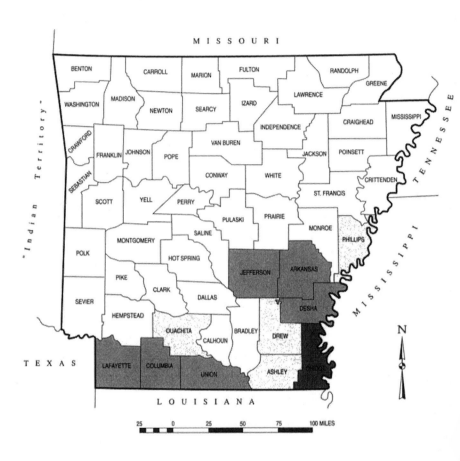

(bushels to bales)

Less than 25:1

26:1 to 50:1

51:1 to 100:1

Greater than 100:1

# Map 3

## Corn-to-Cotton Ratios, 1860

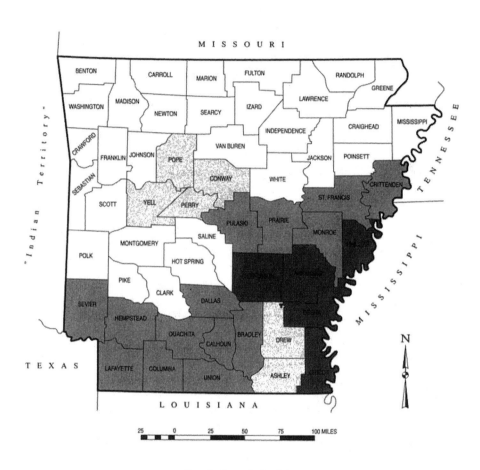

(bushels to bales)

■ Less than 25:1

▨ 26:1 to 50:1

▒ 51:1 to 100:1

□ Greater than 100:1

ratio of bushels of corn to bales of cotton declined from 136:1 to 49:1. A county-by-county assessment of the corn-to-cotton ratios shows clearly the geographic expansion of plantation-type agriculture in the 1850s (see Maps 2 and 3). The trend is particularly apparent in the delta regions along the Mississippi River, the lower Arkansas River, and the Red and Ouachita rivers. By 1860, Arkansas, Chicot, Desha, Jefferson, Lafayette, and Phillips counties evidenced high specialization with ratios of less than 25:1, roughly half the statewide ratio.[10]

Cotton produced the rise of Arkansas plantations. At the same time, plantations drove the boom in cotton production. Plantations, rather than general farms, harvested the vast majority of the cotton produced in the state. This point becomes obvious when one looks at the cotton production of counties with plantation-sized work forces. In 1860, plantation-sized slaveholdings comprised 10 percent or more of the work force in twenty-one of the state's fifty-five counties. These counties produced 284,996 bales of cotton that year, almost 78 percent of the entire crop grown within the state. The sample counties clearly show the relative importance of these plantation-sized operations. In Chicot County, for instance, 79 of 83 owners of plantation-sized slave forces could be located in the agricultural census. These 79 represented 37 percent of the county's 214 landowners. They owned 40 percent of the land but grew 89 percent of the cotton. In Phillips County, 81 of 113 owners with plantation-sized work forces were found in the agricultural census; representing just 11 percent of the landowners and farming 33 percent of the land, they produced 46 percent of the cotton. In every other sample county with a plantation-sized slaveholding, this basic dominance of cotton production was apparent.[11]

Throughout the 1850s cotton production and plantations became increasingly important across much of Arkansas. Only geography and transportation posed any serious limits to the potential for sustained expansion. In terms of soil and growing conditions, a large part of the state was capable of supporting cotton culture. Some of the richest agricultural soils in the nation existed in the state's river deltas, although much of that land was subject to flooding and required investments of capital in levees before it could be used. Such land yielded between one and two bales per acre in the

---

10. The crop mix also provides a means by which to define a plantation. Campbell, *Southern Community in Crisis*, 69, reports corn (bushels) to cotton (bales) ratios for the 1860s in a Texas plantation county to be 23.6:1 for planters with twenty or more slaves, 28.5:1 for planters with ten to nineteen slaves, and 39.2:1 for yeomen farmers.

11. *Eighth Census, 1860: Agriculture*, 7, 224. I used tax records to avoid the problem of matching slaveownership with tax-based landownership.

antebellum years. The prairie and plains regions of the state also sustained cotton, although the soils there were less fertile than in the deltas and production was estimated at only a half bale per acre. Even mountain valleys could support the crop. In 1860 every county in the state except Benton reported some cotton. In the northwestern half of the state, however, large-scale commercial production was not feasible. Much of the land in that area consisted of the uplands of the Ozark, Boston, and Ouachita mountains. Thin and moderately fertile soils in limited areas of the mountains were not enough to attract planters in the antebellum years and helped divide the state into two economic regions, distinguished by small farms in the mountains and plantations elsewhere.[12]

The state's poor transportation system offered a second restriction to economic growth. By the 1850s, only the rivers offered easily accessible and relatively inexpensive transportation. Riverboat transportation was well developed by the antebellum years. Boats steamed up the Ouachita with ease as far as Camden, and at times could reach Arkadelphia. The Arkansas was easily navigated to Little Rock, the White to Jacksonport, and the Red to Shreveport, in Louisiana. The Mississippi River provided ready transportation along the entire eastern border of the state. Transport was extended on these waterways by the use of barges and keelboats, and by the willingness of boat captains to run almost anywhere when the water was high enough. Along these routes customers had relatively efficient and inexpensive contact with markets. White River steamboats charged a typical fee of two dollars per bale for cotton shipped to New Orleans, and a dollar a bale to Memphis.[13]

Away from the rivers, problems of transportation multiplied and the cost of getting goods to market increased. Roads were inadequate, and bad weather made them practically impassable. In 1855, P. H. Wheat of Little Rock advertised that he would ship cotton from Little Rock to the steamboat landing at De Valls Bluff for forty cents per hundredweight. Since a bale of cotton in those days weighed about 400 pounds, Wheat's charges meant that it cost $1.60 per bale to move cotton roughly fifty miles by land, as compared with $2.00 per bale for the remaining five hundred miles from De Valls Bluff to New Orleans. Heavy rains in the autumn of that year caused Wheat to announce an increase in

12. Gerald T. Hanson and Carl H. Moneyhon, *Historical Atlas of Arkansas* (Norman, Okla., 1989), 39.

13. J. W. Smith to T. H. Smith, June 26, 1856, in ISHL; Little Rock *Arkansas Gazette*, June 22, 1855; Little Rock *True Democrat*, October 18, 1854.

his rates for goods other than cotton from seventy-five cents to a dollar per hundredweight.[14]

The significance of transportation problems for agriculture was that arable land away from the rivers was slow to be developed. The best indicator of this fact was the price of land. Throughout the antebellum years, land with easy access to river transportation was more expensive than land without that access. In the 1850s land along the Mississippi sold for from twenty-five to sixty dollars per acre. Along the upper White River at Jacksonport land prices ran around twenty-five dollars per acre. On the less-easily-reached lands of the Red River above Shreveport, bottomlands could be obtained at between eight and fifteen dollars per acre. Away from the rivers, land prices plummeted, ranging from twelve and a half cents to four dollars per acre.[15]

Contemporaries saw the connection between the price of land and access to transportation, and the patterns of development showed that they made decisions on this basis. The editor of the *Arkansas Gazette* believed that land away from the rivers should be selling even cheaper; he blamed speculators, who were counting on the construction of railroads to open these lands for cash crops, for driving up the price. By hanging on to their land, at least according to the editor, these speculators retarded the development of the state by keeping actual settlers from moving into areas that could be put into cultivation.[16] Meanwhile, along the navigable rivers, plantation-sized slaveholdings proliferated (see Map 4). Access to transportation thus added to geographic limitations to split Arkansas into two different economic regions.

Arkansas' economic growth during the 1850s was tied to cotton. The state's and each individual's success were linked to a number of potentially unstable variables associated with cotton and the agrarian economy. The state's economic future consequently always depended upon conditions that were beyond the control of individual entrepreneurs. Weather, the cost of operations, and cotton prices entered into any equation for success

14. Van Buren (Ark.) *Intelligencer* quoted in Little Rock *Arkansas Gazette*, January 9, 1852, July 19, 1854, January 9, June 22, December 14, 1855; Van Buren (Ark.) *Press*, November 9, 1860.

15. John W. Brown Diary, February 4, 1856, in AHC; J. M. Edwards to W. E. Woodruff, June 11, 1858, W. W. Fleming to W. E. Woodruff, December 28, 1856, both in Woodruff Papers; Little Rock *Arkansas Gazette*, September 8, 1854; Sarah A. Nelson to Dear Menecee and Emily, February 22, 1849, in Sarah A. Nelson Letter, Small Manuscripts Collection, AHC; H. P. Montgomery to Dear Brother, November 29, 1857, June 6, 1858, both in Montgomery Family Papers; Agreement between James G. Gordon and Theron Brownfield, March 6, 1854, in Theron Brownfield Papers, UALR.

16. Little Rock *Arkansas Gazette*, February 9, 1855, November 11, 1853.

# Map 4

## Plantation Slaveholdings by County, 1860

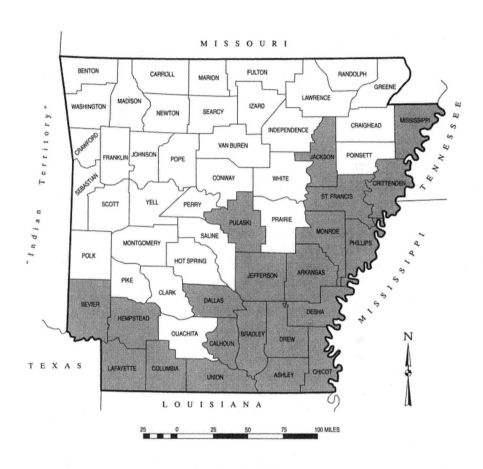

Counties in which 10 percent or more
of slaveholdings were plantation-sized

or failure. During the 1850s most of these factors favored the economic boom that occurred.

Weather was a major force in the cotton economy. A late frost could destroy plants as they came in. Too much rain could wash out early crops, encourage cotton to "grow to weed" (grow tall rather than produce full bolls), cause the plant to sprout in the boll or rot on the stalk, or keep hands out of the field at harvest time. Rain could also bring out boll worms or encourage fungi in the crops. Not enough rain was even worse. Fortunately for the state's farm interests, the weather during the 1850s was relatively benign. True, a cool, wet spring and a wet fall hurt the crop in 1855, heavy fall rains in 1857 and 1859 shortened and reduced the harvest, and inadequate rains in late summer in 1850, 1854, 1858, and 1860 caused the loss of up to one-third of the crop in some sections. Still, farmers never experienced a statewide crop loss during the 1850s. Although a major catastrophe could always happen, nature smiled on Arkansas during the antebellum years.[17]

The Arkansas economy also benefited from good prices for cotton during the 1850s. Throughout the decade prices remained stable and at a profitable level. Generally they fluctuated in the vicinity of ten cents per pound, although in 1860 the average wholesale price reached eleven cents per pound. Like the weather, however, prices were not something that Arkansans could control. Their market was totally outside the state and dependent on national and international conditions.[18]

Factors that affected the cost of operations in an expanding market added to the risks of farming in Arkansas. Although their positive or negative effects varied from individual to individual, acquiring land and labor, procuring supplies, and the marketing of crops were expensive and appear often to have led to debts that threatened the economic viability of those who spent too much or were unlucky.

As has been shown, by the 1850s good cotton land with access to transportation was not inexpensive in Arkansas. Six hundred acres of good land, previously used as a minimum holding for a plantation operation, at twenty-five dollars an acre would cost $15,000. Prime delta

17. J. R. McNeely to J. Sheppard, July 29, 1852, in James Sheppard Papers, DU; B. W. Lee to James N. Lucas, April 30, 1844, in Knight Collection, DU: Johnson Chapman to W. E. Woodruff, February 26, August 6, 1860, both in Woodruff Papers; Little Rock *Arkansas Gazette*, August 30, 1850, July 13, 1855, October 18, December 11, 18, 1856, April 11, May 16, June 6, September 5, November 21, 1857, June 12, 19, August 14, 1858, October 1, 1859, July 21, 28, 1860, June 22, 1861; John Martin to Dear Brother and Sister, April 28, 1853, in Booker and Martin Family Papers; Brown Diary, July 13, October 13, 1852.

18. *Eighth Census, 1860: Agriculture*, 6–9.

land selling at sixty dollars an acre would cost the purchaser $36,000. Both were large sums at the time, and few buyers had that much cash. Many purchases appear to have been on a credit basis, with terms generally ranging from one-half to one-third of the purchase price down, the balance to be paid over time. Interest on land loans ranged from 8 to 10 percent of the unpaid balance each year and added to the cost of annual operations.[19]

A labor force for commercial farming was also an expensive item by the 1860s. Black slaves, legally the property of their masters and unable to seek other opportunities, provided the essential labor force for the cultivation of the state's crops. By 1850 the price of slaves within the United States had reached the highest level of the century, and contemporaries were aware that it was going to go higher. The average assessed value of slaves in Arkansas reflected this rise. Between 1850 and 1860 the average valuation increased from $415 to $741. Market prices for individual slaves were much higher. Skilled workers or those who possessed other desirable traits brought as much as $2,000 and a good field hand around $1,000 by 1860. Twenty slaves for a plantation could cost as much as $40,000, and the use of credit was often necessary for the purchase. Creditors were reluctant to make loans using slaves as collateral, but land or other property could be used instead. Debts acquired in the expansion of the work force added to the overhead of many planters and farmers.[20]

Slave labor presented an additional problem because of the very nature of human property. A runaway slave represented a major potential loss to a slaveowner, and runaways were common during the antebellum years. They might, however, be recovered. The injury or death of slaves caused an even greater problem for the slaveowner. A cholera epidemic in Jefferson

19. Little Rock *Arkansas Gazette*, May 10, 1850, April 22, 1853, August 18, 1854, November 7, 14, 1855; Helena (Ark.) *Shield*, August 25, 1855; W. W. Fleming to W. E. Woodruff, December 28, 1856, in Woodruff Papers; Promissory Note, November 6, 1858, in Samuel W. Williams Papers, AHC; J. G. Gordon and T. Brownfield Agreement, March 6, 1854, in Brownfield Papers.

20. E. W. Wright to Dear Asa, January 5, 1852, in Asa Morgan Collection, AHC; E. Benson to Dear Brother, April 1, 1857, in Benson Papers, DU; Robert F. Kellam Diary, January 2, 1860, in AHC; J. F. Martin to Jared Martin, April 28, 1853, in Martin Family Papers, AHC; *Biennial Report of the Auditor of Public Accounts of the State of Arkansas, for 1859 and 1860* (Little Rock, 1860), 42; Helena (Ark.) *Shield*, February 26, 1853, November 11, 1854; Little Rock *Arkansas Gazette*, December 27, 1850, April 16, 1852; A. Rust to Dear Uncle, June 29, 1850, A. Rust to Dear Brother, March 29, 1850, in Rust Family Papers, J. N. Heiskell Collection, UALR; Orville W. Taylor, *Negro Slavery in Arkansas* (Durham, N.C., 1958), 72–75.

County in 1852 led to the death of seven of John S. Roane's slaves, a loss he estimated at $7,000. John Brown of Camden noted the economic impact of the death of his slave Thomas, drowned while running away from Brown's plantation: "This boy is a loss of $1,200 which would have greatly relieved me in payment of my debts." Such losses could wipe out a slave-owner overnight.[21]

The system of obtaining supplies and marketing crops added to potential problems for the Arkansas farmer. Transportation facilities and sources of capital focused much of the trade of Arkansas through New Orleans. Factors and commission merchants of that city often purchased and forwarded supplies to Arkansas planters and farmers on credit extended against the next year's crop. The factor or merchant then took that crop on consignment, sold it, took a percentage of the sale price for his marketing services, and then charged the planter for the supplies and interest that had been advanced.[22]

The system was not inherently bad, but Arkansans were concerned about their domination by the New Orleans merchants. They feared that the Crescent City's monopoly over their trade allowed the outside merchants to take advantage of them and charge unfair prices. Their complaints had some basis: they paid more for many marketing services than other consumers. The $4.06 per bale paid by one Union County planter for marketing his crop—at a time for which one historian has estimated costs ranging from $2.50 to $4.00 per bale—is typical. Although the cost of dealing through local middlemen helps account for the difference, the price of goods sold at Little Rock compared with the price of the same goods in New Orleans indicates the cost of being a consumer in Arkansas. The markup on most such goods averaged between 100 and 150 percent, but individual items varied greatly. Sugar selling at six cents in New Orleans brought sixteen and a half cents at Little Rock; thirteen-cent coffee brought

21. Brown Diary, March 6, May 9, 1855, June 19, 1859; Little Rock *Arkansas Gazette*, November 1, 1850; E. Hickman to E. H. Fletcher, October 6, 1844, in Fletcher Papers; E. W. Knott to D. T. Weeks, December 5, 1858, J. R. McNeely to J. Sheppard, July 29, 1852, D. T. Weeks to J. Sheppard, July 29, August 10, September 10, 1854, all in Sheppard Papers; Taylor, *Negro Slavery in Arkansas*, 213–32.

22. Little Rock *Arkansas Gazette*, November 21, 1851; Otto and Banks, "Banks Family," 159; A. A. Stith to Mr. Jones, November 21, 1853, quoted in Little Rock *Arkansas Gazette*, December 2, 1853; J. Meek to R. E. Campbell, September 20, 1842, in Meek Letters, Small Manuscripts Collection, AHC; Samuel H. Chester, *Pioneer Days in Arkansas* (Richmond, Va., 1927), 18; J. H. Mann to E. H. Fletcher, October 20, 1857, in Fletcher Papers; Ward and Jonas to John Roark, December 2, 1854, in Brownfield Papers; Gray, *Agriculture in the Southern United States to 1860*, II, 695–96; Harold D. Woodman, *King Cotton & His Retainers: Financing & Marketing the Cotton Crop of the South, 1800–1925* (Lexington, Ky., 1968), 38–42.

twenty-two cents. Merchants attributed their prices to poor transportation and the cost of doing business in Arkansas. Arkansans were never convinced that the outside merchants were not simply gouging them.[23]

Borrowing money to buy land, slaves, and supplies added the cost of servicing debts to the problems faced by Arkansas farmers. Probate files indicate that many farmers were involved in a complex system of borrowing, with debts for land, slaves, and supplies often outweighing debtors' actual resources. Even the richest man in the state, Elisha Worthington of Chicot County, borrowed heavily in the 1850s to acquire more cotton land. His largest single note was for $274,000—used to consolidate other loans and buy more land—that he borrowed from Wade Hampton of South Carolina and Abraham Van Buren of New York City. Typically, loans on land required an interest payment of 8 to 10 percent annually on the unpaid balance of the note.[24]

Heavy debts caused hardship and could be disastrous when market prices dipped, crops were short, or additional supplies had to be purchased to make up shortages or to supplement the foodstuffs produced on the farm. John Brown of Camden spoke for many Arkansans when he complained in his diary that after having reached market too late, his cotton did not produce enough for him to meet his obligations in advances and interest. He wrote, "Now I have to struggle with cash matters for the balance."[25]

By the 1850s some contemporary observers thought that the use of credit had cost the state much of its economic independence. They believed that growth had been based largely on credit and doubted that the accumulated debts could ever be repaid. A Batesville newspaper called Arkansas of 1851 a debt-ridden place, its people indebted to merchants who in turn were indebted to merchants elsewhere. Each January 1, the money made by Arkansans from their crops and produce went to pay off their debts, then moved out of state as merchants settled their obligations. As a result, the state was left with no cash and little accumulated capital. In March, 1857, the editor of the *Arkansas Gazette* made a similar observation when

23. Little Rock *Arkansas Gazette*, November 21, 1851; Glenn G. Martel, "Early Days in Columbia County," *AHQ*, II (1943), 224; H. N. Templeman to J. Sheppard, March 11, 1858, D. T. Weeks to J. Sheppard, July 15, 1855, both in Sheppard Papers; Bill of Sale, in Fletcher Papers; Little Rock *Arkansas Gazette*, June 22, 1855; Woodman, *King Cotton & His Retainers*, 49–51, 76–79; Gray, *Agriculture in the Southern United States to 1860*, II, 715–16.

24. The observation that debt outweighed assets is based on the loose probate records for Pulaski County for the period 1850–1860 and a sampling from other counties. For Pulaski County there are eighty-nine cases on file; Willard B. Gatewood, Jr., "Sunnyside: The Evolution of an Arkansas Plantation, 1848–1945," *AHQ*, L (1991), 9.

25. Brown Diary, May 16, 1854; O. Vaugine to J. N. Lucas, February 15, 1845, in Knight Collection; Woodman, *King Cotton & His Retainers*, 52–53.

he complained that with prices of slaves and land high, many farmers had borrowed money to expand their operations. Fearing a crash, he noted that the one consolation Arkansans would have for their speculation was that "no body among us, has enough, to have laid by any nest-eggs."[26]

Assessing the extent to which contemporaries were correct about the state's having surrendered its economic independence is statistically impossible. It is clear, however, that the forces that directed business activity in Arkansas by the 1850s generally lay outside the state. Investment came from outside merchants, and they usually tied their money to the production of cotton. Goggin, Trader & Holt of Memphis was typical of the companies putting money into the local economy. In an 1859 advertisement Goggin, Trader made the connection between capital and cotton clear, proclaiming "Liberal Cash Advances on cotton and other produce."[27]

Outside domination of the economy had another cost: it limited the growth of the state's own retail and wholesale businesses. The large merchant houses at regional markets usually dealt directly with local planters rather than through local businesses. Although local merchants at times became the agents of outside business, they were usually left to develop trade with a clientele ignored by the bigger houses, such as the farmers and the poor. The Altschul store south of Little Rock was typical and even encouraged trade with neighborhood slaves, opening its doors on Sunday to sell stockings, thread, and ribbons to these customers. Some local merchants prospered, but they generally were left out of the larger trade carried on by the outside concerns.[28]

Aware of the problems of the local economy, some business and agricultural leaders advanced solutions. The development of marketing connections that would break the New Orleans monopoly was one of their goals, and they advocated the construction of railroads as the means to that end. The lack of pools of local capital, along with regional jealousies, prevented a solution to that problem before the war. Although they could raise some money locally, planters tended to be conservative investors and provincial in their outlook. One observer at Arkadelphia noted that "planters do not want capital invested far from them, or where they can not superintend or watch it." Either lacking the capital or not wanting to invest it, Arkansans looked elsewhere for railroad funds but found that outside capitalists had

26. Batesville (Ark.) New Era quoted in Little Rock Arkansas Gazette, November 22, 1851 (see also March 28, 1857).

27. Brown Diary, April 25, 1853; J. Hornor to W. E. Woodruff, June 5, 1860, in Woodruff Papers; Little Rock Arkansas Gazette, September 3, 1859.

28. J. H. Mann to E. H. Fletcher, October 20, 1857, E. H. Fletcher, Jr. to Mr. Haines, December 31, 1858, both in Fletcher Papers; Otto and Banks, "Banks Family," 159.

little interest in investing in an alternative transportation system for the state. The result was that only sixty-six miles of railroad track had been laid in Arkansas by 1861.[29]

Some leaders urged economic diversification, such as the development of manufacturing and mining. A few industries were created, but they were mainly factories for processing raw cotton. The most successful was the Arkansas Manufacturing Company in Pike County, which produced 12,500 pounds of spun yarn per day. Despite many different efforts, however, in 1860 only two spinning plants were operating in the entire state, with an average capitalization of $18,500 and an average work force of twelve.[30] Most other efforts to develop a manufacturing alternative involved even smaller amounts of invested capital and fewer workers per unit. The largest local industry was lumber milling: in 1860 there were 1,877 facilities producing planks, staves, and other raw lumber throughout the state. The average amount of capital invested, however, was only $3,300, and the average mill employed five hands. Flour mills were also important, but the 97 mills in the state in 1860 averaged a capital investment of only $2,391 per unit and a work force of two men. Most attempts to develop mining were never fruitful.[31]

The basic problem faced by those who sought to develop economic alternatives to cotton was lack of capital. Despite promises of returns of up to 25 percent on investments, developers found few investors to back their plans. In one effort, proponents of a cotton factory in Little Rock in 1850 were able to raise only $17,000 of the $47,000 that they needed to construct the plant, and the project had to be dropped. The developers simply could not find enough investors. Those who were ready to invest did not have enough money to make an impact, and those with the money usually had it tied up in cotton.[32]

29. Brown Diary, May 9, 1855, June 19, 1859; J. R. McNeely to J. Sheppard, July 29, 1852, D. T. Weeks to J. Sheppard, July 29, August 10, September 10, 1854, all in Sheppard Papers.

30. Little Rock *True Democrat*, October 26, 1849, July 19, 1854; Little Rock *Arkansas Gazette*, June 7, 1850, January 31, 1851, February 18, citing Van Buren (Ark.) *Intelligencer*; *De Bow's Review*, X (April, 1851), 463, (May, 1851), 564; Fort Smith (Ark.) *Herald*, March 14, 1851; Richard W. Griffin, "Pro-Industrial Sentiment and Cotton Factories in Arkansas, 1820–1863," *AHQ*, XV (1956), 125–27, 131, 135; *Eighth Census, 1860: Manufactures*, Table III, p. 22.

31. *Eighth Census, 1860: Manufactures*, Table III, p. 22; Little Rock *Arkansas Gazette*, September 10, 1852; Van Buren (Ark.) *Press*, July 6, 1859; *Acts of Arkansas, 1853*, 24–26, 138–39, 172–74; *Acts of Arkansas, 1855*, 1224–35; Little Rock *True Democrat*, August 25, 1857.

32. Griffin, "Pro-Industrial Sentiment," 131; Little Rock *Arkansas Gazette*, March 1, 29, May 18, June 7, 1850; Brown Diary, August 14, 1852.

During the 1850s the Arkansas economy prospered, but it was controlled largely from outside the state. The capital was in the hands of the commission merchants and factors at New Orleans, who had little interest in investing in anything locally other than the production of more cotton. As a result, the continued success of the state's economy and its citizens was tied to often-unpredictable factors involved in producing that crop and in its historically undependable price.

Unquestionably, wealth could be made on the Arkansas cotton frontier during the 1850s. Anthony H. Davies of Chicot County came to the state as a bookkeeper in the 1840s. In 1850 he owned over a thousand acres of land and 64 slaves. By 1860 he had increased his work force to 103 slaves and his plantation produced 735 bales of cotton. John M. Hubbard, a native of Ohio, a graduate of Yale College and medical school, moved to Phillips County in hopes of bettering his fortunes. In his new home he practiced medicine, acquired land, and began to cultivate cotton. He had no land in the county in 1850, but by 1860 he owned over 1,500 acres and 66 slaves. Harrison L. Dearing of Union County was a carpenter and a tenant farmer in 1850, but by 1860 he had 2,648 acres and 27 slaves and his plantation produced 172 bales of cotton. Davies, Hubbard, and Dearing exemplified the possibilities present in the Arkansas economy.[33]

An economy based almost totally on cotton, however, was always unpredictable, and individuals encountered problems that the entire system might face if favorable conditions changed. If any part of the equation for success was not present, everything could be lost. The ill-fated John Brown of Camden abandoned active farming in 1853 and took up the law after suffering heavy losses on his cotton. High freight rates caused by low water on the Ouachita River that year, a late arrival of his crop at market, poor prices for it, and the necessity of buying a large amount of corn at high prices because of a failure of his corn crop combined to keep him from grossing enough at the end of the season to repay his merchant for the funds advanced and for the interests that had accumulated. Brown summed up the potential risk involved in the state's agrarian economy when he wrote; "With all my best management, financing and economy such a combination of untoward and unavoidable circumstances makes it a serious season for me. It is obliged to be a losing year any way I can fix it."[34] Much of the success of the local economy depended on luck. The costs and the risks of cotton cultivation simply were not capable of being controlled.

33. G/SA, 1074, 1836; G/EA, 775.
34. Brown Diary, May 17, 1854.

# 2

## ARKANSAS SOCIETY

WHITE SOCIETY IN ARKANSAS IN THE 1850s POSED A PROB-
lem to contemporary observers, many of whom considered the state's population to consist of the dregs of the older sections of the nation. A correspondent of a New Orleans newspaper believed that the character of the
inhabitants had developed as it had because the state attracted the wrong
sort of people. He wrote: "It was . . . particularly unfortunate in its early
settlers, Ishmaels of old, without means or love for civilized life, the wilder-
ness is their home; they scorn the city and multitude; neither have they
house or lands; wherever night overtakes them they pitch their tents and
herd their flocks; 'and when the railroad starts, they will start also, to go
whither it cannot come,' so strong is their love for semi-civilized life, so
great their aversion for improvement of whatever kind."[1]

Others found Arkansans to be more civilized. John Meek, who had just
moved to Union County from North Carolina, wrote: "You have made
a great mistake as to our inhabitants, the people composing our community
are the enterprising Citizens of Europe and America from the first Citys
and countys of Maine & every other state till you reach New Orleans &
for urbanity we think we could compare with any country without a blush.
The people are a Church going people & they are greatly proud in being
orderly when to Church, & our Statute Laws are as good as yours and quite
like them." Samuel H. Chester, who immigrated to Union County with
his family in the 1840s, agreed, remembering that although the local people
had come to a new country, they had brought with them "into their
log-cabin homes the ideals and ways of life of the best people of the older
states."[2]

Arkansas had only been in the Union fourteen years and a focus of
American settlement for a little more than twice that time by 1850, and

1. *De Bow's Review,* XXIII (1857), 209–10; John Kerr to James Kerr, May 25, 1851, in
John Kerr Letter, Small Manuscripts Collection, AHC.
2. J. Meek to R. E. Campbell, September 20, 1842, in John Campbell Letters, Small
Manuscripts Collection, AHC; Samuel H. Chester, *Pioneer Days in Arkansas* (Richmond, Va.,
1927), 10.

society was in many ways still rude. But Arkansas was no longer a frontier community. Observers such as Meek and Chester correctly perceived that the white people who had settled in the state were rapidly shaping their communities into reflections of the world that they had left. Social institutions patterned upon those of the older states emerged, modified by local conditions.

Part of the social ideology brought by settlers was the belief that society was divided into identifiable social groups. That idea remained intact in Arkansas. It was a world that recognized social differences, that accepted the existence of a social hierarchy. The lines that separated these groups were not drawn sharply; differences were best seen in qualities attributed to individuals. Distinctions might not always be evident to outside observers, but they were clear enough to local contemporaries to allow them to place friends, associates, and even passing acquaintances in their social positions.

The basis, ultimately, for the local class system was wealth. Henry Morton Stanley, a young British citizen working as a merchant in southern Arkansas in the 1850s, recognized that fact when he compared the upper class in Arkansas with that he knew in England. He found that the local elite had little but their wealth to set them apart. Those claiming elite status possessed only a thin veneer of the cultural and other attainments that would distinguish them in an older society. A South Carolina physician also recognized the economic character of the elite. Although acknowledging that wealthy individuals lived in the state, he concluded that "there is none of this fool aristocracy to contend with here." Lower-class status also was seen as largely financial. One young immigrant defined the bottom of society as individuals "seeking a livelihood in the sense of bare subsistence."[3]

The top of the antebellum social order consisted of people referred to by contemporaries as belonging to "good society," the "best society," a "respectable" family, or a "genteel" family. Male members were characterized as "High Tone Honorable Gentlemen" or a "Perfect Arkansas Gentleman." A woman was usually called simply a "lady." Mrs. Isaac Hilliard, a planter's wife from Chicot County, described the characteristics of a lady when referring to a friend who was "cultivated & refined without pedantry or fastidiousness, soft & gentle in deportment yet energetic in action."[4]

3. Dorothy Stanley, ed., *The Autobiography of Sir Henry Morton Stanley* (New York, 1909), 154, 156; J. W. Carrigan to Dear Brother, October 20, 1859, in John W. Carrigan Papers, DU; E. B. Dickinson to My Dear Parents, September 22, 1848, in Everard B. Dickinson Papers, J. N. Heiskell Collection, UALR.

4. Stanley, ed., *Autobiography*, 154–55, 170; L. Druker to Dear Brother and Sister, December 22, 1844, in Sandford-Everett Family File, UALR; L. H. Warren to R. K. Jones, December 2, 1855, in Kimbrough Jones Papers, DU; J. C. Davis to Dear Brother, November 18, 1849, in James S. Chambers Papers, DU.

Contemporary accounts often equated membership in the upper class with the ownership of a plantation and slaves. Arkansans frequently were identifying planters when they referred to individuals they considered to be a part of the elite. One young woman who moved to Phillips County in the 1840s wrote that "the best society is those that live on plantations." Equating planter and elite status, consequently, has some basis in contemporary society; however, an absolute equation ignores the complexities of actual membership in the elite.[5]

The available biographies of individuals in the sample counties who in 1860 owned twenty or more slaves and called themselves planters show the danger of relying on those parameters in determining membership in the elite. Most of these individuals were involved in a wide variety of business enterprises and might as easily have identified themselves as something other than planters. Elisha Burke of Phillips County, for example, had 27 slaves and 1,460 acres of land, but in addition to farming, he operated a mill, a cotton gin, and a blacksmith shop, and made wagons. Anthony H. Davies, owning 103 slaves and 1,103 acres on his Lake Hall Plantation in Chicot County, was listed as a planter but had started his career as a book-keeper and remained a merchant while doing his farming. The greatest part of such men's wealth came from planting because it was the most important economic enterprise in the state, but they all engaged in a variety of other ventures, just as their northern contemporaries did.[6]

The complexity of elite activities requires an alternative definition of that class. Taking the earlier definition of a plantation as having at least twenty slaves, and assuming that some individuals might have had enough money to own twenty slaves but chose to use their money in other ways, this study considers the elite, at least for purposes of estimating its size and nature, as consisting of all individuals with wealth enough to own that many slaves and to buy the land to put those slaves to work. Roughly, given the average values for slaves and for land among those with twenty or more slaves in 1850 and 1860, this amount was an assessed tax valuation of $12,500 in 1850 and $25,000 in 1860.[7]

5. L. Druker to Brother and Sister, December 22, 1844, L. Druker to Barnum Sandford, January 18, 1845, both in Sandford-Everett Family File.

6. *G/EA*, 754 (Burke); *G/SA*, 836 (Dearing), 1074 (Davies).

7. In 1850 the average value of slaves in the three counties with the largest slave populations was $469 and the average evaluation per acre of land was $3.98. The average number of acres per slave was roughly 30, so a typical twenty-slave plantation had 600 acres. Multiplying 1850 values times the number of slaves and acres produces $9,372 and $2,387, or a total of $11,759. To take into account plantation animals and other property belonging to members of the elite, I raised this figure to $12,500 as an estimate of the minimum amount of money needed for a plantation.

By 1860 the average value of slaves was $860 and land $11.25. The total value for plantation slaves and land was $22,870, increased to $25,000 to take into account other property necessary to be a planter.

TABLE 5

ELITES IN SAMPLE COUNTIES, 1860

| County | Number in Class | Land-owners | % of Class | Average Acreage | Slave-owners | % of Class | Average Slaveholding |
|---|---|---|---|---|---|---|---|
| Chicot | 81 | 80 | 98.8 | 1,799 | 80 | 98.9 | 58.4 |
| Independence | 7 | 7 | 100.0 | 2,021 | 7 | 100.0 | 24.4 |
| Montgomery | — | — | — | — | — | — | — |
| Phillips | 128 | 126 | 98.4 | 1,297 | 127 | 99.2 | 37.7 |
| Pulaski | 49 | 45 | 91.8 | 1,781 | 45 | 91.8 | 25.6 |
| Union | 30 | 30 | 100.0 | 2,302 | 30 | 100.0 | 35.6 |
| Van Buren | — | — | — | — | — | — | — |
| Washington | 4 | 4 | 100.0 | 2,295 | 4 | 100.0 | 15.8 |

By 1860 members of the elite lived in six of the eight sample counties (see Table 5). Most of them owned land or slaves—97 percent of the total in the group held both forms of property. The size of individual holdings ranged from Elisha Worthington's 11,288 acres in Chicot County to Albert Pike's 40 acres in Pulaski County. Among the slaveowners, several owned only one slave. Elisha Worthington, on the other hand, was the largest slaveholder in the state with 320 slaves. The property value of these men ranged from those who met the minimum requirement to that of Worthington, who was the richest man in the state in 1860, with real and personal property assessed at $2,472,200.[8]

The majority of these men were planters, although some also practiced law or medicine. Whatever they did, they had acquired the characteristics associated with elite status. Anthony Davies, for example, would be remembered as a "man of many fine traits of character and undoubted integrity." Similarly, Lycurgus Johnson of Lakeport Plantation in Chicot County, who owned 4,617 acres within the county and 104 slaves, was portrayed by a biographer as "a gentleman of superior education . . . noted

8. See note 8, chap. 1, for a discussion of the sample counties. The data base included all taxpayers for 1850, 1860, and 1866.

for hospitality, dignity and social culture." Johnson lived "surrounded by all the comforts that wealth can provide."[9]

Some members of the elite chose not to be planters but invested their resources in other enterprises. Fifty-one individuals who meet the financial criteria for the elite in the eight sample counties—that is, about 17 percent of the total—did not have enough slaves to qualify as planters. The largest percentage of these elite nonplanters was in Washington County, but the largest absolute numbers were in Phillips and Pulaski counties. In Washington County members of this subgroup had their wealth primarily in land and livestock. In the other counties they usually were merchants or land dealers. Peter Hanger of Little Rock is typical. Hanger farmed, owning 1,131 acres of land and nine slaves, but most of his wealth came from investments in town lots in Little Rock, from a retail store, and from ownership of a stage line that held the mail contracts for the entire state of Arkansas. A. J. Hutt, also of Little Rock, was one of the city's earliest retail merchants. Hutt had nine slaves, but most of his wealth was based on his ownership of local town lots, the inventory from his business, and invested capital.[10]

As had been noted by Henry Stanley, the elite in general possessed few characteristics other than their wealth to distinguish them from their poorer neighbors. Their education and religious preferences differed somewhat from those of the community at large, but not enough to clearly mark social distinction. The limited biographical information on the members of the elite of 1860 show that few possessed education beyond that provided by the rural schools of the period, although even a modest education set them apart from the poor. There were exceptions, such as Dr. Charles McDermott of Chicot County, who had been sent by his wealthy Louisiana family to Yale for a medical education. More common, however, were men like William Byers of Independence County, who studied law, practiced as an attorney, and was one of his county's largest planters, but who did all of this, in the words of a biographer, after "receiving a limited education, so far as the facilities of schooling were concerned."[11]

By 1860, however, the children of many elite families such as McDermott's and Byers' were receiving an education. Dr. McDermott sent his own son to Tulane at New Orleans to study medicine. One of Byers' sons studied to receive a degree in civil engineering. Members of the elite

9. G/EA, 1074 (Davies), 1076–77 (Johnson).
10. G/CA, 450 (Hanger), 464–65 (Hutt); Little Rock *Arkansas Gazette*, July 31, 1858.
11. G/SA, 1078 (McDermott); G/NEA, 647 (Byers). Elite biographies were obtained by comparing elites defined by the tax rolls with biographies in the 1890 *Goodspeed's* county histories.

sent their children to the University of Virginia, the University of North Carolina, the University of Georgia, and other southern schools. John H. Clopton of Phillips County sent his son William to the University of Berlin. The new generation of the Arkansas elite would be marked by formal education up to and including the college level.[12]

The religious affiliations of the elite were even less distinctive than their level of education. Like the rest of the population, most of the elite were Protestant and belonged to one of the same few major denominations. There was some difference, however, in the proportions within each denomination. In a sample, the largest number of elite church members were Episcopalians, 22 percent of the total, and the second largest were Presbyterians, 16 percent. The Episcopal affiliation was quite disproportionate, since that denomination represented only 0.7 percent of the number of churches in the state and had only 0.8 percent of the church accommodations (the Presbyterians had 13 percent of the churches and 16 percent of the accommodations). Meanwhile elite members of the Methodist and Baptist churches combined were equal in number to Episcopalians, even though in the state overall these two denominations represented 78 percent of the total churches and 75 percent of the accommodations. Wealthy Arkansans thus tended to be distributed more evenly among the state's denominations than was the general population. However, the largest single group of the elite in terms of affiliation, 35 percent, indicated no denominational preference at all.[13]

Education and religion did not mark the elite's uniqueness, but in possessions, particularly homes, and life-style its difference from other groups was conspicuous. Lycurgus Johnson's Lakeport was one of the finest examples of plantation architecture in Arkansas. Built in 1850, the fourteen-room house embodied the Greek Revival style popular elsewhere in the South, the main entrance dominated by a two-story portico topped with a triangular gable. The interior was decorated simply, although the main hall and front parlor contained large chandeliers. Other homes may have rivaled Lakeport's grandeur. Robert Goodwin, owner of 5,040 acres and thirty-seven slaves, had a plantation house described as "one of the largest and finest country homes in Union County." Other members of the elite showed their wealth with equal ostentation.[14]

The elite also owned more household goods than their less-well-off

12. *G/SA*, 836, 844, 1078, 1088; *G/EA*, 760–62, 781, 792; *G/NEA*, 617.

13. *Eighth Census, 1860: Statistics*, 355–56. The sample was members of the elite in the sample counties with biographies in the *Goodspeed's* histories.

14. Information from "Nomination Form—National Register of Historic Places Inventory," in Arkansas Department of Natural and Cultural Heritage, Little Rock; *G/SA*, 839.

neighbors. The household inventory of John Adamson of Pulaski County provides an example of the extent of such property. A sixty-five-year-old planter, merchant, and steamboat owner with land and slaves, Adamson left an estate that included two dining tables, one card table, twenty-three assorted chairs, three large mirrors, a bookcase and books, one mahogany workstand, one green-painted workstand, a dressing table, six different beds, two shuck mattresses, and two cotton mattresses; his dining room contained a bureau, six silver tablespoons, six silver teaspoons, a dozen dessert knives and forks, a half dozen common knives and forks, and a china tea set; the kitchen was outfitted with a cooking stove, crockery, pots and kettles, and utensils. The appraisers even listed the brass andirons, a pair of iron andirons, shovel and tongs, and eighty yards of carpeting. The most valuable item in the list was a silver watch with gold chain and seal, assessed at $30. The estates of other wealthy individuals showed similarly lengthy lists of material possessions.[15]

Among the most-remembered aspects of the elite's life-style are its hospitality and its leisure activities. The life of Mrs. Isaac Hilliard, the mistress of a plantation with more than eighty slaves in Chicot County, exemplified this behavior. She entertained frequently and lavishly: one light dinner that she gave for "ladies" of the neighborhood (who came to visit while their husbands gathered for a feast of wild game) consisted of gumbo, turkey, chicken, beef tongue, guava jelly, vegetables, pickles, plum pudding, and syllabub. At another dinner, for her husband and one of his friends, she served so many courses that both the guest and Mr. Hilliard "turned up their sleeve cuffs and declared they would not eat another mouthful."[16]

The elite also traveled. When Lewis Butler and his father, Alexander, a merchant and planter from Dallas County, visited New York City on business in 1857, Lewis was able to do extensive sightseeing, including a visit to Barnum's museum. Mrs. Hilliard's travels were more elaborate. Her visits to New Orleans included residency at the best hotels, fine dinners, and as many nights at theaters and other entertainments as she could schedule. On a trip to New Orleans in January, 1850, she arrived too late on the first evening to go out, but on the second, after a dinner at the Verandah that was "all shadow, no substance . . . elegantly served but badly prepared," she attended Placide's Varieties. The next evening, a visit by Episcopal bishop Leonidas Polk prevented her attending *Romeo and Juliet* after shopping until 4 P.M. The fourth evening she attended a soiree at the St. Charles

15. Pulaski County Probate Court Loose Records, in AHC.
16. Mrs. Isaac Hilliard Diary, January 22, 1850, March 29, 1850, in LSU.

Hotel, wearing her "Brocade & pearls" and lingering to "sip champaign [and] compliments until my head aches." The final evening Mrs. Hilliard dined with friends, having a "very handsomely served and sumptuous dinner," then attended the American Theatre to see *The Stranger*. All of this was far beyond what was possible for less fortunate members of Arkansas society.[17]

Wealth made it possible for the elite to live in a manner that set them apart, but little else distinguished them. They possessed few other characteristics to single them out, although during the 1850s they were setting themselves off with cultural acquisitions, particularly education, in addition to their material ones. No very substantial cultural divide had been established, however, by 1860.

Beneath the elite was a large class considered by contemporaries to be the backbone of society. It consisted of individuals and families that men like John Meek considered respectable and civilized. They knew what society should be and worked to better their lives. Samuel Chester associated this class with families like the McRaes of Union County, " a sturdy tribe, noted for business sagacity, incorruptible integrity, old-fashioned piety and the absence of any fear complex in their psychological make-up." Like the majority of other settlers, the McRaes came to Arkansas "facing the hardships of pioneer life, partly in the same spirit of adventure that brought their forefathers from across the sea, and partly for the sake of what would come to them and their children in the development of the country." They were propertied, hard-working, and God-fearing, but without the wealth of the elite.[18]

Antebellum observers did not define this less-wealthy propertied class precisely. They recognized that its members were not among the elite but were certainly above the poor and the propertyless. Although generally perceived as a single group, this class is more usefully separated into two for analysis. One subcategory includes those who had acquired at least one slave or who had the wealth necessary to purchase one, but did not have enough slaves or wealth to be members of the elite. In 1860 the minimum worth for this group was about $1,000. That amount was significant because the farmer or merchant who achieved it had made the first step toward controlling the labor of others and had the potential to go further. Such a person also was able to afford a life-style different from that of the second

17. Elizabeth Paisley Huckaby and Ethel C. Simpson, eds., *Tulip Evermore: Emma Butler and William Paisley, Their Lives in Letters, 1857–1887* (Fayetteville, 1985), 20–21; Hilliard Diary, January 28–31, 1850.

18. J. Meek to R. E. Campbell, September 20, 1842, in Campbell Letters; Chester, *Pioneer Days in Arkansas*, 12, 9–10.

TABLE 6

UPPER-MIDDLE CLASS IN SAMPLE COUNTIES, 1860

| County | Number in Class | Land-owners | % of Class | Average Acreage | Slave-owners | % of Class | Average Slaveholding |
|---|---|---|---|---|---|---|---|
| Chicot | 192 | 114 | 59.4 | 337 | 120 | 62.5 | 6.4 |
| Independence | 575 | 505 | 87.8 | 408 | 198 | 34.4 | 3.7 |
| Montgomery | 99 | 83 | 83.8 | 177 | 24 | 24.2 | 3.3 |
| Phillips | 574 | 426 | 74.2 | 315 | 316 | 55.1 | 5.5 |
| Pulaski | 541 | 331 | 61.2 | 404 | 265 | 48.9 | 4.0 |
| Union | 635 | 515 | 81.1 | 514 | 522 | 82.2 | 5.9 |
| Van Buren | 96 | 81 | 84.4 | 271 | 28 | 29.2 | 2.7 |
| Washington | 518 | 478 | 92.3 | 304 | 206 | 39.8 | 3.3 |

subgroup, which consisted of those who did not have a slave or enough money to obtain one but still had property.

Although the terms are not completely satisfactory, these two groups can reasonably be called the "upper-middle class," consisting of those who possessed wealth between $1,000 and $24,999, and the "lower-middle class," made up of those who had property, but valued at less than $1,000.

The upper-middle class in antebellum society looked much like the elite. The most obvious differences were in the amount of wealth they possessed and the sources of that wealth. The elite, with few exceptions, were landowners *and* slaveowners. The same was not true of the upper-middle class: individuals with wealth evaluated between $1,000 and $24,999 were more likely to be landowners than slaveowners. The average amount of property they held was considerably lower than that of the elite. Their largest average property holding was 514 acres in Union County, less than half the smallest county average for the elite, 1,297 acres (Phillips County). Their largest average slaveholding, however—6.4 in Chicot County—was barely a ninth of the average of 58.4 held by the elite in the same county and only about a third of the smallest elite average, 15.8 in Washington County (see Table 6).

For the most part, the members of the upper-middle class were small planters and prosperous farmers. Some of them were very successful. Loderick Matthews, for example, moved to Union County in 1844, purchased 1,200 acres, and then proceeded to expand his operations to the point that by 1860 the family owned 2,480 acres and fifteen slaves locally, with other properties in Texas. He was considered "one of the most extensive planters of that time." More typical of the class were men such as Isaac Wyatt of Independence County, who by 1860 had 486 acres and six slaves. With such resources he was assured of economic success, and at the time of his death he was remembered as "a prosperous and highly respected farmer." Typical of the nonslaveholding upper-middle-class farmers was James W. Headstream, who began farming in Independence County when only eighteen years old. By 1860 he had put together 340 acres and had property valued at $1,552. He was considered a successful farmer, and a man whose "prosperity is the result of many hardships endured and the practice of economy as well as good management and enterprise."[19]

Although the majority of the upper-middle class were farmers, a large number of them were merchants, successful craftsmen, or professionals. One of the more successful men of this type was H. P. Coolidge of Helena. Coolidge had moved from Ohio to New Orleans in 1829, then to Helena in 1842. First renting a store, he expanded his business until, just before the war, he owned five slaves, 960 acres, $13,000 in town lots, and other property assessed at $3,140. Local enterprises offered many opportunities to get ahead for the upper-middle class. Its members worked as blacksmiths, carpenters, tanners, mill operators, and mechanics, as well as merchants and professionals.[20]

As with the elite, separating the upper-middle class into farmers and nonfarmers does not reflect the realities of their lives. They pursued economic prospects in many different ways, and their progress took them into and out of agriculture and other work. The career of John H. Cornish of El Dorado, in Union County, indicates this flexibility. Cornish settled in southern Arkansas in about 1833 when his wagon broke down near El Dorado. He started as a farmer, was elected county sheriff, moved to town in 1846, opened a hotel, acquired a store, and finally sold his hotel to purchase a plantation. Until his death he farmed and ran his store. The tax rolls show that in 1860 he owned 370 acres, three slaves, and property worth $7,409. Cornish changed careers perhaps more than usual, but few individuals pursued one line of work to the exclusion of others. Most sought in every way to maximize their economic opportunities.[21]

Cultural differences also existed between the upper-middle class and the

19. *G/EA*, 772, 774, 777, 793; *G/SA*, 853 (Matthews); *G/NEA*, 725 (Wyatt), 676 (Headstream).

20. *G/EA*, 755, 765, 766 (Coolidge), 771; *G/CA*, 457 (Griffith).

21. *G/SA*, 833–34.

elite. With less money, the upper middle had even fewer educational opportunities. Some of this class had attended college, but the majority had received only a common-school education—roughly the equivalent of elementary school. Isaac Butler Day, son of a prosperous planter in Jackson County, remembered that locally "the schools were poor" and that he did not attend school regularly until he was seventeen years old. John G. Herbert, whose parents owned a farm and fifteen slaves in Izard County, attended school for eight years but remembered that most children went "irregularly on account of having to work." The members of this class understood the value of formal education but found self-education to be the principal avenue available to them.[22]

Religious life of the upper-middle class also differed. Their denominational preferences were less diverse than the elite's and mirrored those of the community at large more closely. A sample showed that a majority of them were Methodists (30 percent) or Baptists (22 percent). Presbyterians constituted the third-largest group, 16 percent. Members of the upper-middle class often were prominent in their local churches, serving in a variety of leadership roles—as organizers, elders, and stewards. As with the elite, however, a large percentage could not be identified as members of any particular denomination—about 21 percent.[23]

Material possessions provided the most visible evidence of the difference in wealth between the upper-middle and elite classes. The homes of the upper-middle class were not as grand. Samuel Chester remembered that most of the houses in the Mount Holly community were built on the same pattern—two large rooms joined by a passageway, shed rooms in the back, and detached cabins for the kitchen, pantry, smokehouse, and children's bedrooms. Jonas Patterson, a nonslaveholding farmer from Charleston, in Sebastian County, lived in a home similar to that described by Chester, consisting of two sixteen-foot rooms on a ten-foot hall. The bedrooms were in the sheds built onto the back. The entire structure was made of hewed logs. The Driver family of Prairie County, with 640 acres and seven slaves, were wealthier than the Pattersons but their home was much the same, a "double log house with 2 shed rooms kitchen and dining room separate from main building and built of logs."[24]

Predictably, the upper-middle class had fewer household goods and less

22. Gustavus W. Dyer and John Trotwood Moore, comps., *The Tennessee Civil War Veterans Questionnaires* (5 vols.; Easley, S.C., 1985), II, 658 (Day), III, 1082 (Herbert); *GINEA*, 670. See also Chester, *Pioneer Days in Arkansas*, 26–30. The educational sample consists of individuals from tax rolls located in the *Goodspeed's* histories.

23. The religious statistics are based on biographies in *Goodspeed's*.

24. Chester, *Pioneer Days in Arkansas*, 16–17; Dyer and Moore, comps., *Tennessee Civil War Veterans Questionnaires*, II, 722 (Driver), IV, 1704 (Patterson).

personal property than the elite. The estate inventory of Dr. Paul Starbuck, a Pulaski County farmer, reflects a typical household. In 1860 his assessed property had been valued at $15,000, consisting of 280 acres of land and several head of stock. At the time of his death he owned one wardrobe, three rocking chairs, one bureau, a half dozen chairs, one card table, a lot of surveying instruments, some new carpet, and few other personal items. William Adamson, another Pulaski County farmer, had 80 acres plus livestock, the total value of the land and animals being $2,160. His estate consisted of two slaves who had not been assessed and the same type of household furnishings as Starbuck's, including five chairs, four bedsteads and bedding, and a wash basin and pitcher. The smaller amount of household possessions—and particularly the absence of items such as gold watches and silverware—indicate that the step from the elite to the upper-middle class was a large one.[25]

The upper-middle class could not afford distant travels and expensive entertainments, but otherwise they engaged in many of the same day-to-day social activities as their wealthier neighbors. Sunday visits and weekend dinner parties were common forms of entertainment. School and church provided other opportunities for social interaction. There were occasional dances. Where dancing was considered morally wrong, the young engaged in similar activities, such as a game called "twistification." Formal balls and parties were more common in towns. John Brown took his daughter to one such occasion at Camden so that she could learn "the forms of society" and acquire the "confidence necessary to be at ease in company." They left at midnight, at which time the too-free use of wine and spirits made it unsafe for "ladies" to remain "with propriety."[26]

The differences between the upper-middle and lower-middle classes were almost as pronounced as those between the two upper classes. Members of the lower-middle class were less likely than those above them to own land, and those who did owned less of it. The largest average landholding among this group was 135 acres in Union County; county by county, the average lower-middle-class holding ranged from about one-fourth to not quite one-half the average among the upper-middle class (see Table 7). There were some slaveholders among the lower-middle class, but only in Phillips County, at 22.8 percent, did they make up more than a tiny fraction of the class as a whole. Moreover, even for the few who did own slaves,

25. Pulaski County Probate Court Loose Records, in AHC.

26. A. Trulock to Dear Sister, November 22, 1847, in Trulock Family Letters, UALR; Sarah A. Nelson to Dear Menecee and Emily, February 22, 1849, in Sarah A. Nelson Letter, Small Manuscripts Collection, AHC; Chester, *Pioneer Days in Arkansas,* 11–20; John W. Brown Diary, September 18, 1853, July 7, September 24, December 27, 1854, in AHC.

TABLE 7

LOWER-MIDDLE CLASS IN SAMPLE COUNTIES, 1860

| County | Number in Class | Land-owners | % of Class | Average Acreage | Slave-owners | % of Class | Average Slaveholding |
|---|---|---|---|---|---|---|---|
| Chicot | 90 | 19 | 21.1 | 76 | 5 | 5.5 | 1.0 |
| Independence | 1,435 | 949 | 66.1 | 128 | 12 | 0.8 | 1.0 |
| Montgomery | 448 | 111 | 24.8 | 83 | 2 | 0.4 | 1.0 |
| Phillips | 381 | 140 | 36.7 | 89 | 87 | 22.8 | 1.1 |
| Pulaski | 614 | 362 | 58.9 | 115 | 11 | 1.8 | 1.8 |
| Union | 549 | 276 | 50.3 | 135 | 11 | 2.0 | 1.1 |
| Van Buren | 491 | 175 | 35.6 | 128 | 2 | 0.4 | 1.0 |
| Washington | 1,073 | 661 | 61.6 | 107 | 26 | 2.4 | 1.1 |

the holdings were very small, ranging from 1.8 slaves per owner in Pulaski County to 1.0 per owner in Chicot, Independence, Montgomery, and Van Buren counties.

The lower-middle class engaged in most of the same economic activities as the upper-middle class, although on a smaller scale. Most of them were farmers, but they tended to move about the countryside more than their more successful neighbors. They were more likely to rent than to own the land that they worked. Anthony Coble of Independence County was typically mobile, moving back and forth and also into and out of landownership. Settling in Arkansas in 1849, he purchased 40 acres in Independence County to farm, but he also worked as a carpenter. In 1860, he sold his farm and moved on to Jackson County, this time renting land and farming as a tenant until 1863. At that time he returned to Independence County and purchased 160 acres, which he farmed until he died in 1881. In the plantation counties, some men of this class also worked as overseers and superintendents of the local plantations.[27]

Nonfarming members of the lower-middle class were more likely to be craftsmen or artisans than merchants. Representative occupations include painter, carpenter, ginwright, miller, wagonmaker, cabinetmaker, black-

27. G/NEA, 654 (Coble)—see also ibid. (Cook); G/EA, 794, 797.

smith, and mechanic. Some individuals were very successful. Bernard Murray, an Irish immigrant, settled in Little Rock in 1857, practically penniless. He went to work as a contractor and hired others to "do the rougher work" while he "put on the finer touches." He was successful enough that by 1860 he had purchased 320 acres of land in Pulaski County and reported property valued at $960. Trades were not the path to great wealth in antebellum society, but they were a good means to acquire a livelihood other than in agriculture and thus provided the economic basis for this part of the lower-middle class.[28]

In their religious life the lower-middle class mirrored the class above them. The majority of a sample were either Methodists or Baptists, with almost 28 percent associated with the Methodist Episcopal Church and another 28 percent being Southern, Primitive, or Missionary Baptists. As among the upper-middle class, Presbyterians constituted the third largest group; 15 percent were members of one of the varieties of that faith. The denominational preference of about 18 percent of the sample could not be determined.

The social life of the lower-middle class was similar to that of the less-wealthy members of the upper-middle class. Visiting was a major social activity and included occasions such as quiltings. "Frolics" or neighborhood dances were also held, although one young woman in Saline County complained that Arkansans did not have as many such events as people in other frontier areas. Church and some school activities also provided social opportunities within communities. Working harder, this class appears to have had less time for interacting with what contemporaries referred to as "society."[29]

Although the life-styles of two middle classes were similar, differences in wealth produced cultural distinctions. Members of the lower-middle class had less education than the upper middle. Except in towns, few of this class received a formal education. Those who did experienced limited schooling. J. R. Bullington, whose father owned 160 acres in Independence County, was typical, remembering that he "passed his school days in picking cotton, gathering corn and clearing new ground." Jasper Farmer of Washington County attended a neighborhood school, but his "early days were divided between attending the common schools and assisting his father on the farm." Jeremiah G. Ellis of Mississippi County, another member of this

28. See G/NEA, 688; G/EA, 750; G/CA, 489 (Murray); and G/NWA, 946, 958, 960, 974.

29. Sarah A. Nelson to Dear Menecee, February 15, 1849, in Nelson Letter; Annie McRae to Dear Fannie, November 2, 1857, in Annie McRae Letter, Small Manuscripts Collection, AHC.

class, also attended school, but spent only four or five months in classes during his entire life.[30]

Housing for the lower-middle class mirrored their relative lack of wealth. For country people, homes usually were log or mixed log-and-frame construction. The houses were very small and often lacked the outbuildings that typified the homesteads of wealthier neighbors. Jeremiah Ellis' entire family lived in a one-room log house that was daubed with mud and had a stick-and-dirt chimney. The family of A. J. Montgomery, small farmers in Craighead County, lived in a similar home constructed of logs, but with two rooms.[31]

The lower-middle class also possessed little personal property when compared with the elite. The inventory of the estate of an attorney from Lafayette County shows the limited property of the class. The administrator reported that in addition to law books, the estate consisted of two tables, a paper case, one washstand with bowl and pitcher, one mirror, one bedstead, a set of fire irons, various articles of clothing, a horse and furnishings, one gold ring, an umbrella, and one "chambre de pot." The household furnishings of James Adams of Pulaski County consisted of five feather beds and four bedsteads, a half dozen chairs, two tables, and one lot of cooking utensils, plus farm equipment and stock.[32]

At the bottom of white society were those who possessed no property at all. Contemporaries often identified them in terms of their life-style and occupations; the "peddler class" and "backwoodsmen & Mechanics" were typical descriptions. The lower class included the people seen by the correspondent of *De Bow's Review* as constituting the majority of people in the state, and its members became the stereotypical Arkansans in the 1830s with the publication of the popular humorous dialogue "Arkansas Traveler." By the 1850s, lack of wealth was commonly used to identify the class, which included those referred to as being of the "hopelessly 'down and out' class" or as being a "Hireling & a slave."[33]

By definition, the lower class of white society was propertyless, but not all who fit within a property-based definition of the lower class were in fact poor. Some personally had no property, but their families did. For example, Young V. Mack of Independence County was twenty-two years

---

30. *G/NEA*, 646 (Bullington); *G/NWA*, 940; Dyer and Moore, comps., *Tennessee Veterans Questionnaire*, II, 76.

31. Dyer and Moore, comps., *Tennessee Veterans Questionnaire*, II, 766 (Ellis), IV, 1558 (Montgomery).

32. Inventory, Borden Estate, in UALR; Pulaski County Probate Court Loose Files.

33. Everard B. Dickinson to My Dear Parents, September 22, 1848, in Dickinson Papers; Chester, *Pioneer Days in Arkansas*, 9.

old in 1860 and showed no taxable property. Mack's father, however, owned 240 acres near Batesville, which Young eventually inherited. Twenty-four-year-old Lemuel T. Darden of Union County was also technically propertyless in 1860 but was actually managing his mother's land and three slaves.[34]

The truly propertyless included individuals who worked as manual laborers or at such jobs as store clerk. Some appear to have been temporarily down on their luck. A few farmed as squatters on unclaimed government land or the property of absentee landowners. One example of the class was Ferdinand La Fayette Neal of Union County. He came from a prosperous family east of the Mississippi River, but he worked as a clerk in a store at Champagnolle, carried the chain for the local surveyor, hunted gold for a time in California, then returned to open a store at Miller's Bluff, in Union County. He had property at times, but in 1860 he had none assessed. Drury D. Smart of Independence County labored as a farmhand, lived in Little Rock for a time working as a stage driver, then returned to Independence County and rented a farm before the outbreak of war. W. W. Black of Pulaski County was seventeen years old in 1860 and worked as an apprentice.[35]

Life was hard for those without property. Their days revolved primarily around work. Their social lives were restricted, although religion provided some opportunities for sociality. Some, of course, such as George Vining of Jefferson County, whose family struggled for survival in the antebellum years, associated with those who spent their free time shooting, racing horses, drinking, gambling, dancing, and fighting. The class had few material possessions. Vining recalled: "It was in some respects the 'simple life'. It was as regarded what they used in their homes, especially the poorer class." They had little that required money. They were not educated, having neither the time nor the resources to attend school. They lacked household goods. Their one-room cabins were usually furnished with benches and stools and a bed with one side pegged into the wall. A young man without property, but whose family had some money, summed up the plight of this class when he informed his parents, "What an inconvenient thing it is to be poor."[36]

The social system thus far described was recognizable statewide, but local

34. *G/NEA*, 692; *G/SA*, 835.

35. *G/SA*, 856–57 (Neal); *G/NEA*, 714 (Smart); Dyer and Moore, comps., *Tennessee Veterans Questionnaire*, I, 324 (Black); George T. Vining, "An Early Settler Remembers," *Jefferson County Historical Quarterly*, VI (1975), 12.

36. E. B. Dickinson to My Dear Parents, January 27, 1849, in Dickinson Papers; Vining, "An Early Settler Remembers," 12, 19 (quotation).

TABLE 8

ALL CLASSES IN SAMPLE COUNTIES, 1860

| County | Elite | | Upper-Middle | | Lower-Middle | | Lower | |
|---|---|---|---|---|---|---|---|---|
| | Number | % | Number | % | Number | % | Number | % |
| Chicot | 81 | 18.6 | 192 | 43.9 | 90 | 20.6 | 74 | 16.9 |
| Independence | 7 | .3 | 575 | 25.8 | 1,435 | 64.3 | 214 | 9.6 |
| Montgomery | — | .0 | 99 | 16.6 | 448 | 74.9 | 51 | 8.5 |
| Phillips | 128 | 8.9 | 574 | 40.1 | 381 | 26.6 | 349 | 24.4 |
| Pulaski | 49 | 3.7 | 541 | 40.8 | 614 | 46.4 | 121 | 9.1 |
| Union | 30 | 2.2 | 635 | 47.7 | 549 | 41.2 | 118 | 8.9 |
| Van Buren | — | .0 | 96 | 15.4 | 491 | 78.7 | 37 | 5.9 |
| Washington | 4 | .2 | 518 | 30.9 | 1,073 | 64.1 | 80 | 4.8 |

TABLE 9

SHARE OF LAND AND SLAVES BY CLASS, SAMPLE COUNTIES, 1860

| County | Elite | | Upper-Middle | | Lower-Middle | | Lower | |
|---|---|---|---|---|---|---|---|---|
| | Land | Slaves | Land | Slaves | Land | Slaves | Land | Slaves |
| Chicot | 78.1 | 85.8 | 21.1 | 14.1 | .8 | .1 | 0.0 | 0.0 |
| Independence | 4.1 | 18.7 | 60.3 | 80.0 | 35.6 | 1.3 | 0.0 | 0.0 |
| Montgomery | — | — | 61.3 | 97.5 | 38.7 | 2.5 | 0.0 | 0.0 |
| Phillips | 52.7 | 72.2 | 43.3 | 26.3 | 4.0 | 1.5 | 0.0 | 0.0 |
| Pulaski | 31.4 | 52.7 | 52.3 | 46.4 | 16.3 | .9 | 0.0 | 0.0 |
| Union | 18.6 | 25.7 | 71.4 | 74.0 | 10.0 | .3 | 0.0 | 0.0 |
| Van Buren | — | — | 49.5 | 97.4 | 50.5 | 2.6 | 0.0 | 0.0 |
| Washington | 4.1 | 7.8 | 64.5 | 88.6 | 31.4 | 3.6 | 0.0 | 0.0 |

economic conditions created at least two different types of communities across the state. Counties with good land and access to transportation attracted people with wealth and created wealth among their inhabitants. In the four sample plantation counties—Chicot, Phillips, Pulaski, and Union—the elite and the upper-middle class represented either a majority or a near-majority of the total population (Table 8). The two upper classes dominated these communities numerically and controlled the basic resources, owning most of the land and most of the slave labor force (Table 9). The nonplantation counties, in contrast, did not have the resources to maintain an elite or a large upper-middle class. Such counties drew people from the lower classes, offering cheap land and some means of securing a livelihood. In the four sample counties without extensive plantation holdings—Independence, Montgomery, Van Buren, and Washington—the majority of taxpayers came from the lower two classes. In these countries the lower classes also owned a greater share of the property than they did elsewhere. They did not have many slaves, but they did own land, and that gave them a stake in the local community. These nonplantation communities were, at least economically, more egalitarian than the wealthier counties.

The differences among classes and between the different types of communities that existed were potential sources of political conflict in Arkansas, but political conflict based on class interests did not develop in the antebellum years. Despite differences, white Arkansas was a relatively cohesive society. The cultural background of Arkansans, the generally shared rural and agrarian life-style, and the operation of the social system prevented the emergence of class friction in the antebellum years. The interaction of these factors created a social ideology that recognized classes but saw the class system as one in which individuals were not fixed permanently within a class but had the opportunity for mobility. Class was not a limiting force but simply reflected gradations in wealth. Individuals had equal opportunities to move up and down within the antebellum world.

The common southern background of most white Arkansans was essential to social cohesion. Most of them came from communities where the ideology of social democracy, a class system with individual mobility, was already in place. These communities embraced the ideals of economic and political democracy as well. In 1860 more than 90 percent of the state's residents were from southern slave states—30 percent from Tennessee, 16 percent from Mississippi, 11 from Alabama, 10 from Missouri, 9 from Georgia, 4 from Kentucky, and another 12 percent from other slave states.[37]

37. Robert D. Walz, "Migration into Arkansas, 1834–1880" (Ph.D. dissertation, University of Texas, 1958), 133, 75. See James Oakes, *The Ruling Race: A History of American Slaveholders* (New York, 1982), 127–28, for a discussion of the egalitarian idea.

Democratic and egalitarian ideology was fostered further by the contin- ued development of Arkansas society in a rural world. By 1860 only Cam- den, Fort Smith, Little Rock, and Pine Bluff had more than 1,000 persons, and these communities were hardly urban. The four had a combined popu- lation of 6,811, only 1.5 percent of the state total. The majority of Arkansans lived in rural isolation, alone except for members of the immediate family and slaves. Henry Stanley believed that this phenomenon added to Arkan- sas' provincialism because people spent too much time within their own fences.[38]

The agrarian base of society added to the dominant social ideal. The plantation, farm, and rural village typified the world of individual Arkansans and provided a setting that reinforced the white egalitarianism of southern culture. The majority of individuals were bound together, from the richest to the poorest farmer, in a common struggle to wrest a living from nature. Their lives were governed by the unvarying cycle of natural events associ- ated with farm life. Even the townspeople were caught up in this cycle, either as farmers themselves or in their business connections with the state's dominant economic enterprise.[39]

The existence of expanding economic opportunities and the consequent social mobility may ultimately have been the most important factors mold- ing the social ideology of antebellum Arkansans. New lands, more slaves, and good prices for cotton produced a steady expansion of wealth for all sorts of people and produced an expanding social order. Arkansans experienced a great degree of social mobility, with comparatively high rates of upward social movement. Through the 1850s the upper classes grew not only in absolute numbers, but also in strength proportional to the rest of the population. This pattern was especially marked in the plantation coun- ties but appeared in all of them. While the upper and upper-middle classes increased in numbers and proportional strength, the lower-middle and lower classes grew in absolute numbers (except in Chicot and Union coun- ties) but declined as a portion of the total population (see Table 10).

The opportunities for social movement can also be seen in figures for persistence and mobility between 1850 and 1860 in the sample counties. A high rate of persistence—survival of an individual or a family in the same county—suggests that people found it relatively easy to achieve economic success there. With new opportunities open elsewhere, those who were

38. Stanley, ed., *Autobiography*. See also I. C. Quinn to Honored Friends, November 7, 1854, in Mary Frances Jane Pursley Papers, DU; Tommy R. Thompson, ed., "Searching for the American Dream in Arkansas: Letters of a Pioneer Family," *AHQ*, XXXVIII (Summer, 1979), 171.

39. *Eighth Census, 1860: Population*, 19. This conclusion is based on sources detailing daily life in antebellum Arkansas.

TABLE 10

GROWTH OF CLASSES, SAMPLE COUNTIES, 1850–1860

| County | Upper | | Upper-Middle | | Lower-Middle | | Lower | |
|---|---|---|---|---|---|---|---|---|
| | 1850 | 1860 | 1850 | 1860 | 1850 | 1860 | 1850 | 1860 |
| Chicot | 57 | 81 | 127 | 192 | 97 | 90 | 80 | 74 |
| (%) | (16) | (19) | (35) | (44) | (27) | (21) | (22) | (26) |
| Independence | 2 | 7 | 232 | 575 | 275 | 1,435 | 162 | 214 |
| (%) | ( 1) | ( 1) | (18) | (25) | (68) | (64) | (13) | (10) |
| Montgomery | 0 | 0 | 41 | 99 | 232 | 448 | 16 | 51 |
| (%) | ( 0) | ( 0) | (14) | (17) | (80) | (75) | ( 6) | ( 8) |
| Phillips | 28 | 128 | 278 | 574 | 367 | 381 | 195 | 349 |
| (%) | ( 3) | ( 9) | (32) | (49) | (42) | (27) | (23) | (24) |
| Pulaski | 15 | 49 | 280 | 541 | 491 | 614 | 275 | 121 |
| (%) | ( 2) | ( 4) | (26) | (41) | (46) | (46) | (26) | ( 9) |
| Union | 29 | 30 | 357 | 635 | 557 | 549 | 281 | 118 |
| (%) | ( 2) | ( 2) | (37) | (48) | (43) | (41) | (18) | ( 9) |
| Van Buren | 0 | 0 | 27 | 96 | 236 | 491 | 50 | 37 |
| (%) | ( 0) | ( 0) | ( 9) | (15) | (75) | (79) | (16) | ( 6) |
| Washington | 4 | 4 | 373 | 518 | 987 | 1,073 | 76 | 80 |
| (%) | ( 1) | ( 1) | (26) | (39) | (68) | (64) | ( 5) | ( 5) |

not satisfied tended to move on. In the sample counties during the 1850s, high persistence rates existed for all classes (Table 11). These rates are generally higher than those discovered in studies of contemporary rural communities elsewhere over the same period. In Trempealeau County, Wisconsin, for example, among those with between $100 and $999 in real property, the rough equivalent of the Arkansas lower-middle class, the persistence rate was 22 percent. In the same county, among those with real property valued between 0 and $99, persistence was 15 percent.[40]

40. Cf. Merle Curti, *The Making of an American Community* (Stanford, 1959), 68; Mildred Throne, "A Population Study of an Iowa County in 1850," *Iowa Journal of History*, VII (1959), 305–30; Howard M. Gitelman, *Working Men of Waltham: Mobility in American Industrial Development, 1850–1890* (Baltimore, 1974), 44–45; and Jonathan M. Wiener, *Social Origins of the New South: Alabama, 1860–1885* (Baton Rouge, 1978), 7–16. See also A. Trulock to Dear Sister, May 21, 1846, in Trulock Family Papers; Mary Owen Sims Journal, May 14, 1859, in AHC.

TABLE 11

PERSISTENCE RATES, SAMPLE COUNTIES, 1850–1860

| County | Elite | Upper-Middle | Lower-Middle | Lower |
|--------|-------|--------------|--------------|-------|
| Chicot | 70 | 36 | 24 | 28 |
| Independence | 100 | 65 | 51 | 51 |
| Montgomery | ★ | 54 | 33 | 13 |
| Phillips | 79 | 51 | 41 | 26 |
| Pulaski | 87 | 63 | 28 | 9 |
| Union | 72 | 47 | 37 | 15 |
| Van Buren | ★ | 59 | 56 | 42 |
| Washington | 75 | 72 | 51˙ | 40 |

★No one in this class in 1850.

Even more telling evidence concerning prewar opportunities appears in the mobility rates from class to class among those individuals who persisted between 1850 and 1860. Many of the new members of the expanding upper classes were local residents who had climbed the social ladder. In counties with members of the elite, between 3 and 28 percent of the persisting upper-middle-class members moved into the elite class during this period. Although persistence rates were not as high for the lower-middle class as for the upper-middle, the upward mobility of this group was greater, between 21 and 55 percent (Table 12).

The system entailed some downward movement as well. Having elite status in 1850 did not ensure that this position could be held through the decade. In Phillips County all of the elite persisted and maintained their position, but elsewhere some persisters did not maintain the wealth necessary to preserve their class position. In Chicot County three of forty failed to stay in the elite class, five of twenty-one in Union County, and two of thirteen in Pulaski County. Generally, however, individuals who lost property would not have remained in a county, so the actual downward movement may have been greater.

Shared backgrounds, common life-style, and the existence of opportunities for economic success and upward social mobility provided the basis

TABLE 12

MOBILITY OF PERSISTERS, 1850–1860 (PERCENTAGES)

| County | Upper | | Upper-Middle | | | Lower-Middle | | | Lower | |
|---|---|---|---|---|---|---|---|---|---|---|
| | 0 | – | + | 0 | – | + | 0 | – | + | 0 |
| Chicot | 93 | 7 | 28 | 59 | 13 | 48 | 48 | 2 | 0 | 100 |
| Independence | 50 | 50 | 7 | 66 | 27 | 42 | 58 | 0 | 89 | 11 |
| Montgomery | ★ | ★ | 0 | 77 | 23 | 25 | 75 | 0 | 100 | 0 |
| Phillips | 100 | 0 | 13 | 74 | 13 | 55 | 34 | 11 | 64 | 36 |
| Pulaski | 85 | 15 | 12 | 79 | 9 | 46 | 50 | 4 | 80 | 20 |
| Union | 76 | 24 | 3 | 83 | 14 | 44 | 52 | 4 | 89 | 11 |
| Van Buren | ★ | ★ | 0 | 75 | 25 | 21 | 72 | 7 | 95 | 1 |
| Washington | 67 | 33 | 7 | 79 | 19 | 28 | 72 | 0 | 100 | 0 |

★No one in this class in 1850.

for a social ideology that made sense in this stratified–democratic society. Arkansans recognized that inequalities of wealth and status existed, but differences were acceptable and understandable as explained by contemporary ideas. In the minds of white Arkansans, social distinctions reflected the rewards of accomplishment rather than of birth or preexisting position. Wealth was available to all, and honest labor produced it. Economic success thus gave the individual the right to distinction in the community. Inequality might exist, but it was not a barrier to individual opportunity and social movement.

Most Arkansans appear to have believed that their community was one in which individuals could rise. Their letters repeat the basic theme, proclaiming Arkansas as a place in which they could achieve new status. A young man wrote from northern Arkansas, "This country on some accounts suits me very well & one reason is this — Everybody is poor alike here — no monopoly of property in the hands of a few. . . . — & I feel certain I can make a living here & lie as well as my neighbours & be independent." Another sought to acquire land to "obtain a foot hold before tis too late."[41]

41. B. Sandford to Friend, July 14, 1849, in Sandford-Everett Family File; E. B. Dickinson to My Dear Parents, September 22, 1848, in Dickinson Papers; Thompson, ed., "Searching for the American Dream in Arkansas," 176.

The key to success was individual effort and hard work, along with a bit of luck. One immigrant to Dallas County wrote to his family, "If you could feald fully persuaded in your mind to bear hardships and move to a new country you could better your family if not your self." One settler expected his community to make rapid advances because of the character of its inhabitants: "This many of them will soon do as they are industrious." Another encouraged his nephew, praising his success and adding that "contentment and perseverance will always succeed." Showing his view of how things worked, the latter writer further informed his nephew that members of his family could rise quickly; all that could possibly prevent such success was themselves, he cautioned, noting the character flaw of one family member when he wrote "if Milton would stop drink." [42]

Any attempt to change this system prompted contemporary ire. Even many of the elite considered it essential to guard against those who might attempt to cut off mobility. The editor of the *Arkansas Gazette* warned Arkansans not to take their society for granted; he proposed an agricultural and mechanical school to provide opportunities for young men and as a means of preventing the possibility that "in imitation of the aristocrats of the old world, snob-aristocrats may form a class in this country, and by their high-sounding pretensions, get an acquiescence in their fraudulent claims to exclusiveness." Another writer indicated that there were present some who did pretend to be aristocrats when he apologized for mistakenly identifying another individual as a part of the "*South Carolina Aristocracy*" and noted that the person was actually "one of the best and most *democratic* (in the devine not the *filthy* political sense of that *pure* word) of men." [43]

During the 1850s few stood up for aristocracy in Arkansas. Even the elite considered the climate hostile to any claims of special distinction. Elliott H. Fletcher, a Mississippi River planter, warned his son that they were "both too exclusive and aristocratic in our personal tastes and sentiments for the circumstances that surround us." As a result, he counseled, "we must yield somewhat to the inexorable necessities of the caste, or else we incur mortifications. We must stoop to conquer sometimes, or else an arrow sped by a vulgar hand may find a crevice in our armor of pride, and wound us to the quick." [44]

Ultimately, white Arkansans were bonded together by a common world

42. E. Benson to Dear Brother, April 1, 1857, in Burwell Benson Papers, UNC; J. Meek to Dear Son, September 20, 1842, in Meek Letters, Small Manuscripts Collection, AHC; W. Carrigan to Dear Nephew, December 28, 1858, February 4, 1860, in Carrigan Papers.

43. Little Rock *Arkansas Gazette,* March 2, 1855; C. C. Scott to David Walker, December 5, 1851, in David Walker Papers, UAF.

44. E. H. Fletcher to My Dear Son, November 25, 1861, in Elliott H. Fletcher Papers, AHC.

view that encouraged them to believe that they, individually, through hard work, could establish a better place for themselves. The world produced social differences, but those differences reflected the worth of individuals, each possessing control of his or her individual destiny. Eugene Genovese has argued that for the South as a whole, the 1850s saw the "easy social democracy, so characteristic of life on the American frontier . . . [give] way steadily before aristocratic pretensions." In Arkansas, however, social democracy still resisted all efforts at suppressing it. For whites, society offered opportunities to all, or at least appeared to. Protecting this society and its openness was a consideration of all through the 1850s; both those who exercised power and those who aspired to power saw this as a principal goal. Politics would focus greatly on making sure that no single group was able to "set themselves apart" as Christopher C. Danley of the *Arkansas Gazette* had warned. Ensuring an egalitarian society for whites required in particular the protection of slavery, the institution upon which the economic and social success of many whites was based.[45]

45. Eugene D. Genovese, *The World the Slaveholders Made: Two Essays in Interpretation* (New York, 1969), 123.

# 3

## SLAVERY AND SLAVES

THE 111,115 BLACK SLAVES WHO LABORED ON THE PLANTA-
tions and farms and in the shops and homes of Arkansas in 1860 lived in
a world considerably different from that of white society. An interplay of
complex forces, including both blacks' and whites' needs, defined the slaves'
place and identity. The demands of whites, because of their relative power,
were perhaps the more critical in creating this world. Whites tried to
limit completely the freedom of blacks, although they could not avoid
recognizing the basic humanity of their slaves. Ultimately, economic needs,
law, and the ideology of paternalism produced the world the slaveholders
attempted to create for their slaves. Black desires to gain some degree of
personal freedom, however, prevented the slaveholders from ever totally
imposing their world upon the slaves. Slaves, within limits, created their
own society, one that kept its own dimensions even while incorporating
some parts of the white society around them. Slaves thus lived in a world
set apart from that of the whites.

For whites the slave system was always foremost an essential means to
wealth. Scholars have debated the profitability of slavery, but there is no
question that individual slaveowners made great fortunes using slave labor.
Their experiences show the profits that were possible. Orville Taylor, the
historian of slavery in Arkansas, used James Sheppard, owner by 1860 of
Waterford and Blenheim plantations in Jefferson County, to show how
one man advanced economically within the system. Starting with a debt
of $15,000 owed for the purchase of a share of a Mississippi plantation in
1847, by 1860 Sheppard was worth more than $90,000 with upwards of
1,600 acres of Arkansas lands and more than a hundred slaves. He invested
tens of thousands of dollars of profits each year in stocks and bonds of
railroads, mining ventures, and insurance companies throughout the South.
Slave labor offered men like Sheppard and other individuals examined in
previous chapters opportunities for considerable economic success.[1]

The steady climb of slave prices during the antebellum years testifies to

1. Orville W. Taylor, *Negro Slavery in Arkansas* (Durham, N.C., 1958), 123–27.

the perceived value of slave labor. The average tax value of slaves in 1850 had reached $415 per slave. In the next ten years the value increased nearly 79 percent, to an average of $741. The actual sale price of slaves was even higher. Taylor estimated that the average price for slaves in Arkansas by the 1840s was $485, with some individuals selling for as much as $1,000. By the end of the 1850s field hands sold for about $1,000 and individual prices reached $2,000 for slaves with desirable skills.[2]

Whether slavery was profitable or not, white Arkansans accepted it as essential to their plantation economy. To whites, black slavery was the only possible way to farm in the delta regions. One correspondent of the *Arkansas Gazette* wrote, "I deny that white men possess the physical ability to cultivate '*profitably*' the bottom lands of Arkansas, or any of the bottom lands of the lower Mississippi and its tributaries." And J. H. Trulock advised a friend: "I will say to you they may preach & pray until their lungs give out and slavery will *exist for centuries* and may be to the end of the world, for aught I know, in some *colour* or *form*. . . . If lands were cheap in old Connecticut and cotton & sugar would grow well there you would soon have slavery either white or black or mongrel."[3]

Although equating slave labor with economic need, whites did recognize that their slaves were not property like livestock. No matter how much whites may have wanted to treat blacks simply as property, their actions often indicated that they saw the basic humanity of individual slaves. They did not accept slaves as equals, but emotional and human relationships developed between members of the two races. Childhood friendships and years of working and living together contributed to these connections. A planter expressed this awareness when, on the death of one of his slaves, he wrote, "He was a honest man as there is in the world none excepted white or black." A slave remembered that her mistress treated her and her family like her own children: "we had feelin's and tastes." Albert Pike publicly recognized these feelings at the American Party Convention in 1856 when he said he "did not consider the slave a mere chattel, but a human being with a soul to be saved and a mind to be cultivated and improved until some day he might be permitted to be free."[4]

Whites reconciled their economic needs with their awareness of blacks

2. *Ibid.*, 77–78; *Biennial Report of the Auditor of Public Accounts of the State of Arkansas, for 1859 and 1860* (Little Rock, 1860), Table J; John W. Brown Diary, January 2, 1860, in AHC.

3. Little Rock *Arkansas Gazette*, November 6, 1858; J. Hines Trulock to Nichols Bardsley, March 28, 1847, in Trulock Family Letters, UALR.

4. E. F. Strong to Dear Sister, March 28, 1854, in Strong-McColloch Family Papers, AHC; Little Rock *Arkansas Gazette*, January 10, 1857. See also Samuel H. Chester, *Pioneer Days in Arkansas* (Richmond, Va., 1927), 42; *ASIAN*, Vol. X, Pt. 5, pp. 232, 302.

as human beings through the ideology of paternalism. This ideology provided the framework for white attitudes about blacks and a rationale for slavery. It did not represent the reality of the system, however. In Arkansas this ideal permeated not only the elite but the entire slaveowning population. Nonslaveholders left little documentation of their attitude toward slaves, but it is possible that at some level even they accepted the paternalistic view of the slave system.[5]

The paternalistic idea included the concept that blacks had been created by God as slaves for white men. Wrote the editor of the *Arkansas Gazette:* "To define our position on the subject of slavery, we will say that we are in favor of it, practically and in the abstract. We consider it morally right, as well as legally so; warranted by God's holy word, and sustained by His law; and we believe that the same God, in His own wise providence, created the African race for slaves." The same editor later affirmed: "The institution of slavery is right. It is an institution of the Bible, both in the Old and New Testaments." An 1859 report by a local Baptist association rehearsed the argument in detail. Blacks had descended from Ham, son of Noah, who had been cursed with servitude for all time. The association concluded: "This race of mankind was appointed to bondage by the Lord."[6]

According to white ideology, blacks should be enslaved because they were racially inferior. Black inferiority was seen as partially intellectual. The editor of the *Arkansas Gazette* asked: "Why have they not been endowed with the intellectual capabilities of the white man? Why is it that we have a record of their existence, as a separate people, for more than three thousand years, without a solitary monument to their wisdom or skill in any art, science, or anything else? Without even an alphabet?"[7]

Whites also viewed physical differences between themselves and blacks as justifying enslavement. They concluded that blacks' physical development qualified them uniquely for hard work in tropical climates. Indicating how quickly the community's ideology was embraced by its members, one transplanted Yankee wrote shortly after arriving in the state, "There seems to be a difference in physical constitution between white and negro races; the whites cannot endure exertion in the hot latitudes and the negro is good for nothing in a climate too cold to grow cotton."[8]

5. Eugene D. Genovese, *The World the Slaveholders Made: Two Essays in Interpretation* (New York, 1969), 98–99.

6. Little Rock *Arkansas Gazette,* November 4, 1853, April 6, 1855; Orville W. Taylor, "Baptists and Slavery in Arkansas: Relationships and Attitudes," *AHQ,* XXXVIII (1979), 221.

7. Little Rock *Arkansas Gazette,* November 4, 1853, April 6, 1855.

8. *Ibid.* November 6, 1858, April 6, 1858; E. Sherman to My Dear Uncle, February 25, 1858, in Sandford-Everett Family File, UALR.

Further proof of black inferiority was seen in character traits attributed to the race. Whites saw them as unruly and violent, characteristics generally expressed in personal rebellion. The white community believed that if allowed to go unrestrained, such expressions could turn into insurrection and mass violence. One wrote, "At home, they are the same savage cannibals which they were when they first became known to the civilized world." Fear of slave violence characterized the white image of blacks throughout the antebellum years and was expressed in recurrent rumors of slave uprisings. No major uprising occurred in Arkansas during these years, however.[9]

Paternalism explained black enslavement, but it also placed limits on how whites could treat blacks and involved a system of mutual responsibility. Whites argued that God had given them responsibility for the black race in order to help it. Whites were permitted to hold blacks as slaves, but they were to treat their property in a Christian and humane manner. Calling on white Christians to bring the gospel to their servants, the Judson Baptist Association reminded them that "no doubt but the Lord has placed them under our charge for a wise purpose." In 1854 the Arkansas Baptist Convention, in a statement titled "On Duties to Servants," urged masters to the "faithful discharge of the fearful duties growing out of this situation. Give your servants that which is just and equal, knowing that you also have a master in heaven." Many owners viewed slaves as members of their family, although as children who must be disciplined and controlled, as were white children during these years. Unlike the white child, however, the slave would be a child for life.[10]

Although blacks would remain slaves and inferiors, paternalists concluded that proper mastery produced good results. The editor of the *Arkansas Gazette* maintained that "when taken and put under the charge of good masters, [Africans] do advance to the utmost point of physical and mental development which they are capable of attaining; and, when emancipated, they relapse into a condition worse, and more degraded than the savage one they originally occupied in their own country." The author of a letter to Christopher C. Danley of the *Arkansas Gazette* presented another idealistic view of slavery:

We believe that the African amid the snowy cotton blooms of the plantations of Arkansas is less a slave than the wan representative of

---

9. Little Rock *Arkansas Gazette*, June 15, 1855, November 2, 1855; Little Rock *True Democrat*, December 16, 1856; Memphis *Eagle and Enquirer* quoted in Helena (Ark.) *Shield*, October 25, 1856; Helena (Ark.) *Shield*, December 20, 1856.

10. Taylor, "Baptists and Slavery in Arkansas," 222; Taylor, *Negro Slavery in Arkansas*, 168.

woman amid the looms and spindles of Massachusetts and New York. We further believe, that the slaves of Arkansas, enlightened and civilized by contact with the anglo-Saxon, are happier than the untutored savage who lies in listless apathy amid the shades of the groves of Angola or mumbles his heathen invocation to some lifeless god of wood or stone amid the jungles of India. So far as the African is concerned, he should thank *the living God* that Providence has placed a number of his race where they may gain a *knowledge of his truth,* and his services are but meagre return for the benefits he has received through the instrumentality of the European race.[11]

Orville Taylor wrote of this elaborate apologia: "Few people in Arkansas vigorously defended slavery—most of them merely accepted it as a part of the pattern of life." Paternalistic attitudes, however, were integrated into white ideas about slavery, and paternalistic sentiments commonly were expressed by slaveholders in statements of affection for their slaves. In their letters, slaveowners often wrote about their slaves as their children and family. Amanda Trulock of Jefferson County typified the paternalistic attitude when she wrote to assure relatives back in North Carolina that "our black family are all well."[12]

Paternalist expressions also appeared in views concerning discipline, particularly when whites justified harsh treatment of blacks. Mrs. Isaac Hilliard wrote: "Idleness is the devil's workshop. I believe it to be my duty, so long as I own slaves, to keep them in proper subjection and well employed. So come what may, I intend to make mine do 'service.'" A complex intertwining of the themes of affection and physical discipline often recurred. An absent master informed his wife, "You must make your two little Darkies do as much of the work as you can and use the rod if necessary. . . . Tell Agnes and Mary they had better be good negroes until I return." Albert Rust of El Dorado reported that upon recovering two runaways he had "inflicted upon them a very severe punishment that I trust will have a beneficial effect upon them as well as the other negroes." Rust later concluded that the desired impact had been made, reporting that one of the slaves had become "interested & very happy in appearances since the rather severe discipline to which he has been subjected."[13]

11. Little Rock *Arkansas Gazette,* June 15, 1855. November 4, 1853, October 9, 1858.

12. Taylor, *Negro Slavery in Arkansas,* 37n2; A. Trulock to Dear Sister, May 25, 1858, in Trulock Family Letters; J. W. Carrigan to My Dear Brother William, May 27, 1853, W. A. Carrigan to Dear Nephew, January 9, 1854, both in John W. Carrigan Papers, DU: E. F. Strong to Dear Sister, March 28, 1854, Strong-McColloch Family Papers.

13. Mrs. Isaac Hilliard Diary, June 29, 1850, in LSU; C. M. Thompson to Dear Wife, January 5, 1858, in Wilcox and Thompson Family Letters, UALR; A. Rust to My Dear Uncle, May 20, July 5, 1857, in Rust Family Papers, J. N. Heiskell Collection, UALR.

In actual operation the slave system could at times approximate the idealistic image created by whites. As practiced, slavery consisted of complex relationships among slaves and masters, and when whites treated their slaves with kindness, those relationships seemed to be working as the paternalistic ideology dictated. At other times, however, the relationships were much different—so different, indeed, as to show that paternalism was little more than a justification of an exploitive labor system.

When times were good economically and a master was so disposed, paternalism was practiced easily. Descriptions of the day-to-day life of many slaves show an existence that was harsh but not inhumane, one much like that of the white lower-middle and lower classes. Labor was hard. The workday was usually sunrise to sunset, especially when hands were clearing new land or during the harvest. Through the year most slaves engaged in the routine activities of farming, preparing the old fields and opening up new ones in the spring, tending to the planted crop through the summer months, and harvesting it in the fall. Women and children went to the fields when necessary, plowing, weeding, threshing wheat, or picking cotton. If the owner needed their work, women labored alongside men in even the heavy tasks of sawing logs, splitting rails, or clearing timber. One former slave remembered the plantation day: "You worked from the time you could see until the time you couldn't see. You worked from before sunrise till after dark. When that horn blows, you better git out of that house, 'cause the overseer is comin' down the line, and he ain't comin' with nothin' in his hand." [14]

White and black accounts suggest that most owners provided adequate housing, clothing, and food, although only adequate. One white Arkansan remembered that his family's slave cabins were similar to the outbuildings in which the boys of the family were placed. Such cabins were usually constructed of logs or planks, sometimes with no chinking between the logs. The furniture was simple: homemade beds with corded-rope springs and a cover of cowhide or grass straw, a stool, and perhaps a table built against the wall. Clothing was functional, with little extra spent by owners to outfit their slaves. Children's clothing usually consisted of long cotton shirts. Most slaves wore some sort of cheap cotton cloth, jean, linsey, perhaps some wool, or a variety of homespun materials. Food was limited, although there was considerable variety in diet according to season, location, and the economic condition of the plantation. Generally, the slaves on interior plantations and farms had a steady diet of staples such as bacon

14. *AS/AN*, Vol. VIII, Pt. 2, p. 180, Vol, IX, Pt. 4, p. 193, Pt. 7, p. 156; Taylor, *Negro Slavery in Arkansas*, 95–102; Farrar Newberry, ed., "A Clark County Plantation Journal for 1857," *AHQ*, XVIII (1959), 401–409.

or pork with corn bread, supplemented with seasonal vegetables and fresh beef or game. The daily fare of the slaves often was similar to that of the owners.[15]

Many masters took seriously the idea that they had obligations to treat their slaves well and to "elevate" them as much as possible. Such idealism was sometimes evidenced by leniency in masters' attempts to ensure obedience and discipline among their slaves. Even the paternalistic ideology assumed that blacks required physical punishment when they did not follow the rules, but paternalism demanded minimum force. According to slave accounts, some masters did exercise restraint in administering physical punishments. Doc Flowers, who was part of a small slaveholding in Washington County, recalled: "I had good white folks. None of dem never struck their colored folks." Peggy Sloan, from a plantation in Dallas County, reported that her masters "never whipped their slaves." Other owners did use physical punishment, but only on rare occasions. William Baltimore of Jefferson County remembered: "Dr. Waters had a good heart. He didn't call us 'slaves'. He call us 'servants'. He didn't want none of his niggers whipped 'ceptin there wasn't no other way."[16]

Some owners tried to avoid punishing their slaves, preferring to motivate them with rewards and special favors. John Brown of Camden provides the best example of such behavior in Arkansas. Brown allowed his hands a vacation for several days during the Christmas season each year, reasoning that "it is a human as well as wise regulation of society to allow them a few days as a Jubilee." When he needed their labor during this time off, Brown paid them. During the 1853 Christmas season he paid some hands as much as $2.37 for splitting rails and others fifty cents a day to haul cotton. On some plantations, slaves were allowed to plant their own gardens either to supplement their diet or to sell their produce. The frequency of this practice is not known, but it appears to have been common enough to create something of a cash economy among slaves.[17]

Numerous owners were conscientious about giving their slaves religious education. Harriett Payne remembered the wife of Colonel Jesse Chaney

15. Little Rock *Arkansas Gazette*, February 8, 1850; *AS/AN*, Vol. VIII, Pt. 2, pp. 12, 172, 328, Vol. IX, Pt. 3, p. 24, Pt. 4, p. 299, Pt. 7, pp. 154–58; *AS/ON*, Vol. XII, Supp. 1, pp. 47, 298; Chester, *Pioneer Days in Arkansas*, 39; Taylor, *Negro Slavery in Arkansas*, 139.

16. *AS/AN*, Vol. VIII, Pt. 2, p. 317 (Flowers), Vol. X, Pt. 6, p. 168 (Sloan), Vol. VIII, Pt. 1, p. 97 (Baltimore). See also Vol. X, Pt. 6, p. 316, and *AS/ON*, Vol. XII, Supp. 1, pp. 50, 298; R. W. Miller to J. Sheppard, June 16, 1859, in James Sheppard Papers, DU: E. H. Fletcher, Jr., to E. H. Fletcher, n.d., in Elliott H. Fletcher Papers, AHC; and Tommy R. Thompson, ed., "Searching for the American Dream in Arkansas: Letters of a Pioneer Family," *AHQ*, XXXVIII (1979), 173.

17. Hilliard Diary, May 19, 1850; Brown Diary, December 25–30, 1853.

near St. Charles: "She was a Christian. I can hear her praying yet! She wouldn't let one of her slaves hit a tap on Sunday. They must rest and go to church. They had preaching at the cabin of some one of the slaves, and in the Summertime sometimes they had it out in the shade under the trees." Eva Strayhorn, a former slave in Johnson County, remembered going to camp meetings with whites, although the slaves sat at the back. When there was no church, her master would call up the slaves for Bible readings and singing. Ellen Thompson's family from Howard County was allowed to attend meetings held by black preachers at Arkadelphia and at Center Point.[18]

A few slaveowners carried their duty of uplifting their servants even to the point of educating them, although the idea caused considerable disagreement among whites. In Arkansas, teaching slaves to read and write was not illegal, but it was not common. Nonetheless, advertisements for runaway slaves indicate that some were literate. Some slaves apparently learned to read along with the white children, or were taught by the white children. Some families taught their slaves to read the Bible, and not infrequently a mistress taught a house servant to read.[19]

Examples also exist of owners who pursued the paternalistic ideal by encouraging and protecting institutions such as slave families. Jesse Chaney in Arkansas County performed the marriage of his slaves himself. One remembered, "They'd stand up before him and he'd read out of a book called the 'discipline' and say, 'Thou shalt love the Lord thy God with all thy heart, all thy strength, with all thy might and thy neighbor as thyself.' Then he'd say they were man and wife and tell them to live right and be honest and kind to each other." Some owners attempted to protect these unions once made. The will of Ira Butler of Chalybeate Springs provided that "Louden and his wife and children are to be sold together and the purchaser will be required to come under obligation not to separate them during the life-time of Louden or Maria, and to treat them with kindness, in a specific manner as to feed, & c." Paternalistic masters were generally reluctant to separate children from their parents, although the particular concern was to keep children with their mothers.[20]

18. *AS/AN*, Vol. X, Pt. 5, p. 301 (Payne), Pt. 6, p. 313 (Thompson); *AS/AN*, Vol. XII, Supp. 1, p. 299 (Strayhorn).

19. *AS/AN*, Vol. VIII, Pt. 2, pp. 181, 279, Vol. IX, Pt. 3, p. 199, Vol. X, Pt. 5, p. 235, Vol. XI, Pt. 7, pp. 7, 154–58; *AS/ON*, Vol. XII, Supp. 1, pp. 28, 199, 299, 356, 798–99; Helena (Ark.) *Southern Shield*, July 9, 1853, December 27, 1850, September 17, 1852.

20. *AS/AN*, Vol. X, Pt. 5, p. 302; Little Rock *Arkansas Gazette*, August 2, 1850; E. Benson to Dear Brother, April 1, 1857, in Burwell Benson Papers, UNC; Helena (Ark.) *Southern Shield*, May 1, 1852; Chester, *Pioneer Days in Arkansas*, 40; Taylor, *Negro Slavery in Arkansas*, 193–94.

Paternalistic behavior suggests a genuine caring about the lives of slaves, but there were other reasons to treat slaves decently. The most important reason was economic. By the 1850s slaves represented an enormous investment, and mistreating them was comparable to damaging one's own property. Concern for protecting this investment was particularly apparent in the conditions slaveowners imposed on those who hired slaves. The contract of Dan, for example, required the person employing him "to cloth boy decently and comfortably, treat him humanely." John Brown of Camden was very cautious. He wrote in his diary that he never received the highest prices because "I have regarded the place I put them as more important than the price of the hire. I want them taken care of and not abused." Whether for paternalistic reasons or out of economic expediency, overworking or abusing laborers was not sound practice.[21]

Still, paternalism was never more than an ideal. When necessary it was pushed aside. In the face of an economic or other crisis in the life of the slaveowner, the ideal could be abandoned for the expedient. Maintenance of family life, kindness, adequate food and clothing, religious education, and restraint in punishment were all easily forgotten in the face of necessity. When mistreated, the slave, unlike the free laborer, had no easy recourse other than submission. As property, the slave could not turn to the law or leave the abusive person. Thus, the paternalistic view offered little protection for the slave.

Whites often blamed improper treatment and abuse of slaves on overseers. Such accusations may have had a degree of truth on large plantations where the slaveowner, the "father" of the system, lived elsewhere or left day-to-day supervision of the plantation to others when he was absent. Under those circumstances, slave conditions were determined by an overseer employed by the master to ensure the efficient operation of the place. The job survival of the overseer depended on the profits shown at the end of the year, not on how he treated the hands. Overseers were more common on plantations with large slaveholdings, so most slaves lived under the control of such managers. (In 1860 only 9 percent of slaveowners had holdings of twenty-five or more slaves, but that represented 46 percent of the slave population. Another 43 percent of slaves lived in holdings of between four and twenty-four. Only 11 percent lived in the small holdings.) The slaves perceived the difference. "They was most generally mean," remembered one former slave of the overseers.[22]

Whether slavery differed materially on smaller holdings or where the

21. Agreement, in Samuel W. Williams Papers, AHC; Brown Diary, January 24, 1861 (see also November 16, December 19, 1853, January 30, 1855, July 12, 1856).
22. *AS/ON*, Vol. XII, Supp. 1, pp. 279, 298; *Eighth Census, 1860: Agriculture*, 224.

master more likely exercised day-to-day control over his slaves is difficult to assess, however. The Arkansas evidence suggests that the experience of the individual slave depended more on other factors than on the size of the holding. In fact, on the small holding the harsh decisions made elsewhere by overseers were required of the individual owner, who often had little time or luxury to be concerned with acting as a paternalistic master. Abuse seems to have taken place at all levels.[23]

Within the context of the paternalistic ideology, the greatest abuse was breaking up slave families. Many masters sold slaves whenever they considered it necessary or expedient, with no thoughts about separating family members from one another. In times of need they considered their slaves as commodities, just like everything else on the plantation, to be used for economic advantage. One farmer placed a thirteen-year-old boy up for sale simply because he had to sell. "I am in debt and want to pay out," he wrote.[24]

Owners often treated slave marriages as conveniences, and they did not allow a ceremony to prevent slave families from being broken up when economically necessary. When Josephine Barnett's master moved from Tennessee to Arkansas, her father was left behind. With seeming acceptance of the action as simply typical, she recalled: "My father belong to Boston Hack. He wouldn't sell and Mr. McNeill wouldn't sell and that how it come." Some owners never bothered to sanction slave marriages with ceremony, and the slaves realized that their unions were different. According to Columbus Williams, "Marriage wasn't like now. . . . Didn't have no ceremony at all. I have heard of them stepping over a broom but I never saw it."[25]

Even efforts to keep slave children with their mothers were abandoned when practical economic matters became important. Especially after a child reached the age of twelve, sales were common, but splitting children away from their mothers at even earlier ages took place. When both parents were separated from smaller children, the children were incorporated into the families that were left behind. The slaves recognized the fragility of their lives together as families. Commenting on the selling of people from her plantation, one former slave remembered that "ever' time dey need some money, off dey sell a slave, jest like now dey sell cows and hogs at de auction place."[26]

23. John Solomon Otto, "Slavery in the Mountains: Yell County, Arkansas, 1840–1860," *AHQ*, XXXIX (Spring, 1980), 52.

24. S. R. Gray to J. Martin, March 18, 1857, in Jared Martin Papers, AHC.

25. *AS/AN*, Vol. VIII, Pt. 2, p. 109 (Barnett); Vol. XI, Pt. 7, p. 157 (Williams).

26. *AS/AN*, Vol. VIII, Pt. 2, p. 347, Vol. IX, Pt. 3, p. 114; *Pyeatt* v. *Spencer*, 4 Ark. 563; *AS/ON*, Vol. XIII, Supp. 1, pp. 29–30.

Although society urged the religious education of servants, many masters neglected such endeavors and some actually objected to them. Columbus Williams remembered of Ben Heard's plantation near Mount Holly in Union County: "We didn't have no church nor nothing. No Sunday-schools, no nothin'. Worked from Monday morning till Saturday night. On Sunday we didn't do nothin' but set right down there on that big plantation." J. E. Caldwell, a Methodist circuit rider, complained that church members had objected to having slave children catechized and had withdrawn from the local church over the issue. Conversely, at least one planter complained that ministers had a pecuniary interest in missionizing the slaves. He complained that Methodist preachers in Jefferson County who were holding meetings for slaves "charge a pretty high price and as far as I have seen done but little good. *They* deem to do it for the money I fear and not for the good of the poor negroes." When whites objected, slaves simply had no access to religion.[27]

Physical punishment was often excessive and violent. Especially at times when their "children" frustrated masters, stern discipline turned cruel. One master complained of a woman on his plantation: "*One* good whipping don't do her. I have to watch and—(not pray) but scold and drub again." Descriptions of slave runaways indicate the extent of violence. The mulatto Joe, for example, was described as "considerably scarred from being whipped." In a particularly brutal incident that was described in court records, the owner was found beating his slave for running away. "He had her stripped, and staked down on the ground; her hands and feet extended, and fastened to stakes; and her face downward. He . . . was whipping her at intervals, using a cowhide, with a plaited buckskin lash about fifteen inches long. . . . Spencer had drawn some blood, but not a great deal. He took salt and a cob, and salted her back." Such behavior indicated the power of owners and the lack of restrictions on their behavior exercised by society or social ideology.[28]

Within the context of this system, in which whites had legally so much control, it is easy to discover what white society thought slavery should be and how whites actually behaved. It is more difficult to discover the world the slaves were creating for themselves. By the 1850s, however, such a world was emerging in Arkansas. Black slaves developed their own ways of changing the conditions of their work and their lives. They appear to

27. *ASIAN,* Vol. XI, Pt. 7, pp. 155–57; James E. Caldwell Journal, June 20, 1861, in James E. Caldwell Papers, AHC.; J. N. Trulock to Dear Brother, February 18, 1848, Trulock Family Letters, UALR.

28. E. H. Fletcher, Jr., to E. H. Fletcher, n.d., in Fletcher Papers; Little Rock *Arkansas Gazette,* September 17, 1852; *Pyeatt v. Spencer,* 4 Ark. 563; Chester, *Pioneer Days in Arkansas,* 46–47.

have created their own society, with its own internal distinctions. They produced an ideology that provided a slave definition of the world around them and how it operated.

Slaves did not possess the means used by whites to change the conditions that they encountered in their work or lives. They could not walk away from bad situations and start again somewhere else. Hard work did not lead to rewards or even a better life. Ultimately, the only ways that slaves could force accommodations were by withholding labor, running away, or gaining skills essential to the plantation or local community. Although the results were limited, such methods did accomplish some of the aims of the slaves.

The most common tool used by slaves to extract concessions from their owners was to stop work. As a group, slaves could sabotage the plantation routine by carefully exploiting white managers. In doing this, the slaves gained control over the work load of the farm. The common use of overseers on larger plantations gave opportunities for such "bargaining." The overseer had to get work done but had limited authority to use punishment to achieve it, since the slaves actually belonged to the landowner. Slaves could secure concessions from an overseer as a result. The effect often was that the amount of work actually desired by the owner was not achieved. Usually the owner blamed the overseer for not being firm enough. One planter complained of his overseer's lack of resolution, "Mr. Bankston . . . has much yet to learn respecting his new undertaking & the negroes are not slow to discern it." John Brown observed "that a very decided and commanding man must be had to make anything on a plantation without the presence of the owner."[29]

Running away was another means slaves had of bargaining with a master or overseer. That bargaining was often the primary goal is indicated by the fact that runaways' efforts usually were not designed to escape to freedom. Many slaves who ran away did not go far, nor did they intend to stay away. Some merely hid in the woods, remaining there until concessions were granted. By withdrawing their labor or by posing a threat to the owner's investment by endangering themselves, slaves sometimes obtained accommodation.[30]

Some slaves secured a better bargaining position by acquiring a valuable skill. Men appear to have had more opportunities than women to advance themselves in this manner. Blacksmithing was one such acquirable skill.

29. E. W. Wright to Dear Asa, January 5, 1852, in Asa Morgan Collection, AHC; Brown Diary, January 1 (quotation), 6, June 1, 1855.

30. Little Rock *Arkansas Gazette*, April 16, 1852; D. T. Weeks to J. Sheppard, September 20, 1854, in Sheppard Papers; *AS/AN*, Vol. VIII, Pt. 1, pp. 311–12.

Other slaves bettered their positions by working as carpenters, chairmakers, basketmakers, and masters of other crafts. In western Arkansas some slaves worked in textile mills, although mostly as manual laborers. In some cases slaves actually managed farms and plantations. Solomon, on the William Newton plantation in Johnson County, learned to read and was used by Newton as the overseer. On the farm of Nat Turner in Phillips County, one of the male slaves, the biggest, was made the whipman and administered punishments. Reuben Dortch of Dallas County was "a regular leader on the plantation—boss of the tool room. He was next to the master of them, you might say. He was a kind of boss." For women, opportunities existed to become cooks, midwives, and seamstresses.[31]

Slaves with skills had numerous advantages and at times received special favors. Andrew, on the Chester plantation in Union County, was allowed to cultivate a piece of land on his own. He produced two bales of cotton annually. It was sold with the rest of the plantation cotton, and he was given the profits to buy Sunday clothing and other goods. Andrew purchased flour and molasses for his wife to bake ginger cakes that were then sold in the community. Andrew was "proud and high-spirited and could never be brought to recognize anyone but his owner as in authority over him." Hampton High, a ginner in Lonoke County, was another skilled slave allowed to have his own money. His owners allowed him to hire out his labor, and his daughter remembered that "they trusted him and I know he did work for pay. On account of the money my father earned he was considered a valuable slave. That's why he could go and eat and drink anything he wanted to."[32]

Slaves who lived in town, since many of them had special skills, had more latitude in their lives than plantation slaves. In 1860 only 3,799 of the 111,115 total slaves in the state lived in towns, but their experiences indicated the opportunities available. Little Rock had a large class of slaves in the building trades and domestic service. Included among the slave occupations were those of brickmakers, bricklayers, carpenters, stonemasons, lathers, and plasters. Skilled domestic servants worked as cooks, maids, gardeners, and coachmen. These jobs were not the only ones available. William Wallace Andrews became well known in Little Rock as a cabinetmaker. The slave sons of Nathan Warren, a free black who owned a confec-

31. D. T. Weeks to J. Sheppard, July 29, 1854, in Sheppard Papers; *AS/AN*, Vol. VIII, Pt. 1, pp. 109, 146, 170, 183, 312, Vol. VIII, Pt. 2, pp. 171, 347, Vol. IX, Pt. 3, p. 19; *AS/ON*, Vol. XII, Supp. 1, pp. 28, 47, 298–99.

32. Chester, *Pioneer Days in Arkansas*, 39–49; Brown Diary, December 25, 1853; Dorothy Stanley, ed., *The Autobiography of Sir Henry Morton Stanley* (New York, 1909), 160; *AS/AN*, Vol. VIII, Pt. 1, p. 110, Pt. 2, p. 183 (High).

tionary shop, performed with one of the best-known musical groups of the period, the Ashley Band. Barbering was another major job opportunity for slaves.[33]

As with skilled laborers in the countryside, skilled slaves in towns held greater bargaining power, which was often used to obtain greater individual freedom. James Alexander of Helena was allowed to run his own barbership; he even advertised in the local newspaper. Many skilled slaves were allowed to hire out their own time for wages. They could decide whom to work for and sometimes even where to live, paying their masters an agreed-upon share of their wages. Hiring out had become such a common practice by the 1850s that white artisans complained that the slaves were unfairly competitive. The practice of hiring out continued until emancipation.[34]

The results of black efforts at securing concessions indicate much about black goals and ideals. The principal goal appears to have been to achieve some sort of control over their individual and family lives. Sometimes their actions were aimed simply at keeping a master or overseer from physically punishing them. A slave in Jefferson County took this sort of step when he ran into the Arkansas River in an effort to avoid being punished by the overseer.[35]

Often slaves were trying to protect or maintain their families. A country slaveowner indicated the importance of this goal to slaves when he tried to recapture a runaway who was probably "lurking about Little Rock" because his wife was there. One slave kidnapped his wife from the David Hunt plantation in Phillips County to improve her living conditions; as Peter Brown remembered this event, "Ma had to work when she wasn't able. Pa stole her out. . . . They went back and they never made her work no more." In Little Rock the slave father of Julia White hired his wife from her master in order that she and their children might move into his home. James Alexander in Helena bought freedom for members of his family, although he himself remained a slave until the outbreak of the Civil War."[36]

By the 1850s both rural and urban slaves were developing a uniquely black society complete with internal social differentiation. Slave recollec-

33. *Eighth Census, 1860: Population*, 19; *AS/AN*, Vol. X, Pt. 6, p. 227, Vol. XI, Pt. 7, pp. 122–24; Paul D. Lack, "An Urban Slave Community: Little Rock, 1831–1862," *AHQ*, XLI (1982), 260–62.

34. Lack, "Urban Slave Community," 282–83; Willard B. Gatewood, Jr., "John Hanks Alexander of Arkansas: Second Black Graduate of West Point," *AHQ*, XLI (1982), 105–106.

35. D. T. Weeks to J. Sheppard, September 20, 1854, in Sheppard Papers.

36. Taylor, *Negro Slavery in Arkansas*, 168; Little Rock *Arkansas Gazette*, November 7, 1851; *AS/AN*, Vol. X, Pt. 6, p. 227, Vol. XI, Pt. 7, p. 122; Gatewood, "John Hanks Alexander," 107.

tions of distinctions among themselves provide the clearest evidence of this system's existence. Charlotte Stephens perceived major differences among slaves and remembered that in Little Rock, "there was class distinction, perhaps to greater extent than among the white people." Rural slaves also saw differences. Eva Strayhorn remembered particularly admiring her master William Newton's black overseer, the aforementioned Solomon, who not only was in a position of authority but also had learned how to read. Charles Dortch recalled that his slave father managed his owner's plantation and that the other slaves respected him: "He was well liked, and then too he was able to take care of himself."[37]

The exact nature of the system emerging among slaves is the subject of scholarly debate and probably can never be satisfactorily reconstructed. Paul Lack has concluded that at least in the urban setting, those slaves who served as intermediaries between black and white society became social leaders. Some evidence suggests that the system was similar in rural settings. Status was based on securing a position that allowed the greatest flexibility in dealing with whites, a position that gave slaves the greatest power. House servants, those who worked with businessmen, those allowed to hire themselves out or to live outside the master's house, slave overseers, and slave managers received the greatest measure of respect within the black community, even though whites ultimately determined who would be allowed access to these avenues of power. Charlotte Stephens equated status with closer contact with the white masters and with imitation of the manners of that class. For her, high status was achieved by those who learned "to speak with a low voice, use good English, [and practice] the niceties of manners, good form and courtesy in receiving and attending guests." The slave Harry Williams, manager for the Williams family's property in Ouachita County, was remembered as a "gentleman" who was sure enough of himself to strike an overseer with whom he disagreed. Lack suggests that all blacks understood that such individuals had achieved important positions that allowed them to contribute to the overall growth and well-being of the black community.[38]

Lack's analysis conflicts with that of other scholars. John Blassingame offers a very different view of the emerging black society, at least on the plantations. According to Blassingame, status derived from physical talent and folk skills. Thus the rebel, the conjurer, the doctor, the hunter, and the storyteller provided the community's leadership. The Arkansas slave

37. Vol X, Pt. 6, p. 228 (Stephens); *AS/ON*, Vol. XII, Supp. 1, pp. 198–99 (Strayhorn); *AS/AN*, Vol. VIII, Pt. 2, p. 170 (Dortch).

38. Lack, "Urban Slave Community," 269; *AS/AN*, Vol. X, Pt. 6, p. 228 (Stephens); Vol. XI, Pt. 7, p. 155 (Williams).

narratives indicate a great deal of respect for the rebel, although providing less evidence about attitudes toward the other roles suggested by Blassingame. Typically, Columbus Williams remembered a slave in Ouachita County who ran away and stayed away for twelve months: "He come back then, and they didn't do nothin' to him. 'Fraid he'd run off again, I guess." One of the few instances suggesting the importance of other talents is the reminiscence of Adeline Blakeley of Fayetteville; she took great pride in her parents, who were of "African stock," and remembered that her mother was much sought out by young slaves for her abilities as a fortune-teller.[39]

Given the nature of slavery, it is probable that neither Lack's nor Blassingame's system existed exclusively. Both accommodation and rebellion were tools used by slaves for the same purposes, and both secured limited independence within an overall system that denied black self-determination. Individual circumstances perhaps best explain why one slave approached this goal through rebellion and another by accommodation. Because slaves ultimately interacted not with white society but with individual owners, the particular problem they faced daily was responding to the peculiar individual character of different white owners. The critical role of the owner helps account for the wide variety of experiences associated with slavery as recalled later by former slaves. As for the overall experience of slavery itself, however, it is clear that its character was created not just by whites but also by blacks.

By the end of the 1850s, slavery in Arkansas was for white society an integral part of the state's economic life. The ideology that embraced it argued that the survival of white society depended upon its existence. Because of this, the protection of slavery was an important factor in the political life of the state during the 1850s. For the slaves, the institution created a mixed legacy. For some few it allowed a degree of self-fulfillment, but for the mass of slaves it separated them from the larger values and ideas of the white community around them. This exploitive labor system left slaves ill-prepared for anything other than slavery.

39. John Blassingame, "Status and Social Structure in the Slave Community: Evidence from New Sources," in *Perspectives and Irony in American Slavery*, ed. Harry P. Owens (Jackson, Miss., 1976), 137–51; *AS/AN*, Vol. XI, Pt. 7, p. 155 (Williams), Vol. VIII, Pt. 1, pp. 14–15 (Blakeley).

# 4

## POLITICAL POWER

AGRARIAN AND COMMERCIAL ELITES DOMINATED AR-
kansas government during the antebellum years, despite the fact that the
electoral process and officeholding were democratic. The political struggles
that took place usually reflected the diverse individual and regional interests
of these elites. Although politicians engaged in often-violent fights among
themselves for power, their broad goals did not vary. The basic agreement
among them, not usually apparent in their efforts to see who would allocate
the state's limited resources, became apparent by the end of the 1850s,
when party and personal differences were put aside to face the outside
threat of abolitionism. Secession marked their essential political unity and
their domination of the political process.

The Arkansas constitution adopted in 1836 established a basically democratic government. The document provided for elections by all free white
adult men, restricted only by a poll tax. Amendments made most county
and state officials elected by the 1850s, and the offices were open to almost
anyone who wanted to run. There were no property requirements, although there were age, residency, and religious restrictions. The only limits
to democracy were imposed by the national Constitution, which provided
for the election of United States senators by the state legislature and the
indirect election of the president.[1]

Arkansans voted with alacrity. Throughout the 1850s elections in the
state produced large turnouts, especially for gubernatorial and congressional
races. In the nonpresidential elections held during the decade, an average
of 75 percent of the eligible voters went to the polls, a voting level equal
to that of other states in their most competitive contests. The 1860 gubernatorial election produced the highest level of participation, with 86 percent
of the state's voters casting ballots in the hotly contested race between
Richard H. Johnson and Henry M. Rector. Interest in elections lagged only

1. *Acts of Arkansas, 1837*, 18, 21, 29, 34–39; Ralph A. Wooster, *Politicians, Planters, and
Plain Folk: Courthouse and Statehouse in the Upper South, 1850–1860* (Knoxville, Tenn., 1975),
25, 86–87, 20, 61.

in presidential contests, where voter participation was lower than in the state elections held at the same time.[2]

The common man also had access to political office. Officeholders came from a broad range of economic and social backgrounds. The historian Ralph Wooster has shown that no set of individuals monopolized state and county offices. Between statehood and 1860, only 51 of 480 county judges and 75 of 331 sheriffs served for more than two terms. Only 51 of 832 men elected to the house served more than one term. In the senate only 3 of 61 men whose terms ended between 1850 and 1860 served again. Further evidence of the turnover in offices is the fact that few county officials moved on to higher service. In the 1850 General Assembly only 8 of 72 house members had county political experience. In 1860 the number was only 7 of 75.[3]

Wooster's analysis also shows that Arkansas officeholders came from no particular class, although on the whole they were wealthier than their neighbors. The median real property holdings in 1860 were $3,000 for county officers, $4,000 for members of the house, and $8,000 for members of the senate, compared with $1,401 for the general population. Median personal property was $5,000 for representatives and $10,000 for senators, compared with $1,389 for the state overall. Forty-two percent of the members owned slaves, compared with about 16 percent of all adult males. On the other hand, the wealthy did not dominate offices. Officeholders varied widely in individual wealth, and some came from the poorer classes. In 1860, 16 percent of the members of the General Assembly possessed no real property at all and the majority did not own slaves.[4]

The vigorous lives of political parties in Arkansas during the antebellum years further reflected the democratic nature of local politics. Active party strife existed despite the fact that the Democratic party dominated, carrying every statewide election, including congressional elections, during these years. Prior to the critical elections in 1860, Democratic majorities ranged from 55 percent in the 1852 gubernatorial campaign to 87 percent in Thomas Hindman's 1858 congressional election. Throughout the 1850s the Democrats never controlled less than 75 percent of the General Assembly, and by the end of the decade they controlled it almost completely. Nonetheless, Whig and American party candidates could show strength, particularly in congressional elections.[5]

2. Brian G. Walton, "How Many Voted in Arkansas Elections Before the Civil War?" *AHQ*, XXXIX (1980), 70, 72–73.

3. Wooster, *Politicians, Planters, and Plain Folk*, 110, 42, 111, 114, 116, 34, 35, 38, 40, 43.

4. *Ibid.*, 160, 169.

5. Walton, "How Many Voted?" 70, 80; Brian G. Walton, "Arkansas Politics During the Compromise Crisis," *AHQ*, XXXVI (1977), 309.

Party operations were also democratic. Although their enemies charged that the state leadership of the Democratic party represented an oligarchy, usually called the "dynasty" or the "family," Democrats recruited party leaders with many different backgrounds and interests. The charge that they were a closed clique came primarily from the connection of some of them, particularly United States senator Robert W. Johnson and Governor Elias N. Conway, to a prominent political family from Tennessee that had exercised great influence in the Arkansas Territory, the Conway-Sevier-Johnson family. No other major leaders in the 1850s had these family ties. William K. Sebastian, who served in the United States Senate from 1848 to 1861, was a planter and attorney from Helena who often pursued policies opposed by Johnson. Alfred B. Greenwood, who represented the First Congressional District from 1853 to 1859, Edward A. Warren, elected to Congress in the Second District in 1852 and then again in 1856, and Albert Rust, chosen in the Second District in 1854 and 1858, were all well-to-do farmers or planters and lawyers who had no close family ties with the "family" leaders. Thomas C. Hindman, First District congressman elected in 1858 and 1860, ran for office as an outright critic of Senator Johnson.[6]

As in the case of Democratic leadership, no single group of individuals monopolized power in the Whig and American parties. These parties attracted a variety of capable individuals. Among the most prominent were Albert Pike, an attorney at Little Rock, and David Walker, a lawyer and farmer at Fayetteville. Both became associated with the Whig party before moving to Arkansas and continued their ties with it afterward. After 1852, William E. Woodruff, a land speculator and sometimes editor of the *Arkansas Gazette*; Christopher C. Danley, also associated with the *Gazette*; and former United States senator Solon Borland all abandoned the Democratic party to become leading proponents of Whiggery in the state. In 1855, many of the Whig leaders moved into the American party. Pike, Danley, and Borland all were prominent in the formation of that new organization.[7]

Democratic institutions, widespread participation in elections, vigorous party contests, and an open party leadership did not mean, however, that the government represented the broad range of economic and social interests

6. *Biographical Directory of the United States Congress, 1774–1989: Bicentennial Edition* (Washington, D.C., 1989), 550, 664, 1092, 1271, 1567, 1775, 1786, 1791, 2010, 2096; Dumas Malone, ed., *Dictionary of American Biography* (New York, 1934), XIV, 150, 593; Michael B. Dougan, *Confederate Arkansas: The People and Policies of a Frontier State in Wartime* (University, Ala., 1976), 38; Brian G. Walton, "The Second Party System in Arkansas, 1836–1848," *AHQ*, XXVIII (1969), 122–23; Michael Dougan, "A Look at the 'Family' in Arkansas Politics, 1858–1865," *AHQ*, XXIX (1970), 99–100.

7. Little Rock *Arkansas Gazette*, May 14, 1852; Harold T. Smith, "The Know-Nothings in Arkansas," *AHQ*, XXXIV (1975), 294, 297; James M. Woods, *Rebellion and Realignment: Arkansas's Road to Secession* (Fayetteville, 1987), 60–61.

present in antebellum Arkansas. Scholars have tried, by examining geographic voting patterns, to determine just what the political struggles of the period did reflect. The pattern through the 1850s was that Democrats usually did well throughout the state but were strongest in the nonplantation and mountainous counties of the north and west. Whigs showed their most strength in counties with larger slave populations and with greater commercial and urban wealth—that is, in the plantation counties of central, southern, and eastern Arkansas. This pattern has led scholars to conclude that the Democratic party, although led by members of the elite, was a party of small farmers. The Whigs, on the other hand, drew their support from the large planters and merchants whose economic interests tied them to the mainstream of the national and world economies. Political conflict thus reflected basic class differences.[8]

The relative strength of Whigs in wealthier sections and Democrats in poorer sections does not prove, however, that wealthy people were Whigs and poor people were Democrats. Support for the Whig and American parties in counties across the state suggests that these parties drew upon a base much broader than the state's economic elite (see Map 5). In the 1851 congressional election, for example, the Whig candidate received 40 percent or more of the vote in twenty-six of the state's fifty-three counties. Widespread Whig support continued in the 1854 state legislative canvass, when one or more Whig legislators were elected in nineteen of fifty-three counties. The American party had a narrower geographic base, but nine counties gave a majority to at least one of the American party candidates for governor or Congress. The figures suggest that class was not in fact a major issue in antebellum state politics.[9]

General geographic support for parties and an examination of party rhetoric, election issues, and legislative disputes suggest that despite conflict, there were few major differences among the parties. Class issues particularly were absent. The parties used different appeals to attract voters, but ultimately they represented the interests of the propertied elites of the state. They might fight among themselves, but only within the context of a basic consensus concerning the role of government. Parties represented the personal, geographic, and specific interests of groups within the propertied class, but not more fundamental social differences.

Party rhetoric and ideology during the antebellum years reflected the basic agreement on the purposes of government held by the leaders of all

8. Walton, "Second Party System in Arkansas," 125–29, 139; Gene W. Boyette, "Quantitative Differences Between the Arkansas Whig and Democratic Parties, 1836–1850," *AHQ,* XXXIV (1975), 214–26.

9. Little Rock *Arkansas Gazette,* August 29, 1851, September 8, 1854.

# Map 5

## Democratic Opposition—Geographic Strength

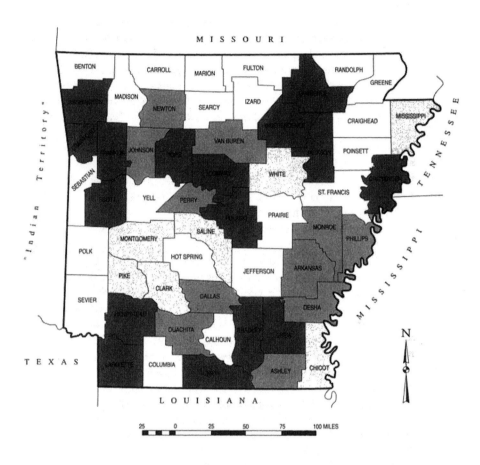

Counties giving 40 percent or more to Whig Congressional candidate, 1851

Counties sending one or more Whigs to General Assembly, 1854

Counties in both categories

Counties in neither category

parties. Democratic, Whig, and American party platforms all endorsed the assumption that government's role was to maintain conditions favorable to economic growth. This stance made it possible for the parties to appeal to existing interests but at the same time play upon the hopes of the majority of people that they would at some future time benefit from particular policies. Legislation helping minority interests, such as those of slaveowning planters, could be advocated as working, ultimately, to the larger public advantage. The principal rhetorical differences among the parties were over specific policies that might work to the state's economic advantage and were linked to political ideas and traditions of national parties. Party ideology was a means of manipulating voters, but it also made clear the common ground upon which political fights took place and the limited range of issues government might address.

Throughout the 1850s the local Democrats tried to link themselves with the ideas of Presidents Jefferson and Jackson and the platforms of the national party. At the heart of the national ideology was the premise that all men were equal and possessed the right to govern their own destinies. From this assumption, party thought reasoned that government existed to ensure individual equality and self-fulfillment, and that the chief means to that end was to interfere as little as possible in citizens' lives. Laissez-faire was the Democratic party's guiding principle, especially for the central government. Limited spending, economy with public funds, and minimum taxation were the best policy. Free of the burden of government, citizens could turn their efforts into economic and social success. Party leaders proclaimed that their party was committed to preserving this ideal and to keeping open opportunities for the mass of the people.[10]

A major corollary to the Democratic philosophy was the principle of states' rights. Party leaders argued that the states were the best protectors of the interests of individual citizens and that the power of the central government should be restricted. Democrats saw efforts at expanding the powers of the central government as threats to individual freedom and property rights. During the 1840s and 1850s local Democrats opposed measures that they thought undermined this principle. In his acceptance of the party's gubernatorial nomination in 1856, Elias N. Conway pointed specifically to efforts at creating a national bank and imposing protective tariffs as unwarranted expansions of federal power. He also opposed federal funding of "local" internal improvements, although arguing that federal

10. Edward Pessen, *Jacksonian America: Society, Personality, and Politics* (Homewood, Ill., 1978), 209.

authorities could support improvements that were clearly national in scope or necessary.[11]

In the early 1850s party leaders focused increasingly on efforts to abolish slavery or restrict its spread; they saw these efforts as the chief threat against individual freedom. During the crisis of 1850, Arkansas Democratic leaders asserted that the Constitution prohibited the central government from doing anything to interfere with slavery. In his 1850 message to the legislature, Democratic governor John S. Roane declared, "The Union of the north with the general government on the slavery question presents a formidable alliance against us, requiring us to do battle not only for our rights of property, but for our very existence as a sovereign state." During the rest of the 1850s the Democrats assumed the role of opposing efforts that would in any way have expanded federal power. The state party platform of 1856 sounded a familiar theme when it argued the equality of the states under the Constitution and concluded that Congress and other federal agencies could not interfere with the domestic institutions of existing or new states.[12]

As early as 1850, however, some Democratic leaders were unsure that national institutions could protect slavery. Congressman Robert W. Johnson was among the first Arkansans to consider secession as the ultimate means to prevent the North from restricting the movement of slavery westward or interfering with slavery within the states. In 1850 the question of secession divided Democrats, drawing strong opposition even from the plantation counties. The moderate party paper, the *Arkansas Gazette*, challenged Johnson's arguments: "It is the universal sentiment that the Union must be preserved and the universal belief that it cannot be dissolved." Nonetheless, the idea that secession might be needed remained an object of consideration.[13]

Certain that the Democratic party provided the best means to secure individual liberty, the party's leaders concluded that their opponents undermined and limited freedom. The editor of a party newspaper, the *Banner*, wrote of the Arkansas Whigs: "They are federalists and whigs still, utterly destitute of political principles as they are, and fighting only for the spoils of office, they really ought to put forward a platform every time they hold a meeting or convention, so that we may know what particular invasions of the rights of the people are on foot." Democrats leveled the same charges

11. Little Rock *True Democrat*, July 1, 1856.
12. *Arkansas House Journal, Eighth Session*, 38.
13. Little Rock *Arkansas Gazette*, March 1, 1850; Woods, *Rebellion and Realignment*, 43–46.

at the American party, or Know-Nothings. Thomas Hindman typified Democratic attitudes when he asserted that the new party's members were nothing more than Whigs and were, as such, pursuing policies that possessed the same evils of their predecessors, National Republicanism and Federalism.[14]

Democratic rhetoric tying the party to the hopes of individual Arkansans and promising advancement based upon limited government posed a difficult problem for the party's opponents. It forced them to try to show that their specific programs provided better opportunities for prosperity. Whig and then American campaign promises agreed that government existed to advance propertied interests. They did not attack the concept of state sovereignty, but they did argue for a stronger central government with a more active role. This stronger central government, with power to carry out internal improvements and impose protective tariffs, would make the United States independent of the Old World and thus better able to protect freedom and democracy. Strengthening the nation would create "an impregnable bulwark for the defense of popular rights." The American party added to the opposition's ideology the idea that preventing foreign immigration would also help protect domestic institutions. Party leaders concluded that the continued immigration of foreigners and the increasing power of the Catholic church, both inimical to southern institutions, would give the North a majority that could "destroy our domestic institutions in spite of us." Restricting immigration and limiting the power of the Catholic church were thus means of keeping the North from becoming more powerful and of protecting the South's institutions.[15]

The Democrats' opponents were also forced to attack that party's claim to represent the people. They did so by charging Democratic leaders with failing to secure internal improvements or to obtain credit for the state. They also accused the Democratic party of being run by an oligarchic "family." In his 1854 campaign for Congress, E. G. Walker called Democratic conventions "self-appointed, self-constituted assemblages of wireworking and office seeking politicians." James Yell, the American party candidate for governor in 1856, contended of his opponents: "For some time past, there have been two kinds of Democracy in this State: the *True* Democracy and the *Pure* Democracy. The *True* Democracy are *true* to Conway, *true* to *Johnson* and *true* to *office*. The *Pure* Democracy are for

14. Little Rock *Arkansas Banner*, June 10, 1851; Little Rock *True Democrat*, March 18, 1856.

15. Little Rock *Arkansas Whig*, July 3, 1851, July 27, 1854; Little Rock *Arkansas Gazette*, September 21, 1855.

*principles*, without regard to men or office. These latter will all be found, soon or late, upon the *American platform*."[16]

In response to the Democratic clamor for disunion, the Whigs and Know-Nothings remained strongly pro-Union, claiming that the Union represented the last hope to maintain slavery, whereas the nation's breakup would destroy that institution. By advocating disunion, they said, the Democrats posed a greater threat than the abolitionists. In 1855, the moderate Democrat and editor of the *Arkansas Gazette* Christopher C. Danley joined the Know-Nothings, claiming that the Democratic party had lost its original principles; he also argued that because the northern wing of the Democratic party had become sectional and abolitionist, the party could no longer protect the South's domestic institution. The Democrats' opponents assured the voters that their parties could protect slavery within the Union.[17]

Agreement among Arkansas politicians ran beyond the protection of property. Most would have concurred with the desirability of the legislative measures requested by Governor John S. Roane in his address to the General Assembly in 1850. Indeed, the goals that Roane outlined would be pursued by politicians throughout the 1850s. Economic success required an expansion of basic services, and the governor pointed to the need for making internal improvements, including roads, levees, and railroads; the necessity of developing a system of education; and the desirability of establishing a geological survey to encourage the use of the state's natural resources. The problem was how to do these things. Arkansas' credit was restricted by an enormous debt owed on bonds issued to fund the state's abortive banking system. Revenues, on the other hand, could not be increased without threatening property. Expressing the concerns of the state's agrarian interests, Roane warned that tax increases would "drive every man of property from the state, and deter others from emigrating to it." In the General Assembly and in Congress, the fight among Arkansas politicians was not over what services were needed, but over who got them and how they would be funded given the state's fiscal troubles.[18]

The heart of the state's development problem was its bank debt. The State and Real Estate banks had been chartered in 1836 and had been funded with state bonds. The State Bank received about half a million dollars, and the Real Estate Bank received two million dollars. Through mismanagement, bad loans, and criminal malfeasance, all in the face of a national

16. Little Rock *Arkansas Whig*, July 27, 1854; Little Rock *Arkansas Gazette*, August 24, 1855.

17. Little Rock *Arkansas Gazette*, August 10, 24, 1855; Little Rock *Arkansas Whig*, May 22, July 3, 1857.

18. *Arkansas House Journal, Eighth Session*, 19–41.

banking panic, the managers of these banks destroyed both institutions within five years. When the state attempted to recoup its losses, it found that many of the loans were made with inadequate or no collateral and that the state would have to pay off the bonds on its own.[19]

Governors Roane and Elias N. Conway agreed that rapidly paying off the debt created by the two banks' failure was impractical and too burdensome for the state's taxpayers. Consequently, they pursued a policy of slowly paying off the debts and husbanding the resources connected with them. With regard to the Real Estate Bank, officials held on to notes and foreclosed lands, hoping that rising land prices would ultimately increase the value of bank property enough to pay off banking debts. This strategy precluded wholesale foreclosures on mortgaged lands because that would dump thousands of acres on the market and drive prices down further, producing the opposite results to those desired. Delay worked to the advantage of the state's propertied interests, allowing mortgagees to hold on to their land and at the same time keeping taxes down. Throughout the 1850s, Democratic administrations placed tighter controls on the banks but did not bring their business to an end, by either defaulting or paying off their indebtedness. By 1860 Governor Conway reported that the current and prospective indebtedness of the Real Estate Bank was $1,922,230, and of the State Bank, $1,287,717. Up to that time the state had paid out $2,341,996 to meet costs associated with the banks and to cancel bonds. All of this had been accomplished without resorting to heavy taxation.[20]

Politicians agreed that taxes should remain low. They viewed taxation as potentially the greatest threat to property and sought every means to avoid increases. A property tax was the main source of state and county revenue during the antebellum period, supplemented by occupation taxes, fees, and county poll taxes. In 1837 the General Assembly set the state property tax at one-eighth of 1 percent of assessed value, and restricted county taxes to a maximum of one-half of 1 percent. The collapse of the banks forced a change in taxes in 1846, but while the General Assembly increased the state tax rate to one-fourth of 1 percent, it decreased the maximum allowed the counties to one-fourth of one percent. Thus, in the midst of a financial crisis, the legislators had actually decreased the overall

19. Ted R. Worley, "Arkansas and the Money Crisis, 1836–1837," *JSH*, XV (May, 1949), 178–91; Worley, "The Arkansas State Bank: The Antebellum Period," *AHQ*, XXXIII (1964), 65–73; Worley, "The Control of the Real Estate Bank of the State of Arkansas, 1836–1855," *Mississippi Valley Historical Review*, XXXVII (1950), 403–26.

20. *Arkansas Senate Journal, Eleventh Session*, 17–18; *Message of Elias N. Conway, Governor of Arkansas, to Both Houses of the General Assembly, November 6, 1860* (Little Rock, 1860), 22–23.

tax rate from five-eighths to one-half of 1 percent. In 1857, as planters were being pressed by a major economic panic, the legislature decreased state revenues even further, reducing the state tax to one-sixth of 1 percent of assessed value while keeping county taxes at the 1847 level. In the next session they attempted further reductions, but the bill was vetoed by the governor.[21]

Refusing to tax their constituency and having lost much of the state's credit because of the banking debt, Arkansas' leaders were forced to look elsewhere for the money to support education and internal improvements. The place they looked was Washington and the federal government. Through land grants, Washington did do much that could have helped the state's development, but local politicians engaged in bitter struggles over the distribution of the federal largess.

Congress provided the means to encourage education in a law that set aside every sixteenth section of the state's townships to support education. In 1843 the state placed the revenues from the sale of these lands in a common school fund. With actual monies to be distributed, state politicians split over how to do it. Local interests fought over the fund and wrote a law that disbursed the money in a way that did nothing to create an educational system. The law provided that the disposal of the land, investment of the revenue, and allocation of available interest would be done in the township where the donated section was located. In 1845 the revenue was so small that the General Assembly mandated that the entire sum be spent for schoolbooks alone. When Congress donated an additional seventy-two sections of land to produce revenue to create a state seminary, the General Assembly divided the funds equally among the counties. Governor Roane summed up the impact of this intensive localism when he noted in his 1850 address: "The fund undivided, was small. . . . But, divide it into fifty-one parts, and you give to each a poor pittance, useless for any purpose whatever."[22]

Efforts at concentrating the school funds repeatedly failed. Educators pushed for a more centralized system, but local interests in the General Assembly always won. In 1853 fragmentation was in part eliminated when township commissioners were replaced with county commissioners. The disposal of land and the investment and use of revenues from it, however, remained dedicated to the county in which the land was located. Ultimately this policy produced some schools, but they were small, isolated, and inade-

21. *Acts of Arkansas, 1837*, 4–23; *Acts of Arkansas, 1846*, 49–51; *Acts of Arkansas, 1857*, 79.

22. *Acts of Arkansas, 1843*, 130, 134; *Acts of Arkansas, 1845*, 60; *Arkansas House Journal, Eighth Session*, 32.

quate. In 1860 there were 727 public schools and 19,242 pupils in Arkansas, an average of 26 students per school. A combination of public funds and tuition payments supported them with an allocation of $6.27 per student. Of this amount, however, only seventy-five cents came from government.[23]

Arkansas also received lands from Congress to encourage internal improvements, but local interests again prevented their efficient use. The state's political leaders believed that roads, levees, and railroads were essential, but limited capital meant construction would be restricted. Regional politicians fought vigorously to preserve their share of whatever funds were available, and through the 1850s local interests triumphed over any statewide scheme of development. Internal improvements were delayed. By the end of the 1850s several railroads, such as the Memphis and Little Rock and the Cairo and Fulton, were under way and could focus internal-improvement resources on themselves—but this concentration of state support was slow to develop.

Arkansas had received its first internal-improvement support from Congress under an 1841 law that donated to the state 500,000 acres of land, money from the sale of which was to be spent on improvements. The fund did not grow quickly, and any chance that the money accumulated might actually be used to promote internal improvements was reduced when in 1848 the General Assembly disbursed it equally among the counties. State leaders condemned such action, but with no effect. In his 1850 message to the General Assembly, Governor Roane asked for a reconstitution of the state fund, attributing the inadequacies of the current system to jealousy among Arkansans that "some particular sections may derive immediate advantages, to the exclusion of others." The Assembly did not, however, revamp the system. Although a few railroad, levee, and other improvement companies were chartered to use the internal-improvement fund, none was successful under the disbursement policy.[24]

A second major grant was bestowed on the state in the Swamp Land Act of September 28, 1850. This legislation gave Arkansas five million acres of overflowed lands to be used to encourage the construction of levees and ditches. Actual land or land scrip was to pay for such works. Again, the General Assembly placed the control of the fund in local hands, where it was the object of great abuse at first, including outright fraud such as the issuance of scrip for work not done. The result was that much of the land

23. *Acts of Arkansas, 1853*, 143–57; *Eighth Census, 1860: Statistics*, 506.
24. *Arkansas House Journal, Eighth Session*, 31.

was squandered without producing a system of levees or in any other way encouraging internal improvements.[25]

By the 1850s interest in internal improvements focused mainly on railroad construction. The state had tried to use the 1841 and 1850 donations, but the revenues were insufficient to bring about any real progress. Again Arkansans turned to Congress for help. The national movement for a transcontinental railroad had gained enough momentum that Congress made additional land grants to promote private construction. Sure that no help would come from the state, internal-improvement interests in Arkansas worked to obtain congressional support for their particular routes and to obtain the corporate privileges for their roads.[26]

By 1853, charters had been given for seven proposed roads in the state, and these showed the major competing interests. The first had been the Mississippi, Ouachita, and Red River line, incorporated in 1851 and proposing a road from the Mississippi River at Gaines Landing to Camden and then on to Fulton on the Red River. The company reflected the interests of south Arkansas planters, blocked from markets along the Red and Ouachita rivers by the unreliability of these streams. The road could ultimately tie in with a transcontinental route. In 1853 the General Assembly created the Arkansas Western Railroad, from Fort Smith to Missouri; the Arkansas Central, from Little Rock to Memphis; the Memphis and Little Rock, also connecting those cities; the Cairo and Fulton, from northeastern Arkansas to Fulton on the Red River; the Mississippi Valley, connecting St. Louis with New Orleans via Little Rock; and the Napoleon and Little Rock, from Napoleon on the Mississippi to the capital.[27]

Of these roads, two put together the best coalition of political support and became the most important: the Cairo and Fulton and the Arkansas Central. The Cairo and Fulton was backed by Senator William K. Sebastian, Congressman (later Senator) Johnson, and Governor Conway. Johnson supported a bill for this route as a member of the United States House of Representatives and continued to push for it in the Senate. Political enemies suggested that this trio supported the Cairo and Fulton because they and

25. Robert W. Harrison and Walter Kollmorgen, "Land Reclamation in Arkansas Under the Swamp Land Grant of 1850," *AHQ*, VI (1947), 369–418. See also Little Rock *Arkansas Gazette*, May 4, 1855.

26. John L. Stover, *Iron Road to the West: American Railroads in the 1850s* (New York, 1978); Eugene Genovese and Elizabeth Fox-Genovese, *Fruits of Merchant Capital* (New York, 1983); Ulrich B. Phillips, "Transportation in the Antebellum South," *Quarterly Journal of Economics* (1905), 19.

27. *Acts of Arkansas, 1853*, 54, 95–104, 108–19, 176–80, 181–91, 201–202; *Acts of Arkansas, 1855*, 204–11.

their friends had interests in land along the route. Johnson explained his support for the C & F with economic and political arguments. He claimed that it offered economic advantages to Arkansas because it would give access to the markets of the North and to the ports of the Gulf and even to Mexico. Politically, Johnson supported the road because it could receive the backing of essential northern Congressmen and would also help the development of northern Arkansas along with other portions of the state.[28]

The Arkansas Central was backed by Whig politicians such as Pike and Absalom Fowler—it was sometimes known as the "Whig road." It was also, however, supported by moderate Democrats such as William Woodruff, Christopher Danley, and Senator Solon Borland. As editor of the *Arkansas Gazette*, Woodruff was a primary spokesman for this line. He believed that a connection with Memphis would tie Arkansas to the rest of the southern slave states through lines that were either proposed or being constructed from Memphis eastward. Woodruff argued that this road would draw cotton out of southwest Arkansas through Little Rock to Memphis and on to other markets—either New Orleans or the East Coast.[29]

On February 9, 1853, the Cairo and Fulton route received congressional approval. Senator Johnson secured passage of an additional bill that gave additional lands to Arkansas for the construction of a railroad. Borland had received a major blow, and he did not even bother to appear in the Senate to vote on the bill. He commented: "The people of Arkansas have no business in Cairo." The bill set out the general route as being from the Mississippi River opposite the mouth of the Ohio River to Fulton on the Red River, via Little Rock. The law also provided for branches to Fort Smith and to the Mississippi River from Little Rock. The branches may have been enough to secure support from other railroad promoters who conceived of their own roads as falling along the proposed routes and thought this would bring them government support. Congress gave the Arkansas legislature the power to determine the actual routes of the line and its branches and to establish the terminus of the Mississippi branch.[30]

The railroad bill gave the state the means to construct railroads but produced political upheaval. By leaving the routes and the terminus of the eastern branch up to the legislature, Congress caused a legislative struggle among local interests. Proponents of a Memphis terminus moved first, urging Governor Conway to call a special session of the legislature to dispose of the lands and establish the eastern branch. The quick move

28. Little Rock *Arkansas Gazette*, March 11, 1853; Little Rock *True Democrat*, November 30, 1852.

29. Little Rock *Arkansas Gazette*, November 21, 1851; October 13, 1854.

30. *Ibid.*, March 11, 1853.

would have cut off the supporters of a Helena route, but Conway refused to call the session—the Memphis supporters accused him of promoting sectional strife. Henry M. Rector, a politician from south of the Arkansas River, charged the governor with delaying to give proponents of a western branch on the north side of that river a chance to gain advantage over Rector's own line. Local interests stalled construction again.[31]

When the General Assembly met in its regular session in November, 1854, settling the eastern-branch route occupied its time. Little Rock, Memphis, and Helena politicians jockeyed to secure their particular plans. The Memphis and Little Rock groups were opposed by legislators from the southeastern, southern, and northwestern sections, but they had support among advocates of the Cairo and Fulton route and politicians from the southwest and west. On January 16, 1855, the Memphis and Little Rock supporters won—the margin of victory in the senate was one vote—and the Assembly named Hopefield, on the west bank of the Mississippi River across from Memphis, as the eastern terminus and bestowed the lands donated by Congress on the company. Six days later the legislators granted the western franchise to the Little Rock and Fort Smith Railroad Company with a route on the north side of the Arkansas River. The Cairo and Fulton, the Memphis and Little Rock, and the Little Rock and Fort Smith received land. The other rival roads were left without government support.[32]

The General Assembly's action did not end the fight. Opponents of the Cairo and Fulton found that the act granting lands to that line was flawed. The language prohibited selling granted lands for the purpose of constructing the roads. Subsequent efforts to straighten out the problem delayed construction. Fights between east-west lines continued when Memphis and Little Rock and Little Rock and Fort Smith officials discovered that the lands granted to them were inadequate to fully finance construction, forcing them to compete for support from towns and counties along their route. The result of the never-ending struggle among local interests was that by the outbreak of the Civil War only one road had started operations: the Memphis and Little Rock opened two of its sections—from Hopefield to the St. Francis River and from De Valls Bluff, on the White River, to Little Rock.[33]

By the end of the 1850s only sixty-six miles of railroad had been built,

31. Memphis *Eagle and Enquirer* quote ibid., December 9, 1853; Rector quoted *ibid.*, December 2, 1853. See also *ibid.*, August 19, 1853.

32. *Acts of Arkansas, 1855*, 149–53, 172–75, 241–50; Little Rock *Arkansas Gazette*, January 19, 1855.

33. *Arkansas Senate Journal, Tenth Session*, 39–40; *Arkansas Senate Journal, Eleventh Session*, 26.

thirty-nine on the Memphis route and twenty-seven on the Mississippi, Ouachita, and Red River line in the southern part of the state. The existing railroad companies—the Memphis and Little Rock; the Little Rock and Fort Smith; the Mississippi, Ouachita, and Red River; and the Cairo and Fulton—appeared, however, to be about to overwhelm the interests that had prevented the concentration of state funds. Seeking direct state funding, these new railroads challenged the dominant fiscal policies of the Conway administration and the hold over state funds by local interests. Henry Rector ran for office that year urging an outright state grant for railroads. In the 1860 General Assembly a coalition of supporters of the M & LR, the LR & FS, and the M, O & RR passed legislation that appropriated $100,000 to the M & LR and the proceeds from the sale of overflow lands and swamplands in two districts to the other two lines. The state was on the verge of a new era of railroad building. The outbreak of the Civil War delayed that occurrence.[34]

Even before the emergence of railroad interests that could subdue the spirit of localism, other concerns had forced local elites to unify. The greatest outside threat to their propertied interests came in the form of the antislavery movement and the emergence of the Republican party. Arkansas' leaders saw these movements as endangering their prosperity. How to meet the menace occupied more and more of their attention and dominated political discussions in the 1850s.

Arkansans had long viewed northern antislavery as a threat, but full awareness crystallized during the crisis of 1850. California's request for admission to the Union as a free state threatened the balance of power between free and slave states. The admission of California would leave the slave states in a minority in Congress and raised questions of how they could protect their peculiar institution. The immediate crisis was resolved with the Compromise of 1850, which admitted California as a free state, created the New Mexico and Utah territories (with their residents to vote on the status of slavery), abolished the slave trade in the District of Columbia, passed a strict fugitive slave law, and paid Texas for surrendering claims to her northern territories.[35]

White Arkansans viewed the compromise with suspicion. The state's

---

34. *Message of Elias N. Conway, Governor of Arkansas, . . . November 6, 1860,* 5–7; *Statistics of the United States in 1860* (Washington, D.C., 1865), 329; George H. Thompson, *Arkansas and Reconstruction: The Influence of Geography, Economics, and Personality* (Port Washington, N.Y., 1976), 192–94; Stephen E. Wood, "The Development of Arkansas Railroads," *AHQ,* VII (1948), 122–23.

35. See Holman Hamilton, *Prologue to Conflict: The Crisis and the Compromise of 1850* (Lexington, Ky., 1964).

leaders expressed their concern in resolutions demanding further action, including indemnification of slaveholders by Congress for fugitive slaves. Senator Rector assailed northerners as thieves for "robbing us of our negro property." A joint committee of the General Assembly appointed to examine the relationship of federal and state governments concluded that the actions taken in the compromise manifested a spirit of aggression against southern rights, violated principles of justice and equity, and represented a spirit incompatible with brotherly love and affection. In his address to the General Assembly in November, 1850, Governor Roane declared that the admission of California was a sign that the majority had embraced the doctrine of abolition and was willing to use the concept of "higher law" to overwhelm the provisions of the Constitution. "Our right to hold property in slaves," he argued, "is clearly recognized in the Constitution; and the right to regulate and control that property, is reserved to the States. Yet Congress, by her action, has evinced a disposition to wrest that controlling power from their hands."[36]

Politicians had to consider how to block the threat. Roane contended that if the northern states attempted to repeal the Fugitive Slave Act, the South would have no choice as to how to act. He told the General Assembly that the person "is a madman who can longer look for justice, or an observance of our rights, at their hands. The repeal of this act should be made to terminate the contest, and secession adopted as the only remedy for the evil." The General Assembly observed that Arkansas cherished the Union but would "never submit to aggression upon her rights, to dishonor or disgrace, except from necessity alone. . . . Arkansas will abide the fate of the majority of the Slaveholding states, and will seek their Destiny."[37]

After expressing their discontent, Arkansas politicians waited to see what would happen next. For a time the issue remained relatively quiet, but it exploded again in 1854 when Senator Stephen Douglas introduced a bill to organize the Nebraska Territory. The Kansas–Nebraska Act allowed the issue of slavery in the territories to be resolved on the basis of popular sovereignty. It repealed the Missouri Compromise, which had prohibited slavery in that area, and appeared to accept the South's view of the limits on the power of Congress to interfere in local matters. Southern representatives applauded the bill while northerners united against it. Northern opposition convinced Arkansans that the mutual consideration essential to maintain the Union was breaking down; the North was seen as refusing to accept

36. *Arkansas Senate Journal, Eighth Session* (Little Rock, 1851), 139, 295; *Arkansas House Journal, Eighth Session*, 38 (Rector quotation).

37. *Arkansas House Journal, Eighth Session*, 40; *Arkansas Senate Journal, Eighth Session*, 246; Little Rock *Arkansas Gazette*, June 20, 1851; Little Rock *Arkansas Banner*, July 6, 1851.

the South's basic rights. The General Assembly passed a joint resolution in 1855 condemning opposition to the bill as a "traitorous blow aimed at the rights of the South, and the perpetuity of the Union." [38]

Arkansans took no action, but the issue continued to fester. Ultimately, two events—John Brown's raid on Harpers Ferry in 1859 and the national elections of 1860—capped this decade of increasing tension and convinced the state's leaders that the growing crisis could not be resolved within the Union. Slave property was no longer safe, not only in the territories but also in the existing states. Richard H. Johnson, of the *True Democrat* in Little Rock and brother of Senator Robert Johnson, responded to the Brown raid with the observation that southerners were foolish if they believed that northern fanaticism would subside. More critically, Johnson linked the raid with the northern Republican party and its political candidates. The editor noted that Brown had fixed "the great crisis in 1860. — With such developments made and the facts before the people of the south, they will not submit to be ruled by a black Republican President, who would promote or connive at such attacks." The editor of the Des Arc *Citizen* agreed. If a Republican candidate were elected president, "the vast power of the Federal Government will be thrown into the scale of abolition." [39]

For Arkansans the chief question was what could be done to protect the state and slavery. Proposals became increasingly radical. Johnson recommended preparation on all fronts and in December, 1859, encouraged the formation of independent militia companies. At the same time, he argued that support of the Democratic party might prevent a Republican victory in the 1860 presidential elections and allow the Union to be maintained. All agreed, however, that something drastic would have to be done if a Republican were elected. A southern convention was considered. All saw secession as a last resort, but also as the ultimate possibility. [40]

The election of 1860 came increasingly to be seen as a critical point for the Union. Democratic leaders worked to make the election a mandate on the slavery question. In the state party convention in April, 1860, they addressed state and federal relations in a series of resolutions that the party insisted be recognized by any Democratic presidential candidate. Among the resolutions, the most critical insisted that neither Congress nor territorial legislatures possessed the power to "annul or impair the constitutional rights of any citizen of the United States to take his slave property into the

38. *Acts of Arkansas, 1855,* 278.

39. Little Rock *True Democrat,* November 23, 1859 (see also November 9, 1859); Des Arc (Ark.) *Citizen,* January 4, 1860.

40. Little Rock *True Democrat,* December 14, 1859, January 4, February 8, 1860; Des Arc (Ark.) *Citizen,* February 8, 1860.

communal territories." The Democratic leadership wanted an unequivocal commitment that the next president would protect slave property.[41]

The Arkansas resolutions, similar to those presented by other southern delegates at the national convention at Charleston, were unacceptable to the party's leading candidate, Stephen Douglas. The convention split between Douglas' supporters and southern-rights proponents. When the majority rejected the southern position, the Arkansans and many other southern delegates walked out, and the convention adjourned without a nomination. Douglas was nominated when delegates reassembled at Baltimore in June, but southerners walked out again and nominated John C. Breckinridge as a candidate who met their criteria and who would make the election a national test of the commitment of the people of the United States to protect the South's slave property. The Democratic party, however, had broken apart.[42]

If Breckinridge was the South's candidate, the Republican nominee, Abraham Lincoln, represented to Arkansans and other southerners all of the forces that threatened the South's future. In the campaign, Breckinridge was portrayed as what the South needed, whereas Lincoln's election was presented as leading to the destruction of the South. Democratic leaders urged Arkansans to unify against such a menace. The Republicans, according to the editor of the Little Rock *Old-Line Democrat*, "no longer deny their original purposes. In the cant of the proverbs, that '*a house divided against itself cannot stand*,' they plainly proclaim their revolutionary aim: that the conflict they have aroused is henceforth 'irrepressible and this government must become either *all free* or else *all* slave.'" The editor of the Fayetteville *Arkansan* warned, "Lincoln elected and no power short of omnipotence can stay the storm. . . . Crush abolition sectionalism, combat anti-slavery, if you would preserve inviolate your sovereign liberties, your household Penates."[43]

The future portrayed by the state's political leaders, if Lincoln were elected, was ominous. The *Old-Line Democrat* predicted that a Republican president would abolish slave labor and "the end will be to curse a paradise of peace and plenty and devastate the garden of the Republic." Arkansans would not submit, the same editor wrote, "to see the great interests, with which are interwove the destinies of Christendom, trodden underfoot; to witness, unmoved, their property arrested from their possession; a numerous servile population turned loose among them, abandoning to waste their fields, polluting their society with idleness, ignorance, and degradation;

41. Little Rock *True Democrat*, April 14, 1860.
42. *Ibid.*, May 12, 19, 1860.
43. Little Rock *Old-Line Democrat*, August 30, 1860; Fayetteville *Arkansian*, July 21, 1860.

calmly behold their happy homes, once the seat of domestic peace, love and virtue, tenantless and desolate."[44]

The worst fears of Arkansans were realized when Lincoln won. They had made the election a test, and they had lost. All leaders saw it as a dire crisis, although they could not agree on what should be done. Most counseled moderation but held little hope for protection with a Republican executive. In his speech to the General Assembly in 1860, newly inaugurated governor Henry Rector expressed his hope that it would be possible to resolve differences but advised the legislators to take steps to protect the state. Arkansas could not do without slave labor, he said, for "without it, her fertile fields are deserts, and her people penniless and impoverished." He concluded that a conflict was inevitable: "sooner or later dissolution must come."[45]

Whigs and American party members took a more conservative stand, arguing that the Constitution and the federal courts remained as a bulwark against illegal action by the Republicans. In the discussion over secession they called themselves—and were called by their opponents—"Unionists," although they were never for the Union at all costs. Perhaps a majority of Arkansans supported this position. What might happen under Lincoln was uncertain. Secession, however, would clearly lead to war, and that would be ruinous to all. Even in the state's plantation regions citizens doubted the advisability of secession. One resident reported from Augusta, in Woodruff County, that many there did not favor secession because "so much excitement effects the cotton market."[46]

Following the secession on December 20, 1860, of South Carolina, the withdrawal of other Deep South states in January and February, and the organization of the Confederate States of America at Montgomery, Alabama, on February 9, 1861, forces in favor of secession in Arkansas became more aggressive. Democratic party leaders pushed the legislature to link the state with South Carolina and the other seceded states. Rector, who had been fairly moderate in his inaugural address, sent a special message to the General Assembly the day after South Carolina passed its ordinance; he stated his conviction that the Union was practically at an end and urged the legislators to arm the militia and prepare for war. Senator Johnson and

---

44. Little Rock *Old-Line Democrat*, August 30, 1860, October 18, 1860.

45. *Arkansas Senate Journal, Thirteenth Session*, 100–101; Little Rock *Old-Line Democrat*, December 6, 1860.

46. J. S. Neill to Dear Brother, January 15, 1861, in Mrs. Walter A. Dowell, ed., "The Job Neill Letters," *Independence County Chronicle*, VIII (October, 1966), 30; Johnson Chapman to William E. Woodruff, January 10, 1861, in William E. Woodruff Papers, AHC; Little Rock *Arkansas Gazette*, November 17, 1860.

Congressman Hindman also asked Arkansans to support South Carolina, call a convention, and secede, considering that to remain in the Union was to surrender to "black Republicanism." Urging white unity, the two politicians warned that even if Lincoln did not interfere with slavery in Arkansas, he would limit the institution's expansion into the West, and the result would be the steady growth of a servile population until the state faced "a conflict for supremacy of races, and the blacks will be exterminated; or else the white man must abandon his country for ever to the negro." Secession was the only way for white Arkansans, whether slaveholder or nonslaveholder, to avoid the catastrophe.[47]

While secessionists urged white unity, Unionists resisted being stampeded. They drew their strength from many sources: ex-Whigs, railroad men concerned about the loss of government support for their projects, and westerners fearful of the problems secession might create on the Indian frontier all added support to the Unionist cause. As the crisis deepened, however, Unionism took on an increasingly class-oriented character. The Unionist editor of the Fayetteville *Democrat* feared that secessionists wanted to establish a government of slaveholders. The editor warned that "the same mob that can make cotton king and Davis President, this same mob can tell you that *only he can be trusted at the ballot box who is a slaveholder*, that a Republican Government based upon the universal suffrage of *white men* is a disgraceful failure." One Unionist in Benton County asked local citizens, "Do you know that in that Confederacy your rights will be respected? That you will be allowed a vote unless you are the owner of a negro?!! These things you do not know!" Unionists argued that the nonslaveholder had little interest in secession.[48]

Unionist feeling was strong enough that as the Deep South moved out of the Union, Arkansans delayed any action. The house of representatives passed a bill on December 22, 1860, calling for a state convention to respond to Lincoln's election, but the senate did not pass the bill until January 16. The act provided for an election on February 18, 1861, in which voters would decide for or against a convention and, at the same time, for delegates to the convention should it be approved. The nature of the election favored the secessionists, Governor Rector nearly provoked an armed conflict between the state militia and federal troops at Little Rock by seizing the arsenal there, and the secessionist press campaigned strongly for action, but the Unionist element prevailed in the balloting: the voters approved a convention but elected a Unionist majority to it. Recent scholarship has

47. Little Rock *Arkansas Gazette*, December 22, 29, 1860, January 5, 8, 1861; Fayetteville *Arkansian*, February 8, 1861.

48. Fayetteville *Arkansian*, March 8, 1861; Dougan, *Confederate Arkansas*, 30.

suggested that support for the Unionist position, which tended to be strongest in the uplands of the state, reflected a basic class division between the yeomanry and the rich. In fact the election showed no simple dichotomy. Both positions had support throughout the state. The northwest went Unionist by only a small margin. Not only the leadership but the voters of Arkansas were uncertain as to the best course to pursue.[49]

In the convention, which began on March 3, economically and politically prominent individuals supported the Unionist position. Among the most widely known was David Walker, a Whig from Fayetteville and a proponent of a north-south railroad along the state's western border. Walker was elected president of the convention. From Van Buren came Jesse Turner, another railroad man with interests in the Indian Territory. There were also prominent attorneys from the state's larger towns, including Augustus H. Garland from Little Rock, William M. Fishback from Fort Smith, and A. W. Hobson from Camden. The Unionists withstood secessionist efforts for fifteen days of debate. In the end, the secessionists secured an election for secession or cooperation—to be held the following August—and a pledge that the state would resist coercion. The Unionists stalled more drastic action and passed resolutions favoring a peaceful settlement within the federal framework.[50]

Ultimately, however, Arkansas Unionists were not for the Union at all costs. They were as convinced as the secessionists that the Republican party posed a real threat to the South. They differed only in how they believed the state's interests might be protected best. They were conservative men, seeing in existing laws the solution to the sectional crisis. In addition, the personal interests of many of them were better served by remaining in the Union. Their position could not be maintained, however, if it appeared that the law would no longer operate to protect slavery in the South. On the first day of the convention Walker wrote to a friend, "Although I am willing to acknowledge that South Carolina has acted hastily and it may be to some extent wrong; yet I have too much southern blood in my veins to sit quietly down and see her contending with the abolition hordes of the North and not wish her God-speed."[51]

The attack on Fort Sumter on April 12, 1861, and President Lincoln's call on April 15 to the loyal states for 75,000 militia to suppress secession

49. Dougan, *Confederate Arkansas*, 46; Woods, *Rebellion and Realignment*, 130–32, 145; Ralph Wooster, "The Arkansas Secession Convention," *AHQ*, XIII (1954), 172–95.

50. Dougan, *Confederate Arkansas*, 38–56; Ralph L. Goodrich Diary, February 8, 1861, in Ralph L. Goodrich Collection, AHC.

51. David Walker to William W. Mansfield, March 3, 1861, in W. W. Mansfield Papers, AHC; Woods, *Rebellion and Realignment*.

prevented Arkansas conservatives from continuing their opposition to secession. John Brown of Camden noted in his diary that Lincoln's action
had spread secessionism to the ranks of the "honest people," and concluded
that the time had come for Union men to "make common cause for the
defense of their section." On April 23 one of the staunchest Unionists,
Christopher Danley, wrote: "From the first, I was for the Union. Now that
the 'overt' act has been committed we should I think draw the sword, and
not sheathe it until we can have a guarantee of all our rights, or such
standards as will be honorable to the South."[52]

Walker, as a result of the developments of April 12 and 15, ordered
the convention to reconvene on May 6, 1861. A remarkable change of
sentiment had taken place. Unionists were aware that they had lost control
and believed that the people of the state now wanted secession. Jesse Turner
informed his wife, "Our people are thoroughly imbued with the revolutionary spirit." On the first day, an ordinance of secession was introduced
and passed. Secessionist and Unionist leaders came together in a common
cause—protection of their state. Only five members opposed the ordinance, and after an appeal for unity by Walker, four of these—all but Isaac
Murphy of Madison County—changed their votes. On the grounds that
they opposed all attempts by the Lincoln government to coerce states that
had seceded from the Union, the convention took Arkansas out of the
Union.[53]

Arkansas seceded to protect what its leaders considered to be property
rights—the right to own slaves and to move them into the national territories—that were vital to the future of the state and ensured by both law and
nature. The leaders had concluded that these rights would not be protected
within the Union. They seceded to protect slavery. Secession was a calculated risk, however. Peaceable secession was recognized as impossible. To
protect their property they would have to fight, and a loss would ensure
the end of slavery. If they remained in the Union there was a chance that
some compromise could be worked out. William Fishback stated the risks
when he encouraged Arkansans to rely on the Constitution, law, courts,
police, and official oaths. Secession would mean, he warned, that "instead

52. C. C. Danley to W. W. Mansfield, April 23, 1861, in Mansfield Papers; John W.
Brown Diary, April 22, 20, 1861, in AHC; Thomas Haney to David Walker, April 17, 1861,
in David Walker Papers, UAF; S. H. Tucker to David C. Williams, May 9, 1861, in D. C.
Williams Papers, Clara Eno Collection, AHC.

53. Jesse Turner to Mrs. Turner, May 8, 1861, in Jesse Turner Papers, DU; Jesse Turner
to D. C. Williams, in Williams Papers; John Campbell to Dear Sir, June 10, 1861, in John
Campbell Letters, Small Manuscripts Collection, AHC; Little Rock *Arkansas Gazette*, May
11, 1861; Dougan, *Confederate Arkansas*, 61–63.

of mobs and [a] few hostile state laws, we should then have a great and powerful nation at our very door seeking to crush our institutions."[54] In the end, Arkansas' leaders put everything on the line and gambled that they and the rest of the South could win a war that would protect slavery and the society they believed slavery made possible.

54. Fishback quoted in David Y. Thomas, *Arkansas in War and Reconstruction, 1861–1874* (Little Rock, 1926), 42–43.

# PART II

## THE CIVIL WAR YEARS

# 5

## CONFEDERATE ARKANSAS

ARKANSAS' LEADERS WENT TO WAR IN 1861 TO PROTECT
their community. They believed it was no longer secure in the Union, and
they chose to protect their future through secession. Their goal required
the state to go to war, and they readily entered the fray united in the
southern Confederacy with other slave states. Probably a majority of the
state's white citizens agreed with their decision and rushed to arms. During
the next four years Confederate Arkansans discovered that even in those
areas of the state that did not experience a Union invasion or a military
occupation, war unleashed disquieting forces. Organizing and supporting
modern warfare produced tensions in an economy that even in peacetime
had been fragile. The same demands also caused adjustments of social relationships among all classes. Confederate Arkansas witnessed change that
undermined the society its leaders had gone to war to protect.

Many Arkansans initially agreed that the war was to protect their way
of life. They were pitted against an "abolitionist horde" of fanatics. They
saw the Yankees as vandals who were hostile to civilization and who had
proved they were out to destroy the South. Mary B. Eskridge of Crittenden
County saw the war as one against the *emissaries of the . . . evil one.*" One
poet composed a poem for the Hempstead Rifles that captured the spirit
of many of the men who marched off in the spring and summer of 1861.
The poem went:

> We go, the Sons of Southern sires
> To meet the hireling Lincoln world,
> To battle for our homes and fires
> 'Neath Dixie's 'stars and bars' unfurled
> And our battle-cry will be
> "Give us death or liberty!"

In such circumstances there could be no slacking. All were expected to
give their wholehearted support.[1]

1. M. B. Eskridge to W. E. Woodruff, June 4, 1861, September 9, 1861, H. A. Whittington
to W. E. Woodruff, May 15, 1861, J. W. Felts to W. E. Woodruff, May 24, July 18, 1862,
all in William E. Woodruff Papers, AHC; Washington (Ark.) *Telegraph*, May 8, 1861 (poem).

Young and old rallied to the cause of the new Confederate nation. Their reasons for enlisting varied, but all were caught up in the wartime hysteria. Some held deep ideological motives. Others went because all the other young men in the community were signing up and the war promised to be an adventure. The rush to the colors was so great that Henry Morton Stanley, living then in Arkansas County, concluded that the entire community would be emptied of men. A military fever touched all. At Little Rock, businessmen closed up shop to go off to war. At Camden, thirteen companies—about 1,300 men—were organized by September, 1861, out of an adult white male population of 1,750. Camden's Judge John Brown wrote: "The excitement intense. The whole country is arising—and our people are perfectly wild."[2]

This fever also infected those who remained behind. Everything possible was done to provide for the soldiers. When one store at Camden refused wholehearted support, the local City Home Guards broke into it and confiscated its goods. Refusal to support the war was a sign of disloyalty, and citizens proposed to run disloyal men out of the state. Hiram Whittington of Hot Springs used $150 of his own money to help outfit a cavalry company. His attitude was typical: "All that are able should give freely for the support of the Government. We must wear our old clothes and use the most rigid economy—make everything we possibly can—and buy nothing we can possibly do without—and let the soldiers and the Government have every spare dollar."[3]

There were some signs of dissent. In October, 1861, officials discovered a large antiwar organization, the Arkansas Peace Society, in Carroll, Fulton, Izard, Marion, Searcy, and Van Buren counties. The government suppressed the society, and individuals associated with it were forced to sign up in the Confederate army. Confined to the mountain counties and consisting of people outside the mainstream of society, the Peace Society reflected changing social relations. Content to be left alone before secession, these mountain men now actively resisted the leadership of the state's Confederate elite. Their resistance raises questions about the common

2. Van Buren (Ark.) *Press*, April 24, 1861; James E. Caldwell Journal, August 1, 1861, in James E. Caldwell Papers, AHC; J. T. Armstrong to My Dear Wife, August 5, 1861, in Armstrong Papers, Southern Collection, UNC; J. W. Felts to W. E. Woodruff, May 24, July 28, 1861, in Woodruff Papers; Dorothy Stanley, ed., *The Autobiography of Sir Henry Morton Stanley* (New York, 1909), 165, 171; John W. Brown Diary, May 30, 1861, in AHC.

3. M. B. Eskridge to W. E. Woodruff, September 9, 1861, in Woodruff Papers; Robert F. Kellam Diary, May 14, 1861, in AHC; H. A. Whittington to W. E. Woodruff, July 6, 1861, in Woodruff Papers.

interests of whites—interests that supposedly held the antebellum community together.[4]

Economic collapse presented a more eminent threat than social conflict in the first year of the war. From the beginning, the sacrifice of manpower and wealth left the state in precarious circumstances. The problem was simple. In arming and equipping the troops, citizens used up much of the cash available in local communities. At the same time, conditions produced a collapse of the credit system. Without cash or credit, civilians were unable to procure necessary supplies and faced immediate shortages that undermined the Confederate cause. John Brown of Camden saw economic disaster ahead in the spring of 1861. He wrote on the day of the election for the secession convention: "We have neither bread nor meat within the State to sustain us above 6 months, — no Banks or moneyed facilities. The State has neither money nor credit — could not on state credit borrow one hundred dollars without her own borders. Nothing but ruin to property holders, and starvation to the poor would be the result of secession."[5]

A shortage of currency in local communities developed almost immediately as Arkansas prepared for war. As early as January, 1861, newspapers noted the annual flow of cash out of state as planters and businessmen settled their accounts. Buying guns and equipment, however, vastly increased this trend. Through the spring, money became more scarce. By June currency shortages existed throughout the state and worsened as public officials encouraged citizens to dig deeper into their pockets to support the military. County courts levied special taxes to provide for arms. Determining the amount of money that went into the state's military organizations is impossible, but it must have been large. John Brown believed the amount spent by that first June was already incalculable.[6]

The use of currency for military supplies caused a major crisis in creditor-debtor relations and a collapse of the credit system. Spring was the season when financial arrangements were made for the whole year. Merchants obtained their supplies from outside the state; planters and farmers in turn acquired what was necessary for putting in crops. At the same

4. Little Rock *True Democrat*, December 5, 19, 1861; Ted R. Worley, ed., "Documents Relating to the Arkansas Peace Society of 1861," *AHQ*, XVII (1958), 86–87; Ted R. Worley, "The Arkansas Peace Society of 1861; A Study of Mountain Unionism," *JSH*, XXIV (1958), 445–56.

5. Brown Diary, February 10, 1861.

6. *Ibid.*, May 20, June 11, September 23, 1861; M. L. Bell to W. E. Woodruff, June 25, October 15, 1861, in Woodruff Papers; Little Rock *Arkansas Gazette*, April 6, 1861, January 5, 1861.

time, debts were being settled from the previous farming season. Arkansans did not have the cash necessary to go to war and carry on normal business too. Debtors were unable to pay their notes, and creditors received requests for extensions of time or, in some cases, found obligations ignored. One debtor was reported as being "absorbed in the Military movements; and appears to have lost sight of his personal liabilities and promises."[7]

Public officials generally sympathized with debtors. The secession convention passed an ordinance protecting the property of men in the service from seizure by creditors. In November, 1861, the General Assembly passed a stay law that forced creditors to accept state war bonds in payment of debts. Debtors were protected further when local courts suspended operations, leaving creditors with no legal recourse. Public attitudes and the law effectively halted efforts to collect debts and protected debtors for the duration of the war.[8]

With no way to collect debts, merchants refused to extend further credit. They requested clients to settle up old debts and announced they would deal on a strictly cash basis. As early as April, 1861, a Little Rock firm announced it would accept only cash because credit was "played out." By November, one Camden merchant noted that all business houses were operating only on cash. Farmers retaliated by refusing to provide produce except for cash. As a result, families without cash had difficulty obtaining all types of supplies even when they were available.[9]

The inability to collect on loans also created a long-term economic problem. Creditors were forced to renew notes, working to secure the debts as best they could. The collection of debts was postponed, but they were not written off. Interest compounded throughout the war, and in southern Arkansas debtors had to pay renewal rates that ran at 2.5 percent per month. By 1865 Arkansans faced the problem of having to pay off debts that had accumulated interest for more than four years.[10]

Confederate and state monetary policy, which might have restored some measure of economic activity, proved a miserable failure. The central and

7. L. Touchstone to W. E. Woodruff, January 20, 1862, in Woodruff Papers, AHC; Brown Diary, May 20, 26, 1861; Kellam Diary, April 17, 1861; J. S. Hornor to W. E. Woodruff, June 15, 1861, in Woodruff Papers.

8. *Ordinances of the State Convention Which Convened at Little Rock, May 6, 1861* (Little Rock, 1861), 35; Kellam Diary, April 30, 1861; Brown Diary, February 4, March 28, 1862; J. S. Hornor to W. E. Woodruff, June 15, 1861, M. L. Bell to W. E. Woodruff, April 24, 1861, both in Woodruff Papers; *Acts of Arkansas, 1861,* 43–47; *Acts of Arkansas, 1863,* 12.

9. Kellam Diary, March 8, 1861; Little Rock *Arkansas Gazette,* May 18, 1861.

10. Brown Diary, May 26, June 3, August 20, 1861; M. L. Bell to W. E. Woodruff, October 15, 1861, in Woodruff Papers; *Biennial Report of the Auditor of Public Accounts of the State of Arkansas, for 1859 and 1860* (Little Rock, 1860), Table H.

state governments printed paper currency to cover their obligations. The value of paper currencies, however, was unstable. From the beginning, merchants discounted government notes and bonds heavily. By the winter of 1862, Confederate Treasury notes were circulating at half their face value. The following spring, those in circulation at Camden were worth only thirty-three cents on the dollar. Official exchange rates meant little, however, because many individuals refused to accept the currency at all. When debtors tried to pay obligations with the devalued currency, creditors usually refused to take payment. Accepting the paper currency offered creditors only one advantage: most of the Confederate, state, and county currencies could be used to pay taxes and other government obligations at par value. A discouraged Confederate soldier wrote from southern Arkansas in 1862, "When it comes to that the citizens refuse to take their own currency I think it is time to quit."[11]

Even this weak and inflated currency might have had some positive effect, but the Confederate government was unable to get much of it into Arkansas. When Major General Theophilus H. Holmes took command of the Trans-Mississippi Department in the summer of 1862, he reported that many of the soldiers in his department had not been paid since the beginning of the war and the government owed them nearly ten million dollars in back pay. In addition, Holmes estimated that businessmen in Arkansas, Louisiana, and Texas were owed some thirteen million dollars for military purchases. If this money had been available when it had some value, a more normal economic life might have been possible. It was not, and the shortage helped produce the general shutdown of economic activity.[12]

The most immediate problems created by the drying up of credit and lack of currency were shortages of supplies. Merchants who might have stockpiled critical items in the spring of 1861 did not do so. Some simply failed to go to market because of the uncertainties concerning demand. Others found northern businesses unwilling to sell goods on credit. As a result, communities experienced shortages immediately. By September, 1862, John Brown listed items that could not be purchased at Camden— cotton combs and cards, pins, towels, coffee, tea, opium, quinine, salt, and the coarse "onasberg" cloth used for slave clothing. Even Confederate troops did not have enough weapons, powder, clothing, and food. Brown reported that soldiers at Camden were poorly clothed and fed and armed

11. Brown Diary, January 7, March 2, 1863; M. L. Bell to W. E. Woodruff, October 9, 15, 1861, in Woodruff Papers; A. O. McCollom to Friends, December 25, 1862, in A. O. McCollom Papers, UAF; David Y. Thomas, *Arkansas in War and Reconstruction, 1861–1874* (Little Rock, 1926), 360.

12. *OR*, XIII, 897.

with old civilian guns. Shortages hindered the war effort and sapped morale.[13]

Arkansans could have produced at home many of the goods that they lacked, but conditions limited their efforts. A lack of capital, skilled craftsmen, and machinery severely circumscribed early attempts to expand textile production in Pike County, for example. When he arrived in Arkansas in May, 1862, Major General Thomas C. Hindman discovered major shortages of all types of supplies and no effort being made to produce them locally. Hindman concluded that the needed facilities had not been developed because "there was neither capital nor sufficient enterprise among the citizens to engage in such undertakings." Increasingly, Confederate authorities resorted to central planning and government industries in order to overcome the shortages that interfered with their efforts to make war.[14]

Food shortages had a more direct impact on civilians than the lack of other supplies. The refusal of merchants and farmers to trade on anything but a cash basis contributed to this problem, but it was complicated by other forces. In part, nature seemed opposed to the Confederate cause from the very beginning. In the summer of 1861 inadequate rain reduced the corn crop. The crops of 1862 were also poor, with regional shortages of corn, wheat, and produce in southern Arkansas; moreover, an epidemic of hog cholera destroyed much of the state's hog supply. Meanwhile, shortages were worsened by speculators who exported large amounts of farm goods to Louisiana, hoping to make more money selling to the wealthier planters there. Many of these problems were regional in nature, but the state's inadequate transportation system made it impossible to move goods around easily and provide relief to the affected areas.[15]

The problems might still have been manageable except that farmers continued to make decisions regarding crops on a nonwar basis. Despite pressing demands for food, many growers devoted their labor force and land to continued production of cotton. By the spring of 1862 public officials and newspapers were pressuring planters to grow less cotton and more foodstuffs. It made military and economic sense. As the editor of the Helena *Shield* concluded, a cotton shortage would place pressure on

13. *Ibid.*, 30, 877–78; M. E. Brodie to Dear Carrie, May 6, June 21, 1862, in Fred J. Herring Collection, Small Manuscripts Collection, AHC; Kellam Diary, November 2, 28, 29, 1861; Brown Diary, March 10, September 19, 1862; Helena (Ark.) *Southern Shield*, February 8, 1862; Little Rock *Arkansas Gazette*, April 6, May 18, 25, 1861.

14. *OR*, XIII, 32.

15. M. L. Bell to W. E. Woodruff, June 25, 1861, F. W. Desha to Woodruff, January 5, 1863, both in Woodruff Papers; W. Chambers to Burilla Chambers, June 12, 1862, in William W. Chambers Papers, UT; Brown Diary, March 21, 24, September 16, October 29, 1862; *OR*, XIII, 30.

England to recognize the Confederate government. Increasing food production would reduce prices and allow the poor men of the army to support their families. At Little Rock, Richard Johnson admonished planters: "No! Put not a single [cotton] seed in the ground." The General Assembly, in an effort to encourage an increase in corn and wheat acreage, made it unlawful to cultivate more than two acres in cotton per hand.[16]

All such efforts were futile. Plantations involved major investments in land and slaves, and most planters were debtors, and few were willing to abandon cotton cultivation completely. Cotton remained the one item that could generate the cash necessary for their operations. In fact, planters in the vicinity of Union forces quickly developed an illegal trade with the Yankees, exchanging cotton for gold. Cotton also had some stable value that could serve as a hedge against inflation. One soldier-planter urged his wife to hang on to their cotton because it would be better than "current money." Planters would not grow more foodstuffs. Danley of the *Arkansas Gazette* raged at planters who "are determined, notwithstanding the prohibition of the Legislature, to plant large crops of cotton. We cannot believe it. There must be some mistake. Cotton planted now is planted for the enemy. Plant grain—so as to support the families of absent soldiers, and feed the soldiers themselves as they fight our battles."[17]

The food shortages and unstable currency combined to produce a runaway inflation in grocery prices throughout Arkansas. Salt, essential for preserving meats, led the way, climbing from a prewar price in Little Rock of two dollars a sack to twenty dollars in eastern Arkansas in November, 1861. Coffee increased from fourteen cents to forty cents per pound. In November, 1861, Confederate authorities made their first effort to control prices by restricting exports, but government orders did not stop the steady price increases. In June, 1862, authorities finally tried to set prices on most commodities. Even this, however, failed to stop the upward spiral. The extent of inflation can be seen by comparing prices in March of 1860 with prices in the same month in 1863, when a sack of salt reached one hundred dollars and coffee sold for seven dollars per pound. Over that same period flour increased from nine cents to a dollar per pound, bacon from fifteen cents to a dollar, and sugar from eleven cents to fifty cents.[18]

Inadequate supplies and high prices hurt those with the least resources

16. Helena (Ark.) *Southern Shield*, February 8, 1862; Little Rock *True Democrat*, April 3, 1862; *Acts of Arkansas, 1862*, 7–8.

17. Brown Diary, May 4, 1861; W. W. Garner to Dear Wife, August 4, 1862, in D. D. McBrien, ed., "Letters of an Arkansas Confederate Soldier," *AHQ*, II (1943), 63; Little Rock *Arkansas Gazette*, May 3, June 7, 1862; OR, XIII, 39.

18. OR, XV, 782; Little Rock *Arkansas Gazette*, March 17, 1860, December 14, 1861.

most. Individuals with cash and foresight had prepared. A Red River planter purchased enough supplies for five years, and a visitor found in 1864 that the plantation still had cloth, shoes, plows, hoes, nails, candles, and even whiskey. The poor did not have the resources to do this, and by 1862 they were hard pressed throughout the state. The fact that the families of the men essential for the Confederate army were suffering persuaded officials to attempt to provide financial aid and donations of food. None of the programs effectively solved the problems. There is no way to know the full impact of the situation on individual families or exactly how they attempted to cope. Nonetheless, they must have depleted their already-minimal resources to survive—consuming their draft animals and breeding stock, and selling land to obtain subsistence.[19]

By the late summer and autumn of 1862, Confederate Arkansas faced a serious crisis. Supporting the war effort had produced major problems within local communities. The state's citizens had no more capital to put into the war or were hoarding what they had. Factories and farms could not provide necessary goods. Among the civilians the poor appear to have been particularly hard pressed, but even those with money found it difficult to obtain supplies. And these problems were just the beginning. A harsh new challenge arose when Union forces under General Samuel R. Curtis marched into northeastern Arkansas. The Federals occupied Batesville and began raiding into the surrounding countryside while Curtis prepared a campaign aimed at Little Rock. Resisting the invaders required the spending of even more human and physical resources and quickened change. From May, 1862, until the end of the war, the Confederate army played a major role in modifying the antebellum community. Under the direction first of General Hindman, then General Holmes, and finally Lieutenant General E. Kirby Smith, the military demanded total mobilization, utilizing whatever civilian resources it needed to stay in the fight. Civilian government, continuing to operate at the state and county level, at first opposed the military's increasing power but after the election of Governor Harris Flanagin in November, 1862, cooperated. The war continued at ever greater costs to Arkansans and their institutions. Even in the areas that remained under Confederate control, war undermined the antebellum community.[20]

Hindman began the increase of military authority within the state in May, 1862. He found a desperate situation. The community was on the

19. G. T. Wright to My Dear Mother, December 15, 1864, in George T. Wright Papers, UT; Little Rock *True Democrat*, March 6, 1862.
20. H. W. Whittington to W. E. Woodruff, October 25, December 10, 1862, in Woodruff Papers; Brown Diary, September 16, 18, 1862; J. D. Brewster to My Dear Sister, October 25, 1862, in J. D. Brewster Papers, UT; *OR*, XIII, 28–44, 877–78, 896–97.

verge of collapse and the state was without military protection. Confederate troops under General Earl Van Dorn had lost the battle of Pea Ridge and were being pulled out of the state, with the enemy that had defeated them still on the northern border. Arkansas' Confederate congressmen protested the abandonment of their state. Governor Rector called for volunteers for a state force that would not be transferred to the Confederate army; he even threatened Richmond with secession. Hindman was sent in authorized to "use every means in your power for the defense of Arkansas."[21]

Hindman made it clear that the whole population and all the resources of the community would be thrown into the conflict. In his first address he outlined his plan to drive out the invader or perish. Success, however, depended on citizens' doing their whole duty. Civilians were expected to contribute every last dollar they possessed, sacrifice all their property rather than allow it to fall into the hands of the enemy, and adhere to the Confederate cause through all difficulties, "for freedom's sake." Hindman may have been speaking to both soldiers and civilians when he pronounced that "there must be efficiency among officers of every rank and obedience among soldiers under all circumstances."[22]

Hindman moved to create stability. He enforced the conscription law passed by the Confederate Congress the previous April, requiring all white males between eighteen and thirty-five to enroll in volunteer infantry companies. Those who did not enroll would be conscripted. Further, he refused to accept substitutes. At the same time, he authorized the organization of independent companies to harass Union forces in the state. Unsure of Rector's support, Hindman forced the governor to abandon efforts to call up the militia and informed him that he alone would conscript any state troops and stores. He ordered new price controls, regularized the impressment of private property, and established facilities near Arkadelphia to produce leather, shoes, harnesses, gun carriages, caissons, powder, shot, shell, and accoutrements. He ordered all cotton in danger of being seized by the enemy to be burned or moved at least twenty miles from enemy lines.[23]

Hindman's most controversial measure was declaring martial law, which he did on June 30. He divided the state into subdistricts under a provost-marshal general. Local provosts were to suppress local anarchy, including increasing opposition to Confederate authority. Hindman hoped military control would stabilize Confederate currency, save civilians from extortionate prices, break up trading with the enemy, and above all prevent the

21. *OR*, XIII, 814–16, 828–29, 831–32, 827–28.
22. *Ibid.*, 830.
23. *Ibid.*, 835; XV, 780–81, 783; XIII, 32, 33–34, 28–29, 831–32, 30; XV, 781–82.

army and civilians from starving. The general accused Rector's government of abdicating its duty and claimed the right to institute an ad interim government to create and maintain his army and exercise the control necessary "for preserving society."[24]

The general's actions produced some positive results. In part, his efforts prevented Curtis' army from linking with a line of supply on the White River and forced the Federals to abandon their campaign against Little Rock. In June they withdrew from Batesville and marched to the Mississippi River, where they established a new base at Helena. Hindman's army was reinvigorated, although it was unable to destroy the Federals as they moved overland to the Mississippi.[25]

At the same time, Hindman's measures provoked a firestorm of protest. His suppression of civil authority and interference with private property—the seizure of cotton—raised the ire of critics. The general dismissed his opponents as "tories, speculators, extortioners, and deserters, and a few of the smaller politicians," but they were not as insubstantial as he claimed. In addition to Governor Rector, the state's congressional delegation expressed concern with Hindman's action. In the Indian Territory, General Albert Pike called the declaration of martial law a "usurpation and the substitution of despotism in place of a constitutional government." The Confederate Congress called on the secretary of war for an explanation of the authority under which Hindman acted.[26]

In midsummer, 1862, Richmond sent General Theophilus Holmes to command the new Trans-Mississippi Department. Hindman was left in command of the Arkansas District, but President Jefferson Davis informed Holmes of the complaints against Hindman and told the new commander to correct the abuses as rapidly as possible. Secretary of War George W. Randolph instructed Holmes to rescind martial law and martial-law regulations, and detailed precisely how the conscription act was to be executed.[27]

Hindman and Senator Robert W. Johnson, the general's principal supporter, won Holmes to their point of view upon his arrival, and the commander delayed carrying out his instructions. Holmes wrote to Davis that martial law had been effective. The continuing opposition caused by Hindman's actions became apparent, however, in the state elections the following October. Candidates openly campaigned on the grounds that they had

24. *Ibid.*, XIII, 39.
25. *Ibid.*, 36–37.
26. *Ibid.*, 39, 44, 856 (Pike quotation); Brown Diary, July 6, 1862; Thomas, *Arkansas in War and Reconstruction*, 320.
27. *OR*, XIII, 874.

not originally supported secession and were opposed to martial law. When the General Assembly met in November, 1862, its members passed embarrassing resolutions condemning the military's "illegal acts" and took the state printing away from Senator Johnson's *True Democrat*, giving it to the anti-martial-law Washington *Telegraph*. On the floor, Representative Augustus H. Garland opposed the reelection of Johnson to the Senate and spoke in "defense of civil law and liberty and against military rule and oppression." A state supreme court justice defected to the Federals at this time because the "military authority" had "overstepped their proper line of operations." Faced with such opposition, Holmes quietly abandoned martial law.[28]

Hindman's star set in the District of Arkansas as the military crisis worsened. Despite his ultimate departure and despite instructions to military commanders to be more attentive to civilian needs, however, the deteriorating military situation meant that his successors would continue to strengthen the authority of the army at the expense of civilians. The military decline began in December, 1862, with the battle of Prairie Grove and the disastrous retreat that followed. Soldiers deserted complaining of poor leadership and inadequate supplies. Hindman suffered another reverse on January 9, 1863, when Federals took Arkansas Post, near the mouth of the Arkansas River. After these defeats Hindman lost his command; Holmes was left in charge of Arkansas but placed under E. Kirby Smith, new head of the Trans-Mississippi Department. On July 4, 1863, Confederate forces suffered another disaster in the battle of Helena, and in September they lost control of Little Rock. Confederate authority in the state now extended only to the southern counties. To protect them, military authorities took whatever radical steps they considered necessary. Hindman was gone, but his policies of total war continued during the remaining years of the war.[29]

Ultimately, the pursuit of military victory changed Arkansas and Arkansans. The overwhelming need for supplies consumed the basic economic resources of the state. The need for soliders and laborers played the greatest role in altering social antebellum relations, as men were pulled away from farm and town jobs. After 1862 many Arkansans realized that conditions

28. J. A. Sedden to E. Kirby Smith, March 18, 1863, in OR, Vol. XXII, Pt. 2, p. 802; T. H. Holmes to Jefferson Davis, August 28, 1862, quoted in Michael B. Dougan, *Confederate Arkansas: The People and Policies of a Frontier State in Wartime* (University, Ala., 1976), 93; Little Rock *Patriot*, November 13, 1862 (Garland quotation); H. F. Fairchild to H. Flanagin, December 12, 1863, in Kie Oldham Collection, AHC.

29. Report of T. H. Holmes, August 14, 1863, in OR, Vol. XXII, Pt. 1, pp. 411–12; E. Kirby Smith to Jefferson Davis, September 28, 1863, *ibid.*, Pt. 2, pp. 1028–29.

threatened the survival of the world they had gone to war to protect. Increasingly they looked for means to ensure that they individually would survive in what they saw as a hopeless fight.

The military's search for manpower presented a profound challenge to Arkansas society. In the spring of 1862 the Arkansas congressional delegation estimated that the state had already sent 30,000 men to the army. Most of these had gone east of the Mississippi River, the last of them with General Van Dorn after the battle of Pea Ridge. When Federal forces invaded the state they found almost no armed resistance. The threat had forced Hindman to enforce Confederate conscription laws vigorously: he reported when he surrendered his command that he had raised thirteen regiments and one battalion of infantry, two regiments of cavalry, and four artillery batteries by his efforts. In addition, he had five thousand men in irregular companies. Holmes tried to carry out conscription in strict conformity with the law at first, but following the battles of Prairie Grove and Arkansas Post his manpower requirements became critical. In February, 1863, Holmes reported 8,475 men present out of 16,990 men on the rolls. To rebuild the army he not only pardoned deserters who returned voluntarily, but also began his own vigorous enforcement of conscription. He allowed enrollment officers to interpret the law broadly. Their efforts left families and communities without the laborers necessary for survival. As a result, Governor Flanagin received a flood of protests.[30]

The zeal of the enrollment officers led to questions concerning the fairness of the law. Some of the officers were ineffective, others open to influence. The poor especially questioned exemptions given to planters and overseers. Rather than continuing to see these men as leaders of society, lower-class critics charged them with shirking their responsibilities. Hostility rose to the point that in some portions of the state conscripts openly and sometimes violently resisted authorities. At Magnolia, in Columbia County, in January, 1863, conscripts stood in line at the local army camp to protest the law. Near Camden, bands ranging in size from twenty to forty men organized to resist enrollment, and a surprised Judge John Brown

30. Congressional Delegation to Jefferson Davis, April 15, 1862, *ibid.*, XIII, 815; General Order No. 2, June 2, 1862, *ibid.*, XV, 780; J. S. Phelps to E. M. Stanton, October 20, 1862, *ibid.*, XIII, 751; Report of T. C. Hindman, June 19, 1863, *ibid.*, 31–32, 43; Report of T. C. Hindman, December 25, 1862, *ibid.*, Vol. XXII, Pt. 1, pp. 138–46; Report of Thomas J. Churchill, May 6, 1862, *ibid.*, Vol. XVII, Pt. 1, pp. 780–82; Abstract of Personnel, February 28, 1863, *ibid.*, Vol. XXII, Pt. 2, p. 793; T. H. Holmes to Jefferson Davis, March 6, 1863, *ibid.*, 797; R. H. Powell to H. Flanagin, May 5, 1863, Wm. P. Fain to H. Flanagin, October 15, 1863, both in Kie Oldham Collection.

found that the opposition had shown a "spirit of disloyalty beyond what was expected."[31]

Still, Holmes's activity was thorough. Returns of the Trans-Mississippi Department for May showed that he had built his force to 22,264 men, with another 12,287 absent. At that point, however, he had effectively exhausted the supply of manpower. In a report to President Davis in June, E. Kirby Smith noted that the fighting population was for the most part already in the army. General Smith observed that the men still available for service were "old men, or have furnished substitutes, are lukewarm, or are wrapped up in speculations and money-making. It will be difficult to develop any force from such material."[32]

Nevertheless, Smith was forced to greater efforts in the summer of 1863 by Federal activity along the Mississippi River and the possibility of a move against Little Rock. On June 3, 1863, he appointed General Elkanah B. Greer commandant of conscripts, with orders to systematize conscription, end abuses, and effectively enlist men. Smith ordered the conscription laws rigidly enforced and established training camps through which the new men could be moved into existing regiments. On June 16 he wrote President Davis and optimistically promised "a force brought into the field." As quickly as men were placed in the ranks, however, they were lost. From July 4 to September 10 the Confederate army sustained major losses. The attack on Helena on July 4, 1863, cost 1,636 men killed, wounded, and missing. The retreat from Little Rock saw the Confederate army of 8,500 men reduced by 1,900 who deserted and another 650 who had been left sick and wounded at Little Rock.[33]

31. L. C. Ross to Harris Flanagin, January, 1863, S. M. Scott to Harris Flanagin, April 27, 1863, both in Kie Oldham Collection; Brown Diary, March 19, 1863; Little Rock *True Democrat*, February 25, 1863; Washington (Ark.) *Telegraph*, January 7, 1863.

32. T. H. Holmes to Jefferson Davis, March 6, 1863, in *OR*, Vol. XXII, Pt. 2, p. 797; Report of T. H. Holmes, August 14, 1863, *ibid.*, Pt. 1, pp. 411–12; Abstract of Personnel, May, 1863, *ibid.*, Pt. 2, p. 851; S. M. Scott to H. Flanagin, April 27, 1863, T. D. Kingsberry to H. Flanagin, August 8, 1863, both in Kie Oldham Collection; E. K. Smith to Jefferson Davis, June 16, 1863, in *OR*, Vol. XXII, Pt. 2, p. 872.

33. E. K. Smith to Jefferson Davis, June 16, 1863, in *OR*, Vol. XXII, Pt. 2, p. 872; General Order No. 15, June 3, 1863, *ibid.*, 853; S. S. Anderson to J. B. Magruder, June 11, 1863, *ibid.*, Vol. XXVI, Pt. 2, p. 47; Report of T. H. Holmes, August 14, 1863, *ibid.*, Vol. XXII, Pt. 1, pp. 411–12; Report of Sterling Price, *ibid.*, 522; E. K. Smith to S. Cooper, July 28, 1863, *ibid.*, Pt. 2, p. 949; H. Flanagin to E. K. Smith, September 22, 1863, in Kie Oldham Collection; Proclamation of the Governor, August 10, 1863, in John H. Reynolds, ed., *Publications of the Arkansas Historical Association* (4 vols.; Fayetteville, 1908), II, 370–71; L. Ewing to My Dear Tom, September 14, 1863, in "Ewing Letters," *Independence County Chronicle*, V (October, 1963), 8; D. McRae to A. McRae, September 18, 1863, in Samuel Spotts Wassell Family Collection, AHC.

After the fall of Little Rock, Smith's measures to fill the ranks of his regiments in the Trans-Mississippi Department were increasingly harsh. State troops who had enrolled solely for service in Arkansas were turned over to the Confederate army. Smith ordered that deserters and absentees return to their regiments or face death. All men liable to conscription were to report for service. To ensure that his orders were followed, Smith instituted determined and stringent measures. To Henry McCulloch, in northern Texas, Smith proposed that the Confederate partisan leader William Quantrill be used to round up men. He also sent enrollment officers into areas evacuated by the Federals to pull in men. The desperation of Confederate authorities can be seen in an order by Brigadier General Joseph O. Shelby ordering the enlistment and conscription of every man in his district between the ages of sixteen and fifty. Shelby's instructions were clear: when men had been ordered to report and failed, "you will use all the force in your power, and when necessary shoot them down."[34]

The number of Arkansas men enrolled into service cannot be known for sure. The enlistment and reenlistment of individuals, the service of men in multiple units, and the existence of state and militia units for which no rosters exist make it difficult to calculate the actual number who served. Conscription officers, however, scoured the countryside well. In 1860 the white male population that might have been liable to conscription by 1865—that is, men aged between ten and fifty—was approximately one hundred thousand. Sixty thousand men, at least, served in the Confederate armed forces. Thousands of others served in state forces. Thus, at least 60 percent of the eligible men in the state served in the military, and the likelihood is that the percentage was larger. Contemporary reports indicate that few of the original male inhabitants were still at home by 1863.[35]

To sustain the war effort, the military also turned to the slave labor force. By the summer of 1862 the army employed large numbers of slaves in the Little Rock area to build fortifications, as teamsters, as blacksmiths, and in a variety of other jobs. The government employed numerous slaves at a salt works near the capital. One of the earliest official requests for slave labor by the government came in April, 1862, when authorities asked for workers for the hospital wards at Little Rock. Military and government employment

34. E. Kirby Smith to Henry E. McCulloch, November 2, 1863, in OR, Vol. XXVI, Pt. 2, pp. 382–83; S. S. Anderson to E. Greer, November 2, 1863, ibid., 387; W. H. Terrell to S. D. Jackman, May 21, 1864, ibid., Vol. XXXIV, Pt. 3, p. 835; General Order No. 13, in Reynolds, ed., Publications of the Arkansas Historical Association, II, 413.

35. Eighth Census, 1860: Population, 12–15; William P. Fain to H. Flanagin, October 15, 1863, R. H. Powell to H. Flanagin, May 5, 1863, both in Kie Oldham Collection.

of slaves furnished their owners with income, and initially the army seemed a secure enough place in the midst of the crisis.[36]

Arkansans soon changed their minds about the wisdom of government employment for slaves. Army employment was particularly harsh, and the slaves suffered. Complaints of bad treatment leading to deaths multiplied. Black laborers, like white soldiers, got sick and died. Charles C. Stuart of Chicot County placed seventeen men in jobs at Little Rock, and within eight months four had died and one was seriously ill and hospitalized. Slaves also escaped to Federal lines or ran away into the countryside. At least one owner hired his slaves to the government only on the condition that they not be used by the army in the field. Johnson Chapman, having lost two of his slaves, attempted to retrieve his other men and asserted his intention to keep his people "as well out of the hands of the military authorities as of the abolitionists."[37]

The deterioration of the southern cause, however, forced the government to use slaves no matter how strong citizen opposition was. In the autumn of 1862 the state legislature authorized military impressment of one male slave for every six male slaves between eighteen and forty-five years of age. Military commanders went beyond the legislative authorization in the numbers that they took. Civilians protested, but with little effect. In July, 1863, General Smith asked Holmes to encourage slaveowners to hire out even more of their hands to be used as teamsters. Smith advised the general to act with caution, but he also instructed Holmes to impress the number he needed if owners did not voluntarily provide them. In September, with Little Rock abandoned and the situation critical, Smith informed General Sterling Price at Arkadelphia that the urgency of the situation required the impressment of blacks for all departments, including hospitals and the Cotton Bureau.[38]

In the summer of 1864 Smith took decisive action when he declared all male Negroes between the ages of eighteen and forty-five subject to conscription and ordered the immediate enrollment of one-fifth of these

---

36. C. C. Stuart to W. E. Woodruff, November 25, December 12, 1862, J. Chapman to W. E. Woodruff, December 5, 1862, all in Woodruff Papers; Little Rock *True Democrat*, April 24, 1862.

37. J. Chapman to W. E. Woodruff, December 5, 1862, R. M. Campbell to W. E. Woodruff, May 15, 1863, both in Woodruff Papers; T. R. Wood to Dear Mother, May 17, 1863, in Wood Family Papers, TSLA; L. Ewing to Dear Tommy, September 14, 1863, in "Ewing Letters," 8.

38. B. F. Askew to H. Flanagin, May 1, 1863, in Kie Oldham Collection; S. S. Anderson to T. H. Holmes, July 7, 1863, in *OR*, Vol. XXII, Pt. 2, p. 987; E. K. Smith to S. Price, September 5, 1863, *ibid.*, 994–95.

men. Property owners objected, seeing this policy as tantamount to the seizure of private property. Justice David Walker concluded that it was probably unconstitutional. Opposition did not halt the conscription of slaves, however, and once the military authorities made this decision, many slaveowners decided that fleeing from Federal forces to protect their slaves was pointless, for slave property was threatened equally by Confederate authorities. The number of slaves used by the Confederacy cannot be known definitely, but in the end the war to protect slavery became one that effectively destroyed the master-slave relationships that underlay the institution. By the last full year of war, Arkansas' General Patrick Cleburne was even promoting the idea of arming slaves for the defense of the South and promising emancipation to those who would serve.[39]

As conditions worsened, Confederate authorities and the Confederate soldier proved as adept at scouring the land for supplies as enrollment officers were in finding men. Especially after the fall of Little Rock, civilians were forced to provide more for the support of Confederate forces, even supplies essential for their own survival. In the autumn of 1863 the defeated Confederate armies moved into southern Arkansas. The government impressed or confiscated whatever it needed, distributing promises to pay or Confederate money for what they took. When commissary officers failed to provide, the soliders procured what they needed. Robert C. Gilliam wrote to his wife from the army as it crossed the southern part of the state: "We are eating everything in our route, even milk cattle. . . . If our own army or that of the Fed pass near you they will eat everything that they can find. If you could hide bread enough to do you it would be well." John Brown likened Confederate soldiers to the "locusts in Egypt." A Federal scout described the result in the spring of 1864: "Arkansas is literally starved out. There is not enough to feed the people on the route between Little Rock and Shreveport, via either Camden or Washington."[40]

Confederate authorities repudiated illegal seizures, but official action was little better than that of the soliders. Authorities took not only foodstuffs but also cotton, hoping to use it to buy from foreign governments

39. OR, Vol. XLI, Pt. 2, p. 1014 (see also J. B. Magruder to R. W. Johnson, November 5, 1864, ibid., 130); D. Walker to J. D. Walker, August 1, 1864, in Walker Papers; Dougan, Confederate Arkansas, 117.

40. R. C. Gilliam to Dear Frances, April 12, 1864, in James J. Hudson, ed., "From Paraclifta to Marks' Mills: The Civil War Correspondence of Lieutenant Robert C. Gilliam," AHQ, XVII (1958), 298; Brown Diary, September 18, 1863 (see also October 13, November 16, December 11, 1863, February 10, 1865). The scout's report is in OR, Vol. XLVIII, Pt. 2, p. 401.

supplies necessary for the army. In General Order No. 34, July 1, 1864, General Smith declared that Confederate authorities would take half of the cotton in the Trans-Mississippi Department, either by purchase or impressment. For a brief period Confederate officials actually traded with Federals to obtain supplies; in January, 1865, Union general Joseph J. Reynolds complained from Little Rock that the Confederates had even gotten guns in this manner. Official seizures fanned civilian discontent. One resident complained that the cotton policy really meant that the government got half of the crop while the cavalry got to burn the other half. With cotton as with foodstuffs, the Confederate military consumed whatever it needed to survive and pushed aside the property rights of civilians.[41]

Confederate conscription, impressment of slaves, and consumption of material resources combined to bring about major changes in antebellum society. Even had they won the war, Confederate Arkansans would have found life in the postwar world different from what it had been before the war. One of the groups most affected was women. The immediate impact of military conscription was to shift their role as laborers. Except in poorer families and more rural areas, women's work had been changing in the 1850s, and their place was becoming defined as in the household and with the children. A man's work was in the fields or at the shop or store. Integration into the market economy had changed household work, especially in towns and for families with money. Household manufacturing had practically ended. Cloth, thread, clothing, shoes, flour, and many foods were no longer made at home, but bought at stores. For a few women, living the idealized life of the "lady" was a possibility. The war, the absence of men, and shortages halted that transition.

War brought swift changes in household work. Pressing shortages forced women to relearn the skills they had abandoned in the previous decade. Home manufacturing became a necessity for town women as well as those of the countryside, for rich as well as poor. Initially women volunteered to sew uniforms for soldiers, but the task soon expanded to include spinning and weaving the cloth as well. As the war progressed, what had begun as volunteer activities became labors of necessity. All had to engage in such work, or they and their families simply had nothing. One woman remembered: "Those that never had to work had to learn very soon or do without

41. General Orders No. 34, 35, June 1, 4, 1864, in *OR*, Vol. XXIV, Pt. 3, pp. 639, 643–44; General Order No. 52, July 12, 1864, *ibid.*, Vol. XLI, Pt. 2, p. 1005; E. Kirby Smith to W. A. Breadwell, June 11, 1864, *ibid.*, Vol. XXXIV, Pt. 4, pp. 666–67; *ibid.*, Vol. XLVIII, Pt. 1, pp. 136, 1364–65, 1318, 1322–23, 1409, 1414–15; J. J. Reynolds to C. Dana, January 26, 1865, *ibid.*, Vol. XLVIII, Pt.1, 650–51; Jno. MacLean to D. H. Reynolds, February 24, 1865, in D. H. Reynolds Papers, UAF.

much clothing. Then they were glad to get their poor neighbors to show them how to spin thread and weave cloth to make their dresses."[42]

On the farms women continued traditional work, attending to the manufacture of household goods and other household activities, but at the same time they took over many of the farm tasks of men. Husbands often tried to supervise the work. Robert Gilliam minutely instructed his wife, Frances, on the crops to plant and the fields to use. For most men, however, maintaining their role proved impossible. William A. Crawford wrote to his wife with a tone of despair, "Sarah, I cannot give you any advice how to proceed at home unless I could be there, and God only Knows when that will be." Women with workers, either slaves or hired laborers, supervised them in planting and other activities, secured essential supplies, and even marketed the goods. Those without laborers had to go into the fields themselves, plowing, planting, cultivating, and harvesting their crops.[43]

Efforts to do the job of two persons often proved inadequate, and many families abandoned their homes and fields. Captain Edward S. Redington of the 28th Wisconsin Infantry found outside of Helena in 1863 that the "country we passed was desolation itself. The road ran through one continued series of plantations of the best land in the world, all deserted, not an acre under cultivation. The houses were almost all empty." In 1864 William A. Crawford, a Confederate soldier, reported after a march through southeastern Arkansas that he found that "thousands of acres of the finest corn I ever saw . . . [are] yet standing in the fields." The area was completely abandoned. The crops were "not gathered nor ever will be."[44]

The effect of this situation on civilians was everywhere apparent. They suffered as their community's economy proved incapable of feeding civilians and making war. In 1862 one Federal wrote home: "All you see is long necked, yellow skinned dirty women, and filthy children. Many of them

42. Kellam Diary, April 30, 1863; M. E. Brodie to Dear Carrie, May 6, June 21, 1862, in Herring Collection; *Confederate Women of Arkansas in the Civil War, 1861–'65: Memorial Reminiscenses* (Little Rock, 1907), 96 (see also 37, 39, 43–44, 46, 63, 95, 97, 133).

43. *Confederate Women of Arkansas*, 27, 51, 63, 95, 133; W. W. Garner to Dear Wife, August 4, 24, 1862, November 21, 1863, 1862, in McBrien, ed., "Letters of an Arkansas Confederate Soldier," 63, 64, 275–77; Vance Randolph, *The Ozarks—An American Survival of Primitive Society* (New York, 1931), 19–21; W. A. Crawford to Dear Wife and Children, February 3, 1864, in Charles G. Williams, ed., "A Saline Guard: The Civil War Letters of Col. William Ayers Crawford, C.S.A., 1861–1865," *AHQ*, XXXII (1972), 82–83; R. C. Gilliam to Dear Frances, January 12, 1864, in Hudson, ed., "From Paraclifta to Marks' Mills," 285–87.

44. E. S. Redington to Dear Mary, May 14, 1863, in "The 28th Wisconsin Infantry at Helena," *Phillips County Historical Quarterly*, XIII (March, 1975), 23; W. A. Crawford to S. H. Crawford, January 30, 1864, in Williams, ed., "Saline Guard," 81.

as innocent of apparel as was Adam and Eve in the days of Paradise." According to S. C. Bishop, an Indiana soldier, the people in the vicinity of Napoleon were "the most poverty stricken of any I've seen yet. . . . One poor woman is literally starving to death." Edward Redington described civilians who passed through Union lines at Helena as "poor, lean, hungry looking creatures we could not help feeling sorry for. . . . Poor things, there is an awful future in store for them. . . . They must suffer this winter, and we shall have to open wide our store houses . . . to keep thousands of our erring brethren from dying of actual starvation."[45]

Little could be done to change these conditions. The legislature appropriated $1,200,000 to help refugees from the northwestern part of the state. Counties tried to provide relief too, but their efforts were inadequate for the problem. For example, the Hempstead County Court enacted a one-half of 1 percent property tax for the relief of the families of volunteers and accepted payment in food and other essential supplies. The county's rolls rapidly expanded to include some 605 indigent families of soldiers—41 percent of the 1,472 families in the county in 1860. Faced with continuing destitution among soldiers' families, counties also attempted to raise funds through subscriptions and other means. No amount of money, however, could buy food and supplies that simply were unavailable.[46]

The change of roles by women during the war was often short-term. The return of a husband, or simply the end of the war crisis, forced many women back into traditional work. The impact that the temporary changes and the physical deprivation had on their attitudes, however, was longer-lasting. For many women the war experience caused the death of an idea— the idea of progress and opportunity. During the antebellum years, people had believed it was possible to improve their position and move forward, or at least to make possible the progress of their children. The war ended that hope and bred in them a new pessimism. Many women felt deprived of some part of their lives. Mrs. E. S. Scott of Camden recalled: "I might have stayed young always and never had to wear glasses, if it had not been for Abe Lincoln and his war making me shed so many tears and read by tallow candles." Mrs. M. C. Hines of Camden remembered years later that

45. William G. Thompson to Mrs. Thompson, October 14, 1862, in Edwin C. Bearss, ed., *The Civil War Letters of Major William G. Thompson* (Fayetteville, 1966), 38; S. C. Bishop to Dear Mother, November 29, 1862, in "Indiana Troops at Helena," *Phillips County Historical Quarterly*, XVII (June, 1979), 37; E. S. Redington to Dear Mary, June 7, 1863, in "The 28th Wisconsin Infantry at Helena," *Phillips County Historical Quarterly*, XIII (September, 1975), 15.

46. *Confederate Women in Arkansas*, 95–96; "Indigent Soldiers' Families," in *Journal of the Hempstead County Historical Society*, XI (Spring, 1987), 34–38; Dougan, *Confederate Arkansas*, 96.

after her husband's death and the loss of relatives and friends, she "clung to my little ones. I was mother, wife, and landlord; had to chop wood, make fires, cook, plow, hoe, card, spin, and weave, running the whole gauntlet, filling all the life's offices, dreading nightfall with all its hideous affliction, and I almost feel the chilly sensations yet."[47]

The war also produced change by weakening the sense of social unity that had existed in the antebellum white community. The struggle turned·neighbor against neighbor as each strove for personal and family survival. The first break was between the civilians left at home and their Confederate leaders, who had led them into a war in which their own government and their own army proved as destructive as the enemy's. Many Arkansans concluded that maintaining the Confederacy had too great a cost. John Brown wrote that because of Confederate plundering in the vicinity of Camden, "there is no doubt the mass of the people would feel more safe, if once reduced to a dependence on the Yankee authorities than our own Cavalry." G. M. Barker asked for government protection in southern Arkansas because "I am afraid this people here will ask for Yankee protection."[48]

As their confidence in the Confederate cause waned, many Arkansans took actions to protect themselves in the face of the inevitable end. The idea of a community bound together by common interests disappeared. One resident of Chicot County complained that the people there had lost all sense of patriotism: "Its get all you can, keep all you get, and 'devil take the hindmost' with them." Those with Confederate money began to dump it wherever they could. John Brown noted that as early as 1863 no one wanted to be holding Confederate currency. Some shrewd operators got rid of it by buying up land, either from public authorities—who had to accept the currency at face value—or from others who needed the money to survive.[49]

Many persons took advantage of official position or access to supplies to speculate in the goods needed by the military and by the civilian population. A problem from the beginning, speculation thrived as scarcity increased. It created widespread ill will among local citizens. Confederate army surgeon

47. *Confederate Women in Arkansas*, 46 (Scott), 51 (Hines). See also *ibid.*, 28, 29, 42, 96.

48. E. K. Smith to Jefferson Davis, September 28, 1863, in *OR*, Vol. XXII, Pt. 2, pp. 1028–29; D. McRae to H. Flanagin, November 14, 1863, in Kie Oldham Collection; Alpha Hibbard Diary, November 23, 1863, January 31, 1864, in Small Manuscripts Collection, AHC; Brown Diary, December 11, 1863; G. M. Barker to A. Garland, January 26, 1864, quoted in *Pulaski County Historical Review*, VI (December, 1958), 7–8.

49. Jno. MacLean to D. H. Reynolds, October 9, 1864, in Reynolds Papers; Thomas, *Arkansas in War and Reconstruction*, 368; Brown Diary, March 23, September 9, 1863; D. T. Ponders to A. S. Morgan, August 15, 1863, in Morgan Papers.

Junius N. Bragg expressed his anger at individuals at Little Rock for whom "this war has been a Godsend, they have risen from penury to opulence." Bragg wanted to see them *"dance* on *air* to the tune of the 'rogues march,' and then let their riches be divided among the widows and orphans, and soldiers' wives from whom they have *stolen* it!" Judge Brown believed that Camden had been the home of so many "swindlers and speculators" that their presence had produced a "prejudice against us in the country and among the soldiers," and that the people might exact some form of vengeance against the town.[50]

Planters, too, looked out for their own futures. Rather than increasing the production of foodstuffs, many continued to grow cotton. Those in southern Arkansas hid their cotton, loaded wagons with what they could keep from Confederate Cotton Bureau agents, and moved it to Matamoras, Mexico, to sell for Mexican gold dollars, a good hedge against the inevitable Confederate collapse. Other planters made a personal peace with the Federals. An extensive trade in cotton developed wherever Federal gunboats and transports could reach. Federal traders met planters anywhere they could, trading cotton for gold or supplies.[51]

As the antebellum community fell apart, class differences like those apparent during the secession crisis reappeared. After exceptions to conscription were made in the fall of 1862, some Arkansans argued that class differences existed and that the interests of one class were not those of others. In southwestern Arkansas in the spring of 1863, men banded together to resist Confederate authorities, and John Brown concluded that the heart of the resistance was "the poorer class." Many common soldiers believed that the rich were not providing adequate support. S. M. Scott informed Governor Flanagin from Arkadelphia in April, 1863, that discontent had reached the point that "the old cry of poor men being obliged to fight for the rich may be heard on all sides." Although the conflict was limited, the perception of class differences indicated a significant change from the antebellum years.[52]

50. J. Bragg to My Love, May 5, 1863, in Mrs. T. J. Gaughan, ed., *Letters of a Confederate Surgeon* (Little Rock, 1960), 135–36; Brown Diary, April 8, July 6, 13, 14 (quotation), May 28, 1865.

51. G. T. Wright to Dear Mother, December 15, 1864, in Wright Papers; J. C. Gray to J. C. Ropes, July 24, 1864, in Henry Steele Commager, *The Blue and the Gray* (New York, 1973), I, 413–14; Jno. S. Phelps to E. M. Stanton, October 20, 1862, in *OR*, XIII, 751–53; R. W. McHenry to J. Davis, January 5, 1865, in *OR.*, Vol. XLVIII, Pt. 1, p. 1316; "Reminiscences of the Late Lon Slaughter as Told to Mrs. E. D. Wall, September 3, 1920," *AHQ*, VIII (1949), 169.

52. Brown Diary, March 19, 1863; S. M. Scott to H. Flanagin, April 27, 1863, in Kie Oldham Collection.

The war also caused changes in slavery, appearing to be on the verge of destroying it even behind Confederate lines. What ultimately might have happened cannot be known, since the Union victory brought an end to the institution, but many Confederates believed that slavery had been weakened. Whites knew in 1861 that the war was in part about slavery, and they believed that their slaves realized the same thing. They feared that slaves would take advantage of the situation and strike out at their masters and for their liberation. Secession in Arkansas was followed by a widespread fear of slave insurrections, and whites strengthened town watches and rural patrols. The immediate fear died out during the first summer of the war, but whites continued to watch. By 1863 many slaves, without violence, were taking greater degrees of freedom. In the summer of 1863 the editor of the *True Democrat* complained that at Little Rock, despite prohibiting laws, "slaves hire houses and have cookshops, beer holes, and other pretended means of support. They are flush of money; buy pistols and horses and get white men to bid for them at auction." Everywhere slaves expressed a new independence. Judge Brown observed that slave discipline had collapsed and that slaves were trespassing on white property and stealing. Maintaining discipline was increasingly difficult even behind Confederate lines.[53]

Slavery continued to exist, but slaves were an increasingly risky form of property. Slave sales continued, but buyers saw the purchase of slave laborers as a short-term proposition. High wages for free workers justified the purchase of a slave for W. W. Garner, who concluded that the sale price would soon pay for itself. However, his advice to his wife about the matter was not sanguine: "Try to get a good one and if he runs off let him go. A negro is as certain as Confederate money." Another man saw a slave as a good use of Confederate money because the slave's labor would at least produce something of value, whereas Confederate money produced nothing at all. Whites perceived the end, and even in Confederate Arkansas rumors circulated that the slaves might be freed as a negotiating point to bring about peace.[54]

53. J. W. Felts to W. E. Woodruff, July 28, 1863, in Woodruff Papers; J. M. Moore to Dear Son, May 10, 1861, in J. M. Moore Papers, UALR; D. McRae to A. McRae, May 6, 1861, in Wassell Family Collection; Caldwell Journal, May 19, 1861; Brown Diary, May 5, 1861, March 6, 1864, July 5, 1865; Des Arc (Ark.) *Citizen*, May 10, 14, 21, 31, 1861; Little Rock *True Democrat*, July 4, 1861, July 8, 1863; Russell P. Baker, ed., " 'This Old Book': The Civil War Diary of Mrs. Mary Sale Edmondson of Phillips County, Arkansas," Pt. 2, *Phillips County Historical Quarterly*, X (September, 1972), 3.

54. B. W. Lee to S. Williams, December 14, 1862, in Knight Papers, TSLA; W. W. Garner to Dear Wife, August 18, 1863, April 3, 1863, in McBrien, ed., "Letters of an Arkansas Confederate Soldier," 182, 65.

Secession and war brought drastic changes in the lives of Arkansans. The antebellum economy proved incapable of sustaining the war effort and at the same time providing for the civilian population. As a result, the military struggled with civilians and civilians fought with one another for supplies. These conflicts undermined the relationships and ideology that had given meaning to antebellum white society. They also brought about an attack upon private property that threatened the institution the war was intended to protect—slavery. Change effected in those areas that remained behind Confederate lines, however, only hinted at the extent of alteration in areas where fighting took place or that were occupied by Union forces.

# 6

## ARMED CONFLICT AND SOCIAL CHANGE
### Arkansas and the Impact of Military Operations

IN 1861, THE FORT SMITH ATTORNEY AND UNIONIST DELE-
gate to the state secession convention William Fishback warned that once
Arkansas had left the Union it would have a "great and powerful nation at
our very door seeking to crush our institutions."[1] By early 1862 Fishback's
warning was on the verge of fulfillment as Federal forces moved into the
northwestern part of the state for the first time. During the next three years
Union armies marched across much of the state. Able to move practically
at will, the Federals did not, however, establish control over the countryside. The marches of these armies, the battles they and Confederate forces
fought, and the power vacuum they created produced conditions that
rapidly tore apart antebellum communities. Material wealth was destroyed.
Thousands of whites refugeed to safer regions, disrupting the communities
they abandoned. The greatest impact of all came when slavery ended where
Federal troops arrived. Although many of the same trends appeared even
within Confederate lines, actual armed conflict hastened the disruption of
antebellum society.

The first Federal troops entered the state when General Samuel R. Curtis
brought his Army of the Southwest into northwestern Arkansas in pursuit
of a Confederate army under General Sterling Price. By March, 1862,
Curtis' ten thousand men were in north central Benton County, with the
main body at Sugar Creek. On March 3, Major General Earl Van Dorn
joined Price's army. Van Dorn took command and determined to stop
Curtis before he could gain too great an initiative in the state. At Sugar
Creek on March 6–8, 1862, the two forces fought the first major battle
on Arkansas soil, the battle of Elkhorn Tavern, or Pea Ridge. After the
Confederates achieved an initial advantage, the battle went badly for them.
Van Dorn withdrew and retreated to Van Buren. Curtis pursued the Con-
federates to Fayetteville but then pulled his army back to Forsyth, Missouri.
The maneuvers of the two armies achieved no military advantage but

1. Fishback quoted in David Y. Thomas, *Arkansas in War and Reconstruction, 1861–1874*
(Little Rock, 1926), 423.

destroyed Confederate authority in the region without replacing it with any alternative government. Locally, the rule of law was replaced by practical anarchy.[2]

Curtis did not abandon his plans to invade Arkansas; however, he decided that the route he had taken would not allow him to move easily into the central part of the state. In April, 1862, the general began a second invasion, this time advancing down the White River in conjunction with the movement of a cavalry force under General Frederick Steele along the Southwest Road toward Pocahontas and Jacksonport. The move had two goals: first, to block Van Dorn from moving into northern Mississippi to reinforce General Albert Sidney Johnston; second, to hit Price's Missouri troops, who were supposed to be located at Jacksonport. Steele failed to stop Van Dorn's army, and when he linked with Curtis they found few Confederate forces near Jacksonport. With the invasion's main objects frustrated, General Henry W. Halleck ordered Curtis to capture Little Rock and then reinforce General Ulysses S. Grant in Tennessee. Because he did not have enough supplies to execute Halleck's order immediately, Curtis encamped near Batesville to prepare his attack on Little Rock.[3]

The Federals waited until June 26 to make their move. Curtis planned to unite with Union naval forces on the White River at De Valls Bluff, where he would receive reinforcements and more supplies, then march on Little Rock. His troops encountered stiff Confederate opposition as they marched. Bridges had been burned and barriers placed across roads. On July 7 the Army of the Southwest was at Cotton Plant, where it fought an engagement at Hill's Plantation. On July 9, Curtis reached De Valls Bluff, where he found additional troops but not his supplies. Concluding that he did not have enough strength to press on, Curtis withdrew eastward to Helena on the Mississippi. Arriving there on July 13 and 14, his force created a permanent base. Along their route the Federals destroyed Confederate resistance and the support to maintain civil authority. As in the northwest, this disruption left a power vacuum in much of the area touched by the invading army.[4]

Union forces made another effort to occupy northwestern Arkansas in the autumn of 1862. General Theophilus Holmes responded by sending a

2. Report of S. R. Curtis, March 9, 1862, Report of E. Van Dorn, March 10, 18, 1862, *OR*, VIII, 190–206, 281–92.

3. S. R. Curtis to J. C. Kelton, April 14, 1862, *ibid.*, XIII, 362; H. W. Halleck to F. Steele, April 15, 1862, *ibid.*; S. R. Curtis to J. C. Kelton, April 28, 1862, *ibid.*, 366–67; S. R. Curtis to W. S. Ketchum, May 5, 1862, *ibid.*, 369; S. R. Curtis to W. S. Ketchum, May 6, 1862, *ibid.*, 370.

4. Report of S. R. Curtis, July 10, 1862, *ibid.*, 141.

# Map 6

## Wartime Arkansas

• Springfield

MISSOURI

Pea Ridge
BENTON
Bentonville •
• Fayetteville
WASHINGTON
MADISON
Prairie Grove
CRAWFORD
• Van Buren
FRANKLIN
JOHNSON
Fort Smith
Roseville ⊚
• Clarksville
SEBASTIAN

CARROLL
NEWTON

MARION
• Yellville
SEARCY

FULTON
IZARD
LAWRENCE

RANDOLPH
Pocahontas •
GREENE

INDEPENDENCE
Batesville ⊚
CRAIGHEAD
MISSISSIPPI

VAN BUREN
• Clinton
• Jacksonport
JACKSON
POINSETT

POPE
CONWAY
WHITE
CRITTENDEN
• Memphis

"Indian Territory"

SCOTT
YELL
PERRY

Cotton Plant
ST. FRANCIS

Brownsville
Little Rock
PULASKI
PRAIRIE
De Valls Bluff
MONROE

MONTGOMERY
SALINE

HOT SPRING
Jenkin's Ferry
Pine Bluff ⊚
JEFFERSON
ARKANSAS
Arkansas Post
PHILLIPS
Helena

POLK
PIKE
CLARK
DALLAS
DESHA

SEVIER
HEMPSTEAD
OUACHITA

Poison Springs
Camden •
CALHOUN
BRADLEY
DREW

TEXAS
LAFAYETTE
COLUMBIA
UNION
ASHLEY
CHICOT

LOUISIANA

TENNESSEE

MISSISSIPPI

N

25    0    25    50    75    100 MILES

Pea Ridge        Battles

•
Camden           Strategic Towns

⊚
Fort Smith       Federal Posts

force under General Thomas Hindman. The Confederates engaged the Union forces of Generals James G. Blunt and Francis J. Herron at Prairie Grove on December 7. The battle left neither army defeated but caused Hindman's withdrawal to Van Buren. The Union force pulled out of the northwest again, but this time a post was created at Fayetteville to control the northern tier of counties of the Ozark Plateau, strategically critical because it was the principal source of wheat and a staging area for Confederate efforts against Missouri. Despite the importance of the post, only one cavalry regiment was assigned the task of controlling nearly 6,500 square miles of mountainous territory. Once again the Federals had invaded the state and left disorder in their wake.[5]

From December, 1862, until the summer of 1863, Union armies in the region engaged primarily in efforts to capture Vicksburg, Mississippi, and Port Hudson, Louisiana. When these posts finally fell, however, the Federals turned upon Confederate Arkansas with two forces, one based at Helena and a second from the Indian Territory. The first, under Steele, left Helena on August 10 and set up a base on the White River at De Valls Bluff by August 23. Leaving that point on September 1, Steele's forces covered the remaining fifty miles to Little Rock against Confederate opposition in ten days, capturing and marching into the city on September 10. Blunt led the second force, leaving Fort Gibson on August 22. After defeating Confederate forces at Devil's Backbone on September 1, Blunt's command occupied Fort Smith. With these victories the Federals established a permanent presence in the interior of the state.[6]

With permanent posts, the Union army was forced to establish some control over the countryside to protect their supply and communications lines. Steele's army had more than fifteen thousand men, Blunt's more than five thousand. Steele fortified the capital and then secured his ties with the Mississippi River by putting the railroad to De Valls Bluff back in operation and constructing fortifications there, as well as by placing troops along the road. Blunt needed to keep the Arkansas River open to secure his supply line, and he and Steele established posts along the river to protect that route. By January, 1864, Federal forces were spread widely across the central part of the state, with posts at Brownsville, De Valls Bluff, Pine Bluff, Batesville, Helena, Fort Smith, Van Buren, Clarksville, Roseville, and Fayetteville.[7]

5. T. H. Holmes to J. C. Pemberton, November 15, 1862, *ibid.*, 897–98; Report of J. M. Schofield, n.d., *ibid.*, 21; Report of H. W. Halleck, November 25, 1863, *ibid.*, Vol. XXII, Pt. 1, pp. 10–11; Report of W. C. Cabell, April 25, 1863, *ibid.*, 312.

6. Reports on the Advance upon Little Rock, *ibid.*, 468–544; Report of J. M. Schofield, December 10, 1862, *ibid.*, 14–15; Report of J. G. Blunt, September 3, 1862, *ibid.*, 601.

7. Report of J. M. Schofield, December 10, 1862, *ibid.*, 14; Abstract of Personnel Returns, September, 1863, *ibid.*, Pt. 2, p. 585; Troops in Arkansas, January 31, 1864, *ibid.*, Vol. XXXIV, Pt. 2, pp. 200–202.

The Federals made no effort to support civil authorities in these areas until 1864, but even then conditions restricted what they did. With his army suffering from disease and unable to procure the essential reinforcements, General Steele adopted a defensive posture after the capture of Little Rock. Steele abandoned this position only after being ordered by Grant to cooperate with Nathaniel Banks's Red River expedition. That campaign took him on an ill-fated march to Camden, where he was unable to link up with Banks and finally had to retreat. After this campaign, a defensive stance was taken again and troops were pulled out of Arkansas. Federal commanders limited their operations to holding posts and maintaining communications. Outside of Federal lines, their authority was minimal.[8]

Invasion, occupation, and the collapse of local political authority caused the devastation of private property and a great increase of civilian suffering through much of the northern half of Arkansas. Invading armies were particularly destructive of property. Federal armies seized what they needed, and individual soldiers took what they wanted as well as engaging in outright vandalism. The ravaging of private property associated with Curtis' operations was extensive. Most of the white population was hostile to the intruding force, and the soldiers responded with equal animosity. One Federal wrote to his wife that every house in the area had been stripped of its contents, even the homes of Union loyalists. When a patrol from the 17th Missouri Infantry was fired upon near Bentonville, the regiment marched into town and burned twenty houses to the ground. At Fayetteville the Union army itself did little damage, but when it threatened to capture the town, Confederate soldiers took what they could before retreating. Neighbors stole from neighbors in the melee.[9]

The advance of the Army of the Southwest toward Little Rock produced similar results. Curtis encouraged destruction of property. In a letter written in April, 1862, he declared his intention that the land he passed over would provide no further support for rebel armies, and his design to support his army from the land. He wrote, "I leave nothing for man or brute in the country passed over by my army, except a little saving to feed the poor, which will hardly save them from suffering." With twenty thousand men marching to the south, his policy produced large-scale destruction. The *Arkansas Gazette* accused his soldiers of taking food, robbing houses, and

8. Report of U. S. Grant, July 22, 1865, *ibid.*, Vol. XXXIV, Pt. 1, p. 33.

9. H. Ankeny to Dear Wife, February 17, 1862, in Florence Marie Ankeny Cox, ed., *Kiss Josey for Me* (Santa Ana, Calif., 1974), 45; F. Wilhelmi to Dear Sister, February 25, 1862, in Clarence Evans, ed., "Memoirs, Letters, and Diary Entries of German Settlers in Northwest Arkansas, 1853–1863," AHQ, VI (1947), 233; W. Washburn to Dearest Susan, March 13, 1862, in Josiah W. Washburn Family Papers, AHC.

burning fences and improvements. Its editor complained, "No country ever was, or ever can be, worse devastated and laid waste than that which has been occupied, and marched over, by the Federal army." Even General E. A. Carr complained about his own troops, in particular about the German regiments from Missouri that broke into the "apartments of ladies and opening trunks and drawers, and ransacking everything and taking away what they wanted." Henry Ankeny of the 4th Iowa Infantry wrote that the path of Curtis' army could "be followed by the burned houses, cotton gins and destruction of all kinds of property, leaving the innocent and helpless to suffer." [10]

Federal and Confederate forces plundered the northwestern part of the state again during the Prairie Grove campaign of 1862. The Confederate army that marched north had no subsistence and was forced to live off of the land. They broke into houses, taking all of the food that they could get. After their defeat, the retreating Confederates took even more. Pursuing Federals took what was left. At the home of Karolina Hermann the Federals took not only food but clothes, including even women's clothing. A soldier of the 19th Iowa described the countryside as having been abandoned by the men, with most public buildings burned. The soldier found the farm of state supreme court justice David Walker in ruins: "Today the fences are burned, his fine meadows and fields are mere camping grounds for Infantry and cavalry, his fine dwelling is a hospital for our sick." [11]

The campaigns against Little Rock and Fort Smith in 1863 did not produce the same sort of looting. Much of the route of the Federal march had already been scoured by earlier raids, but these troops also moved too fast for extensive foraging. The campaign into southwestern Arkansas in 1864, however, again brought about complaints that the Federals took everything that they could find. Mary E. Brodie of Camden wrote that soldiers "nearly took my *wedding slippers*." At Camden the presence of a Confederate army in the year prior to the Union invasion compounded the problem of looting. Nearly all supplies already had been used up. When the Federals did not find enough for subsistence, they even rounded up milk cows and calves. After the Federals left Camden, John Brown noted

10. S. R. Curtis to J. C. Kelton, April 19, 1862, in OR, XIII, 364; Little Rock *Arkansas Gazette,* July 19, 1862; E. A. Carr Report, May 27, 1862, OR, XIII, 86; H. Ankeny to Dear Wife, July 15, 1862, in Cox, ed., *Kiss Josey for Me,* 73.

11. Report of J. M. Schofield, n.d., OR, XIII, 21; Report of H. W. Halleck, November 25, 1863, *ibid.,* Vol. XXII, Pt. 1, pp. 10–11; Karolina Wilhelmi Hermann Diary, November 25, December 14, 1862, in Evans, ed., "Memoirs, Letters, and Diary Entries of German Settlers," 238, 289; Nannie M. Tilley, ed., *Federals on the Frontier: The Diary of Benjamin F. McIntyre* (Austin, 1953), 93 (quotation), 95, 98.

that the residents were left without any livestock or any means to support themselves.[12]

As bad as the damage done by soldiers on a campaign might be, an army that stayed in the same place for any length of time caused even worse problems. Federal troops at Helena, Little Rock, and Fort Smith occupied buildings and homes and seized whatever they needed when they moved in. Later they supplied themselves by foraging from the surrounding countryside. William Barksdale, a minister at Helena, wrote in his diary that "Everywhere they are devouring and laying waste the labor of man's land. . . . Some of my dear brethren are stripped of nearly everything by these northern invaders." At Fort Smith, Federal foragers seized even the goods of loyal civilians. General Cyrus Bussey reported in March, 1865, that "everything had been taken and no receipts given, the people turned out to starve."[13]

Further damage in the vicinity of Federal posts was caused by raiders looking for cotton. Under Federal law, cotton owned by Confederates could be seized as contraband, and Union soldiers devoted much time to running down caches of this lucrative product. The military governor of Arkansas, John S. Phelps, complained in late 1862 that the failure of the Union army to invade the interior of the state was caused by army officers who were devoting their energies to enriching themselves searching for cotton. These raids were accompanied by destruction. Thaddeus Rice of the 11th Wisconsin Infantry wrote home after one expedition: "The white men have all left their plantations. They left a lot of fine furniture in their houses. We tear everything upside down. We dont care for nothing."[14]

The resort of Confederate authorities to partisan or guerrilla warfare to

12. D. C. Gilliam to Dear Friends, April 12, 1864, in James J. Hudson, ed., "From Paraclifta to Marks' Mills: The Civil War Correspondence of Lieutenant Robert C. Gilliam," *AHQ,* XVIII (1958), 298; M. E. Brodie to Dear Sister, July 24, 1864, in Fred J. Herring Collection, Small Manuscripts Collection, AHC; John W. Brown Diary, April 29, 1864, in AHC.

13. Mary Sale Edmondson Diary, November 19, 1863, in AHC; S. C. Bishop to Dear Mother, July 26, 1862, in "Indiana Troops at Helena, Part III," *Phillips County Historical Quarterly,* XVII (March, 1979), 11; *AS/AN,* Vol. VIII, Pt. 1, p. 312, Vol. X, Pt. 5, p. 25; William H. Barksdale Journal, July 19, 1862, in AHC; C. Bussey to John Levering, March 8, 1865, in *OR,* Vol. XLVIII, Pt. 1, p. 1120.

14. Mary S. Patrick Diary, January 19, 1863, in Small Manuscripts Collection, AHC; Alpha Hibbard Diary, March 1, 1863, in Small Manuscripts Collection, AHC; J. Chapman to W. E. Woodruff, April 8, 1863, in William E. Woodruff Papers, AHC; J. S. Phelps to H. W. Halleck, September 28, 1862, in *OR,* Vol. XIII, 683; J. S. Phelps to E. M. Stanton, October 20, 1862, *ibid.,* 751; T. Rice to M. E. Rice, August 11, 1862, in Wilson Powell, ed., "Jacksonport's 'Arkansas Traveler' and the Civil War Letters of Thaddeus Rice," *Independence County Chronicle,* XIII (July, 1972), 10–11.

harass Union forces produced further devastation to the civilian population and its property. Organized resistance of this nature began in the spring of 1862 when General Hindman authorized irregular military units to "annoy" the enemy and encouraged the destruction of any goods that might fall into Federal hands. Cotton, crops in the fields, and foodstuffs were destroyed in counties along the Mississippi and Arkansas rivers to hinder any Federal invasion.[15]

Part of the problem with the use of partisan raiders was that most of these units were under no effective discipline. Reporting on forces in northern Arkansas in the spring of 1864, Confederate General Joseph O. Shelby wrote: "[Their] condition . . . was horrible in the extreme—no organization, no concentration, no discipline, no law, no leader, no any-thing. . . . [They are] sweltering in the hot fumes of Memphis whiskey, and riding rough-shod over defenseless families on stolen horses." Civilians had everything taken from them by such bands, who made few distinctions about the loyalty of their victims.[16]

Federal retaliation against guerrilla raids worsened the situation. Civil-ians were held responsible for attacks by partisan bands, and their property was either seized or destroyed. In June, 1862, residents of Monroe County were informed that they would be held personally responsible for any actions by guerillas on the lower White River. In January, 1863, after an attack by Confederate raiders on military shipping opposite Memphis, the Federals burned the town of Hopefield to the ground because it was a "mere shelter for guerillas."[17]

Ultimately, however, the civilians in the areas left outside of the control of either side suffered the most. For them the war brought not only the loss of property and individual suffering but a considerable amount of personal violence. The first extensive outbreak of violence among civilians took place in northwest Arkansas following the breakup of the Confederate army at Prairie Grove. Confederate sympathizers stole or destroyed the property of many prominent local Unionists, particularly brutalizing the family of Isaac Murphy, whose members were left only with the clothes they were wearing. David Walker reported to Governor Flanagin that Confederate sympathizers robbed the families of men who had gone north

15. Little Rock *True Democrat*, May 8, 25, 1862; Little Rock *Arkansas Gazette*, June 18, 1862; Report of T. C. Hindman, June 19, 1862, *OR*, XIII, 33–34.

16. Report of J. O. Shelby, May 31, 1864, *OR*, Vol. XXXIV, Pt. 1, p. 924.

17. S. R. Curtis to J. C. Kelton, May 19, 1862, *ibid.*, Vol. XIII, 363; "Notice to Inhabitants of Monroe County, June 23, 1862," *ibid.*, 106–107; G. N. Fitch to T. C. Hindman, June 28, 1862, *ibid.*, 109; Report of S. A. Hurlbut, February 20, 1863, *ibid.*, 230; Report of J. H. McGehee, March, 1862, *ibid.*, 232.

or were in the northern armies or were suspected of sympathizing with the Union. Local Confederate officials could do nothing to stop the depredations.[18]

Acts of hostility against friends and families prompted revenge against the perpetrators. Personal attacks escalated quickly. Joseph Peevy reported from the northwest that Federal units were destroying the homes of southern supporters and driving them out. He wrote that Federal raiders had "murdered every Southern man that could be found, old age and extreme youth sharing at their hands the same merciless fate." General W. L. Cabell received numerous requests for help against marauders who were murdering Confederate sympathizers.[19]

Much of the theft and murder that took place ultimately had no military or political motives behind it. In one such raid a band of armed men entered the home of John and Ellen Buchanan of Washington County searching for gold. When the Buchanans refused to tell where their property was hidden, the raiders burned the feet of the mother and father and then hanged one of the sons from a nearby tree. In this particular case all of the family members survived, but in other assaults civilians had all of their property taken from them and many lost their lives. Confederate authorities blamed such actions on bands of deserters and conscripts and professional marauders.[20]

Ultimately, military and personal violence were undifferentiable. Federal authorities tried to solve the problem in northern Arkansas by sending cavalry patrols out of strategic posts to break up all armed bands. Although military law differentiated among insurgents, partisans, brigands, and guerrillas, in the field Union forces made no distinctions and executed anyone suspected of being brigands or bushwhackers. Orders to a Nebraska unit sent on a scout from Batesville were "to spare no bushwhackers." Regular soldiers and civilians were inevitably caught in the imposition of such measures.[21]

The breakdown of law and order and the increase of violence caused many civilians to leave areas that had no political or military authority for safer regions. The result was serious social disorganization and dislocation.

18. Report of J. Stuart, December 23, 1862, *ibid.*, Vol. XXII, Pt. 1, p. 165; D. Walker to H. Flanagin, June 9, 1863, in Kie Oldham Collection, AHC.

19. Joseph G. Peevy to Theophilus Holmes, April 17, 1863, in *OR*, Vol. XXII, Pt. 2, p. 824; W. L. Cabell to Theophilus Holmes, April 21, 1863, *ibid.*, p. 829.

20. W. A. Crawford to Dear Wife and Children, May 15, 1863, in Charles G. Williams, ed., "A Saline Guard: The Civil War Letters of Col. William Ayers Crawford, C.S.A., 1861–1865," Pt. 2, *AHQ*, XXXII (1973), 78; R. W. Mecklin to Kate, September 8, 1863, in Lemke, ed., "Mecklin Letters," 13.

21. W. Baumer Report, February 1, 1864, *OR*, Vol. XXIV, Pt. 1, p. 63.

In the northwest, many counties were practically abandoned. Southern sympathizers began to leave after the battle of Prairie Grove, but an exodus of civilians supporting both sides followed in the summer of 1863. Southerners moved to Van Buren and Fort Smith, then farther south. Union sympathizers left the northwest after the garrison at Fayetteville was temporarily abandoned that summer. The impact of the war on those who fled had already been hard. One observer described the Union families that left as "a filthy, miserable lousy pack of women and children . . . in a state of starvation."[22]

The departure of large numbers of people left those behind to face even harsher conditions. A. W. Bishop of the 1st Arkansas Cavalry (Union) reported that few Union farms remained in western Benton and Washington counties that August. Conditions were desperate. There were few men to cultivate crops. The destruction of fences allowed animals into the fields. A loss of stock prevented those farmers who remained from cultivating anything but small plots. During the winter of 1863–1864 few fields were sown. John B. Sanborn, a Union officer, described conditions in the northwestern counties in February, 1864, observing that although there was adequate forage, farmers were absent and he did not expect any to return until the countryside had been pacified.[23]

In the summer of 1864 many refugees returned to the region, but most lived within the vicinity of a Federal post. That spring, around Fayetteville, Colonel M. La Rue Harrison had located families in small colonies with their fields nearby and had placed forts to protect the dwellings and fields. In the winter of 1864–1865 he promised large crops in areas with garrisons and protection. The rest of the region appeared to be abandoned. The Union commander at Springfield, Missouri, concluded that Marion, Searcy, Newton, and Carroll counties were practically depopulated during the last winter of the war.[24]

The abandonment of rural areas was not confined to the northern tier of counties. Everywhere that military operations brought a breakdown in law and order, the civilian population that possessed the means moved

22. J. B. Sanborn Report, February 19, 1864, *OR*, Vol. XLI, Pt. 1, p. 87; W. L. Cabell Report, April 25, 1863, *ibid.*, Vol. XXII, Pt. 1, p. 312; Wiley Britten, *Memoirs of the Rebellion on the Border, 1863* (Chicago, 1882), 163, 193. The quotation is from R. W. Mecklin to Dear Sister Kate, August 23 (see also August 9), 1863, in Lemke, ed., "Mecklin Letters," 10 (7).

23. Amanda S. Braly to Dear Carrick, October 20, 1863, in Amanda M. F. M. Braly Family Papers, UAF; Britten, *Memoirs of the Rebellion*, 193; Report of A. W. Bishop, August 31, 1864, *OR*, Vol. XLI, Pt. 1, p. 270, see also *OR*, Vol. XLVIII, Pt. 1, pp. 931–33; Report of J. B. Sanborn, February 19, 1864, *OR*, Vol. XXXIV, Pt. 1, p. 87.

24. M. La Rue Harrison to G. M. Dodge, December 22, 1864, in *OR*, Vol. XLI, Pt. 3, p. 917.

elsewhere. Refugee life exerted its own toll on the civilians of Arkansas. Slaveholders who sought to protect their slave property were among the earliest to abandon unsafe areas. Large-scale movement of slaves, especially of younger men who were most likely to escape or to be taken by the Federals, began in the spring of 1862. Most owners headed first for southern Arkansas, then for northern Louisiana or Texas. One public official estimated that at least 150,000 slaves had crossed the Red River by the middle of the war. Resettlement badly disrupted the slave system. Many planters did not have enough land to put their hands to productive work. Breaking up families created serious dissatisfaction among the slaves themselves. Movement also exposed the work force to suffering and disease. Only necessity prompted the continued removal of slaves from Arkansas.[25]

Most white refugees began their migration by moving out of eastern Arkansas for Little Rock or southwest Arkansas. After the capture of Little Rock, however, many considered all of Arkansas to be unsafe and moved on to Louisiana, particularly to Shreveport, or to Texas, where many settled in border towns such as Clarksville, Jefferson, Marshall, and Tyler. On the road to the southwest the refugees encountered numerous hardships. Exposed to the elements and thrown together with new people, many contracted diseases and died on the journey or at their new homes. Although many of the refugees found more supplies and better conditions at the end of their trek, others had difficulty locating good land to farm. They also faced many of the same problems, created by the declining value of Confederate money and a general collapse of economic activity, that they had left in Arkansas. The communities that they abandoned sometimes ceased to exist.[26]

The tax rolls of 1865 provide a measure of the devastating impact of the war on the northern counties. The entire state showed sharp reductions in persons liable to pay polls and in various taxable items, especially livestock

25. W. W. Fleming to W. E. Woodruff, November 30, 1861, C. C. Stuart to W. E. Woodruff, December 12, 1862, both in Woodruff Papers; D. T. Ponders to A. S. Morgan, August 15, 1863, in Asa Morgan Collection, AHC; *OR*, Vol. XLI, Pt. 4, p. 1030; *ASIAN*, Vol. VIII, Pt. 1, pp. 13, 110, Pt. 2, p. 279, Vol. IX, Pt. 4, pp. 3, 212, Vol. X, Pt. 5, pp. 5, 25, 293, 300; *ASION*, Supp. Ser. 1, Vol. XII, pp. 48, 169, 301.

26. Edmondson Diary, August 26, October 21, 22, 1863; Brown Diary, September 7, 13, 1863, April 12, 1864; W. A. Crawford to My Dear Sarah, January 1, 1865, in Williams, ed., "Saline Guard," Pt. 2, pp. 88–89; Mary [Hornor] to My Dear Cousin, July 10, 1864, Jo. [Hornor] to J. J. Hornor, August 11, 1864, in *Phillips County Historical Quarterly*, X (December, 1971), 19–21, 21–22; Joseph M. Horner, "Some Recollections of Reminiscences of My Father," *Phillips County Historical Quarterly*, X (December, 1971), 11–16; Michael B. Dougan, *Confederate Arkansas: The People and Policies of a Frontier State in Wartime* (University, Ala., 1976), 114.

used or consumed by the military and marauders. Statewide, the number of persons liable to pay a poll tax decreased between 1860 and 1865 from 47,317 to 27,246 persons, a 42-percent drop. For the two tiers of counties running along the northern border with Missouri from central Arkansas to the northwest corner—Benton, Washington, Madison, Newton, Marion, Searcy, Fulton, and Izard—losses were much greater. For these eight counties there was a 52-percent loss in men, from 7,234 to 3,747. The number of head of all livestock dropped from 55,666 to 20,293, a 64-percent reduction. Newton County represented an anomaly. Relatively untouched because of its isolation, the county became a haven for residents of the surrounding countryside and for their animals and showed a 9-percent increase in male population and a 4-percent growth in livestock. The other counties showed decreases, with Marion County's 69-percent loss of polls and Marion and Madison counties' 80-percent losses of livestock the greatest.[27]

A comparison of tax rolls between 1861 and 1865 for three counties subject to the constant raids associated with the presence of a Union garrison shows their destruction. Jefferson County, with a Union garrison, had a decline in male population from 1,424 to 456. Sebastian County, near the Union forces at Fort Smith, had a male population loss from 1,209 to 138. Phillips County, site of the garrison at Helena, had a drop in population from 1,008 to 489. These three counties lost over 70 percent of white taxpayers, even more than northwest Arkansas. There were also large losses of animals. The number of horses in Jefferson County went from 1,635 to 604, in Sebastian from 1,664 to 15, and in Phillips County from 1,513 to 840—an overall loss of about 70 percent. Cattle herds declined from 6,804 to 924 in Jefferson County, from 5,046 to 16 in Sebastian, and from 7,266 to 3,317 in Phillips—about a 78-percent reduction. Although the impact was somewhat uneven from county to county, the statistics for these counties show that the heavy price for being in the no-man's-land between Federal garrison and Confederate authority was paid not just in the northwest but in other parts of the state.

The invasion of Arkansas by the Federals brought about considerable destruction of property and a dislocation of the existing society, but the most immediate impact was the end of slavery. Before Lincoln issued the Emancipation Proclamation and before the passage of the Thirteenth Amendment, slaves believed they would be free and saw the instrument of their liberation as the blue-coated army. As many as two thousand blacks

27. The statistical data in this and the following paragraph are from *Biennial Report of the Auditor of Public Accounts of the State of Arkansas, for 1859 and 1860* (Little Rock, 1860), Table H, and *Biennial Report of the Auditor of Public Accounts for the State of Arkansas for 1864, 1865, and 1866* (Little Rock, 1866), Table 9.

accompanied Curtis' column from Batesville in June, 1862. One soldier wrote that slaves came from every mansion and every log cabin with everything that they could carry. He described the scene: "Some were delirious with joy and for a time forgot the hunger which would soon be upon them." A former slave on the plantation of Tom White in Phillips County recalled that Curtis' men told White's bondsmen that they were free and "wid dat de niggers, dat is must of dem, lef' like when you leave de let gate open where is a big litter of shoates and dey just hit de road and commenced to ramble." [28]

The story was repeated wherever the Union army went. Raiding parties brought slaves to Union lines, or slaves slipped away from their masters and escaped to nearby Union posts. The nearness of the Union flag prompted masters to greater activity to ensure that their slaves did not escape, but the slaves found opportunities. When General Steele retreated from Camden in 1864, wagon-train loads of blacks went with his column. One Federal reported that local whites tried to get them to stay, but that "their tears and intreaties have but little impression on the negroes[.] [T]hey seem to have a thirst for freedom." Ultimately, so many attempted to go that Steele, hotly pursued by the Confederates, had to leave many behind. [29]

In making their departures, many slaves exacted a form of payment for their servitude by carrying off the property of their masters. A man in northwestern Arkansas took his owner's horse, saddle, and blanket, rode to a nearby farm, where he picked up a woman, then escaped to the north. Near Helena a white woman complained that when one of her female slaves left she took a horse and saddle. In the same area Federal troops suppressed the plundering of one farm by escaping slaves who carried off all the contents of their master's house. [30]

Some slaves stayed on the plantations, but loyalty to a master was only one reason for such behavior. The old, the infirm, mothers with children, pregnant women, and the very young tended to remain because they did not know where to go or feared that they would be unable to cope with conditions. Reasons for remaining were complex. Cindy Newton of Johnson County refused to leave the farm because she feared that her husband,

28. H. Ankeny to Wife, July 15, 1862, in Cox, ed., *Kiss Josey for Me,* 73; *AS/AN,* Vol. IX, Pt. 3, p. 24.

29. Benjamin F. Pearson, "Benjamin F. Pearson's War Diary," *Annals of Iowa,* XVI (October, 1926), 439–40; A. F. Sperry, *History of the 33d Infantry* (Des Moines, 1866), 94; Brown Diary, April 22, 1864; M. B. Eskridge to W. E. Woodruff, September 10, 19, 1862, C. C. Stuart to W. E. Woodruff, December 12, 1862, J. Chapman to W. E. Woodruff, August 31, 1862, all in Woodruff Papers.

30. Hermann Diary, November 12, 1862, in Evans, ed., "Memoirs, Letters, and Diary Entries of German Settlers," 235; Sue Cook Diary, March 16, 1864, in AHC; *AS/AN,* Vol. X, Pt. 6, p. 214; Report of R. J. Rombauer, June 27, 1862, *OR,* XIII, 176.

who had been taken away earlier by the master, would not be able to find her. She told a Union officer: "Henry is in the South and I'll never see him again if I leave the old home place." The cook of R. C. Mecklin waited until she could find another position before she left for Fayetteville, where a family would pay her more money. Thus, the fact that some slaves remained on the plantation does not necessarily show any great love for their masters.[31]

When the first slaves abandoned their masters, the Federal military had no policy to handle these refugees. As early as May of 1861, General Benjamin Butler seized slaves working for the Confederate army in Virginia, then refused to return them, calling them "contrabands of war." The Federal confiscation act of August, 1861, sanctioned Butler's approach and authorized the seizure of all property, including slaves, used to support the rebellion. These practices applied, however, only to slaves used by the Confederate military. General Curtis, who was a Republican stalwart with some abolitionist sentiments, applied the confiscation law liberally and attacked his enemies as broadly as possible. His promise of "free papers" to all slaves who had been forced to aid Confederate forces created, in his view, a stampede of blacks to his lines at Helena. Papers were given to all blacks who reached his encampment, whether they had worked on fortifications or not.[32]

Thousands of blacks were brought into Helena by Federal raiding parties or fled to the Union lines in the next several months. Blacks escaping from Mississippi swelled the numbers at Helena, and a large community of freedmen established itself on the edges of the army's camp. The pattern was repeated when the Union soldiers marched into the interior in 1863 and thousands of slaves settled around the Federal posts established by Steele. By 1864 there were large slave settlements at Van Buren, Fort Smith, Little Rock, and Pine Bluff. The posts symbolized the end of slavery and served as magnets throughout the war. As Boston Blackwell, who ran away to the post at Pine Bluff, remembered, "Iffen you could get to the Yankee's camp you was free right now."[33]

31. R. W. Mecklin to Dear Sister, September 19, January 28, 1864, in Lemke, ed., "Mecklin Letters," 16, 38; Kate Johnson to Amanda Buchanan, December 19, 1863, in Robert E. Waterman and Thomas Rothrock, "The Earle-Buchanan Letters of 1861–1876," *AHQ,* XXXIII (1974), 144; *AS/ON,* Supp. Ser. 1, Vol. XII, p. 313.

32. J. S. Phelps to H. W. Halleck, September 28, 1862, *OR,* XIII, 684; S. R. Curtis to H. W. Halleck, July 31, 1862, *ibid.,* 525; Special Order No.——, August 15, 1862, *ibid.,* 876–77.

33. T. R. Wood to Dear Mother, May 17, 1863, in Wood Family Papers, TSLA; K. Johnson to A. Buchanan, December 19, 1863, in Waterman and Rothrock, "Earle-Buchanan Letters," 144; William Edward McLean, *The 43d Regiment of Indiana Volunteers* (Pine Bluff, Ark., 1981), 97; J. S. Phelps to H. W. Halleck, September 28, 1862, *OR,* Vol. XIII, 684; *AS/AN,* Supp. Ser. 1, Vol. XII, p. 391; *AS/AN,* Vol. VIII, Pt. 2, p. 173, Vol. VIII, Pt. 1, p. 169 (Blackwell quotation).

The Federals faced a serious problem with the thousands of freedmen. Initially each commander pursued an individual policy. Under Curtis the army used the men for support, putting many to work building fortifications, cutting wood for the Mississippi fleet, working as teamsters, or doing general labor. Curtis favored going further and arming the slaves, and he detailed a Colonel Shaw to organize a black regiment at Helena. Curtis believed this action was only natural: "Free negroes, like other men, will inevitably seek weapons of war, and fearing they may be returned to slavery, they will fight our foes for their own security. That is the inevitable logic of events, not our innovation." When Curtis returned to St. Louis in September, 1862, however, his replacement, General Steele, reversed his orders granting freedom to contrabands and ended Shaw's recruitment of a black regiment.[34]

In August, 1862, the Federal government finally initiated its own policy regarding able-bodied slaves. Efforts had been made to organize black troops in South Carolina and Louisiana in April and July of 1862. In August the policy received official sanction when President Lincoln stated that he believed contrabands should be armed and used militarily. On August 25, Secretary of War William Stanton authorized the recruitment of freedmen in South Carolina for military service. Thereafter there was general recruiting of blacks, although no effort was made in Arkansas until April 6, 1863, when General Lorenzo Thomas arrived at Helena and authorized the recruitment of the first black troops. By August, 1863, Thomas was encouraging Federal commanders in Arkansas to collect as many blacks—men, women, and children—as possible and to organize the able-bodied men into regiments. Ultimately, the Federals enlisted more than 5,500 black troops in the state.[35]

For those freedmen who could not join the army, however, a policy developed more slowly. Many of them searched for jobs as servants with Union troops. They attached themselves to the military camps, where they worked as cooks, laundresses, and general servants. "Uncle Alfred" cooked

34. T. H. Holmes to S. R. Curtis, October 11, 1862, in OR, Vol. XXII, Pt. 2, p. 727; S. R. Curtis to E. A. Carr, October 21, 1862, ibid., 756; F. Steele to S. R. Curtis, November 2, 1862, ibid., 775; AS/AN, Vol. VIII, Pt. 1, pp. 98, 153, 169, Vol. VIII, Pt. 2, p. 349, Vol. IX, Pt. 4, p. 193; M. R. Mann to Dear Elisa, February 10, 1863, in Mary Tyler Mann Papers, LC.

35. "Remarks to Deputation of Western Gentlemen," August 4, 1862, "Reply to Emancipation Memorial," September 13, 1862, in Roy R. Basler, ed., The Collected Works of Abraham Lincoln (9 vols.; New Brunswick, N.J., 1953–55), V, 357, 423; OR, XIV, 377–78; L. Thomas to J. M. Schofield, August 5, 1863, in OR, Vol. XXII, Pt. 2, p. 441; S. P. Curtis to C. Fisk, April 13, 1863, in OR, Vol. XXII, Pt. 2, p. 215; M. R. Mann to Aunt Mary, April 7, 1863, in Mann Papers.

for the white officers of the 112th United States Colored Infantry and bargained with neighborhood cooks for pies and puddings. Blacks associated with the 43d Indiana took care of the officers' horses and did a variety of jobs for officers and men.[36]

First freedom meant hardship and privation because of the failure of the government to develop a policy that dealt with the masses of blacks entering Union lines. The Federal soldiers were liberators but also preyed upon the freedmen. Josephine Barnett remembered that the slaves on the McNeill farm near De Valls Bluff "hated the Yankees. They [the Yankees] treated them mean. They was having a big time. They didn't like the slaves. They steal from the slaves too." Another former slave remembered that the Federals who marched through the David Hunter plantation near Helena emptied the smokehouse. "That turned me agin' the Yankees," Peter Brown recalled. "We helped raise that meat they stole. They left us to starve and fed their fat selves on what was our living." At Helena refugee slave families had their clothing and bedding stolen from them by the soldiers. Marie R. Mann, sent to Helena by the United States Sanitary Commission, described the treatment of the contrabands as barbarous.[37]

The contrabands had almost no resources to fall back on in their new circumstances. The favored few found employment, but most did not, and the first months in camp were difficult. Housing was inadequate. At Helena they crowded into houses with dirt floors and no windows, or tents, where they slept without blankets. Whole families lived in one room. Clothing was difficult to obtain. Few had a change of clothing. Relief agencies provided cloth and clothing, but few of the freedmen possessed the skills to fit the ready-made clothing or to make dresses of the cloth. Food was scarce and the quality poor. The government provided only salt pork and beef. One resident of the camp at Pine Bluff recalled that there was "just enough food to keep the Negroes from starving."[38]

Suffering from malnutrition, with inadequate housing and clothing, without medical attention, the freedmen suffered devastating epidemics. Smallpox, against which few had ever been inoculated, raged through the camps. Diarrhea was rampant and added to the generally unsanitary

36. J. M. Bowler to Lizzie, July 10, 1864, in Edward G. Longacre, ed., "Letters from Little Rock of Captain James M. Bowler, 112th U.S. Colored Troops," *AHQ*, XL (1981), 740; Sperry, *History of the 33d Infantry*, 58; McLean, *43d Regiment of Indiana Volunteers*, 97.

37. *AS/AN*, Vol. VIII, Pt. 1, pp. 110 (Barnett quotation), 312 (Brown quotation); M. R. Mann to Dear Elisa, February 10, 1863, in Mann Papers.

38. K. Johnson to A. Buchanan, December 19, 1863, in Waterman and Rothrock, "Earle-Buchanan Letters," 144; M. R. Mann to W. L. Ropes, April 13, 1863, Mann to Dear Miss Peabody, April 19, 1863, Mann to Aunt Mary, n.d., all in Mann Papers; *AS/AN*, Supp. Ser. 1, Vol. XII, p. 391.

conditions. Marie Mann called the freedmen's camp at Helena a "sickly, pestilential, crowded post." The mortality rates in the camps were high, with as many as 25 percent of the inhabitants dying within the first several weeks. Observing the desperate conditions at the freedmen's camps at Van Buren and Fort Smith, one unsympathetic Confederate woman summed up the harsh realities confronting the former slaves: "This is *Freedom*." [39]

Some freedmen returned to their plantation homes because of the conditions they had encountered. Marie Mann described the events that caused one group of forty slaves who came to Helena to return. On the way to Union lines, they were robbed by Federal soldiers of their bedding and clothing. Only a few found work. Within two months most were sick and thirteen died. Their master came to the post to persuade them to return with him. Mann wrote, "They did not wish to go, faltered, changed their minds daily, for a week, we encouraging them all we could, but as destitution, persecution & death stared them in the face the sad sufferers went back." Mary Breckenridge, a nurse on a Federal hospital boat, reported talking to a slave waiting on the levee to be returned home from Helena. She wrote, " 'Well Uncle,' I said, 'how do you like being free?' 'I haint seen no freedom yet, missis, I'se a gwine home again!' " [40]

Flight to the Yankees ended slavery. It also brought about the collapse of white paternalism. Whites believed that they had been good masters, yet when the Federals came, well-treated slaves left as quickly as others. Many slaveowners felt abandoned and betrayed. James Gill remembered that when the slaves left Tom White's plantation near Helena, "some of dem niggers what belonged to old mars and what he was so good to, dey stole mighty nigh all de mules and rode dem off and mars, he never git he mules back. Naw suh, dat he didn't. De war, it broke ole mars up and atter de surrender he jus' let he Arkansas farm go an' never come back no more." Mary Eskridge claimed that the particular hurt of emancipation came because "those I *trusted most* have deceived me most." Whites concluded that blacks were as deceitful as they had always believed, as uncivilized and inhuman. Paternalism had not paid off. The slaveowners readily abandoned the paternalistic ideal, and in its place emerged only an unameliorated racism. Already white Arkansans looked with horror toward the future as

39. M. R. Mann to Aunt Mary, March 21, 1863, Mann to Aunt Mary, n.d., Mann to Dear Elisa, February 10, 1863, all in Mann Papers; K. Johnson to A. Buchanan, December 19, 1863, in Waterman and Rothrock, "Earle-Buchanan Letters," 144; M. E. Breckenridge to [?], February 4, 1863, in Mary E. Breckenridge, "Adventures on a Hospital Boat on the Mississippi," *Phillips County Historical Quarterly*, I (December, 1962), 36.

40. M. R. Mann to Dear Elisa, February 10, 1863, in Mann Papers; M. E. Breckenridge to [?], February 4, 1863, in Breckenridge, "Adventures on a Hospital Boat," 35–36.

they envisioned a world with blacks no longer restricted by slavery. W. W. Garner concluded in a letter to his wife, written after the Emancipation Proclamation, "Imagine your sweet little girls in the school room with a black wooly headed negro and have to treat them as their equal."[41]

By 1863 the war had consumed the material resources upon which the old society had been based. White society was in disarray, with many members of the antebellum community gone. The internal war had turned neighbor against neighbor. Slavery was gone. A new society would have to be built on the shambles of the old.

41. *ASIAN*, Vol. IX, Pt. 3, pp. 24–25; M. B. Eskridge to W. E. Woodruff, November 20, 1862, in Woodruff Papers; W. W. Garner to Dear Wife, October 8, 1863, in McBrien, ed., "Letters of an Arkansas Confederate Soldier," 282.

# 7

## THE UNION ARMY AND THE FREEDMEN
### Building Black Society

THE CIVIL WAR SHATTERED THE LIVES OF ARKANSANS AND brought their society to the verge of collapse. Yet even while the fighting continued, the process of rebuilding Arkansas began. Antebellum Arkansans played a role in this reconstruction, but in areas as diverse as labor and government the Union army was the major force determining the structure of postbellum life. This was particularly true regarding the place of blacks in society. After 1863 the army became the principal federal agent working to assist blacks in adjusting to their new status. The army was involved initially because of its desire to put blacks to work supporting the war effort, but the desperate plight of the old, the women, and the children forced the development of a more general policy. The army's policy reflected the racist and paternalistic views of northern whites concerning the potential of blacks as much as any humanitarian vision. As a result, the officers of the army limited the freedom of the people they helped to liberate.

The freedmen's program of the government emerged in the spring of 1863, when Adjutant General Lorenzo Thomas, who had been sent to the Mississippi Valley to recruit troops and investigate means to organize the labor of blacks, proposed a plan to deal with the thousands who had escaped to freedom. Thomas proposed to put able freedmen to work, provide relief for those who could not, and educate all. The most immediate goal was putting blacks to work, and in Arkansas a labor policy was the first part of the plan to emerge. Thomas suggested that the government adopt a contraband-labor program similar to that earlier developed by John Eaton, Jr., and used in areas occupied by the armies of General Ulysses S. Grant. Thomas proposed to lease abandoned and confiscated plantations to loyal white men and encourage them to hire blacks as farm laborers. Thomas believed that this plan would prove the effectiveness of free labor. It also relieved the government of the responsibility of supporting the freedmen.[1]

Thomas' labor scheme took further shape in October, 1863, when he

1. E. M. Stanton to L. Thomas, March 25, 1864, in *OR*, Ser. 3, Vol. III, pp. 100–101; L. Thomas to E. M. Stanton, April 12, 1863, quoted in Lawrence N. Powell, *New Masters: Northern Planters During Civil War and Reconstruction* (New Haven, 1980), 3; V. Jacque Voegeli,

announced regulations for freedmen and plantation leases in the Mississippi Valley. The Treasury Department leased lands, and the army controlled the freedmen. On October 24, Thomas issued Special Orders No. 85: "All freed negroes who have sought the protection of the United States, or who have been brought within our lines, are to be put to such labor as they may be competent to perform." Military camps were to be considered places of temporary refuge only; as soon as possible, freedmen were to support themselves. Camp commanders would select commissioners who would provide the workers—men, women, and children—needed to cultivate the plantations. Three days later, Thomas announced regulations for leasing plantations. His primary object was "to line the banks of the Mississippi River with a loyal population and to give aid in securing the uninterrupted navigation of the river, at the same time to give employment to the freed negroes whereby they may earn wages and become self-supporting."[2]

Efforts to organize the freedmen in Arkansas did not begin until after Lincoln ordered Thomas to assume overall supervision of labor and leasing in February, 1864. On March 11, Thomas issued Orders No. 9 for a general system of freedmen's labor. Thomas' orders presented his assumptions concerning labor and the ideas that lay behind his rules. He wrote that "labor is a public duty and idleness and vagrancy a crime. Every enlightened community has enforced it upon all classes of people by the severest penalties. It is especially necessary in agricultural pursuits. That portion of the people identified with the cultivation of the soil, however changed in condition by the revolution through which we are passing, is not relieved from the necessity of toil, which is the condition of existence with all the children of God. The revolution has altered its tenure, but not its law." Having stated his philosophy, Thomas announced that the government would assure order in the contractual relations, protecting each party's contract rights.[3]

Thomas outlined a fair contractual relationship. The standard contract would be for one year. Laborers would provide employers with ten hours of work daily in summer, and nine hours in winter. In turn, the employer was to provide the laborer with just treatment, healthy rations, comfortable clothing, quarters, fuel, medical care, instruction for children, and wages. Wages were reduced to the rates paid the previous year; the minimum wage for males over

*Free but Not Equal: The Midwest and the Negro During the Civil War* (Chicago, 1967), 95–112; Louis S. Gerteis, *From Contraband to Freedman: Federal Policy Toward Southern Blacks, 1861–1865* (Westport, Conn. 1973), 125–26.

2. Special Orders, No. 85, October 24, 1863, *OR*, Ser. 3, Vol. III, pp. 917–18, and Circular, October 27, 1863, *ibid.*, 939.

3. The details of Thomas' plan as given in this and the three following paragraphs are from Orders, No. 9, March 11, 1864, *OR*, Ser. 3, Vol. IV, pp. 166–70.

fourteen was $10 per month, for females of the same age, $7 per month. Children and those too feeble to give full labor were to be paid one-half these rates. At least half of the wages were to be held back until the end of the year, and Thomas urged that no monthly wages be paid. Thomas' orders allowed wages to be reduced when a worker was sick. The plantation lessee could also cut pay because of indolence, insolence, disobedience, or commission of a crime. Corporal punishment of workers was prohibited.

To ensure adherence to the contracts and to exercise other police duties, Thomas placed military police in the neighborhoods of leased plantations. Thomas' provost marshals were to act not only as police but also as judges in disputes between employer and employees. The provost marshals were also to regulate the movement of workers in the plantation districts, preventing their switching from one plantation to another after contracts had been signed.

For those who could not work, freedmen's camps or farms were proposed, to replace the existing refugee communities. The people who lived in these camps could be put to work growing at least their own food. The army could also distribute rations and other supplies to the needy freedmen at these locations. Thomas created a savings bank in which the freedmen could deposit their earnings and learn financial responsibility. He also proposed that the government or lessees provide schools in each police district for the instruction of all black children under twelve years of age in order to encourage the progress of the race.

Thomas appointed John Eaton, Jr., general superintendent of freedmen. Major William G. Sargent received the position of superintendent of freedmen for the state of Arkansas. Sargent opened local offices at Helena, Pine Bluff, De Valls Bluff, and Fort Smith to supplement the state office at Little Rock. Sargent reported that when he arrived, he found the military had attempted to supervise the freedmen around Helena, but nothing effective had been developed. Changes in local superintendents, attacks by Confederate forces, and the lack of systematic management had left the freedmen in a "loose, disorganized condition." No effective means for dealing with the problem of the freedmen had been found. A medical inspection that spring by the surgeon of the 63d United States Colored Infantry found conditions similar in all the camps—housing was poor, clothing was inadequate, and the people suffered from overcrowding. District Superintendent Sargent faced an enormous task with inadequate resources.[4]

4. *Report of the General Superintendent of Freedmen, Department of the Tennessee and the State of Arkansas for 1864* (Memphis, 1865), 6, 11–12; J. I. Harrick to W. G. Sargent, February 1, 1864, David Worcester to W. G. Sargent, February 23, 1864, both in (Little Rock) Field Office Records, Arkansas, BRFAL, RG 105, NA; Joseph Warren, comp., *Extracts from Reports of Superintendents of Freedmen. Second Series, June, 1864* (Vicksburg, 1864), 15–18.

Among his first actions, Sargent created "Home Farms" at the principal posts in Arkansas. This tactic was intended to provide relief for the thousands of refugees crowded at these points. The Home Farms were for those simply unable to secure private employment, and for newcomers, vagrants, and the old, sick, and infirm as well. The government provided seed, farm implements, and draft animals. Rations were supplied to those unable to work. At Helena the military seized the plantation of Confederate general Gideon Pillow because of its location on an easily protected peninsula below the town. Similar Home Farms were created at Little Rock and Pine Bluff. The goal of the army was to make these freedmen more self-sufficient, thus relieving the government from the burden of supporting them.[5]

By April, 1864, Sargent's office had become more concerned with supplying labor for leased plantations as lessees requested workers. Many of the men who applied for leases were former Union officers, although often such leases were signed in partnership with the original landowner. One inspector suspected that some such owners were Confederate sympathizers who made the contracts to ensure that the army did not interfere with their work force. Others who requested workers were local planters or farmers who had remained loyal to the Union. At Helena some freedmen leased land on their own, but only a few such leases were made. So many prospective lessees appeared that the superintendent was unable to satisfy the demand for labor. Ultimately, large numbers of women and children were hired as field hands. At the end of 1864 the freedmen's department at Little Rock reported that more than one hundred plantations had been leased, representing upwards of fifty thousand acres. The work force on these lands included more than ten thousand freedmen.[6]

In 1864 the adjustment of freedmen to free labor began. Ideally, the system should have taught the freedmen the lessons necessary to work as free laborers—how to negotiate contracts, an independent work ethic, means to secure fair treatment, and all of the other things that were part of a free labor system. Events showed that the military supervisors, their subordinates, the landowners and tenants, and the freedmen all had different ideas about what freedom actually meant. The interplay of these interests created new labor conditions for blacks, but the results were a modification of slavery that did not recognize full freedom for black workers. The

5. W. G. Sargent to Col. S. Thomas, February 4, 1864, in (Little Rock) Field Office Records, Arkansas, BRFAL, RG 105, NA; *Report of the General Superintendent . . . 1864*, 69–70.

6. *Report of the General Superintendent . . . 1864*, 36, 37, 64–66. See examples of requests for leases in Kie Oldham Collection, AHC.

freedmen's change was limited by the patronizing attitudes, racism, and exploitiveness of whites. As created, the military's labor program showed the persistence of white beliefs that blacks, either as a race or because of slavery, were neither industrious nor thrifty. Rules for laborers accepted the principle that blacks had to be coerced into work and their activities supervised. The contracts that were signed were not the result of free bargaining between worker and employer to determine wages, terms of work, or even the place of labor. Typically, planters who sought leases stated how many hands they needed. Post superintendents then sent the number required. The freedmen did not have a choice of working for a particular employer or not, nor were they able to decide not to work. Wages were set without any bargaining whatsoever. Workers also had no control over labor conditions. Making the change even more limited, most of the leased plantations organized labor in gangs supervised by overseers, just as in the antebellum years. For the field hand, army-supervised freedom offered few choices. Even some planters felt that the system stifled worker initiative; they added special incentives to their contracts to stimulate more work. The military had little concern for the issue, however.[7]

The lease system worked to no one's complete satisfaction and in practice was modified considerably. As restrictive as the regulations were, most lessees concluded that they were not stringent enough. Many lessees complained that the freedmen were inefficient, and they blamed all problems on the laborers. John Eaton, Jr., and his lieutenants conducted interviews with planters in the autumn of 1864, and those from Helena were particularly vocal. They complained that the freedmen gave no more than four hours of work per week and had poor work habits at that. The lessees' answer was the use of greater force, and they complained that the provost-marshal system contemplated in the regulations had never been put into effect. Although some planters were concerned that the freedmen were not treated well, most believed that the problems were caused by the workers, not themselves or the system.[8]

In fact, leaseholders engaged in extensive abuses that undermined any positive results in helping the freedmen make the transition to free labor. The payment of wages was a part of the planter-worker relationship particularly susceptible to abuse. Under General Thomas' original orders, the leaseholders were to pay half of wages during the year and the other half at the end of the year in order to encourage savings. This procedure made

7. *Report of the General Superintendent* . . . *1864*, 30–31, 36.
8. *Ibid.*, 29, 30, 33–34.

sense considering the cash-flow problems of farmers, but it also reflected Thomas' paternalistic concern with black irresponsibility. In practice, however, many lessees handled the half payment required during the year irregularly. Some planters made no cash payments but reimbursed the freedmen with supplies. Military officials did not ensure that the freedmen received regular pay.[9]

Leaseholders further changed the wage system when they contracted to pay workers a share of the crop, rather than a cash wage. These agreements were advantageous to the planters because they minimized the amount of cash that they needed. After the crop was marketed, planters gave workers the share of the profits for which they had contracted. These arrangements have been called "share-wage contracts" by historians Roger L. Ransom and Richard Sutch. Share-wage agreements helped the lessee but were not equally favorable to the laborers. The contracts gave workers between one-third and one-half of the crop and were potentially lucrative given cotton prices, but share wages usually were used to maintain gang labor and appeared to observers and the freedmen to perpetuate antebellum labor conditions. In addition, workers received no return on their labor until the end of the year. Lessees advanced supplies against the freedmen's share of the crop, but that made possible exploitation of the workers, since planters charged whatever they wanted for the supplies. Even though unpopular among the freedmen, such contracts were used frequently. In one such agreement the post commander at Pine Bluff contracted with freedmen to cultivate and gin a crop in return for a share of the crop and advancement of supplies.[10]

Abuses of the system undermined the morale of workers. At the end of 1864 dissatisfaction grew when few made profits. William Sargent believed that a few would receive cash but many would not. Money and clothing accounted for some of the workers debts, but Major Sargent reported that unspecified debts were the real problem. The question was whether the freedmen were in such an unsatisfactory situation because they had borrowed irresponsibly or because the leaseholders had committed fraud. The military suspected the latter. Investigations indicated widespread fraud. Leaseholders cheated their workers by overcharging for clothing and other supplies. Their markups were high and the quality of goods was poor.

9. *Ibid.*, 31, 67.

10. *Ibid.*, 65; Joseph Warren, comp., *Extracts from Reports of Superintendents of Freedmen. First Series, May, 1864* (Vicksburg, 1864), 31; Statement of Oerin Watson, February 25, 1864, (Little Rock) Field Office Records, Arkansas, BRFAL, RG 105, NA; Roger L. Ransom and Richard Sutch, *One Kind of Freedom: The Economic Consequences of Emancipation* (New York, 1977), 60–61.

Lessees also traded extensively in nonessential items. In addition, local merchants willingly advanced goods against the freedman's share of the crop. At least one officer proposed that in the future, freedmen be allowed to purchase needed goods from the government so that they would be dealing with responsible persons who did not have reason to "cajole them to squander their money, with whom they can take their first lessons in trading with safety."[11]

Other planters took advantage of the freedmen by agreeing only to short-term contracts or refusing to honor contracts at all. Short-term contracts allowed the planters to use workers when they needed them and then turn them back over to the government when labor was not needed. The army accepted such arrangements, although officials did not like them. Workers were not protected, however, even with annual contracts. Colonel Samuel Thomas reported incidents in which leaseholders drove the freedmen back into government camps by cutting rations, provoking quarrels, or creating guerrilla scares, then refusing to settle with the workers because they had not stuck with their work. According to Thomas, leaseholders forgot their contracts in an instant. Freedmen reported abuses but found little help in securing redress.[12]

Testimony indicated that at the end of the first year's experiment, many laborers did not like share wages and wanted some other arrangement. Of the various contracts, most blacks preferred cash wages, which provided immediate rewards. The share system delayed returns and created more opportunities for cheating. Colonel Thomas concluded that abuses caused the workers to be discouraged and that economic reasoning explaining delays in distributing pay escaped them. According to Thomas, the freedman "looks only at results. He sees that the white man has received his labor, and has paid him with food and clothing—about the same he used to get." Regular wages produced different results. Colonel L. B. Eaton reported that planters who paid weekly wages accomplished a third more than those who settled with their workers irregularly. One lessee at Helena remarked: "If labor is paid well, it will work well; if paid poorly, the result will be the reverse."[13]

Colonel Eaton and others believed that in the long run, true freedom required the establishment of the freedmen as independent farmers, rather than wage laborers. Eaton was concerned particularly with the continuation of gang labor and plantation-style operations under the military system. He

11. *Report of the General Superintendent . . . 1864*, 36, 29, 67.
12. *Ibid.*, 67, 35; Report of Lt. J. H. Rains, March 31, 1865, in (Little Rock) Field Office Records, Arkansas, BRFAL, RG 105, NA.
13. *Report of the General Superintendent . . . 1864*, 67, 36, 34.

believed that slavery was not only a bad labor system but also produced a communal life that stifled initiative and smothered the freedmen's advancement. In one report Eaton urged that the freedmen be established on separate farms in order to ensure that they would "grow in domestic virtues and self-reliance." General Superintendent John Eaton agreed with this idea and proposed that the government give assistance to independent black farmers. Some efforts were made, but no assistance was provided. The government leased lands to blacks, who in turn financed operations through local businessmen. The businessmen provided supplies in return for a share of the crop. These contracts were similar to those for share wages and susceptible to the same abuses but were seen as more attractive by military officials because they allowed a different organization of labor. Farmers were relieved of control by overseers or planters and had greater freedom to direct day-to-day farm operations. Although few blacks farmed in this way, the experience had an impact on the development of the postwar labor system.[14]

At the end of 1864 Colonel Eaton optimistically reported that arrangements promoting independent farming were successful and that some farmers had saved enough to buy mules and plows and furnish themselves for the upcoming year. Records indicated that the system was not as successful as portrayed. Blacks who were able to lease land encountered many problems. Creditors and businessmen cheated independent black farmers as readily as they did wage laborers. The system did, however, have a greater appeal to the former slaves themselves. In July, 1865, the Freedmen's Bureau agent at Helena noted that those who were renting worked very satisfactorily. Those who had not rented desired to obtain land, and many were "able" to cultivate small tracts.[15]

Most military and Treasury Department officials were not interested in promoting a social revolution. Despite the optimism of Eaton and the hopes of blacks, the policies implemented preferred the lease of large tracts of land and restricted small holdings. After his 1864 inspection Colonel Eaton charged that the Treasury Department in particular was fixing on the South the same pattern that had existed in the antebellum period. He wrote: "As it is, the great plantations of the old regime are scarce ever broken."[16]

14. *Ibid.*, 12, 37, 73; Case of Washington Keatts v. Thomas Bass, in T. D. Y. Yonley and John Wassell to J. L. Chambers, November 8, 1864, (Little Rock) Field Office Records, Arkansas, BRFAL, RG 105, NA.

15. *Report of the General Superintendent . . . 1864*, 73; Report of Henry Sweeney, June 30, 1865, p. 17, in (Little Rock) Field Office Records, Arkansas, BRFAL, RG 105, NA; *House Reports*, 39th Cong., 1st Sess. No. 39, pp. 77, 71, 73.

16. *Report of the General Superintendent . . . 1864*, 73.

Despite discontent among all parties, the military in January, 1865, renewed leases and contracted labor along the same lines as in 1864. Although lessees complained about the inefficiency of free labor, they were more than ready to try again and vied with one another for the services of the freedmen. Major Sargent reported that all the hands who wanted to work had been hired. As a result, the system inaugurated in 1864 was the one in place at the end of the war and was taken over by the Bureau of Refugees, Freedmen, and Abandoned Lands—the Freedmen's Bureau—in May, 1865.[17]

The experiences of 1865 added to the conviction of the supervisors of the freedmen that the best way to help the freedmen was to lease or sell small parcels of land to them. The agents of the Freedmen's Bureau adopted this view as well. In 1865 the head of the bureau, General John W. Sprague, reported that the best results had been achieved where black farmers had leased small parcels of land because the policy created "industrious, prosperous, and *loyal communities.*" Sprague also concluded that the policy produced greater self-sufficiency among the freedmen and required less supplies furnished by the government. He urged that black lessees be given preference over whites who wanted to farm large plantations. Even some white leaseholders agreed with Sprague. At Helena leaseholders furnished land and supplies to individual black farmers, then allowed the freedmen to farm on their own. This program was similar to the system of sharecropping that eventually developed in the state and may have been the model for it.[18]

The 1865 season showed that the interest in using freedmen to farm small units was as strong among the freedmen as among military officials or white lessees. Military reports indicated that a growing number of freedmen wanted to farm on their own and that they wanted to work without the control of overseers. Since they usually could not buy land, the lease of small plots was the best means that they had to achieve work freedom. Further, the freedmen believed that they could make more money under such conditions and that they were taking a step toward actual landownership. A Union army surgeon leasing land in Pulaski County reported that he had attempted to hire a successful black farmer at $100 a month to supervise his plantation but the man refused because he could make more money renting land and farming it on his own than as someone else's employee.[19]

17. *Ibid.,* 36; Circular No. 1, June 10, 1865, in *House Executive Documents,* 39th Cong., 1st Sess., No. 70, pp. 67–68; Circular No. 8, August 21, 1865, *ibid.,* 70–71.

18. "Report of Missouri and Arkansas, July 17, 1865," "Report of Missouri and Arkansas, January 10, 1866," *Senate Executive Documents,* 39th Cong., 1st Sess., No. 27, pp. 136–39, 27–29; *House Reports,* 39th Cong., 1st Sess., No. 30, p. 74.

19. *House Reports,* 39th Cong., 1st Sess., No. 30, pp. 77, 71, 73.

By the end of the war, wartime experiments had answered many questions concerning black free labor. The most important was that blacks would work as free men; indeed, the labor force under the military's control showed that they would work as hard free as they had as slaves. A few planters complained that they could not get enough out of their hands, but the consensus was that the system functioned well. E. Darwin Ayres, treasurer of the loyal state government of Governor Isaac Murphy, testified in Congress that he knew men who got more work from their hands after freedom than before. "The story that they won't work," he said, "is gotten up by those who said that free labor could not be made to pay, and who wanted it to come out so."[20]

The end of slavery was more than the end of a labor system, although whites were more concerned with that issue than with others. It had also been a social system relegating blacks to a permanent lower class. That status was ensured by law but also reinforced by the denial to slaves of elementary tools necessary for full social and economic freedom, particularly education. As a free people, blacks needed to master skills such as mathematics, reading, and writing. The freedmen perceived that need. For the whites charged with supervising them during the war, however, such considerations were secondary. Still, in 1863 military officials began to plan for a system of education. In that year General Superintendent Eaton invited northern groups to send teachers to aid the freedmen. In December, 1863, the first teachers arrived in Arkansas, sent by the American Missionary Association. By March, 1864, thirteen AMA teachers were at work in schools at Helena, Little Rock, and Pine Bluff. Three other AMA schools opened that spring at Island No. 63, White River Island, and De Valls Bluff. The Friends Freedmen Committee entered the field in April, 1864, when they opened an orphanage and school at Helena.[21]

Religious spirit was the primary motive for most of the teachers who came to Arkansas. Caroline H. Moffatt, who taught at Little Rock, was typical. Describing her work, she wrote: "My heart is given to this work and my prayer to God is that he will give me health & strength sufficient to labor efficiently for the elevating of this long oppresed [sic] and downtrodden race." Their educational effort, however, took them into a broad variety of areas and was limited by their attitudes about the character and deficiencies of blacks.[22]

20. *Ibid.*, 72, 74, 77, 80, 126.

21. W. G. Sargent to John Eaton, March 1, 1864, in Warren, comp., *Extracts . . . May, 1864*, 24–29; Larry Wesley Pearce, "The American Missionary Association and the Freedmen in Arkansas, 1863–1878," *AHQ*, XXX (1971), 124; Thomas C. Kennedy, "Southland College: The Society of Friends and Black Education in Arkansas," *AHQ*, XLII (1983), 209.

22. Carrie H. Moffatt to George Whipple, March 2, 1864, D. T. Allen to C. H. Lowery, January 1, 1864, in American Missionary Association Papers, ARC.

The heart of the educational effort was instruction in basic skills such as arithmetic, reading, and writing. In addition to these skills, one Little Rock school added geography, singing, and Scripture memorization. Students made rapid progress in these areas and the teachers were pleased with the results. Little Rock teachers reported that after only three months of work, they had pupils halfway through *McGuffey's First Reader* and some into *McGuffey's Second Reader*. Students at Pine Bluff had learned in the same time to spell words of up to three syllables, and a few had achieved significant reading skills.[23]

The teachers considered instructing in morality to be equal in importance to teaching basic skills. All of them were sent by religious groups, and that accounts in part for this view. They distributed religious pamphlets and had students memorize Scripture. They tried to get the freedmen to formalize slave marriages. At the same time, however, these teachers believed that morality included learning self-discipline and the work ethic. They believed the freedmen had neither and that they also lacked regard for contracts, failed to fulfill obligations, were wasteful, and demanded immediate gratification. As a result, instruction included lessons in the value of looking to future results, delaying gratification, practicing honesty, being prompt, fulfilling commitments, and doing hard work for an employer. Colonel L. B. Eaton agreed with the need to emphasize these virtues and believed that the very presence of the teachers had moral value because it exercised an "elevating and restraining influence."[24]

The students often indicated that they did not want all that the teachers had to offer. Some teachers concluded, like the masters of slaves, that physical punishment was necessary to instill self-discipline. The desire of some freedmen to break up their slave marriages exasperated teachers. On the whole, however, teachers were impressed with how widespread the desire for education was among the freedmen. After only three months in operation, one Little Rock school reported an average daily attendance of 130 students, including young, old, and the soldiers from black regiments being formed in the city. Teachers found the same to be true wherever they opened schools. Carrie Moffatt reported from Little Rock that her students came to her "with tears coursing down their cheeks" and told her "how *long* they have prayed for and *expected* this time to come."[25]

23. Pearce, "American Missionary Association and the Freedmen in Arkansas," 128, 132.

24. *Ibid.*, 129, 138, 134–35, 137; *Report of the General Superintendent . . . 1864*, 23, 69; David Todd to George Whipple, June 2, 1864, in American Missionary Association Papers.

25. Pearce, "American Missionary Association and the Freedmen in Arkansas," 127–28, 132; S. H. Young to C. H. Fowler, February 4, 1864, Carrie H. Moffatt to George Whipple, March 2, 1864, both in American Missionary Association Papers.

Teachers had a mission to educate the freedmen, and the students appeared to respond, but both were hindered from the beginning by inadequate resources. Town schools often met in black churches that did not have enough room for all the prospective scholars who wanted to attend. Schools on the Home Farms were often taught in the cabins of individuals. Educational materials were in short supply, particularly books. Some of the material used was inappropriate. One teacher complained to the AMA that the books that had been sent to teach the freedmen to read had words that were too difficult, and requested books with two- and three-letter words.[26]

The school effort also lacked continuity. The teachers, although paid, were really volunteers who had no intention of making the education of freedmen a full-time career. As a result, turnover was great. At the end of the spring term in 1864 most of the teacher corps returned north to escape the southern climate, avoid disease, or handle personal matters. Few of them returned that autumn, and the schools were forced to build a teaching staff from scratch.[27]

Conditions among the freedmen created further problems. In the summer of 1864 freedmen's communities across the state were hit by epidemics of mumps, measles, whooping cough, dysentery, and pneumonia. Overall, one-eighth of the population in the camps died. At the Pine Bluff Home Farm nearly one-sixth of the inhabitants died in May and June. Suffering from inadequate food, clothing, and shelter, blacks were highly susceptible to contagious diseases. Fearing the risk to themselves, the teachers closed the schools during the summer.[28]

In the autumn of 1864 military officials and northern agencies renewed the school effort, but the problems remained unsolved. The number of freedmen seeking an education increased with the collapse of the Confederacy, but school facilities were not expanded and remained inadequate. The book shortage had not been dealt with. There were not enough teachers; in an effort to get more, military officials encouraged various northern groups to send them and also allowed blacks such as Little Rock's Andrew Wallace to open their own schools. To provide more funding, some schools began to charge tuition. At Pine Bluff students paid one dollar per month.[29]

Despite the problems, teachers and military supervisors remained optimistic about the schools and their impact. At the end of the fall term in 1864, an inspector reported that the freedmen continued to throng to the

26. Pearce, "American Missionary Association and the Freedmen in Arkansas," 132, 134, 136.

27. *Ibid.*, 129, 133.

28. *Ibid.*, 135.

29. *Ibid.*, 139–40, 140–41; *Report of the General Superintendent . . . 1864*, 68, 69.

schools. Those who attended "enjoyed and appreciated" the privilege. He found that soldiers and workers could be seen everywhere carrying their spellers and readers, and were heard reciting to one another from them. The bureau agent who moved to Helena at the end of the war reported: "It is extraordinary to see with what avidity the little ones pursue knowledge and how rapidly they learn." In addition, the teachers and supervisors believed the freedmen were learning proper moral conduct. A visitor to Little Rock approved of the "good taste and practical sense of the negroes," who were scorning extravagant clothing for the dress "becoming their avocations."[30]

Hopes rose even more in January, 1865, when the general superintendent of freedmen assigned a full-time officer to take charge of educational activities in Arkansas. Joel Grant, who had been an officer in the 12th Illinois Infantry, received the position and promised to expand the number of schools and teachers as fast as possible. The problems that plagued the schools persisted, however, and limited what he could achieve. In addition to all of the other difficulties, in the spring of 1865 the army stopped providing rations to teachers, forcing three to leave in the middle of the term. At the end of his first month in Arkansas, Grant reported that there were eleven schools, twenty-two teachers, and about one thousand students attending the schools daily. At the end of the spring term, the total number of schools had increased only from eleven to fourteen and the number of teachers had actually declined to twenty-one. This was the school effort for an uneducated population that prior to the war had numbered more than 100,000.[31]

In the end, the impact of freedmen's education during the war was limited. Without enough teachers, schools, or supplies, little was accomplished in providing even basic educational skills to them. The labor system created by the freedmen's office also affected only a few of the former slaves. The labor experiments, however, did produce new ways to approach the labor problems of the South in the various contract arrangements that were tried. The legacy of these experiments lasted into the postwar years. Perhaps as important as any lesson taught the freedmen was the hard fact

30. *Report of the General Superintendent . . . 1864*, 68, 69; Report of Henry Sweeney, June 30, 1865, p. 7, in (Little Rock) Field Office Records, Arkansas, BRFAL, RG 105, NA.

31. Special Orders, No. 3, January 5, 1865, in (Little Rock) Field Office Records, Arkansas, BRFAL, RG 105, NA; Joel Grant to W. G. Sargent, February 28, March 31, May 30, 1865, *ibid.*; Report of Henry Sweeney, June 30, 1865, pp. 16–17, *ibid.*; Pearce, "American Missionary Association and the Freedmen in Arkansas," 144, 258. Pearce concludes that AMA efforts in Arkansas were successful. The prewar population figure is from *Eighth Census, 1860: Population*, 16–17.

that their liberties would not be protected by the federal government, nor would they receive the support essential for them to protect their freedom themselves. They were fair game in a free labor market. The results were observed by Captain Henry Sweeney, an officer of the 60th United States Colored Infantry and a bureau superintendent at Helena. Sweeney wrote in July, 1865: "The mass of colored people look with suspicion on every one who can read and write, and fully appreciate their own ignorance in that very great distrust, as they know that in all written documents (such as contracts to labor & c.) they are liable to be swindled by unprincipled white men."[32]

32. J. W. Sprague to O. O. Howard, July 11, 1865, in "Reports of Assistant Commissioners of the Freedmen's Bureau," *Senate Executive Documents*, 39th Cong., 1st Sess., No. 27, p. 138; Report of Henry Sweeney, June 30, 1865, p. 17, in (Little Rock) Field Office Records, Arkansas, BRFAL, RG 105, NA.

# 8

## RECONSTRUCTION OF LOYAL CIVIL GOVERNMENT
### Lincoln, the Army, and Arkansas Loyalists

AFTER THE UNION ARMY CARVED LARGE AREAS OF ARKANsas away from control by the Confederate state government, the Federal military and local citizens began reconstructing the civil government in the occupied areas. Citizens in these areas were remarkably receptive to the turn of events, sometimes even welcoming the Federal troops. New leaders emerged ready to restore the state government and its relations with Washington. As with efforts directed toward the freedmen, the course of political reconstruction was limited by Federal policy. Civilian loyalists had a chance to produce significant political change, but the army was no more interested in a political revolution in the state than it had been in a social one. Thus, the shaping of loyal government resulted from the interplay of civilian, military, and federal governmental interests, and a new political world emerged even while the outcome of the war was still uncertain.

When Federal forces reached Batesville in May, 1862, General Curtis discovered strong Union sentiment. He concluded that the people of the state were ready to abandon the Confederate cause and were cheered by the return of the old flag. Crowds of people took the oath of allegiance and expressed their desire for a provisional government. Curtis urged General Henry W. Halleck, commander of the Department of the Mississippi, to reestablish civil authority as soon as the army entered Little Rock. On May 12, 1862, Halleck named Curtis military governor to direct civil affairs.[1]

Curtis never reached Little Rock, but the Lincoln administration remained interested in establishing civil government in Arkansas. The restoration of loyal government would strengthen the president's political position. In addition, it would please Missourians who saw the stabilization of Arkansas as essential to their state's protection. On July 19, 1862, the president appointed John S. Phelps military governor of Arkansas. In August Phelps went to Helena, where he urged General Curtis to invade the interior and tried to organize a government. Phelps and Curtis were imme-

---

1. S. R. Curtis to W. Scott Ketchum, May 5, May 6, May 7, 1862, in *OR*, XIII, 369, 370–371; H. W. Halleck to S. R. Curtis, May 12, 1862, *ibid.*, 378.

diately at cross-purposes because Curtis had no interest in the invasion. Phelps complained that the general had abandoned local Unionists to their fate.[2]

Phelps ultimately left Helena because of illness and ran his military government from St. Louis, maintaining his control through his secretary and adjutant general, Amos P. Enos. Enos continued pressure on the army for an invasion and in January, 1863, General John A. McClernand proposed an attack on Little Rock as a part of the campaign against Arkansas Post. Enos packed the papers of the military governor and readied himself to move, but the army did not advance and Enos returned to Helena. The military governor was helpless until the army moved. Without much notice, Lincoln revoked Phelps's and Enos' appointments in July, 1863, and the military government was abolished.[3]

The Unionist sentiment that encouraged Curtis and the president was widespread and strong. Military officials found most Unionists in the northern counties, but reports also indicated Union militancy in Sebastian County, around Fort Smith, in the Magazine Mountain area in Logan and Yell counties, and in Clark County in the southwestern part of the state. An entire regiment was supposed to have been organized among residents in the Ouachita Mountains but had been broken up by Confederate authorities. Unionism was not just a mountain phenomenon. One Federal officer returned from an expedition into Mississippi County and reported: "The people of Arkansas I found to be much more loyal than those residing in Missouri, and it is my firm and decided belief that the people residing in the neighborhood of the [Arkansas] river, in that State, only require a show of protection to establish their loyalty and fidelity to our Government."[4]

Arkansas Unionism had no obvious social or economic base. A Union

2. J. S. Phelps to H. W. Halleck, August 17, September 28, October 18, 1862, *ibid.*, 577, 683, 685; J. S. Phelps to S. R. Curtis, October 1, 1862, *ibid.*, 698; J. S. Phelps to E. M. Stanton, October 20, 1862, *ibid.*, 751; H. W. Halleck to J. S. Phelps, August 21, 1862, *ibid.*, Ser. 3, Vol. III, p. 429; E. M. Stanton to J. S. Phelps, in *Report of the Adjutant General of the State of Arkansas, for the Period of the Late Rebellion, and to November 1, 1866* (Washington, D.C., 1867), 3; B. Gratz Brown to Abraham Lincoln, December 3, 1862, in Robert Todd Lincoln Collection (hereinafter cited thus) of Abraham Lincoln Papers, LC. For Curtis' statement on the idea of an invasion, see *OR*, Vol. XXII, Pt. 1, p. 75.

3. *Report of the Adjutant General of Arkansas*, 4; J. M. Schofield to J. S. Phelps, January 2, 1863, *OR*, Vol. XXII, Pt. 2, p. 8; A. F. Enos to E. M. Stanton, January 13, 1863, *ibid.*, 39–40; J. A. McClernand to S. P. Curtis, January 14, 1863, *ibid.*, 41.

4. E. E. Brown to J. M. Schofield, June 22, August 17, 1862, in *OR*, XIII, 444, 581; S. R. Curtis to W. S. Ketchum, June 5, 1862, *ibid.*, 418; J. G. Blunt to J. M. Schofield, November 9, 1862, *ibid.*, 788; W. H. Pierre to S. R. Curtis, January 13, 1863, *ibid.*, Vol. XXII, Pt. 2, p. 37; W. A. Phillips to J. G. Blunt, March 19, 1863, *ibid.*, 162; Report of J. I. Worthington, January 8, 1864, *ibid.*, Pt. 1, p. 781; Report of F. R. Poole, October 1, 1863, *ibid.*, 616 (quotation).

officer described one party that sought his protection: "These people who came out with me are hardy, vigorous, and resolute men; they represent every trade, pursuit, and profession of life, and in intelligence and appearance are equal to the same number of men in any country." Cincinnatus Vann Meador, editor of a Little Rock Unionist newspaper, the *National Democrat,* concluded that pro-Union support derived from four different groups. There were the unconditional Unionists who had opposed secession and been forced to flee the state or go into hiding. There were secret sympathizers who had supported secession to avoid persecution. There were secessionists disillusioned with the war because of the "selfishness" of the "rich men" who conducted it. Finally, there were those "without principle," shifting their allegiances as the course of the war changed. There was no single reason underpinning Unionist sentiment.[5]

Army correspondence suggested that many Unionists were not so much pro-Union as anti-Confederate or antiwar. Confederate conscription was a major source of this hostility. Union commanders reported an increase in refugees after Confederate authorities began enforcing conscription in June, 1862. The vigor of enforcement made resisters more militant and changed their loyalties. The commander of an expedition through Hot Spring, Clark, Pike, Polk, and Montgomery counties found that Unionists had been persecuted and that "every conceivable means has been used to force these loyal men into the rebel service; they have been hung by scores; they have been hunted down with bloodhounds by the slaveholding rebels of Red River Valley; they have been robbed of their property, chained and imprisoned." Such actions appear to have made them more than ready to take up arms against their persecutors.[6]

The military encouraged Unionist activity because it promoted recruiting. In January, 1863, M. La Rue Harrison, who organized the 1st Arkansas Cavalry (Union), encouraged Fayetteville citizens to hold what was probably the first wartime Union meeting in the state. Those who attended petitioned Congress to allow them to elect a member of Congress and passed resolutions of loyalty. When the Federal forces withdrew, men who had expressed their Unionism often had to leave to protect themselves, and some joined the departing army. This situation was common. William Phillips, commander of the districts of western Arkansas in the Department of the Missouri, wrote that loyal men often made open demonstrations of their feelings upon the arrival of Federal soldiers, leaving them little choice

5. Report of H. C. Caldwell, November 18, 1863, *OR,* Vol. XXII, Pt. 1, p. 54; Little Rock *National Democrat,* May 28, October 4, 1864.

6. E. B. Brown to J. M. Schofield, June 22, 1862, in *OR,* XIII, 444; Report of H. C. Caldwell, November 18, 1862, *ibid.,* Vol. XXII, Pt. 1, p. 754 (quotation).

but to join the army when it left. Politics and recruiting for Federal regiments thus went together.[7]

The second major effort to restore civil government in the state began after the Federals captured Fort Smith and Little Rock in September, 1863. On October 19 and 24, Unionists held mass meetings at both towns. Those who attended asked military officials to hold elections for Congress. At the same time, Senator William K. Sebastian, who had never resigned his seat, proposed to return. Elections would have presented Congress with a loyal delegation that, if seated, effectively would have restored normal relations with the Union. A committee appointed at Little Rock assured the president of the loyalty of the state and asked for his assistance in restoring the government.[8]

The Union movement divided almost immediately over what plan would best accomplish their goal. The divisions reflected major differences over who should be allowed to participate in the government and hold power in the future. William M. Fishback, colonel of the 3d Arkansas Infantry and later the 4th Arkansas Cavalry, headed one faction. Fishback, a Fort Smith attorney, had been in the secession convention and had voted against secession initially. When war broke out he went to St. Louis, where he took the oath of allegiance, worked for the St. Louis *Democrat,* and became involved in Unionist politics. Fishback's circle included Isaac Murphy from Huntsville, the only delegate to the secession convention not to vote for or sign the ordinance, Elisha Baxter of Batesville, who had almost been tried for treason by Confederate authorities; and Edward W. Gantt, colonel of the Confederate 12th Arkansas Infantry, who shifted his support to the Union with a ringing denunciation of Arkansas' Confederate leadership in the summer of 1863.[9]

When President Lincoln announced his Ten Percent Plan in December, 1863, the Fishback group moved. Excepting only high-ranking civil and military officials of the Confederacy, the president's plan offered a pardon and the restoration of rights to all who swore an oath of future loyalty to the United States and accepted the end of slavery. When a number equal to 10 percent of the votes cast in 1860 had established their loyalty, they

7. M. La Rue Harrison to J. S. Phelps, January 27, 1863, *ibid.*, Vol. XXII, Pt. 1, p. 78; W. A. Phillips to S. R. Curtis, March 9, 1863, *ibid.*, 149.

8. J. M. Schofield to E. M. Stanton, December 5, 1863, *ibid.*, 731; Little Rock *National Democrat,* October 20, 1863; New York *Herald,* November 9, 1863; New York *Times,* January 4, 1863.

9. Harry W. Readnour, "William Meade Fishback," in Timothy P. Donovan and Willard B. Gatewood, Jr., eds., *The Governors of Arkansas: Essays in Political Biography* (Fayetteville, 1981), 92; William L. Shea, "Isaac Murphy," *ibid.*, 39–40; Michael B. Dougan, "Elisha Baxter," *ibid.*, 56–57; Memphis *Daily Bulletin,* November 1, 1863.

could organize a new state government. Fishback's supporters urged the loyal people of the state to organize and call a constitutional convention. The convention would revise the constitution to make it acceptable in the North—particularly by abolishing slavery. The people would then vote on the constitution and elect officials. If the referendum approved the constitution, the state could present itself to Congress with officers in place, ready for a full restoration of normal relations with the Union.[10]

An examination of their rhetoric and activities shows the Fishback faction was motivated largely by hostility toward the antebellum elite. They pushed for changes that would have ended slavery and also democratized the government. Valentine Dell, editor of Fishback's Fort Smith newspaper, the *New Era,* proclaimed: "Our chains are broken at last. . . . We again belong to, enjoy the honors, privileges, and advantages of that country which has stood pre-eminent among all nations of the earth in freedom, happiness and power." Dell attacked the men whose "selfish, diabolical ambitions, covetousness and lust of power" had brought on a war that had "no other object in view than the disfranchisement and degradation of the great mass of the people of the South." The people would change that. In one of its first numbers, Fishback's *Unconditional Union* at Little Rock proclaimed: "Not only will the loyal men of Arkansas fight the fight on the ensanguined battlefield, but they will fight a great battle at the ballot box which will result in total abolishment of slavery in all its phases, and the introduction and establishment of free institutions in this state, which shall, by their sunny influence, disperse the cloud which has heretofore hung like a pall over the people and destinies of the people of Arkansas." William Walker offered a hostile comment on the origins of Fishback's group when he wrote that "there is not a single Union citizen of any social prominence or respectability who has any connection with the Union Club here."[11]

A more conservative group within the Union party opposed the Fishback faction. Its members included Dr. Meador, the newspaper editor; Charles Bertrand, a Little Rock businessman; and Anthony A. C. Rogers, a planter and slaveowner from Pine Bluff. They used Meador's *National Democrat* to advocate the appointment of a military governor, urging Rogers for the position, and a delay in reorganization. Meador supported the Ten Percent Plan but argued that the state did not have enough voters who could take the oath to meet its minimum requirements. The faction also opposed the convention movement. The conservative Unionists were a

10. Memphis *Daily Bulletin,* November 14, 1863.

11. Fort Smith (Ark.) *New Era,* October 8, 1863; Little Rock *Unconditional Union,* January 28, 1864; W. Walker to D. C. Williams, January 26, 1864, in D. C. Williams Papers, Clara Eno Collection, AHC.

minority, but Meador and Rogers had a powerful ally in General Steele, commander of the Army of Arkansas.[12]

The conservative Unionists wanted political reorganization supported by all who were willing in 1863 to support the Union, not just original Unionists. Rogers' opponents considered him a "copperhead," a label used in the North for Democrats who opposed the war, because of his willingness to allow these others into the party. Rogers and the other conservatives also pushed for a moderate reconstruction and particularly rejected the class appeal of Fishback and his supporters. In one editorial in the *National Democrat,* Meador presented the faction's views on reconstruction. He wrote: "Oppression and punishment of those not found in armed rebellion, has not been the policy of the government, whatever may have been their political opinions in the past. Justice may have demanded a sterner policy, but mercy ever residing with a generous and victorious army has been extended, even to these remaining at home, who have been the unholy means of bringing on a cruel and desolating war." Steele agreed with these views, and he opposed Unionists who he believed attempted to "create prejudices against one class or the other; to create divisions where none should exist."[13]

The proconvention group organized Union clubs and prepared for a constitutional convention without Steele's support. In mid-December, the Central Union Club at Little Rock asked loyal citizens to choose delegates for a convention at the capital on January 8, 1864. Meetings were held throughout the state in areas occupied by Union forces and delegates selected. At the same time they sent Colonel Gantt to Washington to ask President Lincoln to support the convention and the government organized under a revised constitution. Gantt went with letters from General John W. Davidson, head of Steele's cavalry division, introducing the former Confederate to prominent Republicans and condemning General Steele's "conciliatory policy."[14]

In January, delegates began to arrive at Little Rock. When the convention began, the members quickly revised the 1836 constitution to abolish slavery and limited the use of indentures. They also declared the acts of the

12. Memphis *Daily Bulletin,* October 28, 1863; Little Rock *National Democrat,* December 26, 1867.

13. Little Rock *National Democrat,* October 20, December 26, 1863, February 20, 1864; J. Snow to Dear Governor [William H. Seward], May 10, 1864, in Robert Todd Lincoln Collection; C. C. Andrews to A. Lincoln, June 5, 1864, in *OR,* Vol. XXXIV, Pt. 4, pp. 231–32.

14. Frank Moore, comp., *Record of the Rebellion* (New York, 1866), Vol. VIII, Doc. 40, pp. 324–26; F. Steele to S. H. Boyd, January 18, 1864, in *OR,* Vol. XXXIV, Pt. 2, p. 104–105.

secession convention null and void and repudiated all debts contracted by the state in support of the war. Efforts at democratizing state government reflected the Fishback faction's broader agenda. The new constitution provided for the election of the secretary of state, state auditor, treasurer, attorney general and state attorneys, and supreme and circuit court judges. It created a new elected office of lieutenant governor and allowed the legislature to override a gubernatorial veto with a simple majority. As a last act, the delegates selected Isaac Murphy as provisional governor. When they adjourned, the delegates provided for an election on the constitution and for state officials to be held March 14, 15, and 16.[15]

Lincoln had already ordered the registration of voters and prepared for an election to be held on March 28. When he heard of the convention's actions, he was delighted and instructed Steele to harmonize his and the convention's plans at all costs to avoid dividing Union supporters. In a letter to Isaac Murphy, General John M. Thayer, and William Fishback, Lincoln declared that he had no intention of opposing the will of the state convention. In his final instructions to Steele, the president insisted again on cooperation and wrote: "It is probably best that you merely assist the convention on their own plan, as to election day & all other matters."[16]

After receiving Lincoln's instructions, Steele acted to carry out the convention's plan despite his personal opposition to it. On February 2, 1864, the general designated the posts at Little Rock, Helena, Pine Bluff, Van Buren, Fayetteville, Dardanelle, Lewisburg (now Lewisville), Batesville, and De Valls Bluff as points where citizens could come to take the oath of allegiance. On February 29, he proclaimed an election to be held beginning on March 14. As registration progressed, Steele reported that large numbers of prominent citizens were daily taking the amnesty oath, including many "Rebel" families who had fled Little Rock when it was occupied. Still, the commander was only a reluctant supporter of the president's and the convention's program. In a letter to General Nathaniel Banks he stated his reservations: "Without the assistance of the troops to distribute the poll

15. *Journal of the Convention of Delegates of the People of Arkansas Assembled at the Capitol, January 4, 1864* (Little Rock, 1870); *New Constitution with the Acts of the General Assembly of the State of Arkansas . . . 1864, 1864–65, 1865* (Little Rock, 1865), Articles VI, VII.

16. A. Lincoln to F. Steele, January 5, 27, 30, February 17, 1864, in Roy P. Basler, ed., *The Collected Works of Abraham Lincoln* (9 vols.; New Brunswick, N.J., 1953–1955), VII, 108–109, 154–55, 161, 190–91; A. Lincoln to F. Steele, January 20, 1864, *ibid.*, 140–41; "Lincoln to Arkansas Delegation," January 22, 1864, *ibid.*, 144; Lincoln to I. Murphy, February 8, 1864, *ibid.*, 173–74; Lincoln to J. M. Thayer, February 15, 1864, *ibid.*, 185–86; Lincoln to W. M. Fishback, February 17, 1864, *ibid.*, 189–90.

books, with the oath of allegiance, and to protect the voters at the polls, it cannot succeed."[17]

While publicly supporting the convention, Steele privately warred against his enemies. His most important victim was Davidson, whom Steele considered to be disloyal. In the midst of the political machinations, Steele asked Halleck for the authority to relieve Davidson of his command and protested: "He is the only discordant element in [my command]. He will intrigue against me." Steele was a friend of General Ulysses S. Grant's and General Halleck's and generally had their support in departmental affairs, and he was authorized to let Davidson go. Davidson lost his command.[18]

The convention faction responded by trying to get Steele removed from his command of the Army of Arkansas. Davidson attempted to go to Washington to appeal his case to the president, but Halleck denied him permission. Davidson then sent a letter to Lincoln and included correspondence from Provisional Governor Murphy that expressed the governor's concern about Steele and the tension between the civil government and the military. Murphy wrote: "Any action against him [Davidson] will be against the Union element here." By February, tension had reached the point that the president considered sending General Daniel Sickles to Little Rock to investigate what was happening and prevent trouble. Murphy and his supporters did not desire such intervention, and backed away. Ultimately, all parties assured Lincoln that there was no conflict.[19]

When the election took place, it was more successful than the Unionists had predicted. Large crowds jammed the polls. At Batesville the military commander reported: "The election here has been a great success and passed off very quietly. The cowed and downtrodden people came flocking from all parts, and there was universal astonishment among them at seeing so great a crowd as filled the streets of Batesville during the three days of the election." Replying to telegrams from an anxious Lincoln, Governor Murphy reported that in some areas guerrillas had attempted to prevent a fair election but that the turnout was heavy. On March 22 he informed Lincoln that more than 8,000 votes had been counted, more than enough

17. F. Steele to N. Banks, February 28, March 10, 1864, in *OR*, Vol. XXXIV, Pt. 2, pp. 448, 542; General Orders, No. 2, *ibid.*, 225; F. Steele to H. W. Halleck, February 25, 1864, *ibid.*, 423.

18. F. Steele to H. W. Halleck, January 28, February 23, 1864, *ibid.*, 175, 403; Special Orders, No. 48, *ibid.*, 187.

19. J. W. Davidson to A. Lincoln, February 26, 1864, *ibid.*, 427; Little Rock *National Democrat*, February 27, 1864; A. Lincoln to F. Steele, February 25, 1864, in *OR*, Ser. 3, Vol. IV, p. 133; I. Murphy to A. Lincoln, February 24, 1864, *ibid.*, 127.

to meet the 10-percent requirement, and that the majority favored the new constitution. The president received official results in April—12,179 for the constitution and 226 against it.[20]

On April 11, Murphy announced the election of constitutional officers, and three days later the General Assembly was organized. On April 18 the new state government inaugurated Murphy as governor amidst a great show of support by the military and the civilian population of Little Rock. In his address, Murphy restated his faction's commitment to changing the political system. He lashed out at "a class of people, that seek their own selfish ends, rather than the prosperity of the people; who, when the rebellion was strong were rebels, and used the rebellion for their profit; but when the rebellion grows weak . . . they become at once loyal, and use their loyalty in the same way." At the same time he criticized the president's "too lenient amnesty proclamation" for making this behavior possible. As to specific measures, the governor asked the General Assembly for laws granting equal protection to the freedmen, although he did agree that measures compelling the freedmen to adhere to contracts might be needed. He asked for revenues to support the government, a fair system of taxation. He recommended the organization of a loyal state militia, to be armed and supported by the federal government, to suppress violence and protect the state's loyal citizens.[21]

The General Assembly did little to implement the governor's program. The Fishback faction elected Fishback and Elisha Baxter to the United States Senate over the opposition of the conservative faction headed by the General Assembly's speaker of the house, Horace B. Allis. After disposing of that business, however, members accomplished little else. They authorized the collection of taxes on all personal property except livestock but suspended the collection of real-estate taxes until a later date except for those in arms against the government. Displaying hostility toward their rebel neighbors, they suspended the sale of lands for debts, excepting the land of those who had not taken an oath of allegiance, and barred "forever" the collection of debts by persons still in arms. Facing the opposition of the military commander, the legislature decided not to organize the militia but asked the president for permission to do so. They passed no laws regarding the freedmen.[22]

20. R. R. Livingston to W. D. Green, March 18, 1864, in *OR*, Vol. XXXIV, Pt. 2, p. 647; A. Lincoln to I. Murphy, March 16, 1864, in Basler, ed., *Collected Works of Abraham Lincoln*, VII, 240; I. Murphy to A. Lincoln, March 16, 17, 22, April 15, 1864, in Robert Todd Lincoln Collection.

21. *Arkansas House Journal, 1865*, 35; *Arkansas Senate Journal, 1865*, 15–27; Little Rock *National Democrat*, April 23, 1864.

22. *New Constitution with the Acts of the General Assembly . . . 1864, 1864–65, 1865*, 40, 41, 44–45, 51–53; *Arkansas Senate Journal, Sessions of 1864, 1864–65, and 1865*, 65, 87; J. Snow to Dear Governor [William H. Seward], May 10, 1864, in Robert Todd Lincoln Collection.

Without revenues and with no militia organized, the Murphy government had to rely on the military's cooperation to suppress violence and extend civil authority into the countryside. But relations with the commanding general did not improve. Steele did little to support the restoration of civil government outside of the capital. Following Steele's retreat from Camden in the disastrous Red River campaign, Murphy asked the president to remove the general from his command because the army and citizens had lost confidence in him. The governor complained that Steele had failed in his invasion of Confederate Arkansas and had made no effort even to pacify the areas occupied by Union forces. Murphy wanted a more active man and more troops in order to bring peace to the restored sections of the state. Unionists felt betrayed by the national government. In a letter to Lincoln written in June, Murphy went further: "Encouragement was given to hold elections and organize a State government. With trustful hearts it was done—not by the aid of military unwillingly given, but such aid as positive orders from the President must enforce with unwilling minds. Notwithstanding 12,000 votes were given, a civil government erected on advanced principles, and which, if it had been sustained by the heart cooperation of military authorities here, would have been a complete success, but the military are confined to a few posts." The state government and the military had come to cross-purposes.[23]

Little could be done. When Congress, as a result of disputes between itself and the president, refused to seat the men elected from the state, the state government lost most of its leverage with the military. Lincoln instructed Steele to support and protect the Murphy government, but the governor had no influence over Steele's policies and the general refused to take a more active stance in the state after the spring debacle. Steele's men sat in their entrenchments at Little Rock and seldom ventured out. Posts in the western part of the state were unsupplied and weak. Fortifications that had been started remained unfinished. Recruitment of black troops languished. Joseph Trego of the Quartermaster's Department wrote: "The troops under Steele's command are doing nothing but laying in camp letting their horses starve while rebels are burning hay which they need here so much. . . . The men, being idle, spend their wages for liquor, get drunk, raise a row and get into the guard house. I have heard no reasons assigned for such mismanagement except that the officers . . . prefer remaining in the city and Steele dont like to incur their displeasure by ordering them away." John Gray, a civilian, suggested that Steele wished to avoid discomfort, writing: "General Steele at Little Rock lives quite like an Eastern

---

23. I. Murphy to A. Lincoln, May 11, 1864, in Murphy-Berry Family Collection, AHC; I. Murphy to A. Lincoln, June 29, 1864, in OR, Ser. 3, Vol. IV, pp. 460–63.

prince with his harem, wines, dogs, horses, equipages, and everything in great style." To make matters worse for Murphy, Steele refused to create and equip the militia.[24]

Steele's inaction severely hindered the civilian government because its authority could not be extended beyond the military posts. Steele's policy also undermined the Union movement. General Christopher C. Andrews complained to the president that rebel spirit was resurging. Union citizens were leaving large parts of the state, and those who remained were more timid, while the rebels were bolder. Murphy agreed and informed Lincoln that one hundred Unionists were leaving the state each day, "broken-hearted and hopeless." Murphy continued to believe that his government could be a success, but only if the military gave it more support.[25]

The military implications of Steele's inaction became apparent in the autumn of 1864 when Sterling Price staged a massive raid into Missouri that passed unmolested through eastern Arkansas. Defeated, Price then took his army back through western Arkansas with little opposition. The effects of Steele's policies on local civil government were not considered important by his superiors, but his failure to stop Price was. In December, General Joseph Reynolds replaced Steele, much to the distress of his civilian allies. Charles Bertrand appealed to the president to intervene, complaining that Steele understood the local situation and would be irreplaceable, and at Little Rock a public meeting on December 8 protested the removal. The action Governor Murphy had been unable to achieve, however, was finally accomplished by a Confederate general. Steele was gone.[26]

Steele's removal did not solve the civil government's problems. General Reynolds presented a new problem when he began to implement the army's plan of concentrating troops in the state at only a few easily defended and supplied posts and withdrawing many units for use in Sherman's army in the Carolinas. The posts at Fort Smith and Van Buren were to be abandoned. The initial orders were given to Steele, but Reynolds was the one who had to carry them out.[27]

24. A. Lincoln to F. Steele, June 29, 1864, in OR, Ser. 3, Vol. IV, p. 460; C. C. Andrews to A. Lincoln, June 5, 1864, in OR, Vol. XXXIV, Pt. 4, pp. 231–32; U.S. Grant to H. W. Halleck, January 1, 1865, ibid., Vol. XLVIII, Pt. 1, p. 391; J. H. Trego to Dear Little Wife, August 28, 1864, in Kansas Historical Quarterly, XIX (November, 1951), 391; J. C. Gray to J. C. Ropes, July 24, 1864, in Henry Steele Commager, The Blue and the Gray (New York, 1973), II, 413–14.

25. C. C. Andrews to A. Lincoln, August 1, 1864, in OR, Vol. XLI, P. 2, p. 562; I. Murphy to A. Lincoln, June 20, 1864, ibid., Ser. 3., Vol. IV, p. 463.

26. C. P. Bertrand to A. Lincoln, December 12, 1864, in OR, Vol. XLI, Pt. 4, pp. 835–38.

27. H. Halleck to J. Schofield, November 16, 1864, ibid., Vol. XXII, Pt. 2, p. 709; E. R. S. Canby to F. Steele, November 16, 1864, ibid., Vol. XLI, Pt. 4, p. 682; M. L. Harrison to G. M. Dodge, December 22, 1864, ibid., 917.

The state's Unionists believed the military had betrayed them. Thousands of refugees had moved to these posts for protection. Murphy sent Adjutant General A. W. Bishop to Washington to get the order reversed. From Fayetteville the post commander complained to General Grenville Dodge: "In the name and for the sake of the thousands of families who will be left to the tender mercies of assassins and robbers, in the name of this beautiful country which will be left a desert, in the name of humanity I beseech you to try and have the order countermanded." Bertrand protested to the president: "Does he mean to abandon the State? And if such is his purpose, will you allow him to do it? Do you know that this abandons one entire Congressional district and the whole of another, save two or three counties, and that two-thirds of the members and perhaps three-fourths of the legislature, now in session here, are furnished from the district of country thus to be abandoned and given up?" The Unionists' only hope was the president, and they flooded him with pleas for a reversal.[28]

On December 27 Bishop met with Lincoln, along with the congressional delegation from Missouri. Lincoln asked Halleck to see what could be done. As a result, the orders to abandon the area were reversed. General Ulysses S. Grant ordered that all of the posts be held and those already abandoned be reoccupied. Reynolds gave grudging assent to the orders, informing Halleck: "These posts cannot afford the least protection to Kansas or Missouri. They have been sustained at enormous cost, but will be reoccupied and held."[29]

Grant's orders came too late to prevent further suffering for the Unionist population. Even though he received unofficial information that the evacuation order had been rescinded, John M. Thayer moved his command out of Fort Smith. Hundreds of Unionists fled with the army. Governor Murphy complained to A. W. Bishop that the army had behaved little better than a lawless mob and that soldiers had robbed starving women and children of everything. The political implications for the civil government were stark. Loyalty and support of the Union offered no protection. The Murphy government could not even ensure that a military force would remain in the state to protect civilians.[30]

28. M. L. Harrison to G. M. Dodge, December 22, 1864, *ibid.*, Vol. XLI, Pt. 4, p. 917; C. Bertrand to A. Lincoln, December 12, 1864, *ibid.*, 836; *Report of the Adjutant General of the State of Arkansas,* 4.

29. H. W. Halleck to U. S. Grant, December 28, 1864, in *OR,* Vol. XLI, Pt. 4, p. 946; U. S. Grant to H. W. Halleck, *ibid.*, Vol. XLVIII, Pt. 1, p. 391; H. W. Halleck to Commanding Officers, January 10, 1865, *ibid.*, 473; J. J. Reynolds to H. W. Halleck, January 14, 1865, *ibid.*, 515. See also *Report of the Adjutant General of the State of Arkansas,* Appendix B.

30. J. M. Thayer to W. D. Green, January 9, 1865, in *OR,* Vol. XLVIII, Pt. 1, p. 466; Orville Gillett Diary, January 30, 31, 1865, in Orville Gillett Papers, AHC; I. Murphy to A. W. Bishop, February 15, 1865, in Murphy-Berry Family Collection.

When General Reynolds turned his attention to the Unionists, he found a critical situation. The people the Murphy government depended on for support had been neglected to the point that they were in desperate straits. At Fort Smith one group requested help from the president, claiming that more than two thousand loyal citizens were on the verge of starvation. They wanted seed for planting and food to help them survive until the spring, and they concluded that unless given help they would have to abandon the area. One sympathetic Federal supported their claims, reporting that many faced starvation. At Little Rock, Reynolds found nearly seven hundred destitute women and children.[31]

Given the extent of the problem, Reynolds was forced to give Murphy some of the things that the state government had wanted. The development of armed farm colonies, which had been used to support and protect the freedmen, was attempted with white civilians. Such measures had been tried in northwestern Arkansas in the spring of 1864 by Colonel La Rue Harrison and had seemed to be successful. That March, Harrison reported that he had fourteen agricultural settlements in the northwest. They successfully protected the colonists and allowed them to support themselves, which freed the military from the need to provide for them. Harrison claimed he had some 1,200 men armed, and projected that his colonies would farm 15,000 acres. Harrison's experiment involved some coercion of settlers that headquarters did not approve, but despite abuses, Reynolds accepted the idea of armed farm colonies. At Little Rock he seized a farm and moved Unionist refugees to it and provided them with the seeds and tools for gardening. Reynolds sent one hundred refugees back to Van Buren to another farm.[32]

The military's greatest concern about the farm colonies was arming their inhabitants, and Reynolds tried to retain close control over them. In February, 1865, army officers began to form local military companies at Fort Smith and in the northern counties. Governor Murphy authorized these companies. Although called "state militia," they were under the orders of the nearest Federal military command and the Union army furnished them with smoothbore weapons and ammunition. Reynolds refused

31. A. O'Bryan and W. F. Owens to I. Murphy, February 4, 1865, in OR, Vol. XLVIII, Pt. 1, pp. 742–43.

32. Ibid.; C. Bussey to J. Levering, March 8, 1865, ibid., 1120; M. L. Harrison to W. A. Phillips, March 15, 1865, ibid., 1179; M. L. Harrison to I. Murphy, March 15, 1865, ibid., 1177–78; C. Bussey to J. Levering, May 3, 9, 1865, ibid., Pt. 2, pp. 305, 368–69; J. J. Reynolds to [?], March 18, 1865, ibid., Pt. 1, p. 1210; C. Bussey to J. Levering, March 14, 1865, ibid., 1169; Michael A. Hughes, "Wartime Gristmill Destruction in Northwest Arkansas and Military-Farm Colonies," AHQ, XLVI (1987), 167–68.

to provide food or supplies to them, insisting that they support themselves. He remained uneasy about these companies, and when he received reports that one of them was engaged in plundering, he ordered that no more be formed without his personal authorization.[33]

The Murphy government could do little for the Unionists, since the army had the sole authority to arm local communities. The military also was the only institution capable of providing relief to the starving thousands. The General Assembly tried to raise money with new taxes on wartime commerce and money on hand over two hundred dollars, plus an income tax on revenues above six hundred dollars. The income generated by these taxes was not enough, however, to finance the government, much less solve its many problems. The legislators ultimately borrowed the money to maintain governmental operations. In the last year of the war the Arkansas General Assembly was able to do almost nothing. In its April session in 1865, however, the members did ratify the Thirteenth Amendment.[34]

Ultimately, the Murphy government had the possibility of representing a large portion of the antebellum population. For that to have taken place, however, all of the instruments of the federal government would have had to support and encourage the Union movement. That did not happen. The military looked upon Murphy and his supporters as nuisances. There were no rewards for Unionism. Except in the northwestern portion of the state, the federal government never effectively differentiated between loyalists and rebels in its actual programs. As the war came to an end the pro-Union government was in place, but its constituents had been badly treated by their friends, and Murphy must have realized how frail were its supports.

The war ended quietly in Arkansas in May, 1865, a marked contrast to the bombast with which the state had entered the fray. When General Kirby Smith pulled his army into Texas and prepared to hold out despite the surrender of Confederate armies east of the Mississippi River, Confederate state authorities negotiated a separate peace. Governor Harris Flanagin sent representatives to Little Rock and proposed a plan to ensure "the restoration of peace and good order in society and the due administration of the laws, and to induce all citizens of the State to return to their homes and resume peaceful avocations." Flanagin's plan called for convening the Confederate

33. Reynolds Orders, in *OR*, Vol. XLVIII, Pt. 1, p. 848; Levering Endorsement, March 8, 1865, *ibid.*, 933; C. Bussey to M. L. Harrison, March 15, 1865, *ibid.*, 479; J. Levering to C. Bussey, March 10, 1865, *ibid.*, 1139; *Report of the Adjutant General of the State of Arkansas*, 4–5.

34. *New Constitution with the Acts of the General Assembly . . . 1864*, 75–76.

legislature to repeal acts related to secession; then the legislature and Flanagin would resign. This would leave the Unionist governor, Murphy, in control, and he would recognize county officials holding office under the Confederate state government. Flanagin's goal was to maintain the continuity of local authority. He made no pretense that a Confederate state government existed, which might have encouraged the raising of guerrilla bands. For Flanagin, restoring civil government and ensuring that all Arkansans regarded themselves as subject to law was paramount.[35]

General Reynolds did not accept Flanagin's plan, stating that the federal government would not recognize the legitimacy of any Confederate civil officers. Reynolds, however, was as concerned as Flanagin with rapidly restoring order and getting the people back to their peacetime endeavors. To help, he ordered the issue of seed corn to returning Confederates and allowed them to keep the army animals that they brought home with them. His main concern, however, was the ability of the Murphy government to ensure order and hold power. Overlooking how little had been done to support the Unionists, Reynolds strongly criticized them: "The loyal people of this State are deficient in self-reliance. They are timid and discouraged, and require for a time strong aid from the United States."[36]

Reynolds provided some aid. Although Congress had refused to seat the delegation elected from Arkansas in 1864, Reynolds recognized the legality of the Murphy government and at the war's end helped that government extend political control into the areas that had remained under Confederate domination. Reynolds asked army officers to provide information on local aspirants to office; he then furnished Murphy with the names of men whose loyalty was unquestioned, and Murphy appointed them. Reynolds reported that the return of civil government was moving smoothly and that the maintenance of loyal government might be possible. In one letter he wrote: "People are returning to their homes in every direction, and thus far I see no reason to anticipate any serious trouble in pacificating the State."[37]

At Camden, John Brown chronicled a return to peace that suggested Reynolds had a basis for his optimism and that revealed few problems. It was almost as though the war had not happened. Business and commercial activities livened up quickly. The freedmen presented few problems. On July 6 Brown noted that the military was helping to restore order among blacks. He wrote: "The Feds have got the negroes and they don't know what to do with them. They are adopting a strict police regulation with

35. H. Flanagin to A. H. Garland, May 22, 1865, in OR, Vol. XLVIII, Pt. 2, pp. 626–28; J. J. Reynolds to Adjutant General, May 27, 1865, ibid., 228–29.
36. J. J. Reynolds to Adjutant General, May 27, 1865, ibid., 226–28.
37. J. J. Reynolds to J. Pope, June 15, 1865, ibid., 705.

them, and urging them to go back to their former owners for the present." The Unionist county government was operating. On July 13, Brown wrote: "The State Government is organizing the County and Court System again. Most of the County officers have been commissioned, and we are gradually getting back to our old condition." Brown and others appeared ready to return to peaceful pursuits. What that desire meant regarding society, political power, and economic life in Arkansas unfolded over the next fourteen years.[38]

38. John W. Brown Diary, July 6, 13, June 27, 1865, in AHC.

# PART III

## POSTWAR ARKANSAS

# 9

## ARKANSAN SOCIETY AT THE WAR'S END

ARKANSAS IN 1865 FACED A WORLD THAT HAD CHANGED
greatly. The extensive material loss suffered during the war was the most
obvious manifestation of change. Armies had stripped the countryside of
animals. Buildings had been destroyed or were in disrepair. The antebellum
labor system was gone. Government was in the hands of different men.
Despite their altered circumstances, the former Confederates enjoyed a
unique situation. Federal policy left the reconstruction of their community
largely up to them. Except for temporary restrictions on the political rights
of Confederate leaders and some encouragement to recognize the freedom
of the former slaves, the remnants of Arkansas' antebellum white society
were able to begin rebuilding their lives. The war's survivors made the
decisions and the policies that created postwar Arkansas. Who survived and
with what resources were critical to the process.

The sacrifices caused by the war appeared to many contemporaries,
and to later historians, to be general. Reports of devastation came from
throughout the state and from members of every class. W. W. Fleming, a
hotelkeeper, returned to his home at Fort Smith to find his property "torne
all to peaces." Daniel Ringo, a wealthy attorney at Little Rock, reported
that his property there had been stolen or seized by authorities and that his
properties along the Mississippi River had been "burned and made desolate
and waste." At Batesville and Augusta, Andrew N. Carrigan found the
properties of his dead brother in disarray. He wrote: "He has nothing left
but his land and town property, and I cannot tell whether it is worth
anything or not. His place was pretty well ruined, orchard destroyed,
paylings broken down, and his beautiful little residence injured very much
I suppose."[1]

1. J. P. Walworth to W. E. Woodruff, July 6, 1866, W. W. Fleming to Woodruff,
December 15, 1866, E. H. Howell to Woodruff, August 25, 1865, all in William E. Woodruff
Papers, AHC; D. Ringo to S. Wheat, July 13, 1866, in Wheat Family Papers, Southern
Collection, UNC; A. N. Carrigan to My Dear Brother, June 2, 1866, in John W. Carrigan
Papers, DU; J. Page to Dear Son and Daughter, November 14, 1866, in *Arkansas Family
Historian*, XX (June, 1982), 126.

County tax assessments in 1865 versus those for 1860 indicate the extent of material losses. The number of horses and mares counted across the state decreased nearly 50 percent, from 68,918 to 34,533 head. Mules, essential to the resumption of postwar agriculture, dropped 39 percent, from 24,407 to 14,221. Assessors found 43 percent fewer head of cattle, a reduction from 247,417 to ·141,973. The number and value of household goods declined. The number of pleasure carriages dropped from 2,779 to 1,321. Furniture value decreased from $109,845 to $60,634, probably representing a loss of items as well as an adjustment of value. The value of jewelry, dropping from $240,666 to $91,646, also probably indicated partially a loss of items.[2]

For many white Arkansans the single largest property loss came with the emancipation. In 1860 the 60,799 slaves listed on the tax rolls were assessed at $45,075,417—the most valuable property in the state. The real value of these slaves, based upon an average 1860 price of $1,000, was more than $60 million. The total number of slaves actually counted in the census—111,115—using the same average price, were worth more than $100 million. For all slaveowners, the war destroyed the value of this property and all of the capital that had been invested in it.[3]

The end of slavery also undermined the value of real property. The land was still arable, but doubts concerning the reliability of the former slaves as free laborers reduced real and assessed values. The number of acres assessed increased between 1860 and 1866, but the average value dropped from $5.32 to $2.21 per acre. The number of town lots reported also increased, but the average value of each lot dropped from $276 to $198. The loss in value of all land was almost $34 million.[4]

Changes in life-style mirrored the material losses. The lives of wealthy families changed most radically, but all classes experienced changes caused by their loss of resources. The family of John S. Roane, one of Jefferson County's largest planters and an ex-governor of the state, were forced to live in the cabins of their former slaves. Daniel Ringo ended up renting a room in his old house; he had the family silverware, but no furniture and no money. For the wealthy slaveowners, the loss of slaves as household workers was a common complaint. Hamet Pinson, a small planter, ob-

2. *Biennial Report of the Auditor of Public Accounts for the State of Arkansas for 1864, 1865, and 1866* (Little Rock, 1866), Table 9; *Biennial Report of the Auditor of Public Accounts of the State of Arkansas, for 1859 and 1860* (Little Rock, 1860), Table H.

3. *Biennial Report of the Auditor . . . 1864, 1865, and 1866; Biennial Report of the Auditor . . . 1859 and 1860.*

4. *Biennial Report of the Auditor . . . 1864, 1865, and 1866; Biennial Report of the Auditor . . . 1859 and 1860.*

served; "Many of *our* ladies who were once wealthy now have to do their own housework." Typical of many less-wealthy Arkansans, E. H. Howell, who had owned a small farm near Brownsville, returned to find all of his personal property gone. Assessing his situation, he complained that he was not "worth enough to buy clothes enough to keep me warm this winter." George Pendleton, a small landowner in Union County, put his family in an unoccupied slave cabin and went to Texas to earn some money as a teacher. His wife found conditions unbearable; she could not purchase supplies to farm and had to sell butter to buy the paper and envelopes she used to write him. In one of these dearly purchased letters she complained: "I had rather take my hoe and folar you rou for rou than this way of living." The degree of change was not the same for all, but almost all Arkansans found their lives altered.[5]

A heavy loss of population within the state added to the sense of change experienced by Arkansans. Almost every contemporary source recognized that many of the people he or she had known before the war were no longer there. A correspondent of the *Arkansas Gazette* who visited Pine Bluff in the summer of 1865 reported. "New faces met me at every turn, with now and then a familiar one. The Old merchants with but few exceptions have passed away, and new ones filled their places." For individual families the loss was more personal. William H. Barksdale of Helena wrote to his sister in Tennessee for the first time since 1861 to inform her: "My brothers have all been killed and relatives not a few. . . . Alas! how many Mothers mourn in sadness on the desolate hearth-stone of their once happy homes. Fathers, husbands and sons all—all gone!" Congressman-elect E. Darwin Ayres estimated that the total population of the state may have been reduced by at least half, basing his conclusion on reports indicating that the voting-aged population had declined from 54,000 to 25,000 between 1860 and 1865.[6]

A comparison of poll taxes in 1860 and 1865 suggests that contemporary impressions were accurate. The number of polls collected in 1865 was 37 percent below that of the last prewar year, a drop from 43,181 to 25,518.

5. H. Pinson to My Dear Friend, February 1, 1867, in Pinson Papers, LSU; E. H. Howell to W. E. Woodruff, August 24, 1865, M. L. Bell to Woodruff, December 22, 1865, January 3, 1866, all in Woodruff Papers; D. Ringo to S. Wheat, July 13, 1865, in Wheat Family Papers; M. A. Pendleton to My Dear Husband, June 27, 1868, in George M. Pendleton Family Papers, LSUS; F. Fletcher to Dear Mother, November 9, 1865, in Elliott H. Fletcher Papers, AHC; J. L. Cheatham to Dear Dave, June 4, 1867, in *Clark County Historical Journal* (Winter, 1979–1980), 108.

6. Little Rock *Arkansas Gazette*, May 19, 1865; "The Rev. William Henry Barksdale," *Phillips County Historical Quarterly*, XV (December, 1976), 45; *House Reports*, 39th Cong., 1st Sess., No. 30, p. 72 (Ayers).

Comparing the names of taxpayers in 1860 with those who paid in 1866 in the eight sample counties shows an even more dramatic loss. In only one of the counties was the decline less than 50 percent: Washington County's 1866 rolls showed 59 percent of the 1860 taxpayers still present. In the other seven counties Phillips County had the greatest decrease—64 percent. The losses were 63 percent in Montgomery, 58 percent in Pulaski, 57 percent in Van Buren, 56 percent in Independence, 53 percent in Union, and 52 percent in Chicot.[7]

A decline in the black population paralleled that among whites. Contemporary observers such as Governor Murphy believed that less than one-half of the antebellum black population remained in 1865, a decrease of some fifty thousand individuals. The absence of an official enumeration of blacks in 1865 makes a systematic assessment of these observations impossible, but the evidence provided by the army, various agencies trying to provide aid for the freedmen, and individual examples suggests that Murphy's perception was correct.[8]

The war had produced many different problems that caused this population loss. Service-related deaths helped to explain the decline in population among young white males. William L. Fox estimated that 6,862 Arkansans died in battle or from disease while in the Confederate service. Blacks pressed into the Confederate service also died in great numbers because of poor working conditions and exposure. Federal records indicate that 1,713 white Arkansans died in the Union army; 30 percent of the 5,000 black Arkansans in the Federal army also died. The total number of white deaths constituted more than 12 percent of the 69,016 white men in the state between the ages of fifteen and forty. Others who served in the army simply chose not to return to Arkansas at the war's end. Joel C. Barlow of Helena was one of these, moving to Memphis after his service with the 2d Arkansas Battery because it offered greater business opportunities. Sheppard H. Blackmer of Washington County settled in Springfield, Missouri, after he left the 1st Arkansas Infantry, to learn the trades of brickmaking and plastering. Death and other factors help account for the fact that in some cases fewer than one of ten men who had joined the army in 1861 ever returned to their home counties.[9]

7. *Biennial Report of the Auditor . . . 1864, 1865, and 1866,* Table 9, pp. 32–34; *Biennial Report of the Auditor . . . 1859 and 1860.*

8. *House Reports,* 39th Cong., 1st Sess., No. 30, p. 126 (Murphy estimate).

9. William L. Fox, *Regimental Losses in the American Civil War* (Albany, N.Y., 1893), 553, 554, 527; *Report of the Adjutant General of Arkansas for the Period of the Late Rebellion, and to November 1, 1866* (Washington, D.C., 1867), 256; *House Reports,* 39th Cong., 1st Sess., No. 30, pp. 125, 79, 72, 154; *G/EA,* 749–50 (Barlow); *G/NWA,* 916–17 (Blackmer); *AS/AN,* Vol. 8, Pt. 2, p. 4 (Fitzhugh).

Conditions among civilians further decreased the population. Deaths among white refugees and those who remained at home were high. Black refugees also died in large numbers. Federal officials reported death rates in freedmen's camps as high as 50 percent. No one counted deaths among the slaves carried to Texas and Louisiana by their masters. Rates for whites and blacks may have been higher than they had been in peacetime because of the dislocation that all suffered, forcing them to deal with innumerable hardships. Many refugees decided that opportunities were better outside of Arkansas and either remained where they had settled or moved on to other states. The wife and children of Norfleet H. Cotton, a landowner in Monroe County, moved to Tennessee to live with his parents in 1863. At the end of the war, Cotton rejoined them briefly and, after checking on his property in Arkansas, decided to keep them where they were because he considered local conditions to be unstable. Many of the freedmen who had been refugees also made decisions not to return to Arkansas and instead sought new opportunities outside the South, remained where they had been taken, or tried to find family members in the older states.[10]

Across all classes, Arkansans had been hurt badly by the Civil War. The large numbers of people who perished, the many who were displaced and never returned, and the material losses weakened and changed the old community. Evidence of widespread individual tragedy does not support, however, the conclusion that the war brought about the total destruction of all characteristics or elements of antebellum society. A closer look at the eight sample counties indicates that the war's effects differed among individuals and individual families, and that membership in a particular class had an impact on what happened. Generally, wealthy individuals and families survived the war years and maintained control over their property better than their poorer neighbors. The loss of their slaves had a major economic impact, but they were still in a better position than others to reestablish their lives and fortunes. Poorer individuals and families did not have as much to lose, but their losses were more disastrous, often involving everything. They were less likely to still be in their home county at the

10. Susan Elizabeth Miller—Her Story," *Stream of History*, XX (Winter, 1985), 8, 10; Russell P. Baker, ed., " 'This Old Book': The Civil War Diary of Mrs. Mary Sale Edmondson of Phillips County, Arkansas," *Phillips County Historical Quarterly*, XI (December, 1972), 3–5; Joseph M. Hornor, "Some Recollections of Reminiscences of My Father," *Phillips County Historical Quarterly*, X (December, 1971), 15; Carolyn R. Cunningham, ed., "The Legacy of Love—The Cotton Correspondence: Part I," *Phillips County Historical Quarterly*, VI (March, 1968), 34–37; *AS/AN*, Vol. VIII, Pt. 1 (Blakely), Vol. IX, Pt. 3, p. 199 (Hatchett); Vol. X, Pt. 5, p. 15 (Rassberry), Vol. XI, Pt. 7, pp. 9 (Wesmoland), 85; *AS/ON*, Vol. XII, Supp. 1, p. 391; David Todd to George Whipple, June 4, 1864, in American Missionary Association Papers, ARC; *House Reports*, 39th Cong., 1st Sess., No. 30, p. 126 (Henry).

TABLE 13

PERSISTENCE RATES, 1860–1866, COMPARED WITH PROJECTED RATES FOR A
SIX-YEAR PERIOD BASED ON PREWAR RATES

| County | Elite | | Upper-Middle | | Lower-Middle | | Lower | |
|---|---|---|---|---|---|---|---|---|
| | A | P | A | P | A | P | A | P |
| Chicot | 88 | (82) | 52 | (62) | 32 | (54) | 18 | (51) |
| Independence | 86 | (100) | 62 | (79) | 33 | (71) | 26 | (57) |
| Montgomery | * | * | 58 | (72) | 34 | (60) | 20 | (48) |
| Phillips | 77 | (87) | 52 | (71) | 24 | (67) | 10 | (56) |
| Pulaski | 76 | (92) | 61 | (78) | 41 | (57) | 13 | (45) |
| Union | 83 | (83) | 57 | (68) | 38 | (62) | 25 | (49) |
| Van Buren | * | * | 52 | (75) | 42 | (74) | 32 | (65) |
| Washington | 100 | (100) | 57 | (83) | 51 | (71) | 18 | (64) |

*No one in this class in 1860.
A=actual persistence rate, 1860–1866.
P=projected rate over six-year period.

end of the war. Class thus played a role in how the war affected the members
of the community (see Table 13.)[11]

Postwar tax rolls show that large numbers of taxpayers who reported no
property in 1860 failed to reappear in the lists made in 1866 and their
persistence was less than that projected from prewar figures. This group
statistically should have survived to 1866 at a rate of 56 percent, but in the

11. The following text and associated tables reflect the percentages of individuals who,
having appeared on the 1860 tax rolls, appeared again on the 1866 rolls. Since the tax rolls,
rather than the census, were used, family persistence was difficult to measure except in obvious
cases.

A measure of normal persistence was necessary to measure the actual rates to determine
how the war may or may not have affected survival. Unfortunately, there is no standard
formula for determining persistence rates for periods of less than ten years, and establishing
such a formula is made more difficult since the rate of persistence in even normal times would
decrease each year over a ten-year period. To establish a projected normal persistence rate
based on prewar rates, I simply divided the prewar rate by 10 to establish an annual persistence
rate, then multiplied that rate by 6 to establish a projection for the period 1860 to 1866.

sample counties only two out of every ten individuals in this class in 1860 remained in 1866. Biographical material offers no ready explanation for what happened to the propertyless, but it does provide a basis for speculation. Many in this class in 1860 were young men. In Phillips County, where tax rolls were matched with census records, a sample showed the average age of those without property was thirty, whereas the property-holding population had an average age of thirty-six. The propertyless were also more likely to be unmarried than those with property. Younger and without family ties, they may have joined the army at the outbreak of the war in greater numbers and, as a result, suffered disproportionately the impact of service. They also would have been more likely to seek new opportunities elsewhere if they had not established themselves in a county before the war.[12]

A few individual cases suggest that the search for opportunity elsewhere was a common reason for not returning to a county. Thomas H. Patterson of Searcy was twenty-three years old when he joined the 7th Arkansas Infantry and left his job as an overseer. With no property in Arkansas, at the end of the war he returned to his family home at Henderson, in McNairy County, Tennessee, where he worked as a store clerk, then moved to Mississippi to teach school. W. W. Black, another propertyless individual, had been bound out as a laborer in Little Rock before the war. In 1862 he joined the 1st Arkansas Infantry. After the Confederate surrender, Black stayed when his unit passed through Memphis; he took a job cutting crossties for the railroad. He remembered, "I had no home to go two [sic]."[13]

If an absence of responsibilities or opportunities at home drew the propertyless elsewhere, the presence of these circumstances helps explain the individuals from the class who remained in a county. Many who had no property in 1860 but who reappeared in the 1866 rolls obtained real or personal property during or just after the war. They did so in a variety of ways. William H. Renfro, a plantation manager in Phillips County, joined the army, but his family purchased a farm during the war. Renfro returned to that farm afterward and in 1866 reported ownership of 240 acres. Lemuel Darden of Union County came back from the 3d Arkansas Infantry to take possession of a 240-acre farm owned by his mother. Alexander C. Jones,

---

12. Analyses were based on the 1860 and 1866 tax rolls.

Tax rolls and census material were correlated for only one county. The number of people on the tax rolls and not on the census and the number on the census but not on the tax rolls suggest that neither source should be considered other than a rough estimate of population and that any conclusions based on them are also rough approximations of population characteristics.

13. Gustavus W. Dyer and John T. Moore, comps., *The Tennessee Civil War Veterans Questionnaires* (5 vols.; Easley, S.C., 1985), IV, 1704–705 (Patterson), I, 324–25 (Black).

a Union County carpenter, returned and married a widow with property. All these men were propertyless in 1860 but had prospects for advancement in 1866.[14]

Others had families or already-existing business ties in a community. Jesse C. Shell of Phillips County had no property, but he had business and political connections. He was orphaned when only twelve years old but later found work as a plantation manager. He also served as a deputy sheriff. When Shell returned after the war, he reestablished these connections and became a prominent politician. Ferdinand L. Neal of Union County had no property before the war, but he had established himself as a clerk in a grocery and also worked as a timberman and in the stave business. In 1865, he came back and opened a business of his own and in 1866 reported personal property valued at $230.[15]

Among the propertyless class, those who persisted in Arkansas had in some way established ties in a community either before or during the war. Persistence among this class was, however, the exception. For a large majority of the propertyless, the war brought devastation and dislocation, and they never returned to their antebellum homes. Even if they survived the war, they saw their future and opportunities elsewhere. The antebellum world, promising economic and social advancement for even the poorer members of the community, had disappeared.

Possession of any property increased the probability that individuals would reappear in the 1866 tax rolls. Individuals fitting into the lower-middle class, with property valued between $1 and $999, persisted at an average rate of 37 percent. Although this rate was greater than that for the propertyless, the difference between projected and actual rates for the lower-middle class was larger. The group should have survived at a rate of 65 percent. The actual rates varied from a high of 51 percent in Washington County to a low of 24 percent in Phillips County (see Table 13).

Patterns varied county to county, but most lower-middle-class survivors had improved their personal- and real-property holdings during the war. Their lack of large slaveholdings accounts for relatively small declines in personal-property values; in some counties the average value of their personal property increased (Table 14), reflecting an actual expansion of personal-property owned by the class, particularly livestock holdings. Losses tended to take place only in those counties subjected to a sustained military occupation.

14. G/EA, 794–95; G/SA, 835, 845–46.
15. G/EA, 797; G/SA, 857–58.

TABLE 14

PERCENTAGE CHANGES IN PROPERTY, 1860–1866, LOWER-MIDDLE CLASS

| County | Real Property | Personal Property | Land | Horses/ Mules | Cattle |
|---|---|---|---|---|---|
| Chicot | +74.3 | –14.0 | +929.7 | –5.9 | +147.6 |
| Independence | +10.6 | +20.0 | +49.1 | +44.2 | +6.3 |
| Montgomery | +12.2 | +13.6 | +41.4 | +15.4 | +45.9 |
| Phillips | +104.3 | +89.0 | +192.8 | +125.0 | +17.2 |
| Pulaski | +18.9 | –54.8 | +71.0 | –50.0 | –69.4 |
| Union | –46.6 | –12.6 | +84.6 | +38.5 | +11.5 |
| Van Buren | –21.4 | –3.6 | +80.3 | –7.7 | –8.7 |
| Washington | +23.7 | –13.5 | +20.9 | 0 | –3.4 |

For the upper-middle class—the group possessing $1,000 to $24,999 in property—the persistence rate was higher than for the lower-middle, although not matching projected rates. In this class, the majority of individuals persisted. Overall, 56 percent of the upper-middle class survived, compared with a projected rate of 73 percent. The higher rate of survival suggests that wealth was certainly a factor in wartime resiliency (Table 13).

The upper-middle class, of course, possessed more property in 1860 than the lower classes, and consequently the war produced greater losses for them. They suffered their greatest loss in the value of personal property, where emancipation hit them much harder than it did the classes with few or no slaves (see Table 15). Reduced personal-property values, however, also reflected an actual decline in personal-property items, with large losses in livestock herds. Again, the greatest declines tended to take place in those counties experiencing a long-term military occupation.

Among the state's antebellum elite—that is, those with property valued in excess of $25,000—survival rates were the highest of all (Table 13). In five of the six counties with members of this group in 1860, persistence rates neared or equaled the projected rate of 82 percent, and in the sixth, Chicot County, the survival rate of 88 percent actually surpassed the projection. Even in Pulaski County, which had the lowest rate, more than three-quarters of the elite persisted.

TABLE 15

PERCENTAGE CHANGES IN PROPERTY, 1860–1866, UPPER-MIDDLE CLASS

| County | Real Property | Personal Property | Land | Horses/ Mules | Cattle |
|---|---|---|---|---|---|
| Chicot | –67.4 | –87.4 | + 5.2 | – 8.3 | –12.7 |
| Independence | –18.9 | –82.0 | + 4.4 | +41.2 | –61.8 |
| Montgomery | –48.9 | –73.4 | –27.7 | –24.2 | –33.7 |
| Phillips | –49.6 | –90.7 | +28.2 | –11.1 | –30.8 |
| Pulaski | –34.5 | –90.6 | – 1.2 | –71.4 | –73.3 |
| Union | –77.3 | –93.7 | – 6.8 | –30.3 | –38.6 |
| Van Buren | –38.7 | –78.3 | +47.5 | –18.8 | –42.0 |
| Washington | –42.9 | –85.2 | – 8.5 | –44.3 | –46.9 |

TABLE 16

PERCENTAGE CHANGES IN PROPERTY, 1860–1866, ELITE

| County | Real Property | Personal Property | Land | Horses/ Mules | Cattle |
|---|---|---|---|---|---|
| Chicot | –65.1 | –96.8 | + 4.8 | –61.3 | –72.9 |
| Independence | –34.3 | –80.2 | – 2.7 | –54.1 | –73.1 |
| Montgomery | ★ | ★ | ★ | ★ | ★ |
| Phillips | –66.7 | –97.1 | +16.2 | –62.0 | –76.4 |
| Pulaski | –50.6 | –98.5 | +23.7 | –78.4 | –82.0 |
| Union | –78.5 | –95.5 | –12.4 | –67.9 | –48.5 |
| Van Buren | ★ | ★ | ★ | ★ | ★ |
| Washington | –71.3 | –49.5 | –65.4 | –84.6 | +15.6 |

★No members of elite class in 1860.

As might be expected, the decline in the value of property owned by members of the elite was heavy, and the greatest loss was in the value of personal property, although the decline in the value of their real property was also higher proportionally than among other classes (Table 16). Real-property values appear largely to have reflected a simple devaluation of land. Personal-property values, however, mirrored major losses of livestock and other personal-property items. Still, despite their losses, the elites emerged with more personal property than the classes below them. Although livestock herds had declined, the elite still possessed sizable holdings.

A sense of what occurred among the elite can be gained by examining the wealthiest persisting individuals in each of the six counties with members of this class—Elisha Worthington of Chicot County, Gideon J. Pillow of Phillips, Thomas Keessee of Union, Richard Fletcher of Pulaski, Morgan Magness of Independence, and William Wilson of Washington. All of them suffered serious losses of personal property. Worthington may have had the greatest loss: in 1860 the county assessed his personal property—including 175 horses and mules, 150 head of cattle, and 320 slaves—at $247,100; in 1866 he, like the other wealthiest individuals, listed no personal property at all. Although all six men lost large amounts of personal-property wealth, most of them added to their landholdings. Worthington owned 11,288 acres of land valued at $225,100 in 1860. In 1860 the tax rolls showed that the value of his real property had dropped to $81,042, but the actual amount of land had increased to 11,576 acres. The largest gains were made by Fletcher, of Pulaski County. In 1860 he had 1,579 acres worth $19,609. In 1866 his real estate was valued at $24,685 and included 4,886 acres. The only major loser was Magness, of Independence County, whose holdings declined from 4,019 acres worth $14,867 in 1860 to 2,885 acres worth $14,623 in 1866. The landholdings of the rich remained relatively unchanged or actually increased.

The elite was hard hit financially by the war, but the conflict did not change the basic structure of antebellum society. The elite lost more than did those beneath them, but they had more to begin with and could afford to lose considerably and still maintain their position in the community. The persistence figures indicate that the poor and those with less property did not survive the war years intact, for whatever reason. The wealthy, on the other hand, persisted and within their counties retained their relative positions in terms of wealth. They were on the top before the war and they were still there after the war.

An examination of the twenty wealthiest individuals in each of the sample counties highlights the persistence of status by the antebellum elites.

The pattern is particularly pronounced in the plantation counties. In Chicot County all twenty of the wealthiest individuals in 1866 had been members of the antebellum elite. In Phillips County sixteen of the twenty had been members. In Pulaski County thirteen of twenty came from the prewar elite. Only in Union County did fewer than half of the twenty wealthiest come from the prewar elite. In short, in the plantation areas the men and families that dominated the communities after the war generally came from the same group that had exercised control before the war.

The prewar elite remained relatively strong in the nonplantation communities as well. In these counties the prewar social elite belonged primarily to the upper-middle class. In Van Buren, Montgomery, Independence, and Washington, most of the wealthiest people in 1866 came from that same class; usually, in fact, they were the same people. In Montgomery County all but three of the wealthiest members of the community in 1866 had been part of the upper-middle class in 1860. In Van Buren County the twenty wealthiest consisted of at least sixteen members of the upper-middle class of 1860. Thus, even in these counties, wealth was a factor in persistence through the war years.

The elite survived for many reasons. Even though they often contributed extensively to the Confederate cause, they still had the resources necessary to protect themselves and their interests during the war years. The example of Judge John S. Hornor of Helena illustrates the measures they could take. Hornor was a Unionist in 1861, but all of his sons joined the Confederate cause, and Hornor himself contributed greatly to it—although he refused to turn his gold over to Confederate authorities. He remained in the county, hung on to his slaves, and continued farming despite the Union occupation of Helena. He decided after the failure of the Confederate attack on Helena in 1863, however, that he could not continue to operate, and he moved his slaves and his families to Davis County, Texas. There he purchased land and put his slaves to work raising produce, cotton, and cattle. At the end of the war he sold his cattle and returned to Phillips County, with his workers, and began planting. Hornor may have been more successful than others in holding on to his wealth, but many members of the elite pursued the same course and, despite the loss in the value of their property, faced the postwar years with their resources, land, and access to labor only minimally diminished.[16]

The war did not destroy how wealth was distributed, but it did undermine some of the ideas that had created social peace in the antebellum

16. Hornor, "Reminiscences of My Father," 10–17.

years. The belief that Arkansas offered all comers some degree of economic opportunity persisted, but that faith was no longer as certain. Further, antebellum belief in the possibility of upward social mobility was dampened. Prewar statements of optimism gave way to statements of hope— usually that the individual simply could survive or retain a position in society—but postwar Arkansans seldom spoke of improving their status. Poor whites left little evidence of their perception of conditions immediately after the war, but their horror of being forced to compete with the freedmen expressed their pessimism regarding the future. State supreme court justice Charles Harper reported that the poor men of the state feared that they would be brought to a level of equality with the freedmen. He thought that the poor were "willing to have slavery abolished; but they want the negro out of the country."[17]

Optimism also lessened among the state's small property owners. The Fort Smith hotelkeeper W. W. Fleming hoped "with care and prudence to survive our misfortunes and repair damages, so that we can be comfortable again." J. L. Cheatham, a small farmer from Dallas County, wrote several years after the war: "I have made some money since the war, and if I can collect what is due me [from before the war] I will have sufficient means to live comfortably on until I can make some more." The editor of the *Gazette* believed that returning soldiers were "laboring with fervidness to get ready for the good time which they hope to see next year." For those who were not wealthy, success and social mobility were still possible, but the imminence of such movement was no longer so apparent.[18]

Even the planters lost some of their antebellum expectations for rapid increases in wealth and power. Judge Hornor informed William Woodruff that he hoped only "that with proper energy and industry on my part I shall be able to make a comfortable living for my family." Andrew Carrigan, a planter from Hempstead County, wrote that he had given up getting rich and intended only to "enjoy as much of life as God's will is I should." A year later, he was even more pessimistic. He expressed the shift in mood felt by others when he wrote: "Before the war, I felt independent, I knew if God spared my life & the lives of my servants, that I would in a few years be well enough off, but that is all gone, & I know my family have to be supported by my individual effort. So I am laying on right manfully. I know

17. *House Reports*, 39th Cong., 1st Sess., No. 30, pp. 7 (Harper), 120.

18. W. W. Fleming to W. E. Woodruff, December 15, 1866, in Woodruff Papers; J. L. Cheatham to Dear Dave, June 4, 1867, in *Clark County Historical Journal* (Winter, 1979–80), 107; Little Rock *Arkansas Gazette*, August 22, 1865.

how to work. I know how to carry on work."[19] In every quarter of the state, this perceptible shift in the attitudes of the elite had taken place.

The idea of economic and social opportunity was tarnished, and the loss of faith created, at least initially, concern among members of the elite that society might come apart. The thoughts of the poor are hard to determine, but the wealthy made it clear that they feared class forces had been unleashed. Observers believed that the war had convinced many of the people at the bottom of society that they shared few of the interests of their wealthier neighbors. One soldier expressed such a sentiment as early as 1862, writing: "The rich sit back and seem to regard a wet and hungry soldier as something beneath their notice. They will certainly receive their reward." H. Hayes of Chicot County also perceived a breakdown in the unity of poor and rich whites at the war's end when he wrote of the wealthy in his county: "The planters of this region have no patriotism. It's get all you can, keep all you get and 'devil take the hindmost' with them." The conflict over issues such as taxation and conscription added to this coming apart of the antebellum ideological consensus.[20]

Members of the elite believed that wartime experiences could produce continued social friction. John Brown, the Camden merchant, concluded that the swindles and speculations of the rich had "gotten up prejudice against us in the country and among the soldiers." The men who feared the hostility of the poor never stated how they believed this feeling might be acted upon, but unquestionably, in a democratic society the enmity of the poor toward the rich potentially threatened the political power of the elite and thus their ability, critical to their success, to control their environment. No one feared class warfare. The elite did seem to believe, however, that they would face a challenge to their political hegemony. The importance of class conflict as a potential basis for political division was an issue awaiting the restoration of political life, but in 1865 a persistent economic elite looked at the shambles within the society beneath it and at the weakening of the ideas that had created prewar unity, and wondered about the future.[21]

The war brought about change, but the elite was unwilling to accept much of it. The individuals who had been at the top of the antebellum

19. J. S. Hornor to W. E. Woodruff, October 10 (quotation), December 12, 1865, in Woodruff Papers; A. N. Carrigan to My Dear Brother, June 2, 1866, August 13, 1867, in Carrigan Papers.

20. R. A. S. Park, ed., *"Dear Parents": The Civil War Letters of the Shibley Brothers of Van Buren* (Fayetteville, 1963); H. Hayes to D. H. Reynolds, October 9, 1864, in D. H. Reynolds Papers, UAF.

21. John W. Brown Diary, May 28, 1865, in AHC.

system were in place and ready to put things back in place. Judge Hornor expressed a typical view of the task facing them when he concluded that "we may ere long get the old order of things properly resumed." The elite set out to do that. Contemporaries soon recognized how little had changed within white society in the state. Wealth continued to be the basis for differentiation among whites; wealth determined class; wealth determined social standing. Enoch K. Miller, an educational supervisor of the American Missionary Association, recognized the persistence of the old system in his travels across the state in 1867. Miller wrote: "Taking one of these long tours you behold human nature in all its phases. You meet the intelligent educated men who dwell for the most part on the rivers, and own large plantations. You meet the unlettered yet industrious poor white men who work small farms in the hills, and you find also the poor 'white trash,' who stay (but can scarcely be said to live) anywhere and everywhere and eke out a miserable existence by fishing, hunting and stealing."[22] Miller's observations indicated how well the old system had survived. The white social world continued to be one in which variations in wealth created remarkably different social groups.

More than the system had survived, however. In 1865 the state's antebellum elite—the very people who had directed its destiny before the war, the wealthy, the large landowners—were still on top, in position to control the economic and political reconstruction of the state. Only the unsettling questions of how to manage labor, restore economic activity, and handle potential class hostility remained to prevent achieving Hornor's goal of getting the old order of things "properly resumed." How the elite handled these issues determined the development of the state for the next century. The leaders of the Old South were the ones who took the state into Reconstruction, the New South, and beyond.

22. J. S. Hornor to W. E. Woodruff, September 21, 1865, in Woodruff Papers; E. K. Miller to J. R. Shipherd, January 15, 1868, in American Missionary Association Papers.

# 10

## RECONSTRUCTION OF POLITICAL POWER
### Arkansas Politics, 1865–1868

THE PERSISTENCE OF THE ANTEBELLUM ELITE ASSURED that they would try to regain political power. The uncertainties of the postwar economy made their control of the government even more imperative. That they could regain power was uncertain, however, because of wartime political changes. The government of Isaac Murphy was in power, supported by the federal government and unsympathetic with the elite and their interests. The war had also undermined the society and the ideas that had made the elite's rule possible. On the other hand, the reconstruction policies of President Andrew Johnson, placing few requirements on the southern states for restoring normal relations within the Union, encouraged them. In the autumn of 1865 the antebellum elite started their effort to recapture political power.

When the war ended, the state government was controlled by Unionists who stood between the old elite and political office. The administration of Governor Isaac Murphy had taken the position that the war should end slavery and make the state government more representative of the interests of the masses of Arkansans. The latter goal was expressed in the election law enacted in May, 1864: it required each elector to take an oath, sometimes called the "test oath," that he had not voluntarily borne arms against the United States or the State of Arkansas and that since April 18, 1864, he had not aided the Confederacy indirectly or directly. Arkansas Unionists thought that only the old leaders had voluntarily supported the war, and the intent of the law was to prevent this class from returning to power.[1]

In setting out to build a party, the Unionists appealed particularly to the lower classes, who they believed had been alienated from the old leadership. Although some poor whites may have provided early support for secession, Unionists concluded that those who did so had been duped by secessionist leaders. The refusal of the secession convention to submit the ordinance of secession to a popular vote convinced them of a conspiracy and allowed

---

1. *New Constitution with the Acts of the General Assembly of the State of Arkansas . . . 1864, 1864–1865, 1865* (Little Rock, 1865), 17.

them to hang on to the belief that most white Arkansans had remained loyal. Looking particularly at the mountain counties, Unionist leaders thought that secession sentiment was dead and that their candidates could be elected to office even if all citizens were allowed to vote. Congressman-elect George H. Kyle summed up their view when he concluded that prewar leaders such as Senator Robert W. Johnson and others who had controlled the destiny of the state could not be elected to any office. Kyle told a congressional committee in February, 1866: "The people are done with such men. . . . I do not believe the people will elect those old politicians and secessionists."[2]

The Unionists recognized, however, that they faced problems in attracting lower-class voters. The potential gains of appealing to class hostility were limited by a factor that crossed class and sectional lines: the experiences of the men who had fought. Despite public assertions to the contrary, Unionist politicians recognized that many former Confederates were not willing to forgive and forget. Kyle recognized the common bond generated by service in the Confederate army when he observed: "I am inclined to think that a great many of the persons who were in the rebel army would vote for a candidate who had believed with them, who had been on their side of the question, as we call it, sooner than they would for me." General James S. Brisbin refused to credit the loyalty of Confederate Arkansans, finding instead "an almost universal disposition among them to elect to all their offices persons, who have served against the government during the late war, and to exclude Union officers and Union men from any participation in public affairs."[3]

Friction between Unionists and Confederates appeared in numerous ways. A common problem was the inability of Unionists to obtain justice in counties where former Confederates regained control of offices. An army inspector who crossed northeastern Arkansas in the fall of 1865 found that "prominent rebels" had already taken over the local civil offices. Colonel W. H. Whipple reported that "their sympathies are with those who have been connected with them in the rebellion, and they show but little regard for that class of men who stood firmly by the government." Local judges enforced civil judgments and criminal indictments rendered by local Confederate courts against Union men in Jackson, Lawrence, and Randolph counties. Unionists found no such help. In Izard County another officer concluded, "It seems to me that here offences . . . are only prosecuted against Union men and not against those who are rebels."[4]

2. *House Reports*, 39th Cong., 1st Sess., No. 30, pp. 53, 74, 80, 119–20, 128, 154.
3. *Ibid.*, 128, 51 (Kyle quotation), 70 (Brisbin quotation).
4. *Ibid.*, *House Miscellaneous Documents*, 39th Cong., 2d Sess., No. 15, p. 2.

An outbreak of violence that began in the fall of 1865 and continued into 1866 destabilized Unionist efforts and was directed primarily at them. The crimes included the murder of Captain Dodson Napier, an officer of an Arkansas Union regiment who was serving as sheriff in Pope County, in October. After that, Adjutant General A. W. Bishop received numerous reports that Union men had been murdered and complaints of personal violence against Unionists from throughout the state. Governor Murphy authorized the organization of Home Guard units to suppress the violence, but the Guards were unsuccessful in ending the disorders. Murphy requested federal troops to carry out the task in January and August, 1866, but not enough were sent to put an end to the virtual civil war. By March, 1866, a resident of Pope County wrote: "The people here were divided during the war. About one fourth going with the Yanks, the people here call them mountain Boomers. A good many of the Boomers have been killed since the war. Some have left and now this is as peaceful country as any." Such actions undermined Union strength and organization.[5]

Despite Confederate loyalty and the violence in the countryside, Unionists believed that they could secure a majority in an election. As part of their strategy, they tried to get support from moderate Democrats as well as from lower-class whites. They courted the moderates by arguing that the Murphy government had President Andrew Johnson's backing, which would facilitate a rapid restoration of normal state-federal relations. Former Confederate general Edward Gantt was among the most active Democrats, encouraging the president to indicate his support of Murphy by pardoning the leaders whose support the Unionists sought. Gantt specifically advocated a pardon for Confederate senator Augustus H. Garland. Unionists urged the president to declare the insurrection at an end in Arkansas and counsel Arkansans to support the Murphy government and constitutional law.[6]

Unionists were secure enough in their position that, at the end of the summer of 1865, Murphy proclaimed an election for Congress for the second Monday of October. He asked Arkansans to select no one who was disqualified by law from holding office and urged citizens to put old issues

5. *House Reports*, 39th Cong., 1st Sess., No. 30, pp. 71, 75, 80, 97, 119; J. E. Lindsay to N. B. Eison, March 16, 1866, in James R. Eison, ed., "A Letter from Dardanelle to Jonesville, South Carolina," *AHQ*, XXVIII (1969), 74.

6. E. W. Gantt to A. Johnson, June 29, July 4, 1864, J. J. Reynolds to Johnson, July 8, 1865, I. Murphy and H. C. Caldwell to Johnson, July 8, 1865, all in Andrew Johnson Papers, LC; Little Rock *Arkansas Gazette*, August 8, 1865; Washington (Ark.) *Telegraph*, August 16, 1865; John W. Brown Diary, July 13, 1865, in AHC; *House Reports*, 39th Cong., 1st Sess. No. 30, pp. 48, 51, 83, 181–82.

behind them. Murphy asked the people to "choose those whose disposition and capacity are to build up and restore. Shun all those whose inclinations lead them to tear down and destroy; we have had enough of that."[7]

Unionists nominated candidates in all three congressional districts. In the Second District, composed primarily of southern counties, they ran Kyle, a prewar Whig who had been in the Tennessee legislature before he moved to Arkansas in 1858. Kyle had opposed secession in 1861. In the Third District, covering the northwestern counties, Unionists put forward Colonel James M. Johnson, commander of the 1st Arkansas Infantry (Union). In the First District, consisting of eastern counties, Unionists divided. They had splintered before the war and could not agree on a candidate now that it was over. Murphy supported the candidacy of Dr. Thomas M. Jacks, who had been elected to Congress in 1864. A splinter group pushed William Byers of Batesville, a "conservative Union man" and prewar district judge who had served as a judge during the war but refused to swear an oath of allegiance to the Confederacy.[8]

Unionists carried on their most organized campaign in the Little Rock district where Kyle ran. On August 29, they held a mass meeting of "National Union Men" at Little Rock. This meeting stated precisely the platform of the Unionists. They asked for the support of all men who regarded "the people of the United States as a great nation, and not as a confederacy of independent States." They insisted that the old leaders must remain disfranchised (although only temporarily) because their return to power would threaten the safety of the state and any chance of obtaining early recognition by the federal government. They recognized emancipation and argued that blacks should have rights, particularly rights of personal security, personal liberty, and private property. With regard to voting, Kyle argued: "Let the future determine the *status* of the negro in this respect." He insisted, however, that white Arkansans accept the fact that "the negroes were free, have been made free by the fortunes of war, and cannot be re-enslaved."[9]

At the National Union meeting in Little Rock the party declared its support for a variety of social and economic programs designed to develop the state. The platform encouraged the creation of educational institution to promote the interests of the people, particularly a "judicious system of

7. Little Rock *Arkansas Gazette*, August 15, 1865.

8. Little Rock *Unconditional Union*, August 10, October 5, 1865; *House Reports*, 39th Cong., 1st Sess., No. 30, pp. 48, 59, 98, 128.

9. *House Reports*, 39th Cong., 1st Sess., No. 30, pp. 54, 55, 51. See also Little Rock *Daily Pantograph*, August 31, 1865; Little Rock *Arkansas Gazette*, August 15, 1865; and Little Rock *Unconditional Union*, August 10, 1865.

free schools." It also advocated policies that would encourage immigration, foster manufacturing and commerce, improve river navigation, and ensure the construction of railroads. Party members were optimistic about opportunities in the state but believed that government must take an active role to bring growth. They concluded: "The State is capable of immense development. The eyes of thousands are already fixed upon it, and whether we will it or not, the capital and industry of the north are coming here."[10]

Despite the limits imposed by disfranchising legislation, Democratic leaders organized a Conservative party to oppose the Union movement that summer. Their strategy included fusion with wartime Unionists who opposed Murphy and his colleagues. They also promoted unity with prewar Whigs. Unionists such as Cincinnatus Vann Meador were put to the front, but behind them were prominent Democrats such as Robert W. Johnson. Whig leader Augustus Garland also actively participated behind the scenes. The coalition avoided appeals to prewar ideologies, instead asking "conservative" men to unite to reclaim control of the government. Like the Unionists, they organized most completely in the Second District. The Unionist candidate Kyle faced five Conservative opponents, including Meador and Lorenzo Gibson, a prominent antebellum Whig.[11]

The Conservatives emphasized the war, race, radicalism, and their own friendship with President Johnson. The problem of the test oath was the central issue. Conservatives protested that the oath was unconstitutional and urged prospective voters to disregard it. The editor of the Washington (Arkansas) Telegraph observed that an unjust law was not "binding upon the consciences and conduct of the people of the State." Other Democrats argued that the president's amnesty of May 29, 1865, restored full political rights, not just property rights, to former Confederates who were not excluded from it. They urged all ex-Confederates to vote in the October election.[12]

An appeal to white racism was also an important part of the Conservative campaign. The party identified Unionism with abolitionism and asserted that a Unionist victory would cause a full-scale race war and the collapse of society. They opposed an expansion of civil rights for blacks, but they particularly objected to extending the right to vote. The editor of the Washington Telegraph, J. R. Eakin, objected to giving the black man the

10. *House Reports*, 39th Cong., 1st Sess., No. 30, pp. 54, 55.
11. Little Rock *Unconditional Union*, August 24, 1865, Washington (Ark.) *Telegraph*, August 23, 1865.
12. Washington (Ark.) *Telegraph*, August 23, September 27, October 4 (quotation), 1865; Little Rock *Arkansas Gazette*, August 31, October 9, September 11, 1865; *House Reports*, 39th Cong., 1st Sess. No. 30, pp. 51, 55.

vote because "he is utterly unfit for it." Some candidates even suggested blacks might be reenslaved. In one speech Meador concluded that he "could not say that slavery might not exist again if the people wanted it." The particular audience for such rhetoric was the state's white poor, who the Conservatives argued would be most affected by an expansion of black rights. The *Telegraph* insisted on support for Conservatives to bring about "the defeat of the wild visionary and oppressive theories of those who, not satisfied with the freedom of the negro, would make slaves and menials of the working men of the South." [13]

Finally, the Conservatives stole part of the Unionist campaign program. They claimed that they, rather than the Unionists, were the true friends of President Johnson. Johnson had called for a reconstruction based on liberality toward the defeated South, and the Conservatives claimed that their ideas matched the president's principles. Supporting Conservative candidates, they maintained, would ensure a rapid restoration of the state to the Union and a return to peaceful government. [14]

The election held on October 9 passed quietly. Many Conservatives stayed away from the polls rather than take the voter's oath, although some election judges refused to administer it. Unionists, however, were dispirited by the rapid resurgence of the Conservatives. The actual turnout was small: about six or seven thousand votes were cast, considerably fewer than in the election held by the Murphy government the previous year. In the First District, William Byers reported that 2,500 votes had been cast and that he had received 1,800 of them. In the highly contested race in the Second District, only 2,500 voters went to the polls, and only 500 of them voted for Kyle. In the Third District no reliable returns were ever received. Explanations for the small vote varied, but in the end, the small turnout caused Congress not to seat the successful candidates. As a result, Arkansas remained outside the Union. [15]

The 1865 election and its result were critical for the state. When Congress refused to recognize the men elected, the Murphy government's claims of a special relationship with Washington were weakened. The election also demonstrated Conservative strength and encouraged their

13. Washington (Ark.) *Telegraph*, August 23 (first quotation), September 6 (second quotation), 1865; Little Rock *Daily Pantograph*, August 17, 31, September 6, 9, 28, 1865; *House Reports*, 39th Cong., 1st Sess., No. 30, p. 51.

14. Little Rock *Arkansas Gazette*, September 4, 11, 1865; Little Rock *Daily Pantograph*, August 27, 1865; Washington (Ark.) *Telegraph*, October 4, 1865.

15. Fort Smith (Ark.) *Weekly New Era*, November 4, October 14, 1865; Little Rock *Arkansas Gazette*, October 11, 1865; *House Reports*, 39th Cong., 1st Sess., No. 30, pp. 51, 57, 82.

organization. Despite disfranchisement, Lorenzo Gibson, a man who could not take the test oath, had received a majority in the Second District. The state election commission overturned the results, but given the restrictions on the franchise, Gibson's showing indicated impressive Conservative strength. Unionists predicted in the spring of 1866 that they could carry the First and Third districts, but the situation was changing rapidly. The old political interests made rapid strides to recapture power.[16]

Following the October election, the Conservatives' organizational efforts intensified. The Little Rock *Daily Pantograph* called for the organization of a "Great Constitutional Party." The new party would support the president's liberal reconstruction policies, align with Johnson in his battle with Congress, and unite all whites against the imposition of black suffrage. The party met in convention at Little Rock on December 11. The delegates invited Generals William T. Sherman and Joseph Reynolds to address them. Sherman advised them to attend to personal affairs, rather than bothering about political matters. They decided to ignore this suggestion and prepared to actively contest future elections.[17]

Conservative optimism was reinforced by a decision in the state supreme court that December declaring the disfranchising law of 1864 unconstitutional. The case of *Rison* et al. v. *Farr* was one of several filed after the October election challenging disfranchisement. Farr, who had not been allowed to vote, argued that the election oath illegally altered the provisions of the 1864 constitution in defining the qualifications of electors. The constitution stated that "every free white male citizen of the United States who shall have attained the age of twenty-one years, and who shall have been a citizen of the state six months next preceding the election, shall be deemed a qualified elector." The Pulaski County Circuit Court and then the state supreme court ruled in favor of Farr. The judgment made it possible for all former Confederates to vote in the next election.[18]

Conservative leaders prepared cautiously for the elections planned for August, 1866. Their strategy remained much the same as it had been, although they focused more on linking themselves to the president in his fight with Congress. Johnson, for political and ideological reasons, adopted a strong stand against congressional efforts to change his reconstruction policies so as to provide better protection to the freedmen. In February,

16. Fort Smith (Ark.) *Weekly New Era*, November 4, 1865; Little Rock *Arkansas Gazette*, October 1, 1865; *House Reports*, 39th Cong., 1st Sess., No. 30, pp. 51, 72.

17. Little Rock *Daily Pantograph*, October 18, November 14, 16, 1865; Augustus H. Garland to Andrew Johnson, October 24, 1865, in Johnson Papers; Little Rock *Arkansas Gazette*, October 23, 26, 1865; Washington (Ark.) *Telegraph*, December 20, 1865.

18. *Rison* et al. v. *Farr*, 24. *Ark. Reports*, 161–76.

1866, he vetoed bills extending the life of the Freedmen's Bureau and defining civil rights on constitutional grounds. In March, he vetoed modified versions of the same bills. The president's actions moved his position closer to the national Democratic party and farther from the Republicans. Conservatives in Arkansas, who were largely Democrats, saw that the president's success would allow them to return to the Union on favorable terms. Johnson also provided them with an issue to stabilize their fragile coalition of Democrats and Whigs—a fight for constitutional liberty. James D. Butler of the *Pantograph* contended: "The great issue is constitutional liberty, based upon popular will, as maintained by President Johnson and the great mass of the people, or concentrated power assumed by the very few who are in public places, in contravention of the Constitution, and for the purpose of domineering over the helpless who are not in power." [19]

In March, Conservatives held demonstrations across the state to show their support for the president. A combined meeting for Arkansas County and Prairie County passed typical resolutions, endorsing the president's policies and his stand in resisting "the storm of fanaticism that threatens the overthrow of the last vestige of Republicanism found on the American continent." Conservatives also supported the president by backing the National Johnson Club's call for a convention at Philadelphia in the summer. The latter move uncovered some of the friction that remained between the Whig and Democratic factions within the Conservative movement when ex-Whig Lorenzo Gibson received a commission to organize a local Johnson Club and appointed only Whigs to attend the convention. Gibson's action led Robert W. Johnson to hold his own convention at Pine Bluff, which nominated only Democrats to the convention. Johnson ultimately withdrew his delegates, but in a letter to his distant cousin the president, he warned that he did not believe the old Whig leaders could be counted on. [20]

The Conservatives used support for the president as their primary campaign issue in the canvass for state offices in the summer of 1866. They and the president, they maintained, had to win to keep Congress from punishing the South with Negro equality and suffrage. Party newspapers de-

19. Little Rock *Daily Pantograph*, February 19, 1866; Van Buren (Ark.) *Press*, March 3, 17, 24, 1866; Little Rock *Arkansas Gazette*, July 19, 1866. For a discussion of affairs in Washington see LaWanda Cox and John H. Cox, *Politics, Principle, and Prejudice, 1865–1866: Dilemma of Reconstruction America* (New York, 1963), David Donald, *The Politics of Reconstruction, 1863–1867* (Baton Rouge, 1965), and Eric L. McKitrick, *Andrew Johnson and Reconstruction* (Chicago, 1960).

20. Van Buren (Ark.) *Press*, March 10, 24, July 21, August 4, 1866; Little Rock *Daily Gazette*, April 13, May 1 (quotation), July 12, 26, 31, 1866; Van Buren (Ark.) *Press*, August 4, July 21, 1866; R. W. Johnson to A. Johnson, July 23, 1866, in Johnson Papers.

manded that Conservative candidates make their positions on national issues clear. John S. Denham, editor of the Van Buren *Press*, declared that he wanted clear statements, that he wanted to know whether candidates were "pig or puppy." William E. Woodruff, Jr., having taken over the *Arkansas Gazette* in early July, warned readers that if they did not support Conservatives, Radical rule would come to pass in the South. "If the President's policy is defeated," he wrote, "it will sound the knell of conservatism."[21]

Support of the president was their central campaign theme, but the Conservatives developed other issues as well. They did not let their appeal to racial fears drop. They insisted that the Murphy government and the Unionists were radicals on the issue of race whose continued power would ensure black suffrage and black equality, both of which they themselves opposed. Their position appealed to those who feared that full black freedom might challenge their own place in society, those who held to antebellum ideas of black inferiority, those who wanted no changes in the antebellum political status quo, and those whose economic interests would not be served by empowering blacks.[22]

A new issue raised in 1866 was the charge that the Murphy government and Unionists were fiscally irresponsible. The Conservatives asserted that the men who supported the Murphy government were the scum of society, seeking to obtain power and impose heavier taxation upon their betters. Murphy's government had created a fiscal crisis, they argued, and the political triumph of the Conservative party was the only means of solving that crisis; they promised tight control over expenditures and a reduction in taxes. The editor of the *Arkansas Gazette* asked citizens to consider only candidates who would overhaul taxes, encouraging them to believe that existing taxes were an onerous burden. "The taxes must be reduced," he wrote, "as they are greater than can be borne."[23]

The charges of radicalism and fiscal irresponsibility undercut the claims of the Murphy administration to exercise legitimate authority. State Conservative leaders may not have intended it, but their rhetoric was used as justification for an escalation of violence against Unionists during the campaigns in the summer of 1866, which in turn worked to the advantage of the Conservatives. In his message to the legislature in November, 1866, Governor Murphy concluded that conditions amounted to a virtual civil war. He summed up the situation:

21. Van Buren (Ark.) *Press*, July 21, 28, 1866; Little Rock *Daily Gazette*, July 19, 1866.
22. Van Buren (Ark.) *Press*, June 30, July 28, 1866.
23. Van Buren (Ark.) *Press*, June 30, July 7, 21, 1866; Little Rock *Daily Gazette*, March 14, 1866.

For a short time, kind and harmonious feelings seemed to be restored between the late warring elements.

A change came slowly, but decidedly; and, during the last three or four months, a proscriptive party spirit has developed itself to an alarming extent, in portions of the State, threatening an appeal to arms, and in a different shape.

In a private letter the governor claimed: "The feeling towards Congress is more hostile than during the war, and hatred of Union soldiers and Union men is a matter of ambitious pride."[24]

The Conservatives quickly developed the advantage in the political fight that took place in 1866. Unionists believed that they had little chance to win. The resources of the elite were arrayed against them. A list of newspapers supporting the National Union Convention at Philadelphia indicates that Conservatives controlled most of the Arkansas press. The only openly Unionist and pro-Murphy newspaper by the summer of 1866 was the Fort Smith *New Era*. Conservatives drew their nominees for the state election from among the antebellum representatives of the elite, the prewar Democratic leaders. A large number of former state officials and wartime political leaders, including Senator Robert W. Johnson, who ran for the state senate, composed the Conservative slate.[25]

Unionists did not respond directly to Conservative charges but argued that President Johnson's victory against Congress was not a foregone conclusion and that the existing state administration offered a clear path to Arkansas' rapid restoration to the Union. The governor asked David Walker to encourage former Confederates to spend their time restoring the state's economy and to "shun all party and political excitement." Political agitation, he perceived, was a very dangerous thing, and he concluded that unless the Conservatives were willing to establish justice at home and secure equal rights to all citizens, the state would not be allowed to return to its normal position within the Union. He noted: "As to affairs at Washington City, we had better let them pass, at present, without much comment. Our position there depends on our behaviour here. . . . If we secure to all the good citizens of the state equal rights, the state is sure to obtain her just rights—in haste."[26]

Unionist efforts indicated, however, that the leadership was disheartened. Organization for the campaign did not begin until June, when a

24. *Arkansas House Journal, Seventeenth Legislature*, 30; I. Murphy to J. M. Tebbetts, February 26, 1866, in *House Reports*, 39th Cong., 1st Sess., No. 30, p. 154.

25. Little Rock *Daily Gazette*, July 24, 1866; Memphis *Daily Argus*, August 10, 1866.

26. I. Murphy to D. Walker, May 16, 1866, in A. Howard Stebbins Collections, AHC.

Union League club organized in Van Buren County. A "Radical" party organized in Sebastian County the next month. Unionists confined their efforts largely to the western part of the state, where they again nominated Colonel James Johnson for Congress in the Third District and several members for the legislature in the Fort Smith and Van Buren districts. Johnson announced that he was a Radical Unionist and ran on a platform that advocated the enfranchisement of blacks as the only means that would allow loyal Arkansans to maintain control of their state and local governments. In the Second District, George Kyle again ran as a Unionist candidate. In the First, William Byers, who had won the vote as a Unionist in 1865, tried again for the district's congressional seat, but this time he moved toward the Conservatives and ran as a supporter of President Johnson against Dr. P. Van Patten, a former Confederate. At the local level the Unionists ran few men for legislative or county positions.[27]

Realizing that they would lose the election and control of state government, Unionists sought congressional intervention. General Edward W. Gantt publicly stated at Washington, D.C., that he thought Arkansans had not accepted the results of the war and had shown their attitude in the election. Governor Murphy believed the same thing. In a letter to a friend, Murphy predicted that the "rebel element" would have full control of the election except in a few northwestern counties. The tone of the Conservatives had become "venomous and disloyal."[28]

Election results confirmed Unionist fears. The Conservatives swept to victory. In the First Congressional District, Byers defeated Van Patten, but his victory offered little encouragement to the Unionists because of his overtures to the Conservatives. In the Second District, Conservative Anson W. Hobson defeated another Conservative after the regular Unionist candidate, Kyle, withdrew from the race disputing the legality of the election. In the Third District, former congressman Alfred B. Greenwood easily defeated Colonel Johnson, who carried only Sebastian County. The three positions on the state supreme court went to Freeman W. Compton, a member of the Confederate state court; David Walker, who had abandoned his Unionism to support the Confederate state government; and John J. Clendenin, a prewar attorney general and circuit court judge who had represented Governor Flanagin in efforts to have the Confederate state government recognized in 1865. William R. Miller, Confederate state auditor, gained that position again. Of the better-known members elected

27. Van Buren (Ark.) *Press*, June 30, July 21, 1866; Little Rock *Daily Gazette*, July 7, 14, August 4, 1866.
28. Little Rock *Daily Gazette*, August 4, 1866; I. Murphy to D. H. Bingham, August 2, 1866, quoted *ibid.*, August 22, 1866.

to the twenty-five seats in the state senate, three had served in the Confederate legislature, one had been a Confederate brigadier general, and three had served as colonels of Confederate regiments.[29]

To contemporaries, the Conservative victory meant the old leadership was back in power. From Crittenden County, a Unionist reported a quiet election in which "all the 'elect' were active co-workers in the late (so-called) 'lost cause.'" At Fayetteville, Unionists met to discuss means to protect themselves after the election of "notorious rebels and bushwhackers to the various offices." In a note to General E. O. C. Ord, Governor Murphy recognized Confederate political successes throughout the state and complained that the murder and harassment of Union men had begun. Reluctant to organize the militia because of the internal conflict such a move might cause, he asked instead for mounted troops from the United States Army to be sent to various points. The Conservative editor William E. Woodruff, Jr., assessed members of the incoming legislature as men "who have been prominent in our state for their natural abilities and personal merit. In view of the peculiar state of affairs, it is a matter of congratulation that so much of our best talent will be assembled in the next Legislature." The editor of the Little Rock *Conservative*, started by former senator Robert W. Johnson in the summer of 1866, called the same men "reliable, conservative, and public spirited." The antebellum elite appeared to have regained the power lost with military defeat.[30]

The election showed Conservative strength. More than 34,000 votes were cast on August 9, 1866, five to six times more than in 1865. Few Unionists voted. Kyle's withdrawal and Byers' association with Conservatives blurred the results in the First and Second districts. In the Third, however, Colonel Johnson received only about 30 percent of the vote, and most of his support was extremely localized. Sebastian County provided him a majority. Pope County gave him his next highest percentage—40 percent. Elsewhere, his strength was limited. In Benton County, Johnson's total was only 3 percent of the ballots cast. Even in the areas that they had expected to carry, Unionists had a small showing.[31]

The victorious Conservative coalition moved quickly to stabilize condi-

29. Little Rock *Daily Gazette*, October 9, 1866. Comparisons of elected officials are in Janice Wegner, ed., *Historical Report of the Secretary of State of Arkansas, 1978* (3 vols.; Little Rock, 1978), I, "Historical Roster of County Officials."

30. Fort Smith (Ark.) *Weekly New Era*, September 5, 1866; Memphis *Daily Argus*, August 18, 1866; Isaac Murphy to E. O. C. Ord, August, 1866, in L. C. Gulley Collection, AHC; Little Rock *Daily Gazette*, November 3, 1866; Little Rock *Daily Conservative*, November 1, 1866.

31. Based on returns published in Little Rock *Daily Gazette*.

tions that threatened them and property in the state. The Conservative majority in the Sixteenth General Assembly, in session from November 5, 1866, to March 23, 1867, acted in behalf of the state's major propertied interests and Confederate constituents. Democrats and Whigs put aside disagreement over means in order to achieve ends they both desired. Much of their activity provided relief to their constituents from the burdens created by the war. The legislators passed several bills helping Confederate soldiers and officials. One bill dedicated 10 percent of the state's revenues to a fund to support wounded and disabled Confederate soldiers. The General Assembly passed another law that pardoned and granted amnesty to Confederate soldiers who had taken actions liable to prosecution, with the exception of rape, if done while serving in the army or acting as an official of the Confederate government. The Conservatives in the legislature passed both bills over Governor Murphy's veto.[32]

A major concern of landowners was tax relief. The tax bill approved on January 21 reduced state taxes to one-half of 1 percent and county taxes to a maximum of 1 percent on assessed valuation. The same act also eliminated the three-dollar-per-acre minimum evaluation on land and required that land be assessed at "true" value. Another bill exempted taxpayers from having to pay any state or county taxes levied prior to 1865 and provided landowners relief from paying the backlog of taxes that had built up during the war.[33]

The General Assembly also provided protection for debtors. One bill relieved the obligation of those indebted to the common-school fund, the internal improvement fund, and all other state and county public funds. The bill, passed over the governor's veto, also recognized the validity of payments made in Arkansas war bonds or treasury notes or Confederate States treasury notes made between May 6, 1861, and January 1, 1865. Another relief measure provided that in addition to written agreements, verbal agreements would be accepted in proceedings determining whether contracts intended that payments for debts be made in Confederate money or paper currency. If a debtor could prove that a contract had assumed payment in Confederate money, the debt could be paid in the value of that money at the time of the contract. The General Assembly also extended the state's exemption law, prohibiting the sale under execution of most household property, a family's home, and the lot upon which the home stood.[34]

32. *Acts of Arkansas, 1866*, 90–96, 169; Little Rock *Daily Gazette*, October 12, 1866; Little Rock *Daily Conservative*, November 1, 15, 24, December 3, 1866.

33. *Acts of Arkansas, 1866*, 67–68, 96.

34. *Ibid.*, 170–72, 195–96.

The General Assembly devoted considerable attention to measures intended to regulate the state's labor system. On the surface, the law appeared to be fair. It required that all contracts for a period longer than one month be made in writing. It gave the laborer and employer a lien upon the product raised or manufactured as surety against labor done or supplies advanced. If a laborer abandoned an employer prior to the expiration of a contract, he was liable for the full amount that would have been provided up to the end of the contract, and the employer could recover that amount from future wages. If an employer dismissed a worker without good cause, the laborer had the right to take out of the goods produced full restitution for the work done. The problem with the law was that jurisdiction on labor issues was placed in the hands of local justices of the peace, men who were usually allies of local landlords. That aspect of the law gave landowners a powerful tool in dealing with laborers.[35]

The actions of the legislature showed that although the Conservatives represented the traditional sources of power within the state, they were not completely reactionary. The war had brought some basic changes in the attitudes of political leaders about the role of government. Perhaps because of the crisis they faced, the Conservatives turned to the state government to encourage economic development. Particularly revolutionary was a bill allowing the state to provide financial support to private enterprises. After two decades of conflict over using the state's resources to aid railroads, the legislators advanced an ambitious plan to bail out the existing roads and to give them and new companies financial backing that would speed the laying of rails. The General Assembly confirmed previous charters, allowing the roads to claim lands allocated to them by Congress prior to the war. The legislators also extended the time allowed to these roads to begin construction, to ensure reception of federal funds. The railroads received further relief with a bill that approved payment on loans from public funds in depreciated wartime money at the full dollar value.[36]

The most radical of these measures was direct funding of railroad construction. The first bill passed by the legislature allowed counties and cities to issue coupon bonds bearing interest up to 10 percent per annum to purchase stocks in the Iron Mountain and Helena road. A second bill gave any railroad that had completed forty miles of track $10,000 for each mile, in the form of 8-percent state bonds. For each additional ten-mile section, the company could obtain $10,000 per mile more. Such support potentially involved the state in issuing hundreds of thousands of dollars in bonds. State

35. *Ibid.*, 298–300; Little Rock *Daily Conservative*, October 30, 1866.
36. *Acts of Arkansas, 1866*, 57–64, 87–88, 189–95, 170–72, 303–304, 409–15.

losses from these bonds were to be minimized, however, as the General Assembly reserved to the state the first lien on the property, rights, and credit of companies that received state aid.[37]

Governor Murphy vetoed the second bill with a message that would have done credit to his prewar Democratic predecessors. Murphy protested that these bonds would create an enormous potential debt and destroy the credit of the state: "If all the projected railroads in the State should bring themselves within the terms of this act, the people would be saddled with an amount of debt that would cripple the energies of the State for generations, without any corresponding benefit to the State, as the depreciation of the bonds would be such that their influence would not advance the completion of any of the contemplated roads an hour." The assembly wanted no more of prewar caution, however. By a vote of 43 to 11 they overrode the governor's veto.[38]

The new attitude toward government also focused on diversifying the state's economy. Part of the program was aimed at encouraging development by creating a favorable tax climate. One bill gave any cotton or woolens factory constructed within three years of April 1, 1867, a five-year tax exemption. More critically, however, the assembly moved to solve the state's debt problem in order to restore state credit so that new bonds could be issued to support internal improvements and manufacturing enterprises. The assembly set up a commission charged with refunding the state debt by issuing new bonds. Retiring the bonds that had been issued to the State Bank and the Real Estate Bank meant that state credit would be stronger and that the state, rather than the bondholders, could gain control over the assets put up as collateral against these bonds.[39]

Attitudes toward the railroads, diversification, and the state's role in these areas was new. Wartime experiences forced changes in perspectives, linking prewar Democrats and Whigs and submerging the differences between them. In 1866 the editorial pages of Robert Johnson's Little Rock *Conservative* and Woodruff's *Arkansas Gazette* could have been written by the same editor, despite their prewar political differences. On railroads, Woodruff counseled that "no argument is necessary to convince the most cautious skeptic that railroads are the source of incalculable wealth, and that there is not a possibility of losing a dollar invested in them." At virtually the same time, Johnson's paper concluded: "We are for railroads and for State aid." The new Conservative coalition looked to the future in their

37. *Ibid.*, 100–101, 428–32.
38. *Arkansas House Journal, Sixteenth Legislature*, 946–49, 962.
39. *Acts of Arkansas, 1866*, 166–67, 488–91; Little Rock *Daily Gazette*, December 11, 1866.

policies. Taxes might increase, but the Conservatives believed that the benefits to the overall economy, in terms of expansion of the tax base caused by economic growth, would make any short-term problems acceptable.[40]

The war had helped cause this shift. As one man writing to the *Conservative* stated: " 'We should learn even from our enemies.' And we of the South should learn as soon as possible, that the North has become rich and great by manufacturing wool, cotton, and everything else, even down to wooden nutmegs and axe handles, and we should profit by their example." Woodruff wrote in a similar vein: "Our people, during the war, traveled about the country considerably and all have learned to appreciate the difference between the energetic man and the laggard, whether in the army or in civilian life." A letter to the *Conservative* put it more directly, insisting that "the times have changed, and if we are wise we will change with them." Another letter to the same paper explained the change: "I believe the late disastrous war has, perhaps, done some good, in this, that our people are more united, more public spirited, and feel a greater interest in those measures which will redound to the interest of the whole state." The state's leaders emerged from the war with changed minds on issues that had limited antebellum development.[41]

The Conservatives won in 1866, but before they could implement their political program the battle between the president and Congress came to a head. Johnson's National Union movement failed. National Republican politicians disagreed about how to proceed with reconstruction, but Johnson's failure and Republican gains in the 1866 elections indicated that most northerners wanted a harsher policy, and this perceived desire resulted in congressional intervention. The Thirty-ninth Congress took up reconstruction measures in December, 1866.[42]

Congressional intervention in the South ended the restoration of antebellum political leadership. On March 2, 1867, moderate and radical Republicans passed a reconstruction bill that was vetoed by the president, then passed over his veto on the same day. The bill divided all of the southern states except Tennessee among five military districts and declared their existing civil governments to be provisional. To have their representatives readmitted into Congress, these states had to call constitutional conven-

40. Little Rock *Daily Gazette*, December 6, 18, 1866; Little Rock *Daily Conservative*, December 3, 1866.

41. Little Rock *Daily Conservative*, October 11, 1866; Little Rock *Daily Gazette*, October 5, 1866; Little Rock *Daily Conservative*, November 3, 27, 1866.

42. For a discussion of the failure of the Johnson movement and the outcome of his struggle with Congress, see Eric Foner, *Reconstruction: America's Unfinished Revolution, 1863–1877* (New York, 1988), 261–67.

tions, write constitutions that included black suffrage, and ratify those constitutions and the Fourteenth Amendment. The Fourteenth Amendment, emerging out of the Civil Rights Act of 1866, defined national citizenship and prohibited the states from abridging the rights of citizenship without due process of law, making unlawful any laws discriminating among citizens on the basis of race. It also disqualified from holding office persons who had taken an oath to support the Constitution and subsequently had broken that oath. Under the Reconstruction Act, those disallowed from holding office by the Fourteenth Amendment were not allowed to vote for delegates to the constitutional conventions or upon the constitutions themselves.[43]

Conservative political hegemony had been overturned. In other areas, however, the people behind the Conservative politicians had reestablished control that would not be challenged. Securing their labor force and beginning economic reconstruction were essential as they emerged from the destruction of the war. In these areas they moved as quickly as they had toward political restoration. Their efforts did more to create the conditions that formed Arkansas for the rest of the nineteenth century than any particular destruction visited upon the state by the Civil War.

43. For the development of the Congressional Reconstruction program, see *ibid.*, 271–80.

# 11

## RESTRICTIONS ON BLACK FREEDOM, 1865–1867
### From Slavery to Tenantry

THE POSTWAR YEARS BROUGHT CONTINUED CHANGES IN the social and economic positions of the freedmen as they moved from slavery to freedom. Their place emerged out of a struggle between blacks seeking the fullest freedom possible and whites determined to deny that freedom and protect their own economic and social interests. That struggle was not an equal one. Slavery and the war had left the freedmen with few economic resources other than their labor. Whites, on the other hand, held the chief economic assets, particularly the land. Adding to the forces at work were the operations of the Freedmen's Bureau. Charged with protecting the interests of the former slaves, the bureau in fact offered only limited help because of its meager funding and the restrictions imposed by the attitudes of the national government and individual bureau agents. The interplay of the freedmen, local whites, and the Freedmen's Bureau produced a place for blacks in society that was somewhere between slavery and full freedom, a freedom that was always restricted.

Freedom for blacks at the end of the war meant that they should have been able at least to move about as free laborers, selling their labor to the highest bidder. Contemporary reports recording a flood of former slaves from rural areas into towns and cities seem to suggest that the freedmen exercised that right. As conspicuous as this movement was, however, it did not reflect what took place for the majority of blacks. Towns in fact offered few opportunities. Jobs were unavailable, especially with the departure of Federal troops. In addition, the army discouraged blacks' relocation to towns. Economic survival meant that the majority of freedmen had to make some sort of labor arrangement with local landowners. The majority settled down where they were and worked for their former master or the master's neighbors, at least during the first years of freedom. Anthony Taylor was typical. A slave on a plantation in Clark County owned by a man named Bullock, Taylor recalled that "we stayed on the old plantation for seven or eight years before we had sense enough or knowed enough to get away from there and git something for ourselves."[1]

Whites recognized the essential economic limits on the freedmen, despite their open concern about the dislocation of blacks in 1865. Individual whites acknowledged the basic immobility of the freedmen when they recognized the role that their former servants played in helping reestablish farm operations after the war. Both large planters and small farmers had similar experiences. Andrew Carrigan, on his small plantation in Hempstead County, was able to start farming again in 1865 because some of his former slaves remained with him to gather the crops in the field at the end of the war. John Brown of Camden congratulated himself that many of his servants had remained with him and that he had suffered no interruption about his home. General John W. Sprague of the Freedmen's Bureau perceived the economic constraints on the freedmen when he denied that they were forsaking the farm and flocking to towns. Sprague reported: "They are somewhat *bewildered* by their sudden change from slavery to freedom; but very few, indeed, are willing to be paupers."[2]

Restricted mobility did not mean that there was no movement at all. The editor of the *Arkansas Gazette* observed: "Many of the colored population seem to think that their freedom is not complete unless they get sight of the commanding officer of some military post." Some former slaves did leave, like those on Mary Eskridge's plantation in eastern Arkansas, who "scattered—here and there to find better times." Although it did not take place on a large scale, movement confirmed whites in their fears that blacks would not work as free men. The editor of the *Ouachita Herald* commented that at Camden "the negro, his faults, his laziness, his thefts and impudence form the popular theme of discussion in every crowd." Otis Hackett, an Episcopal priest at Helena, found that the labor question "perplexes and staggers the most hopeful." Hackett believed with most other whites: "As their own masters they [the freedmen] are restless, shiftless, and idle. They

1. Little Rock *Daily Gazette,* July 6, 1865; General Orders, No. 68, June 30, 1865, *ibid.;* John W. Brown Diary, June 13, 29, 30, July 6, 1865, in AHC; *House Reports,* 39th Cong., 1st Sess., No. 30, pp. 52, 154; *AS/AN,* Vol. X, Pt. 6, p. 259 (quotation)—see also Vol. VIII, Pt. 1, 147, Pt. 2, pp. 171, 341, Vol. IX, Pt. 3, pp. 24, 30, Vol. X, Pt. 5, pp. 47, 219, Pt. 6, pp. 15, 165.

2. A. N. Carrigan to My Dear Brother, in John W. Carrigan Papers, DU; Brown Diary, July 11, 1865; *Senate Executive Documents,* 39th Cong., 1st Sess., No. 27, p. 138; see also *House Reports,* 39th Cong., 1st Sess, No. 30, p. 77.

are slow to learn that there can be any connexion between liberty and labor."[3]

These racial attitudes created the framework within which whites developed their own beliefs about what freedom should mean for the freedmen. They were willing to grant certain basic rights. Witnesses before Congress noted that the state constitution of 1864 granted basic civil rights—including the rights to make contracts, sue and be sued, acquire and dispose of property—and that most whites accepted these. In addition, most whites favored some sort of educational opportunities for blacks. William Byers reported that whites wanted black schools, so long as they were separated racially. General Sprague reported in January, 1866, that many planters had established schools on their plantations at the request of the freedmen, some doing it grudgingly, others willingly. Bureau officials recognized that this phenomenon involved considerable self-interest on the part of the planters, who by providing schools could acquire more workers. At the same time, the planter could control education on the plantation school, ensuring that the freedmen would receive lessons that would make them more pliant workers.[4]

There was, however, almost total opposition to extending the basic political right of the vote. Unionist politicians attributed this resistance to poor whites who feared that blacks might be manipulated if they had the vote. Yet even those Unionists who considered the possibility of extending limited suffrage based on educational or property qualifications believed that their stance would divide their own party. S. R. Harrington, who had served in Arkansas as an officer of the 5th Kansas Cavalry, found that qualified suffrage had a respectable number of supporters but unqualified suffrage had few. "There is a strong prejudice against the colored man in that respect," he noted.[5]

Whites assumed that direct control was necessary to make free blacks

3. Little Rock *Daily Gazette*, July 6, 1865; Mary B. Eskridge to William E. Woodruff, May 30 (quotation), August 29, 1866, M. L. Bell to Woodruff, October 12, 1865, January 3, 1866, all in William E. Woodruff Papers, AHC; *House Reports*, 39th Cong., 1st Sess., No. 30, pp. 74, 75, 81, 99, 126, 154, 155, 169; *Ouachita Herald* (Camden, Ark.) quoted in Little Rock *Daily Gazette*, August 9, 1866; Lou to Dear Cynthia, 1866, in Earle-Ward Family Papers, AHC; "Missionary Report, January 1, 1866," in Otis Hackett, "Excerpts from the Diaries and Letters of Reverend Otis Hackett," *Phillips County Historical Quarterly*, I (1962), 38–39.

4. *House Reports*, 39th Cong., 1st Sess., No. 30, pp. 53, 58–59, 81; *Senate Executive Documents*, 39th Cong., 1st Sess., No. 27, p. 28; *Report of the Commissioner of the Bureau of Refugees, Freedmen, and Abandoned Lands for the Year 1867* (Washington, D.C., 1867), 68.

5. *House Reports*, 39th Cong., 1st Sess., No. 30, pp. 53, 58, 72, 75, 81, 120 (quotation), 155.

good laborers again and to make coexistence with them in society possible. General James Brisbin concluded that Arkansans still believed some sort of coercive system was essential to secure labor. Brisbin observed, "I think many of the people entertain the belief that if the State was once more in operation under a State government, and in full practical relation with the federal government of the United States, and they had all the civil officers they are entitled to, they could then regulate the black population by a system of vagrant laws amounting to slavery."[6]

Whites also continued to believe that physical force was necessary to ensure labor and conformance to contracts. Former Confederate general Gantt, a Freedmen's Bureau agent in Hempstead County, carried on an educational campaign to convince his neighbors that "*bodily coercion* fell as an incident of slavery." Although some conceded his point, Gantt found that "others growl and wish to be allowed to *enforce* their contracts, the simple English of which is to '*whip the nigger*.' " The meaning of a Jefferson County planter was clear when he complained of the influence of black troops stationed at a nearby post and stated his hope, "if ever we get clear of the negro troops to be able to get them a little under discipline."[7]

Whites desired to limit freedom for the former slaves, but the freedmen wanted freedom in its fullest sense. By 1865, at least among black political leaders, full freedom meant control over their own labor and economic independence. Despite recurring rumors that the government might provide them with land and help—the proverbial "forty acres and a mule"—those who understood the situation had no illusion that this would happen. Instead, they focused on actions that would help them to help themselves. How that was to be done had been considered in the areas under Union control at the end of the war. In the first years of peace, blacks emphasized education, protection from violence, fair treatment in labor relations, and acquisition of land as their primary goals, providing themselves with the tools necessary for economic independence.

The belief in the importance of education had been apparent among the freedmen in the latter years of the war. All observers saw the continued strength of this belief. The efforts of the Freedmen's Bureau and private agencies were limited by inadequate funds and a shortage of teachers, but where they did establish schools, the freedmen attended eagerly, particularly in the towns. Visitors to the Little Rock schools found the buildings full to capacity and the students well motivated. August Strickland, a teacher

6. *Ibid.*, 70.
7. *Report of the Commissioner of the Bureau of Refugees, Freedmen, and Abandoned Lands for the Year 1867*, 28 (Gantt's emphasis); M. L. Bell to W. E. Woodruff, October 12, 1865, in Woodruff Papers.

in a freedmen's school in Jefferson County, believed that the amazing progress the freedmen demonstrated resulted from their desire for education. He reported: "I never saw people learn so fast. It generally took me three months to teach what they learn in ten or fifteen days. But I am satisfied the difference is caused by more intense application."[8]

The freedmen wanted education because they believed it was essential for individual advancement. As long as they lacked education, they were condemned to manual labor on the plantations and farms and in the towns, and they desired other opportunities. Delegates to a Convention of Colored Citizens in Little Rock on November 30, 1865, asked that the state legislature educate their children. They did not challenge white beliefs that blacks should remain at the bottom of society, but they argued that the future prosperity of the entire state could not "afford to rest upon ignorant labor." Education of the black work force improved the chances for statewide economic growth, according to the delegates. Of course, economic development promised to change their own opportunities and conditions.[9]

The freedmen also believed that they had to have protection. For most blacks this meant that they be allowed to work and be treated fairly on the job. It also meant defense against violence. They thought government recognition of their full legal and political equality was the best way to secure that end. William H. Grey of Phillips County stated this desire in a speech before the Convention of Colored Citizens: "We don't want anybody to swear for us or to vote for us; we want to exercise those privileges for ourselves; and we have met here . . . to ask the people of Arkansas . . . to give us those rights. By giving us those rights they will give peace and quiet to the State." In the convention's memorial to the state legislature and Congress, the delegates stated their belief that protection would come only when they had equal rights before the law and representation in government. They petitioned the government to "clothe us with the power of self protection by giving us our equality before the law and the right of suffrage."[10]

Acquisition of land was the third essential goal seen by blacks. They impressed observers with their desire to have property. The freedmen saved as much money as they could to buy their own land, and some actually purchased it in the first year after the war. Obtaining land made the

8. *House Reports*, 39th Cong., 1st Sess., No. 30, pp. 80–81, 99, 126, 77, 74, 126; A. C. Strickland to Dear Brother Shipard, July 9, 1867, in American Missionary Association Papers, ARC.

9. *Proceedings of the Convention of Colored Citizens of the State of Arkansas, Held in Little Rock, Thursday, Friday, and Saturday, November 30, December 1, and 2* (Helena, Ark., 1866), 11.

10. *Ibid.*, 7, 10; *House Reports*, 39th Cong., 1st Sess., No. 30, pp. 70, 72, 74.

freedmen independent of the control of the landowners and gave them the freedom to direct their own destinies. Their perception of the relationship between land and freedom was expressed by a freedman in a conversation with a Union officer at Fort Smith. The officer asked what the freedman needed, if freedom alone was not enough. The freedman replied, "Yes, sir, you set me free, but you left me there." "What do you want?" the officer repeated. "I want some land," the freedman told him. "I am helpless; you do nothing for me but give me freedom." "Is that not enough?" "It is enough for the present; but I cannot help myself unless I get some land; then I can take care of myself and family; otherwise, I cannot do it."[11]

Their different views of black freedom placed black laborers and white landowners at odds immediately. In 1865, the Freedmen's Bureau was the intermediary between the two, and its policies and the activities of its agents helped to determine how the conflict was resolved. Congress charged the bureau with the massive task of supervising all abandoned lands and controlling all subjects relating to refugees and freedmen. The bureau's mission included the important task of overseeing the labor contracts and educational activities pertaining to the freedmen. The bureau was under the control of the army.

In June, 1865, General Sprague assumed duties as assistant commissioner of the Freedmen's Bureau assigned to the district of Missouri and Arkansas, and he initiated bureau work in Arkansas. In October, 1865, the district was reduced to include only Arkansas, and Sprague established his head-quarters at Little Rock. In circulars No. 15 and 16, issued on October 25 and 26, 1865, Sprague instructed local officers in their duties and indicated the critical role that the bureau had assumed in adjusting the relationship between whites and blacks, between landlords and workers. In addition to local bureau agents' work in restoring or otherwise disposing of abandoned lands, Sprague encouraged them to establish schools in rural districts and on plantations. He also published guidelines for contracts that agents would negotiate between the freedmen and landowners, and admonished agents not to interfere with contracts unless the freedmen were being wronged. Sprague also appointed superintendents "empowered to administer justice," who were to be "governed by the laws now in force in Arkansas, except so far as these laws make a distinction on account of color"; the last clause was necessary because state law prevented blacks from equal access to the civil courts.[12]

As bureau operations developed, the agency's regulations imposed limits

11. *House Reports*, 39th Cong., 1st Sess., No. 30, pp. 77 (the quoted conversation), 81, 99; *Senate Executive Documents*, 39th Cong., 2d Sess., No. 6, p. 30.

12. *House Executive Documents*, 39th Cong., 1st Sess., No. 70, pp. 67, 73, 75–78, 77.

upon the freedmen that were much like those desired by whites. Although individual agents and assistant commissioners were often sympathetic with the freedmen, overall policy restricted what could be done to help. Black desire for land was dashed when President Andrew Johnson restored property rights to former rebels under the terms of his general and special pardons. White landowners complained that the bureau did not return the land fast enough, but in fact the agency returned it as fast as the owners could prove that they had always been loyal citizens or that they had received a presidential pardon. Freedmen who had been farming these lands were allowed to gather their crops, but then they had to leave. In his report issued in October, 1866, Sprague reported that the bureau had returned 105 dwellings and 95,443 acres of land to prewar owners. Still registered were only 32 houses and 29,838 acres of land. The surrender of abandoned lands deprived the bureau of its only major source of revenue, which created additional problems, since the loss of income further restricted the agency's ability to help the freedmen.[13]

Limited funding meant that bureau efforts to create schools for the freedmen were inadequate. Without a sure source of revenue, the work depended upon benevolence. Sprague appealed to "intelligent and Christian citizens" to assist in educating the freedmen, but the response was not good. In its history, the bureau never had more than thirty-six teachers at one time for all its schools in Arkansas. School operations in 1866 cost only twelve thousand dollars, two-thirds of which was raised by northern benevolent organizations; the other third came from the students, who were charged fifty cents a month to attend. Despite the desire by bureau officials, teachers, and freedmen for more schools, few students ever had access to a schoolhouse. For the 1865–1866 school year, the superintendent reported an average attendance throughout the state of only 1,233 students. The system peaked in 1868, when, excluding those students attending Sabbath school, enrollment reached 1,672. As with the wartime school effort, the resources dedicated to education were inadequate to the huge task, and the bureau schools only scratched the surface.[14]

Conditions within the state sharpened the dilemma faced by bureau school officials. Despite the freedmen's desire for education, economic pressure forced many of them to abandon hopes of education in order to provide for themselves. Julia Fortenberry went to a school in Ashley County, but only for four seasons and only during "vacation" when the

13. *Ibid.*, 71; *Senate Executive Documents*, 39th Cong., 2d Sess., No. 6, p. 24.

14. *House Executive Documents*, 39th Cong., 1st Sess., No. 70, p. 78; *Senate Executive Documents*, 39th Cong., 2d Sess., No. 6, pp. 28–29; John W. Alvord, *Sixth Semi-Annual Report on Schools for Freedmen, July, 1868* (Washington, D.C., 1868), 46.

family was not farming. A slave from Jefferson County wanted to attend school. He remembered: "I went about a month after peace was declared. Then papa died and mama took me out and put me in the field." John Jones, from another Arkansas River plantation, attended school for only seven days; then, being the oldest boy in the family, he "had to plow." Either schools were unavailable or the prospective students did not have the leisure to attend.[15]

The limited potential for blacks to acquire either land or an education presented major barriers to their economic development, imposing restrictions on black freedom that served the interests of local whites. The contract system of labor developed during the war and used by the bureau afterward, however, proved to be the chief means that helped landowners restore a measure of control over the freedmen. Under the administration of local bureau agents, laborers and employers signed written contracts for periods of not longer than one year. Terms were to be negotiated by laborer and employer without bureau intervention. The bureau did assure adherence to contracts. A lien upon crops was security for the laborer's wages. At the same time, the local agent was to ensure that workers complied with contracts. The bureau's attitude toward compliance was much like that of the landowners. Sprague ordered agents to inform the laborer that "he is to work under the direction of his employer; that he is to render good and faithful service, and not leave the plantation or place of his employment in working hours without permission, unless he is treated with cruelty."[16]

At first the system appeared to work well. The freedmen negotiated contracts in early 1866 that promised very high wages, largely due to a shortage of workers. Bureau officials believed the freedmen would make profits and be able to save part of their income. In January, 1866, Sprague reported that first-class hands received wages of twenty dollars per month and board, cabins, fuel, medicine, and medical treatment. Other reports noted pay as high as twenty-five dollars per month plus living provisions for good field hands, and fifteen dollars per month for women who could work in the fields. Generally these rates were comparable to those for white laborers and made possible greater savings than in other states. General James Brisbin told the Congressional Reconstruction Committee: "They save their money, and I believe some of them will become very wealthy men. I know a great many negroes in Arkansas who have made from $700

---

15. *AS/AN,* Vol. VIII, Pt. 1, p. 64, Pt. 2, p. 329 (Fortenberry), Vol. IX, Pt. 3, p. 199, Pt. 4, p. 150 (Jones), Vol. X, Pt. 5, pp. 26, 121.

16. *House Executive Documents,* 39th Cong., 1st Sess., No. 70, pp. 77–78.

to $800 and $1,000, and in rare cases $1,500 during last year [1865], by growing cotton on shares with their former masters."[17]

Planters seemed pleased with the new system after their experiences with it in 1865, and bureau agents thought that relations between the freedmen and landowners were more amicable than elsewhere in the South. The shortage of workers was believed responsible, at least in part, for this situation. The bureau's agents believed that landowners would not take advantage of their workers because they needed them and could not replace them. One former Union officer thought that the planters realized "what is really the case, that if they fail to treat the negroes kindly they will be unable to secure their services in the future." How much the planters' acceptance reflected acquiescence and how much it represented a wait-and-see attitude are hard to determine. Few employers found the bureau to be a problem, at least initially. Agents provided what local landowners wanted, namely, some means of forcing blacks to work. One planter thought the bureau unnecessary but conceded that the majority of people had no objections to it and that "honestly administered, it promptly settles disputes between master and servant, fixes wages, gives both an inexpensive court of appeal in the nature of arbitration, and, in the existing condition of the African race, affords certainty to labor and investment."[18]

In practice, bureau agents often favored planters and farmers over laborers. Sprague's orders made clear his interest in restoring economic activity in the state, and agents accepted contracts that allowed landowners to exercise extensive power over their workers. Agents had little concern other than that the contracts be signed and adhered to. The primary test of fairness was that the worker receive a just return for the work. Most of the contracts made in the winter of 1865–1866 contained few explicit provisions concerning planter-worker relations, but those that did showed what planters expected of the system and what the bureau would accept. The contracts signed by workers on the Peter McCollum plantation in Ouachita County imposed restrictions on the freedmen typical of an ante-bellum plantation. McCollum provided his workers with housing, rations, medical attention, and clothing. In turn, they worked under his direction. They were to rise at daylight and feed the stock; they were to go to the fields at a half hour after sunup; they had three-quarters of an hour for

17. *Senate Executive Documents,* 39th Cong., 1st Sess., No. 27, p. 28; *House Reports,* 39th Cong., 1st Sess., No. 30, pp. 74, 77, 80, 81, 126, 51, 71 (quotation), 72.

18. *House Reports,* 39th Cong., 1st Sess., No. 30, pp. 99, 120, 126 (first quotation), 52, 58, 70, 80 (second quotation); *House Executive Documents,* 39th Cong., 1st Sess., No. 11, p. 32.

lunch in the winter and one and a half to two hours in the summer. They were to have no visitors and were prohibited from using indecent language, swearing, or being impudent. The freedmen were to "submit cheerfully to the . . . rules and regulations," and McCollum could fine them for transgressions. Few contracts were this specific, but the intent of all was the same. Those signed by workers for D. H. Freeman in Lafayette County stated conditions with simplicity: "They are to labor as they formerly did." [19]

The contracts negotiated under bureau supervision in the winter of 1865–1866 showed that relations between landowners and laborers had not been completely resolved. Whereas planters initially preferred some sort of wage system that allowed them to use their laborers much as they had slaves, the freedmen desired to farm on their own. In the first planting season after the war, about 30 percent of the contracts were agreements to farm on shares, rather than for wages. Most of these contracts were for "share wages"—that is, the workers received a share of the crop at the end of the year, rather than a set wage. About 6 percent of the contracts, however, involved share tenantry, in which the laborer was given a plot of ground to farm independently, with the landowner receiving a share of the crop as a form of rental. Which of the systems would ultimately win out remained undetermined at the end of 1865. [20]

Farming operations in 1866 settled many of the issues that remained unresolved concerning the relationship between the freedmen and land-owners. The year provided a real test for free labor because unfavorable weather seriously threatened the crops planted that spring. In such trying circumstances, the freedmen in general worked well. Some planters reported success despite weather problems; however, a Pine Bluff planter found that everyone had a different story about the performance of the freedmen. General Sprague noted in August, 1866, that "reports of employers of Freedmen are almost as various as the number of individuals making them." Sprague held on to the belief that performance was related to treatment. He wrote that "when men have a decent regard for justice and fair dealing and tact in managing and dealing with labourers there is no difficulty in preserving order or obtaining faithful labor." [21]

19. *House Executive Documents,* 39th Cong., 1st Sess., No. 70, pp. 77–78; Records Relating to Freedmen's Labor, Labor Contracts, Records of the Assistant Commissioner of the State of Arkansas, in BRFAL, RG 105, NA.

20. Records Relating to Freedmens Labor, Labor Contracts, Records of the Assistant Commissioner of the State of Arkansas. See also A. E. Habicht to F. W. Thibaux, November 20, 1866, in Letters Sent/Received, (Arkadelphia) Field Office Records, BRFAL, RG 105, NA.

21. Little Rock *Daily Gazette,* August 24, 1866; J. W. Sprague to O. O. Howard, September 1, 1866 (see also J. W. Sprague to O. O. Howard, November 5, 1865), in Reports of Bureau Operations, Records of the Assistant Commissioner of the State of Arkansas, BRFAL, RG 105, NA.

For the many threatened planters, however, the freedmen could not work hard enough. Andrew Carrigan of Hempstead County concluded that the freedmen were "not doing very well. A great many are leaving the men they have contracted with, in some instances all have left, leaving the employer in the grass." As a result, employers increasingly resorted to physical force to get their workers to perform. Sprague reported in September, 1866, that a few landowners were good with their workers but that the majority believed "the only way to manage niggers is to whip them and make them *know their* places." Complaints against planters indicated that punishment of freedmen for a variety of transgressions and designed to ensure their labor or keep them in their place increased through the summer of 1866.[22]

The planters discovered another way to manipulate free labor during the harvest season of 1866. With short crops and the uncertainty of profits, many employers endeavored to deprive their laborers of their wages or their share of the crops. Some drove their workers from the farms, charging that they had failed to honor their contracts. Others refused to pay their laborers, citing a variety of reasons for not complying with the agreements. Sprague thought that the freedmen would be cheated out of as much as one-third of what employers owed them. He reported: "Men who profess to be honest and honorable cannot understand that there is any moral wrong in *robbing and cheating* a negro."[23]

The bureau protested the mistreatment of the freedmen but could do little to prevent it; the agency did not possess the personnel or the resources to intervene effectively. From the beginning of their operations, bureau heads and local agents in the state had complained that they did not have enough men to adequately supervise their assignments. Enforcement of bureau decisions in contracts cases was impossible. An agent at Hamburg could not proceed against a local planter because the witnesses had been "intimidated and prevented from coming," and he was unable to move ahead on his own because "the want of troops prevent further investigation." Where troops were available, the army provided only infantry even

22. A. N. Carrigan to Dear Brother, June 22, 1866, in Carrigan Papers; J. W. Sprague to O. O. Howard, October 17, 1865, March 20, June 7, September 1, 1866 (quotation; Sprague's emphasis), in Reports of Bureau Operations, Records of the Assistant Commissioner of the State of Arkansas, BRFAL, RG 105, NA. See also "Wells v. Wells," August, 1866, (Hamburg) and "Bureau v. B. Adams," July, 1866 (Arkadelphia), in Registers of Complaints, Field Office Records, Arkansas, BRFAL, RG 105, NA.

23. "Sparks v. Davis," December, 1866, and "Bureau v. B. Adams," July, 1866, in (Arkadelphia) Register of Complaints, A. E. Habicht to G. I. Williams, November 22, 24, 1866, (Arkadelphia), all in Field Office Records, Arkansas, BRFAL, RG 105, NA; "Letter from E. O. C. Ord in Relation to the Treatment of Freedmen in Arkansas, November 24, 1866," *House Miscellaneous Documents,* 39th Cong., 2d Sess., No. 14, p. 2.

when the distances and conditions encountered required the use of mounted infantry or cavalry. The situation did not change. In March, 1867, General Ord complained, as had other officers before him, that he could not carry out his mission: "I have just ten men to the thousand square miles, and not more than one of these is mounted."[24]

In the first year's experimentation with free labor, the bureau forced blacks into contracts with landowners but provided only limited protection of their rights. Freedmen were bound legally to work, while the landowners used extralegal means to assert their preeminence in contractual relationships. By subtle pressure, intimidation, or violence, the landowners seized control over labor conditions and the distribution of profits. Certainly this employer domination of laborers resulted at least in part from the bureau's lack of strength, but the landowners' position was further bolstered by the actual support of the bureau when the agency began to encourage share tenantry in the contracts negotiated at the beginning of the 1867 planting season.

Bureau support for share tenantry developed out of observations of the first full year of operations. Local agents believed that the freedmen working for an interest or share in the crop did better as workers and in fulfilling their contracts than those working for wages. They linked this performance with the freedmen's desire for land and thought that share tenantry gave blacks a sense of farming on their own. The bureau agent at Arkadelphia remarked in December, 1865, on the general disposition "prevalent among the Freedmen to become planters by renting land or making crops on shares." As a result, bureau officials concluded that share tenantry or renting land was the best means of strengthening black freedom and economic ambition while assuring the state a steady source of labor.[25]

Landowners favored the share system as well, or at least bureau officers thought that they did. The advantage to the landowner was that no cash had to be advanced or distributed to the workers during the year. Although bureau officials did not cite it as an additional benefit, planters were aware that the possibilities for cheating the freedmen were greater in such a system, especially in accounting for the costs of supplies advanced during

24. "Letter from E. O. C. Ord," 2; W. A. Britton to E. W. Gantt, December 19, 1865, (Arkadelphia) Field Office Records, E. O. C. Ord to O. O. Howard, March 15, 1867, Reports of Bureau Operations, Records of the Assistant Commissioner of the State of Arkansas, both in BRFAL, RG 105, NA.

25. J. W. Sprague to O. O. Howard, February 27, 1867, in Operations Reports, Records of the Assistant Commissioner of the State of Arkansas, W. A. Britton to E. M. Gantt, December 18, 1865, in (Arkadelphia) Field Office Records, "Report of Freedmen in Eastern District of Arkansas, June 30, 1865," in (Helena) Field Office Records, all in BRFAL, RG 105, NA.

the year. Whether because the system produced more labor, allowed the employer to deal in credit rather than cash, or permitted greater fraud, many planters did seem to embrace share tenantry. By January, 1867, farming on shares had come to mean farming on shares as a tenant. The editors of the Little Rock *Conservative* observed that farm conditions for 1867 were still unclear, but that it was "generally conceded that the system of planting on shares is the most successful, as well as the most advantageous to both planter and laborer."[26]

Bureau officials knew of the potential danger in share tenantry. W. A. Britton, the bureau agent at Arkadelphia in December, 1865, reported that he found many freedmen wanting to make rental or lease contracts, but that he discouraged them and refused to approve or register such contracts. The agent warned the Little Rock office that without subsistence, the freedmen would buy their provisions from the landowner, purchasing them at exorbitant prices and paying for them when the price of their crop might be low. He thought that this would put them "in the *power* of the white man, when he keeps a running account against them for a whole year's experience, & can bring them in debt to him." Unless the freedmen had the means to begin with, he concluded, they could never step into the shoes of the planters and compete with whites. Although concerned about the share tenant contracts, bureau officials decided that they were better than alternative methods and encouraged the freedmen to sign such agreements in 1867.[27]

The new contracts made in January and February, 1867, showed the impact of the bureau's decision. Share tenantry had become pervasive throughout the cotton-growing region. General Ord reported in February, 1867, that most of the contracts signed up to that point had been made for a share of the crop, and that such arrangements were generally agreed to be the best for all parties. Individual contracts do not always show clearly the transformation from share wages to share tenantry, but Ord's description of the common form of the contracts does. Noting that details varied greatly in these contracts, Ord observed that usually the planter provided land, stock, feed for the stock, house and quarters, all necessary fuel, all cotton and other seeds, bagging and rope, and advanced necessary rations and clothing during the year. Ord cited the plantation of W. S. Whitley in Monroe County as a model one, indicating that Whitley purchased provisions at New Orleans and St. Louis at wholesale and furnished them to his tenants at his cost plus freight. In turn, for laboring, the freedmen received

26. Little Rock *Daily Conservative*, February 2, 1867.

27. W. A. Britton to E. M. Gantt, December 18, 1865, in Letters Sent/Received, (Arkadelphia) Field Office Records, BRFAL, RG 105, NA (Britton's emphasis).

about one-half of the crop, against which was held the amount advanced during the year. The new system prevailed in the area of smaller plantations. It made inroads even into the large-plantation counties, where some planters gave up their efforts at working the freedmen in gangs and broke up their lands among tenants.[28]

That spring, local agents were optimistic about the new system. From Arkadelphia, A. E. Habicht observed that share contracts gave the freedmen a chance to lessen their reliance on whites and taught them to depend on their own management. The optimism disappeared when bureau officials began to receive complaints of the problems that W. A. Britton had predicted. In August, 1867, General C. H. Smith, who had replaced Ord as head of the bureau in the state, reported that planters had found many ways to cheat their tenants. Once the crop had been put in, cultivated, and laid by, planters began campaigning to get their hands to break their contracts and lose their rights to a share of it. At Arkadelphia, Habicht's predictions of self-reliance for the freedmen gave way to reports that employers attempted to defraud the tenants in every way possible when they settled with them on the cost of supplies. The system had turned into another means by which the landowners could tighten their control over their laborers.[29]

The freedmen understood what was happening. No matter what system of labor was used, they would be cheated and nothing could be done to prevent it. Distrust of whites became a part of their view of the postwar world. Anthony Taylor described the system when he recalled the landowner for whom he worked in Clark County:

> He was a pretty good man. Of course, you never seen a white man that wouldn't cheat a little. He'd cheat you out of a little cotton. He would have the cotton carried to the gin. He would take half the corn and give us five or six shoats. After he got the cotton all picked and sold, the cotton it would all go to him for what you owed him

28. (Lake Village) and (Arkadelphia) Registers of Contracts, A. E. Habicht to O. O. Howard, January 2, 1867 (Arkadelphia), S. Hersey to E. O. C. Ord, February 28, 1867 (Lake Village), all in Field Office Records, Arkansas, BRFAL, RG 105, NA; Little Rock *Daily Conservative*, February 2, 1867; E. O. C. Ord to O. O. Howard, February 22, 1867, in Reports of Bureau Operations, Records of the Assistant Commissioner of the State of Arkansas, BRFAL, RG 105, NA.

29. A. E. Habicht to O. O. Howard, January 2, 1867, Habicht to Michael Bozeman, November 21, 1867, Habicht to Nathaniel May, October 6, 1867, all in Letters Sent/Received, (Arkadelphia) Field Office Records, BRFAL, RG 105, NA; C. H. Smith to O. O. Howard, August 21, 1867, in Reports of Bureau Operations, Records of the Assistant Commissioner of the State of Arkansas, BRFAL, RG 105, NA.

for furnishing you. You never saw how much cotton was ginned, nor how much he got for it, nor how much it was worth nor nothing. They would just tell you you wasn't due nothing. They did that to hold you for another year. You got nothing to move on so you stayed there and take what he gives you.

The freedmen realized that they had become trapped in a system that would not deal with them fairly.[30]

The experiences of 1867 established the labor relationships that connected blacks and landowners in Arkansas into the next century. The majority of blacks became tenant farmers tied to the land by a continuing indebtedness. The development of these peculiar economic bonds meant more than simple impoverishment and economic subordination. The economic relationship entailed social subordination as well, since maintenance of the inferiority of blacks was so central to the white society's goal of economic control. This was not a return to slavery, and political developments in 1867 promised long-term change that might expand the black workers' freedom, but in the short term they had few options. They were free, but subject to social and economic controls that squelched full freedom. In his report of August, 1867, bureau chief C. H. Smith summed up their condition: "Freedmen in many places are still *freedmen* not *freemen*. The white man still arrogates the rights and powers of masters while the freedmen half acknowledge them." White landowners had, however, achieved what many of them had feared would be impossible as slavery collapsed. They had within two years reestablished control over black labor.[31]

The future of Arkansas society, both white and black in 1865, depended upon the economic reconstruction of the state. After 1867, perhaps even more than for whites, the future of blacks was bound to the future of agriculture, and particularly of cotton. As long as whites needed workers in the fields, and as long as they possessed the power to control labor, the condition of black Arkansans was related closely to the economy of the state. The antebellum elites worked at rebuilding their economic fortunes as they restored their political fortunes and resecured control over the work force. Their success in the latter two areas was not paralleled in the former, ensuring poverty for blacks and for the state as a whole.

30. *ASIAN,* Vol. VIII, Pt. 1, p. 184, Vol. XI, Pt. 7, p. 157, Vol. X, Pt. 6, p. 262.

31. C. H. Smith to O. O. Howard, August 21, 1867, in Operations Reports, Records of the Assistant Commissioner of the State of Arkansas, BRFAL, RG 105, NA.

# 12

## EMERGENCE OF THE POSTWAR ECONOMY
### The Triumph of Cotton and Its Impact

FOR ARKANSANS IN 1865, ECONOMIC PROSPECTS WERE bleak. Stock and farm implements were gone, destroyed or taken. Fences were down and farms grown up in weeds. Capital had been squandered on the lost cause. Slavery was gone. Still, the problem of recovery was not overwhelming. Arkansas' primarily agricultural economy could be rebuilt without heavy capital investment. Stock would replenish itself naturally. Farm equipment was simple and inexpensive, and much of it could be fashioned locally. The labor situation was not as hopeless as many initially feared, and the landowners quickly regained control over the labor force. There were problems. Financing renewed operations was the most critical, and it was complicated by uncertainty regarding land titles, taxes, and debts. Once these problems were solved, however, crops could be planted, and good crops promised rapid recovery. Restoration of agriculture would bring a subsequent recovery of business. Planters, farmers, and businessmen began to reconstruct their economic lives in the summer of 1865, and the decisions they made had implications for the state's development into the twentieth century.

Much of the state's best agricultural land was in the hands of the United States government in 1865, but regaining control over it was one of the easiest tasks confronted by landowners. Most Arkansans who had property confiscated reclaimed it quickly. If the government had not already acquired title to the property, local officials of the Freedmen's Bureau returned it when the owner claimed it after the federal government decided that the presidential amnesties restored property rights. If the government had already acquired title, the owner had to apply to the district bureau superintendent and provide proof of title and evidence that the applicant had sworn the amnesty oath or had been pardoned by the president. If the military was using the property or if it was under cultivation by loyal refugees or freedmen, restoration was delayed, but usually only for a short time. Indicative of the ease and speed of land restoration, Confederate general Gideon J. Pillow of Phillips County had the freedmen's colony on his land gone, his control restored, and preparations for cultivation under way in the autumn of 1865.[1]

A more difficult problem was the complicated tax situation. Federal victory invalidated Confederate state taxes, but Confederates owed state and county taxes levied by the Murphy government after 1864, as well as the 1861 United States direct tax. The state and local taxes were each 1.5 percent on each hundred dollars' worth of property—a combined rate of 3 percent, as compared with only .5 percent in the 1850s. The direct tax was .37 percent. Finding the cash to pay these taxes was difficult, yet tax collectors actively pursued collection and confiscated property upon which taxes had not been paid. Payment of the taxes redeemed the land but involved the owner in problems in the courts. Still, most landowners settled their tax bills, although often through borrowing money.[2]

Paying or renegotiating personal debts assumed before and during the war was an equally critical requirement for economic recovery. Property owners had to deal with creditors who, now that the war was over, demanded immediate payment of their loans, which they had been unable to take to court during the war, plus the interest accumulated over the previous four years. The Freedmen's Bureau agent at Hamburg suggested the extent of the problem when he estimated that nine out of ten men in Ashley County emerged from the war heavily in debt, with a majority insolvent. The complications were endless. William E. Woodruff, Sr., owed northern clients money that he had collected before the war but that had been seized by Confederate authorities. John Hornor of Helena, who cosigned a friend's purchase of slaves in 1858, was saddled with responsibility when the friend was killed in the war and his land was not valuable enough to pay the debt. M. L. Bell, a businessman and planter in Jefferson County, summed up the significance of postwar indebtedness when he wrote, "I shall be embarrassed by some debts that were of no consequence before the war."[3]

1. Circular No. 15, October 25, 1865, *House Executive Documents*, 39th Cong., 1st Sess., No. 70, p. 75; W. E. Woodruff to W. Elliott, August 8, 1865, J. S. Hornor to W. E. Woodruff, December 12, 1865, both in William E. Woodruff Papers, AHC; D. C. Watkins to D. Walker, July 12, 1865, in David Walker Papers, UAF; G. H. Pillow to D. C. Douglas, November 2, 1865, in Douglas-Maney Papers, TSLA.

2. W. E. Woodruff to T. S. Ayres, November 19, 1866, J. S. Hornor to W. E. Woodruff, June 12, 1866, both in Woodruff Papers; D. C. Watkins to D. Walker, July 12, 1865, in Walker Papers.

3. J. S. Taylor to J. Tyler, November 30, 1866, in Operations Reports of Subordinate Offices, Arkansas, BRFAL, RG 105, NA; J. Hornor to W. E. Woodruff, August 17, November 4, 30, 1866, Ed. H. Howell to W. E. Woodruff, April 28, 1866, W. E. Woodruff to W. Elliott, August 8, 1865, M. L. Bell to W. E. Woodruff, April 15, 1867, all in Woodruff Papers.

The importance of the debt problem was reflected in the efforts by debtors to secure legal relief. Some appeals were of the most tenuous nature. Garland H. Dorris, who purchased a slave in Jefferson County in August, 1863, asked to have the debt invalidated, claiming that President Lincoln's Emancipation Proclamation had ended slavery in the county and the contract could not be legal. Elisha Worthington of Chicot County pleaded that the statute of limitations had run out for his creditors, who had not moved against him in the courts during the war. In Pulaski County, Lemuel Filkins tried to have a judgment by a Confederate court overturned on the grounds that the court was illegal. The courts generally favored creditors, and debtors found little relief.[4]

Debtors had to pay off their notes or renegotiate them before they could begin farming again. Creditors generally were willing to renew notes because foreclosing would leave them with the debtor's land, an item of uncertain value in 1865. The elder William Woodruff, who was a creditor on numerous land being purchased throughout the state, gave extensions if the debtor paid interest on the note and paid the taxes on the land. Renegotiation of debts provided immediate relief but left farmers owing so much that they had little margin between potential profits and losses. It is impossible to determine the full extent of indebtedness in 1865, but probably most farmers renewed were heavily burdened with new debts pyramided upon the already-existing ones. Still, credit was available and Arkansans were able to find the capital necessary to begin farming again.[5]

Agricultural activity renewed on a larger scale than during the war almost with the first day of peace. Where wives, children, and slaves had begun crops, returning Confederate soldiers stepped in to ensure that the crop already planted was taken care of; some tried to expand production by putting in late crops of cotton and corn. Andrew Carrigan saved his corn crop, which allowed him to begin his personal economic recovery. Carrigan sold the corn for cash and then used his profits to buy drugs so that he could resume his profession as a doctor; he also purchased supplies that allowed him to put in a new crop in 1866. Elliott Fletcher, whose wife stayed on their Mississippi River plantation during the war, found cotton in the field when he returned. He supervised its harvest, delivered four bales to Memphis in December, 1865, and promised more.[6]

Where farms had been abandoned, returning farmers faced greater prob-

4. *Arkansas Reports,* 210–15, 326–36, 286–326, 487–95, 91–95, 556–60.

5. Ed. H. Howell to W. E. Woodruff, April 28, 1866, in Woodruff Papers, W. A. Britton to E. K. Miller, April 3, 1867, in Enoch K. Miller Papers, AHC.

6. A. N. Carrigan to Dear Brother, June 2, 1866, in John W. Carrigan Papers, DU; E. H. Fletcher to Dear Sirs, December 18, 1865, in Elliott H. Fletcher Papers, AHC.

lems. Cotton could still be put in if seed could be found in May, but those who got back later were forced to cultivate a late crop of corn. The experiences of James Hudson of Jefferson County indicate the frenzy with which operations were renewed and what could be accomplished. Hudson, who served with the 2d Arkansas Infantry, returned after Appomattox to his father's farm. Although it was late in the spring, he plowed up twenty-five acres of corn that had been planted and replaced it with cotton. After putting in the crop, Hudson helped his father move back from Texas. He brought in beef cattle that the elder Hudson had acquired there and sold them at Pine Bluff. In addition, Hudson helped harvest wheat in Union County in return for wages. As a result of his efforts, the family had cash from the cattle and his labor, and fifteen bales of cotton that Hudson sold for three thousand dollars. Recovery could be quick.[7]

The rapid regrowth of agriculture in 1865 convinced many that a full economic recovery was possible. The editor of the *Gazette* reported that the cotton crop was not big, but that it held promise for the future. With cotton prices at fifty cents per pound and looking up, the editor thought farmers could pay the wages asked by freedmen and still make profits. The editor optimistically predicted that by 1866 "the agricultural productions of Arkansas will not be materially less than it has been in years previous to the war." With bonanza prices for cotton, optimism spread quickly among farm interests in the cotton-planting region.[8]

Optimism generated activity, and planters were busy in 1865 and early 1866 lining up financial backers and preparing to resume full-scale farming. General Pillow informed a partner that he had found a factor in Memphis willing to give what was needed to restore his plantations. Further, Pillow observed: "There is a great rush to the Arkansas River. Several Gentlemen left today for the purpose of renting." At Pine Bluff, M. L. Bell, who was pessimistic about farm prospects in September, 1865, had caught the fever by the next month. He found a partner who provided financial backing, and he wrote hopefully: "I am going to try the cotton question next year. . . . If I can get the *freedmen* to do a little over half work I think I can make some money next year if cotton keeps up to 25 cts." Not only Arkansans became caught up in the desire to make their fortunes with cotton: many of the backers of planters and farmers were northerners. One Freedmen's Bureau officer wrote that the "whole country is filled with southern men

7. "William R. Young Memoirs," 69, in William R. Young Papers, AHC; "Post Civil War Reminiscences of James Madison Hudson," *Jefferson County Historical Quarterly*, VII (1978), 6.

8. Little Rock *Daily Gazette*, October 6, 11, 1865.

and northern officers or men acting as partners in their business matters."[9]

Small farmers had more problems than large farmers in finding financial backing after the war. They were in debt relative to their resources to much the same degree as their wealthier neighbors. Finding a line of credit to provide the capital and supplies necessary to renew farming was difficult, however, because the credit system upon which they had relied before the war was in disarray in the summer and autumn of 1865. They had usually depended upon local planters or country merchants for their credit, but both of these sources had dried up. Planters put everything they could into restoring their own lands. The merchants had much of their capital tied up in uncollectable prewar and wartime loans and had problems reestablishing their commercial ties with outside business houses and securing credit to restock their shelves. When contemporaries noted a shortage of money, they meant that the outside firms that extended credit to the town merchants—and thereby to country merchants—were not yet in the local market. The complaint was common in the fall of 1865.[10]

Informants for the state's newspapers reported, nonetheless, that farm interests showed considerable activity. Early estimates suggested cultivation of cotton would be extensive in 1866. General Sprague of the Freedmen's Bureau predicted that as much as three-fourths of the acreage cultivated in 1860 would be planted in 1866. After a trip through eastern Arkansas, another officer estimated that most plantation land would be used, except along the Mississippi River where levees had been broken during the war. By the middle of the summer, observers lowered their estimates of the land being cultivated to from one-half to two-thirds of that cultivated in 1860, but all were still positive about the size of the crop that would be produced.[11]

In general, landowners who renewed their efforts in 1866 farmed as they had before the war. In the plantation region, landholding patterns remained

9. G. H. Pillow to D. C. Douglas, November 2, 1865, in Douglas-Maney Papers; M. L. Bell to Woodruff, September 6, October 12, 1865, in Woodruff Papers; *House Reports,* 39th Cong., 1st Sess., No. 30, p. 98.

10. John W. Brown Diary, June 27, 1865, in AHC; M. L. Bell to W. E. Woodruff, July 7, September 6, 1865, Ed. H. Howell to W. E. Woodruff, April 28, 1866, all in Woodruff Papers; A. N. Carrigan to My Dear Brother, June 2, 1866, in Carrigan Papers; "W. R. Young Memoirs," 69; Little Rock *Daily Gazette,* March 10, 1866.

11. Little Rock *Daily Gazette,* January 27, 1866, Camden (Ark.) *Eagle* quoted *ibid.,* August 23, 1866; Washington (Ark.) *Telegraph* quoted *ibid.,* August 31, 1866; Helena (Ark.) *Shield* quoted *ibid.,* August 9, 1866; Memphis *Daily Argus,* June 24, 1866; E. G. Barker to J. W. Sprague, July 31, 1866, in Operations Reports of Subordinate Offices, BRFAL, RG 105, NA; J. W. Sprague to O. O. Howard, March 20, 1866, in Reports of Bureau Operations, Arkansas, BRFAL, RG 105, NA.

TABLE 17

HOLDINGS OF LAND OVER 600 ACRES, 1866

| County | Landowners | | Land | |
| --- | --- | --- | --- | --- |
| | No. | (%) | Acres | (%) |
| Chicot | 125 | (45) | 218,871 | (86) |
| Independence | 75 | (6) | 176,318 | (26) |
| Montgomery | 1 | (1) | 669 | (3) |
| Phillips | 256 | (33) | 287,993 | (69) |
| Pulaski | 119 | (13) | 159,782 | (49) |
| Union | 160 | (20) | 210,318 | (56) |
| Van Buren | 23 | (6) | 21,331 | (24) |
| Washington | 46 | (4) | 38,034 | (17) |

unchanged and large operations dominated (Table 17). In some plantation counties the percentage of land in plots of six hundred acres or more actually increased. The concentration of land in large holdings does not indicate what kind of agricultural operations took place on them, but it does show that in the plantation areas agricultural wealth remained concentrated. Most of the owners tried to use their laborers as they had their slaves, working them in gangs under overseers. Lycurgus Johnson, a planter in Chicot County who had owned more than a hundred slaves before the war, retained them as free laborers, except for fifteen who had "died, strayed, or been stolen." Outside the plantation region, small farms continued to be the dominant unit. Small farmers sought a few hands to help put in their crops, or depended upon themselves and their families to begin their operations anew.[12]

One change did take place that had long-term implications. The high price of cotton encouraged both planters and farmers to put more land into that crop and less into corn or grains, thus risking self-sufficiency in the hope of reaping cotton profits. In January, 1866, the editor of the *Arkansas*

12. E. G. Barker to J. W. Sprague, July 31, 1866, T. J. Able to Sprague, September 30, 1866, both in Operations Reports of Subordinate Offices, Arkansas, BRFAL, RG 105, NA; MS Tax Rolls, 1850, 1860, 1866, in Arkansas County Records, AHC.

*Gazette* predicted that because "cotton is high; and is *the* great article of commerce, we may look for exertions as have never before been put forth by the people of the country." Upon this effort hinged the hopes of the community that "the grand side-wheeler and the little dinky may find freight enough of the usual sort to pay them well for venturing upon our dangerous waters." In an item that appeared the next month, the same editor observed that "many who never raised a cotton plant, excited by the high prices, are exerting themselves to the end that a few bales may gladden their pocket this coming fall." Cultivation of cotton intensified everywhere in the state. No county statistics exist for 1866, but the trend was apparent by 1870. The ratio of corn to cotton declined as farmers dedicated more land to cotton. Statewide, the ratio of bushels of corn to bales of cotton edged up to 54:1, compared with 49:1 in 1860. However, the number of counties with a ratio of less than 50:1 increased from nineteen to twenty-six, and specialized agriculture moved into the interior of the state (see Map 7).[13]

The scramble to grow cotton caused a slight boom in land prices and rents. One prospective purchaser found a plantation off the river in Jefferson County valued at thirty-two dollars per acre. Along the lower Arkansas River, land rented for ten dollars per acre. Upriver a report indicated that open land with river frontage sold for twenty-five dollars per acre and rented for six. It is impossible to reconstruct average purchase and rental prices in 1865 and 1866, but a few examples indicate prices comparable with those of 1860.[14]

As farmers prepared for the 1866 season, town economies surged. After a slow start, business activity was brisk in most towns. In August, 1865, Christopher Danley of the *Arkansas Gazette* found that money was being made by dry goods merchants, grocers, and restaurant owners and saloonkeepers. The Union army was gone, but business had not been hurt. In October, M. L. Bell reported that trade was lively in Pine Bluff and that merchants were looking for a quick return to prosperity.[15]

Hopes grew, but nature intervened in the late spring of 1866 to threaten the entire recovery. Rain fell statewide beginning in the middle of May and

13. Little Rock *Daily Gazette,* January 24 (emphasis in original), February 8, 1866.

14. J. H. Haney Diary, October 7, 1865, in AHC; J. E. Lindsay to N. B. Eison, March 16, 1866, in Lindsay Letter, Small Manuscripts Collection, AHC; L. Musgrave to John Routh, May 27, 1866, in Theron Brownfield Papers, UALR; M. L. Bell to W. E. Woodruff, July 7, October 14, 1865, in Woodruff Papers, AHC; Memphis *Daily Argus,* June 24, 1866.

15. Haney Diary, June 27, 1865; Little Rock *Daily Gazette,* August 18, 1865 (see also June 24, August 5, 19, 1865); M. L. Bell to W. E. Woodruff, October 14, 1865, in Woodruff Papers.

# Map 7

## Corn-to-Cotton Ratios, 1870

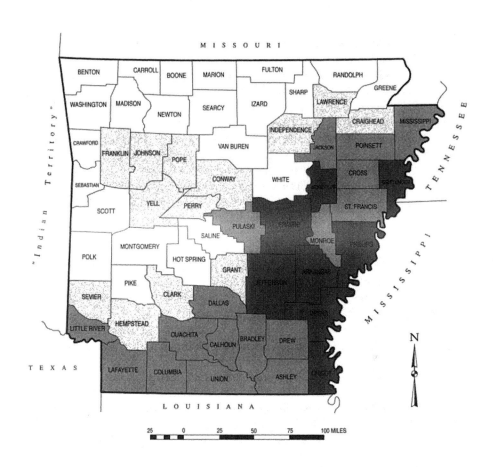

(bushels to bales)

Less than 25:1

26:1 to 50:1

51:1 to 100:1

Greater than 100:1

continuing into early summer. Every major river overflowed, although southern Arkansas suffered the most. Fields were washed out, and in Union County one planter reported rain so heavy that it had packed the ground too hard for his cotton to come up. With continued rain and flooding, farmers could not get into the fields, and grass sprouted and established itself where the topsoil was not washed away completely. General Sprague reported that the problem was worse than usual because the land had been left uncultivated for years and was stocked with grass and weed seeds. When the weather moderated, planters acted quickly, sometimes hiring extra hands. At Helena one planter even hired soldiers from the local garrison. Bureau officials reported that the freedmen worked for days in mud and water trying to save the crops. Despite these efforts, a correspondent of the Memphis *Daily Argus* advised his readers that crops were "backward, grassy and weedy." [16]

Farmers had an additional setback when they discovered that many of the seeds they had used for their first planting were defective. On some plantations second and third plantings were necessary because the seeds would not germinate. Combined with the problem of flooding, the replanting of fields exhausted the available supply of seed, and many farmers were unable to replace lost crops. Others found seed but spread it more thinly than usual. Seeds were usually sown close together so that when the plants came up they supported one another. This time the stands were not thick enough and the cotton did not grow properly. [17]

After a brief period of fair weather, conditions worsened. In late June counties on the southern border and in the Arkansas and Mississippi river valleys saw the start of a drought that lasted through most of the summer. Heat and dry weather caused the cotton to "cast off," that is, to lose the blossoms that would become the cotton boll. Then, beginning in late August, some areas had almost six weeks of rain, prompting a second growth of the cotton with resulting loss of bolls. In September army worms that stripped the plants overran the drought- and rain-stricken areas, and nothing could stop the pests. T. J. Abel, bureau agent at Luna Landing in Chicot County, found that the worms had left the fields "as naked as they usually are in January." [18]

16. J. W. Sprague to O. O. Howard, June 7, July 11, 1866, in Reports of Bureau Operations, Arkansas, BRFAL, RG 105, NA; L. Musgrave to John Routh, June 19, 1866, in Brownfield Papers; A. N. Carrigan to My Dear Brother, June 2, 1866, in Carrigan Papers; Little Rock *Daily Gazette*, May 12, June 9, 23, 1866; Memphis *Daily Argus*, June 24, 1866; *Senate Executive Documents*, 39th Cong., 2d Sess., No. 6, p. 32.

17. Memphis *Daily Argus*, June 24, 1866; *Senate Executive Documents*, 39th Cong., 1st Sess., No. 6, p. 32; W. J. Davis to J. Tyler, November 30, 1866, in Operations Reports of Subordinate Offices, Arkansas, BRFAL, RG 105, NA.

18. W. J. Davis to J. Tyler, November 30, 1866, H. Sweeney to Tyler, December 31, 1866, T. J. Abel to J. W. Sprague, September 30, 1866, all in Operations Reports of Subordinate Offices, Arkansas, BRFAL, RG 105, NA.

The harvest in the fall of 1866 was far short of early predictions. Reports indicated that less than one-half of the hoped-for yield had been realized. The failure was not statewide; some areas harvested two-thirds of the planted crop. In the south and along the major river valleys, however, there were disaster areas. William Pickett of Calhoun County claimed that it was the worst cotton crop he had ever seen. The corn crop was also less than expected—a particular problem because it meant that many farmers would suffer from a shortage of food in the coming year. In Jefferson County one observer estimated that fewer than one in ten planters had made enough corn to supply their own needs and would be forced to buy provisions. *Banker's Magazine* estimated that the crop was 11,585,332 bushels, one-third less than in 1860.[19]

The short crop of 1866 varied in its impact. Some farmers and planters lost their entire crop, while others salvaged large parts of theirs. As early as that spring, one newspaper correspondent estimated that because of the cool temperatures, the rains, and other problems, only about one-fourth of the planters in the Pine Bluff area would make a profit for the year, and the remaining three-fourths would only make expenses. The family of Governor John S. Roane was one of the more famous losers. The Jefferson County family lost heavily because the partial failure of their crop made it impossible for them to handle existing debts. The overall situation for the large planters is difficult to determine, but many suffered the fate of the Roanes and were destroyed financially. From Hamburg, bureau agent J. S. Taylor noted that "the short crop will prevent many from operating next year." Helena agent Henry Sweeney concluded that the planters had experienced serious losses and that "in some cases all that was invested has been lost and the parties left in debt."[20]

Small farmers may have been hurt even worse. William R. Young of White County attempted to make a crop, but its failure forced him to sell his land to pay his debts and to go to work as a schoolteacher. George R.

19. E. D. Newell to J. Routh, October 5, 1866, in Brownfield Papers; W. J. Pickett to My Dear Sister, November 7, 1866, in William J. Pickett Papers, DU; T. J. Abel to J. W. Sprague, September 30, 1866, E. G. Barker to J. W. Sprague, July 31, 1866, both in Operations Reports of Subordinate Offices, Arkansas, BRFAL, RG 105, NA; L. Hersey to John Tyler, January 1, 1867 in (Lake Village) Field Office Records, BRFAL RG 105, NA; R. Wallace to William E. Woodruff, June 24, 1867, in Woodruff Papers; *Ouachita Herald* (Camden, Ark.) quoted in Little Rock *Daily Gazette,* August 9, 1866; Washington (Ark.) *Telegraph* quoted in Little Rock *Daily Gazette,* August 31, 1866; Little Rock *Daily Gazette,* October 2, 1866, April 2, 1867; Pine Bluff (Ark.) *Dispatch,* January 12, 1867; *Banker's Magazine,* October 5, 1867, compared with *Eighth Census, 1860: Agriculture,* 7.

20. Little Rock *Daily Gazette,* August 24, 1866; M. L. Bell to W. E. Woodruff, April 15, 1867, in Woodruff Papers; J. S. Taylor to J. Tyler, November 2, 1866, in Operations Reports of Subordinate Offices, Arkansas, BRFAL, RG 105, NA.

Pendleton, who had owned 280 acres and several slaves in Union County before the war, failed and moved to Texas to teach, leaving his wife and children behind in a slave cabin to make what money they could while trying to collect debts owed to the family. How many small farmers went under in 1866 is not clear, but newspaper columns and correspondence reflect a sense of disaster that pervaded the community. The editor of the *Conservative* at Little Rock predicted that many people would be prosecuted because they could not pay their debts, and that sheriff's sales would be widespread. He wrote: "Time will be denied Debtor Classes, however industrious or hopeful that class may be. And many are the unfortunate families, that will be driven out from their last shelter within the next two years."[21]

Crop losses also devastated the freedmen. Bureau agents reported that freedmen who worked on shares had made scarcely enough to pay back landowners and merchants for supplies. A. S. Dyer wrote from Jacksonport that in his area "the Freedmen owing to the contracts which were made with them at the beginning are badly worsted." In addition, especially in the southern parts of the state, the bureau received large numbers of reports that landowners were driving their workers away. Complaining that freedmen had gotten to work late, left early, and were careless, employers blamed them for their problems and asked permission to annul contracts or to levy charges for damages against wages. In some cases planters who leased land ginned the cotton, took it to market, and left without paying their workers. From Helena, agent Sweeney complained that planters had devised innumerable "excuses and devices for cheating them [workers] out of what little they could get."[22]

Still, planters and farmers had weathered agricultural reverses before the war, and some found reasons for hope now. The extent of individual indebtedness had some correlation to the impact of the short crop. If a grower had heavy debts, setbacks meant that the cost of the debt outweighed income. With less debt, continued high prices for cotton meant that that unless a crop was lost completely, profits could still be made. Despite general farm problems and individual losses, the value of the crop approached or perhaps even exceeded that of 1860 because prices were

21. Little Rock *Daily Conservative*, December 6, 1866; Lease in George M. Pendleton Family Letters, LSUS; J. L, Cheatham to D. M. Patterson, June 4, 1867, in *Clark County Historical Journal* (Winter, 1979–80), 107; Little Rock *Daily Gazette*, July 4, August 18, 1866.

22. L. Hersey to John Tyler, January 1, 1867, in (Lake Village) Field Office Records, A. S. Dyer to [?], January 8, 1867, in (Jacksonport) Field Office Records, H. Sweeney to J. Tyler, October 31, December 31, 1866, in Operations Reports of Subordinate Offices, Arkansas, all in BRFAL, RG 105, NA.

more than three times higher. If prices held, landowners and laborers, planters and farmers, believed that their loses could be recouped the next year.[23]

Thus 1867 was critical to the future of the state's economy. Could farms and plantations turn the profit that would spark recovery? In February the editor of the *Conservative* concluded that planters and farmers had learned important lessons in 1866 and looked forward to the coming year. Those with labor were going to "work with more than ordinary confidence of success." Planters and farmers echoed this positive outlook. M. L. Bell took over the operations of the Roane plantation for Mrs. Roane and predicted that the family's debts and mortgages could be paid with the current crop "if we have any success." W. A. Britton, a former Freedmen's Bureau agent who was planting in the Pine Bluff area, found that few planters paid expenses in the first year's operations, but because most of them had been in debt at the end of the war and were still in debt, they would continue to use free labor and grow cotton "in hopes they *may* make a good crop some future day, and pay their debts."[24]

A few negative voices urged farmers to proceed cautiously. Recognizing that many planters had not raised enough corn to supply their own needs, they urged that all farmers try to be more self-sufficient by raising more corn and less cotton. The editor of the Fayetteville *Arkansian* called on the state's farmers and planters to abandon their reliance on cotton. "We do not hesitate to insist again and again," he wrote, "that our people should change the suicidal, cut-throat policy they have heretofore pursued of over-cropping, over-trading, and everlastingly raising cotton, cotton, cotton, to the exclusion of everything else, and thus, still remaining for years to come, as we have been, to our sorrow, in years past, 'hewers of wood and drawers of water' for our northern master."[25]

Some changes did take place as operators prepared for 1867. Many planters, as has been seen, abandoned efforts to use farm labor in gangs and

---

23. The 367,000 bales of cotton produced in 1860 was worth $14,680,000 if sold at the average rate of eleven cents per pound. If only one-half of the 1860 crop was planted in 1866, the potential harvest was 183,500 bales. A loss of one-third of that crop would have produced a harvest of 121,110 bales, which at thirty-seven cents per pound would have been worth $17,924,280. Even if one-half of the crop had been lost, the crop would have been 91,750 bales, worth $13,579,000. Given the probable reduction of numbers of individuals engaged in planting, these prices should have produced a profit for most planters unless their debt was considerably greater than that of 1860 planters.

24. Little Rock *Daily Conservative*, February 2, 1867; M. L. Bell to W. E. Woodruff, April 15, 1867, in Woodruff Papers; W. A. Britton to E. K. Miller, April 3, 1867, in Miller Papers.

25. Pine Bluff (Ark.) *Dispatch*, January 12, 1867; Fayetteville *Arkansian* quoted in Little Rock *Daily Conservative*, January 1, 1866; Little Rock *Daily Gazette*, March 19, 26, 1867.

contracted with workers as share tenants, rather than for wages or share wages. The system of supplying these tenant farmers also changed. Many landowners stopped furnishing tenants and instead encouraged merchants to establish stores on their plantations to provide supplies. In some cases landowners were partners of the merchants. In typical contracts the landowner received half of the crop for the land while the tenants mortgaged their share of the crop against the supplies they received. Freedmen's Bureau officials worried about this practice because they believed the merchants charged exorbitant rates and took every opportunity to cheat the freedmen. The bureau did not stop the development of the system, however.[26]

Hopes were dashed once again in 1867 by the weather. The spring was cooler than usual, and heavy rains fell throughout it and into early summer. All the major rivers again overran their banks, and plantations along them remained underwater through much of the spring. Crops that had been planted were washed out. With desperation, tenants and landowners tried to recover after each flood. In Clark County farmers planted cotton three successive times after fields washed out. Rain through June turned into drought in July that damaged cotton, corn, and every other crop, particularly in eastern Arkansas. In July and August the parched fields were assaulted by caterpillars, which destroyed the fraction of the crop that had survived the spring floods. One planter reacted to this new plague with despair: "Surely the Almighty intends chastising us in every possible manner. I expect we are guilty of many sins."[27]

In June many planters who had been renting land let their workers go, concluding that the crop would not justify further expenditures. Along all the rivers, farmers and planters were ruined. The editor of the *Arkansas Gazette* concluded that the failure to produce a crop was "particularly unfortunate, as some had mortgaged everything to procur enough to work

26. A. S. Dyer to [?], January 8, 1867, V. V. Smith to J. E. Bennett, October 1, 1867, both in Operations Reports of Subordinate Offices, Arkansas, BRFAL, RG 105, NA; W. J. Pickett to My Dear Sister, November 7, 1866, in Pickett Papers.

27. Bureau reports and letters from May through August, 1867, in Operations Reports of Subordinate Offices, Field Office Records, and Reports of Bureau Operations, Arkansas, BRFAL, RG 105, NA, chronicle the weather problems of 1867. See also A. N. Carrigan to My Dear Brother, April 10, August 13, 1867, in Carrigan Papers; DU; *Chicot Press* quoted in Little Rock *Daily Gazette,* August 28, 1867; Magnolia (Ark.) *Vindicator* quoted in Little Rock *Daily Gazette,* September 20, 1867; Searcy (Ark.) *Record* quoted in Little Rock *Daily Gazette,* August 31, 1867, October 8, 1867; Little Rock *Daily Gazette,* May 17, 19, 30, August 6, 31, September 3, 10, 18, 24, 1867; and Hamet Pinson to Miss Hessie, August 17, 1867, in Pinson Papers, LSU.

their fields this year." Labor was demoralized. In some cases, realizing no profits would be made, they walked away from their contracts. The bureau agent in Pulaski County reported after the disasters that the freedmen "do not now labor with the energy and cheerfulness manifested earlier in the year."[28]

Landowners, merchants, and workers all maneuvered to minimize their losses in the face of a terrible harvest. By June neither tenants nor landowners were able to obtain further advances for supplies from merchants who were unwilling to risk anything more against a crop that promised to be extremely short—many feared they had already advanced more than the crop would return. At the same time, landowners who had encouraged their tenants to obtain their supplies from merchants moved to protect their share of the crop against the merchants' claims. The bureau was an ally in the latter effort and in May issued a circular instructing local agents to make sure that merchant liens against crops did not interfere with the lien of the planter. Landowners also tried to get workers to break their contracts to avoid having to settle with them. Workers had little protection as landowners and merchants contrived to safeguard their own interests at the expense of the laborers.[29]

Fears about the cotton crop proved warranted. It was severely short, with newspapers estimating a harvest of less than two-thirds of the amount expected in the spring. In some hard-hit areas the crop was even smaller. Continuing high prices meant, however, that any cotton at all could help pay off advances and loans. Unfortunately, a further crisis developed as the crop went to market. Even with production reduced throughout the Mississippi River Valley, prices for cotton collapsed that autumn. Farmers had planted expecting prices to remain close to what they had been in 1866, about thirty-seven cents a pound, but October prices in 1867 were at only seventeen and eighteen cents. Prices were low and there was little demand. The combination of the short crop and the decline in prices produced a drastic loss in the value of the state's cotton. General C. H. Smith estimated

28. Little Rock *Daily Gazette,* June 6, 1867. Conditions are documented in letters filed in Operations Reports of Subordinate Offices, June and July, 1867. The observation on the freedmen is from E. O. C. Ord to O. O. Howard, July 23, 1867, in Reports of Bureau Operations, Arkansas, BRFAL, RG 105, NA.

29. *Report of the Commissioner of the Bureau of Refugees, Freedmen, and Abandoned Lands for the Year 1867* (Washington, D.C., 1867), 68; Circular No. 8, May 25, 1867, in Little Rock *Daily Gazette,* May 30, 1867; Little Rock *Daily Gazette,* August 31, 1867. See also reports filed for June, July, August, and September in Operations Reports of Subordinate Offices, Arkansas, BRFAL, RG 105, NA.

that it was 75 percent less than what farmers had expected as late as July.[30]

So the hoped-for profits for planters and tenants did not come in 1867. Instead, their already-large debts increased. In southern Arkansas, Andrew Carrigan, who besides being a small planter had set up as a country merchant, speculated that few people would be able to pay their debts. He wrote: "I have a good deal owing to me in this country, and it keeps increasing, and how the people are to pay me I cant see." When the crops failed to produce expected profits, both planters and their creditors were in trouble. Many who had survived the catastrophe of 1866 now lost everything. At Helena one planter found that times were very hard; he calculated that nearly half of the population were petitioning for bankruptcy. General Smith reported in December, 1867, that "the cotton planters as a rule will have nothing at all for themselves or hands, and in most cases both parties are hopelessly in debt."[31]

The economic disaster hit the entire state and all classes. Increased cultivation of cotton by tenants and small farmers as well as by planters spread the effects of the price collapse to almost everyone. J. C. Esselman of Pocahontas informed a friend that "the decline in the price of cotton has ruined a great many persons in this particular section and as this is not a cotton county you can readily imagine how the people in such localities will be affected." An attorney, Esselman indicated that many individuals were being forced to declare bankruptcy, including some of his own debtors. Across the state at Van Buren, L. C. Southmayd concluded that "very few planters here abouts will be able to meet their *last years* liabilities." Bureau agents estimated that few freedmen would be able to repay the debts that they had contracted and would enter the next year with obligations still owed for 1867. The year marked the beginning of a cycle of indebtedness by farmers of all classes to outside creditors and local merchants.[32]

30. William Meyer to J. E. Bennett, October 27, 1867, S. Geismiller to J. E. Bennett, October 1, 1867, both in Operations Reports of Subordinate Offices, Arkansas, BRFAL, RG 105, NA; C. H. Smith to O. O. Howard, December 28, 1867, in Reports of Bureau Operations, *ibid.;* Little Rock *Daily Gazette,* September 3, October 24, 1867; J. C. Esselman to Dear "Cam," December 13, 1867, in Campbell Brown and Richard Ewell Papers, TSLA.

31. A. N. Carrigan to Dear Brother, August 13, 1867, in Carrigan Papers; R. Wallace to W. E. Woodruff, November 25, 1867, in Woodruff Papers; C. H. Smith to O. O. Howard, December 28, 1867, in Operations Reports, Arkansas, BRFAL, RG 105, NA.

32. J. C. Esselman to Dear "Cam," December 13, 1867, in Brown and Ewell Papers; L. C. Southmayd to Albert Wallace, August 9, 1867, in Walker Papers; C. H. Smith to O. O. Howard, December 28, 1867, in Reports of Bureau Operations, Arkansas, BRFAL, RG 105, NA. For reports of financial problems of the freedmen, see J. W. Carhard to J. E. Bennett, September 30, 1867, J. C. Predmore to J. E. Bennett, October 1, 1867, both in Operations Reports of Subordinate Offices, Arkansas, BRFAL, RG 105, NA.

The disastrous season had other side effects. Among the most trouble-some was a decline in land prices. By the autumn of 1867, a correspondent of William Woodruff, Sr., reported that good land in Lafayette County brought as little as one dollar per acre in specie, but that little demand for farmland existed. Farm leases also declined. Plantation land below Little Rock that had leased for ten to fifteen dollars in 1867 dropped to three to four dollars in 1868. One farm lease in Union County went for only thirty-five cents per acre. With land as one of the few pieces of collateral available, other than crops, the decline left merchant loans made in 1868 even less protected than before and constricted the already-low credit base for plantation operations.[33]

With land prices down and landowners and workers already heavily in debt, merchants were reluctant to make further loans. In the winter of 1867 and spring of 1868, few farmers or country merchants could get credit. One writer concluded that money matters in the southwest part of the state were "closer than since the surrender." Any money made in cotton had to be used to settle existing debts and pay for supplies for the next year. Many individuals liquidated what holdings they had to obtain operating funds. George Pendleton informed his wife: "It is the tightest times. . . . To my certain knowledge Mr. Brown is offering a portion of his team for sale at a mere nominal price for the sake of getting some money to buy provisions." Many stores refused to sell anything on credit. By June, 1868, one observer found that in Lafayette County there was not enough money in circulation to pay local taxes.[34]

Particularly important, because of the political implications, the eco-nomic problems of 1867 created a challenge to the survival of the state's landowning elite. The belief that the Arkansas economy could rapidly recover died with the crops in the field and the prices at market. As early as May, 1867, the editor of the *Arkansas Gazette* had written: "The day of making sudden fortunes in agricultural pursuits has passed, and hereafter wealth will be accumulated by slow and steady accretions. . . . Let planters first raise what is necessary for their own support, and then produce to sell." M. L. Bell of Pine Bluff wrote: "Really I cannot see what is to become of

33. Alex Byrne to W. E. Woodruff, November 19, 1867, Mrs. E. P. Moore to Woodruff, January 5, 1868, Michael Bozeman to Woodruff, January 1, 1869, W. J. Bronaugh to Wood-ruff, December 19, 1872, M. L. Bell to Woodruff, July 7, 1874, all in Woodruff Papers; E. Jane Smith to Dear Friend, January 4, 1867, in E. Jane Smith Letter, Small Manuscripts Collection, AHC; A. N. Carrigan to My Dear Brother, April 10, 1867, in Carrigan Papers; Lease with James M. Welch, in Pendleton Family Letters; L. C. Southmayd to L. R. Evans, January 7, 1867, in Walker Papers.

34. Alex Byrne to W. E. Woodruff, November 19, 1867, June 15, 1868, in Woodruff Papers; G. M. Pendleton to My Dear Little Wife, May 25, 1868, in Pendleton Family Letters.

our country. . . . Ruin seems to stare us in the face, our country is ruined & I fear the town with it." A resident of southwest Arkansas saw thousands who had failed economically and did not know how they were going to survive. Many planned to move elsewhere, discussing spots as close as Texas and as far away as Honduras and California.[35]

Merchants were not as pessimistic about conditions, although their position depended on how much credit they advanced. At Camden, Robert Kellam's firm purchased local cotton for between fourteen and fifteen cents per pound and hoped to sell it at New Orleans for twenty, making a profit even though the farmers were not. Henry Butler, a merchant at Tulip in Dallas County, was in trouble, however, because he was having difficulty collecting debts. He informed his brother-in-law William Paisley, a merchant at Dobyville: "There will be much I won't collect at all, and much I will have to wait another year and maybe longer. . . . Times look squawly indeed, with a 'squawlier' prospect ahead." Butler congratulated Paisley for doing better since he had not gone so "heavy" into the credit system, although even the conservative Paisley had debtors not paying their bills.[36]

Yet even after the debacle of 1867, credit was ultimately available for the 1868 farming year. In fact, new sources of money and competition for the trade of Arkansas caused by the expansion of transportation kept interest rates down despite farm problems. Northern markets pursued Arkansas' merchants and businessmen and fed their credit into the state and sparked competition by New Orleans merchants. Many firms sent representatives into the state to trade directly with farmers. At Camden, Robert Kellam complained about outsiders, in this case "the Jews," who by getting hold of local trade were threatening to "gain upon the American merchant." Credit could be obtained, but the collateral for it was invariably a field planted with cotton. If landowners wished to continue to farm, the price was sticking with cotton.[37]

With its emphasis on cotton, the Arkansas economy was buffeted about

35. Little Rock *Daily Gazette*, May 30, 1867; M. L. Bell to W. E. Woodruff, November 28, 1867, M. Bozeman to Woodruff, May 8, 1868, both in Woodruff Papers; J. Everett to B. Sandford, February 3, 1868, in Sandford-Everett Family File, UALR; Hamet Pinson to My Dear Friend, September 21, November 8, 1867, February 1, 1868, in Pinson Papers.

36. Robert F. Kellam Diary, February 28, 1868, in AHC; H. Butler to W. Paisley, February 7, 1868, S. Williams to W. Paisley, February 27, 1868, both in Elizabeth Paisley Huckaby and Ethel C. Simpson, eds., *Tulip Evermore: Emma Butler and William Paisley, Their Lives in Letters, 1857–1887* (Fayetteville, 1985), 104, 105.

37. Kellam Diary, November 12, 1869; J. B. Rumph to R. W. Golsen, August 5, 1869, D. Newton to R. W. Golsen, July 30, 1868, both in Golsen Brothers Papers, LSU; W. J. Bronaugh to W. E. Woodruff, November 26, 1873, in Woodruff Papers.

by the problems connected with that crop after 1867. Weather conditions continued to be bad, with either late springs, flooding, or drought in 1868, 1869, and 1874. Cutworms were particularly bad in 1869. Worse, the market for cotton remained soft and prices low. For several years after the price collapse of 1867, market prices ranged between 12 and 18 cents per pound, although individual farmers could seldom count on those prices, since they usually dealt with local merchants paying prices 25 percent less than at market. In 1874 cotton hit 11.1 cents a pound, then began a precipitous fall that bottomed with the disastrous price of 5.8 cents a pound in the period from 1894 to 1897.[38]

By the end of 1867, the basic pattern of the Arkansas economy was set largely as it remained for the rest of the century. Potential had existed for another course of development. Many had urged caution, self-reliance, and diversification. In 1866 editor William E. Woodruff, Jr., asked Arkansans: "Shall we be actors in this drama, builders of this realm? or, shall we continue impotent grovelers and let *others* speculate upon our wealth." The editor of the Fayetteville *Arkansian* called for diversification and turning away from cotton, warning that to fail to do so would make the farmers captives of the credit system. Few farmers listened. They went back to cotton to restore their wealth. The disasters of 1866 and 1867 fixed cotton cultivation on them. Farm operators were in debt and required credit each year. The price for the new credit was growing cotton to settle the obligations, and the crop spread across the state. By 1880 the number of counties with a cotton-to-corn ratio of 25:1 or lower, showing the abandonment of self-sufficiency and increased emphasis on cotton, had increased from eight to twenty-six (Map 8). Those with a ratio between 26:1 and 50:1 actually declined from eighteen to fifteen, as the number with even greater emphasis on cotton increased. The number of counties with ratios between 51:1 and 100:1 expanded from twelve to seventeen. (The fact that ten new counties were created between 1870 and 1880 is not of great significance to the trend suggested by the foregoing statistics; only four of the new counties were in the cotton-plantation region.) Nature and the price of cotton were critical factors in the state's postwar economic

38. D. Newton to R. W. Golsen, August 31, 1868, August 27, 1869, J. B. Rumph to R. W. Golsen, August 8, 1869, all in Golsen Brothers Papers; M. L. Bell to W. E. Woodruff, July 7, September 12, 1874, in Woodruff Papers; M. Pendleton to Dear Husband, June 27, 1868, in Pendleton Family Papers; M. N. Love to Father and Mother, March 8, 1868, in Mathew N. Love Papers, DU; J. H. Anderson to Dear Brother, May 20, 1873, in Anderson Papers, AHC; Little Rock *Daily Gazette,* May 26, 1868, March 19, May 25, 27, 29, July 13, August 6, September 9, 1869, July 26, 1870.

life, but the decision of Arkansans in 1866 to emphasize cotton culture helped tie their farms to a crop that languished for the next hundred years and left Arkansas a legacy of poverty.[39]

For the state, a lack of capital and credit meant that little changed economically or socially over the next decades. Arkansas remained primarily agricultural. There was some manufacturing growth. The number of manufacturing firms increased from 518 in 1860 to 1,079 in 1870, then steadily expanded to 4,794 in 1900. The capital invested in manufacturing grew in the same period from $1,316,610 in 1860 to $1,782,913 in 1870, then to $135,182,170 in 1900. Relative to the overall economic picture, however, these changes had little significance. In 1860 capital invested in manufacturing represented 1.4 percent of the combined value of farms and manufacturing establishments. In 1870 manufacturing capital had increased to 5.3 percent and by 1900 to 21.0 percent of the combined totals. Much of this relative growth, however, came because the value of farm products declined rather than because of any significant increase in manufacturing.[40]

With the economy agrarian, the population remained rural. In 1860 the town dwellers reported by the census constituted only 0.9 percent of the total population. By 1870 the percentage had grown to 2.6 percent. There was a steady growth of towns through the rest of the century, but no major change in where the majority of Arkansans lived. By 1900 the urban population was only 8.5 percent. Most people still lived on farms or in small rural communities long into the twentieth century.[41]

The economic crisis set the stage for the political drama that took place in Arkansas between 1867 and 1874. Pushed to the wall economically, the state's landed interests saw their very survival threatened, both as individuals and as a group, by the intervention of Congress in reconstruction in 1867. The new system could destabilize labor and add to the financial burdens of this elite. They had been pushed from political power. The situation demanded quick maneuvering to minimize the threat and recapture political control. Politics between 1867 and 1874 largely reflected that effort by the elite to regain command of the state government and use it to protect themselves.

39. Little Rock *Daily Gazette*, July 4, 1866; Fayetteville *Arkansian* in Little Rock *Daily Conservative*, January 1, 1867; J. Turner to W. E. Woodruff, March 22, 1870, in Woodruff Papers; Kellam Diary, August 2, 1869; D. Newton to R. W. Golsen, July 30, 1868, J. B. Rumph to Dear Bob, August 8, 1869, both in Golsen Brothers Papers.

40. Donald B. Dodd and Synelle S. Dodd, *Historical Statistics of the South, 1790–1970* (University, Ala., 1973), 8–9.

41. *Ibid.*, 6–7; *Ninth Census, 1870: Compendium*, Table IX; *Tenth Census, 1880: Compendium*, Pt. 1, Table XIX.

# Map 8

## Corn-to-Cotton Ratios, 1880

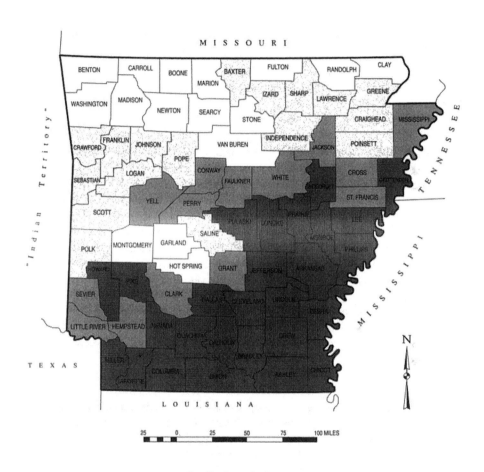

(bushels to bales)

- Less than 25:1
- 26:1 to 50:1
- 51:1 to 100:1
- Greater than 100:1

# 13

## RADICAL RECONSTRUCTION AND REDEMPTION, 1867–1874

IN 1867 CONGRESSIONAL RECONSTRUCTION REOPENED the question of governmental authority in Arkansas. Congressional intervention took place at the same time that the disasters of 1866 and 1867 threatened the economic and social survival of the state's economic elite, who had done much to stabilize their position in the immediate postwar years. Given the enormity of the crisis for the elite, they engaged in almost frantic efforts to ensure that Congress did not worsen their problems. Fighting with fierce determination, they made certain that Congressional Reconstruction was short and that, in the end, it did not change their control over political power. The defeat of Congressional Reconstruction was the last step for the elite in consolidating their place after the war and limiting the changes brought about by that conflict.

The first Reconstruction Act placed Arkansas with Mississippi in the Fourth Military District, commanded by Major General E. O. C. Ord. Military intervention put on hold the measures passed by the Sixteenth General Assembly, and Ord refused to allow the legislature to reconvene in July, 1867. The general prepared for a new constitutional convention to consider changes required by Congress by appointing boards of registration to administer the prescribed oath to prospective voters and register them. The process continued until September, when Ord ordered an election for November, 1867, to consider holding a convention and to choose delegates to it. The registration pushed the political interests of the state to organize.[1]

Congressional intervention gave Unionist opponents of the Conservatives a new life. In April, 1867, many of them gathered for the boisterous first state convention of the Republican party of Arkansas. The delegates charged that the Conservatives had caused secession and were now trying

---

1. *Senate Executive Documents,* 40th Cong., 1st Sess., No. 14, p. 157; *Debates and Proceedings of the Convention Which Assembled at Little Rock, January 7, 1868* (Little Rock, 1868), 27–31; Thomas S. Staples, *Reconstruction in Arkansas, 1862–1874* (New York, 1923), 132–77.

to avoid the consequences of their defeat. The Republicans endorsed the intervention of Congress and called for a new state government that was loyal, that was economical and would restore the public credit, and that would support railroads and other internal improvements, create a system of public schools, and encourage immigration to and investment in the state.[2]

Three different groups that formed the basis for the new party were represented at the convention. The president, James M. Johnson, a physician and 1836 settler in Madison County, was typical of the antebellum white element who came to be known as "scalawags." Many of them were wartime Unionists who had become Republicans because they believed that congressional policy, particularly black suffrage, was necessary for their own protection and to ensure loyal state government. After the return of the Conservatives to power, Fort Smith Unionists concluded: "Nothing is left us but to apply to Congress for redress and help. . . . Let us go back therefore and build up the house of state on a new foundation, removing the decayed and rotten timbers." Unionist Elisha Baxter counseled unity: "The only hope for protection to Loyal men in this state is to organize a Loyal state government under the military bill by the aid of the negrow [sic] vote. I hope there fore we will have no prating among our friends about the negrow [sic] vote since to lay aside all other considerations it is the only salvation for the Loyal people of the State."[3]

Many northerners who had settled in the state after the war joined the scalawags in the Republican party. They were called "carpetbaggers." The most prominent of them was General Powell Clayton, who came to Arkansas as colonel of the 5th Kansas Cavalry and became commander of the post at Pine Bluff. After the war he married an Arkansas woman and started a plantation along the Arkansas River. He became involved in politics, according to his own account, because his Confederate neighbors treated him so badly that he had to take a stand for "the preservation of his life and property." Other carpetbaggers had come during the war and remained, hoping to find new opportunities.[4]

Newly enfranchised blacks were the third group represented in the convention. Blacks provided the voting strength of the party, but only three black delegates attended the convention. John Peyton of Pulaski County

2. Little Rock *Daily Gazette,* April 3, 4, 5, 6, 9, 1867.

3. *Ibid.,* April 9, 1867; Fort Smith (Ark.) *New Era* in Van Buren (Ark.) *Press,* November 30, 1866; Elisha Baxter to Calvin C. Bliss, April 12, 1867, in Calvin C. Bliss Papers, AHC; Powell Clayton, *The Aftermath of the Civil War, in Arkansas* (New York, 1915), 299.

4. Little Rock *Daily Gazette,* April 9, 1867; Clayton, *Aftermath of the Civil War, in Arkansas,* 299–302.

was the most visible, serving on the committee on resolutions and the state central committee. A Missourian, Peyton had come to Little Rock as a slave in 1832. With freedom, he became a prominent minister and gained widespread respect among blacks. Loudly cheered by a crowd of freedmen on the convention's first day, Peyton admonished his audience to listen closely to the debates and to "rightly use the freedom" they now had.[5]

The convention was the first step toward active organization throughout the state by a state executive committee headed by Benjamin F. Rice, a northern attorney who had settled in Little Rock after the war. Party efforts focused on mobilizing the newly enfranchised black voters through mass meetings and the use of a network of secret political clubs, the Union League. The committee sent representatives through the state to charter local chapters. Their efforts were only partially successful. The Conservatives charged that the Union League had extensive power, but Freedmen's Bureau agents found that it was thoroughly organized only around Little Rock. In rural areas individual planters exercised considerable control over their workers' political behavior.[6]

During the campaign the ideas of the new party matured and the threat to Conservative interests became clearer. The Republicans advocated internal improvements similar to those backed by Conservatives, but argued for their development throughout the state rather than only in favored sections: in an editorial on October 29, 1867, the party's Little Rock *Republican* asked readers, "Do you want good roads *throughout* the state?" In addition, party leaders proclaimed themselves the representatives of the poor and maintained that their economic and social programs would help the working class. Advocating free education, Washington County Republicans urged taxing the state's wealthy to give the "neglected children of poor men an equal opportunity for education with those of the rich." "Times are changing," wrote "Progress" to the *Republican*; "the people will soon learn that no one class are entitled to a monopoly of rights to the prejudices of those of other classes." Republicans promised new taxes, equally applied to all classes. The reasons for this class appeal are unclear, but during the war Unionists had believed that lower-class whites were loyal. This program offered hope to poor whites as well as to blacks.[7]

5. Little Rock *Daily Gazette*, April 4 (quote), 9, 1867.

6. Recommendation for A. K. Davis and J. Helm, August 15, 1867, copy in G. W. S. Bensen to C. H. Smith, September 27, 1867, Letters and Telegrams Received, Assistant Commissioner, Arkansas, BRFAL, RG 105, NA (see also August–November, 1867, files for political reports); Little Rock *Evening Republican*, May 2, August 5, 21, September 24, December 16, 1867; Clayton, *Aftermath of the Civil War, in Arkansas*, 301.

7. Little Rock *Evening Republican*, July 2, October 29, December 5, 1867, January 11, 1868.

Conservatives considered the Republican program threatening. Taxes posed a potential burden, especially given the economic crisis. Schools and diversified economic development could undermine the stability of the labor force. Of immediate concern, however, was the impact on labor of Republican efforts to organize black voters. An editor of the *Arkansas Gazette* complained that the Republican state convention caused workers to abandon plantations all around Little Rock and that "they left their work at a time, when by reason of the late season, they were most needed in the fields." S. R. Cockrill of Pine Bluff complained to President Johnson that Republican efforts were preventing restoration of order in the work force. He concluded: "The idea of *voting*, has had a most demoralizing influence." Even a sympathetic Freedmen's Bureau agent reported that "many have . . . joined the Union League or the Grand Army of the Republic; they are becoming quite enthusiastic and are getting rather over zealous in attending barbecues and other political meetings . . . to the detriment of their crops."[8]

Despite their concerns, the Conservatives were not unified on how to respond. Former congressman and Confederate general Thomas C. Hindman advocated that party lines be drawn to contest the convention election, but others did not want to turn the election into a party issue. Some Conservatives concluded that the convention could be defeated by refusing to register to vote, but other leaders wanted a full registration and a vote against the convention. Among the latter, the editors of the *Arkansas Gazette* warned that not voting contributed "to the success of radicalism and the triumph of the negro suffrage party." They and John Denham of the Van Buren *Press* encouraged county meetings to nominate candidates for the convention who opposed black suffrage. The Conservatives never effected a statewide organization, but local meetings were held that nominated men adhering to the party line. In Pulaski County the Conservatives selected three Union army officers to run, who according to the *Arkansas Gazette* were "of a different class from the political incendiaries and agitators who consort with negroes and endeavor to climb into office on their shoulders. These candidates . . . oppose the establishment of negro governments and the scheme of the radical party to give control of the state to the African."[9]

Conservative newspapers united in their attack upon the convention, emphasizing racial issues and asserting that the convention was the first step toward black domination. They also assaulted the carpetbaggers, maintaining that they were unsuccessful men who had come to Arkansas to

8. Little Rock *Daily Gazette*, April 4, 1867; S. R. Cockrill to A. Johnson, January 9, 1868, in Andrew Johnson Papers, LC.

9. Little Rock *Daily Gazette*, October 29, 1867; Van Buren (Ark.) *Press*, April 26, October 25, 1867; Little Rock *Daily Gazette*, October 30, 1867.

exploit the state. Conservatives declared their preference even for continued military rule, rather than a restored civil government run by blacks or
carpetbaggers.[10]

Local Conservative partisans attacked Republican efforts to organize
black voters. They gave out misinformation about registration and voting.
For example, rumors were spread that the registration was actually a Yankee
trick to get blacks drafted into the army or to tax them. The Conservatives
also tried to undermine black trust of Republican organizers by characterizing them as Yankees with no real interest in the complete freedom of
blacks. They asked black farmers to compare their relative impoverishment
as freedmen with their condition as slaves and asked what the Yankees had
accomplished. At times whites resorted to violence against Republican
organizers, attacking them and driving them from counties.[11]

The Conservatives failed to block the convention. Their own disorganization, white disfranchisement, the black vote, and political lethargy ensured approval of the convention, and Republicans got a majority of the
delegates. The convention met between January 7 and February 14, 1868,
and the Republicans produced a document that, although generally unre-
markable, prescribed significant changes. Its political keystone was its
suffrage provision, which extended the vote to all adult males, regardless
of race, but also disfranchised all who had taken an oath to support the
government of the United States and then voluntarily violated it, who had
violated the rules of civilized warfare, or who were disqualified from voting
by the proposed Fourteenth Amendment. Combined with later legislative
enactments governing registration, the disfranchising rules gave the Republicans a strong tool against a resurgence of the Conservatives.[12]

Having failed to prevent a convention, the Conservatives were determined to prevent the ratification of a new constitution. They held a prelim-
inary organizational meeting at Little Rock on December 2, 1867. Chaired
by Colonel Francis A. R. Terry, a Civil War veteran and prewar Democratic
state senator, the meeting recommended that Conservatives "co-operate
with the national Democratic party, by a thorough organization in every
county and township in the state." The assembly named nine members to

10. Little Rock *Daily Gazette*, October 29, 30, 1867; Pine Bluff (Ark.) *Dispatch*, October
12, 1867; Van Buren (Ark.) *Press*, September 20, August 23, 1867.

11. J. Geisreiter to J. E. Bennett, August 31, September 1, 1867, I. W. Carhart to J. E.
Bennett, August 31, 1867, G. W. S. Bensen to C. H. Smith, September 27, 1867, all in Letters
and Telegrams Received, Assistant Commissioner, Arkansas, BRFAL, RG 105, NA.

12. For a discussion of issues and debates in the convention, see Staples, *Reconstruction in
Arkansas*, 217–47, and *Debates and Proceedings of the Convention Which Assembled at Little Rock,
January 7, 1868*, 878–79. For assessments of the election turnout, see Little Rock *Daily Gazette*,
November 8, 12, 1867, and Pine Bluff (Ark.) *Dispatch*, November 23, 1867.

serve as a Democratic State Committee. The tone of the Conservative defense was signaled by the *Arkansas Gazette*, whose editors declared: "From this day hence, the line of party is drawn. On the one side will be found the enemies of the constitution and advocates of negro domination; and on the other, the friends of constitutional liberty and supporters of a white man's government. There is no neutral ground between; therefore choose ye the household to whose fate you will unite your fortunes." [13]

The central committee called another state convention to organize the party. Gathering at Little Rock on January 27, 1868, the convention was dominated by prewar and wartime Democrats. Prewar federal officials such as Senator Robert W. Johnson, Congressmen Albert Rust and Edward A. Warren, District Judge Daniel Ringo, and United States Attorney John M. Harrell attended. Former state officers included Jordan E. Cravens, representative; Elbert H. English, chief justice of the state supreme court; Samuel W. Williams, attorney general and representative; and George C. Watkins, attorney general and chief justice of the supreme court. Several Confederate military leaders were delegates, including Colonel Lucien C. Gause of the 32d Arkansas Infantry and Colonel Robert C. Newton of the 5th Arkansas Cavalry. It was not a completely Democratic show, however. Symbols of the Whig coon and the Democratic rooster along with a motto—United in a Just Cause—decorated the stage of the Little Rock city hall, and the antebellum Whig and wartime congressman Augustus H. Garland participated actively in the proceedings. [14]

The delegates established the platform of the postwar Democracy. Their first resolution declared their intent to maintain a "WHITE MAN'S government in a WHITE MAN'S COUNTRY," and others argued the inferiority of blacks. The convention recognized the equality of blacks before the law but denied their rights to make those laws or to possess social equality. Trying to block reconstruction under a revised constitution, the delegates proposed that the Constitution of 1864 be accepted as the new state constitution. Before adjourning they proclaimed that those who opposed their platform were "enemies of the country" and charged the central committee to organize the state to ensure success of the "great white man's party." [15]

13. Little Rock *Daily Gazette*, December 3 (first quotation), 7 (second quotation), 11, 1867.

14. Little Rock *Daily Gazette*, January 28, 29, 1868. For biographies of many of the prominent prewar politicians who attended the convention, see Clio Harper, comp., "Prominent Members of the Early Arkansas Bar: Biographies of 1797–1884" (Undated manuscript in AHC), 93, 116, 132, 133, 136, 168, 190, 264, 303, 312, 317, 365, 383, 386, 395.

15. Little Rock *Daily Gazette*, January 30, 1868.

The Republicans also met while the constitutional convention was still in session. They prepared for an election to ratify the new constitution and elect officers to a new state government. With some conflict between the scalawag and carpetbagger factions, the delegates who assembled at Little Rock on January 15, 1868, nominated a full ticket headed by Powell Clayton for governor and Dr. James M. Johnson for lieutenant governor. Their platform reasserted the position taken the previous spring supporting Congressional Reconstruction, internal improvements, free schools, economical government, and the civil and political equality of all men.[16]

When the constitutional convention adjourned, Republican candidates stumped the state, and party newspapers editorialized in favor of the proposed constitution and the Republican slate. Speakers and writers continued to emphasize old themes: their party stood for the interests of poor whites and blacks against the Democratic party's support of the old elite. They promised rapid political reconstruction, economic growth, and peace and prosperity. While canvassing the state in favor of the constitution and party ticket, Republican leaders also renewed efforts to organize blacks.[17]

The Democrats were better organized than in 1867 and campaigned vigorously, urging electors to vote down the proposed constitution. Democratic newspapers violently attacked the document, and Democratic speakers traveled the state trying to arouse voters. They argued that the constitution was not republican in form because it disfranchised many white citizens. They also claimed that by enfranchising blacks the constitution would encourage social equality. They attacked its fiscal provisions, which they charged would place the entire burden of taxes on whites, would void debts for the purchase of slaves, and would compel whites to support a public school system their children would not attend. Above all else, they appealed to racism. In a typical speech, John M. Bradley, a Conservative delegate to the convention despite his service as a Freedmen's Bureau agent, called upon voters to oppose the constitution "if you do not want to be compelled to send your children to school with niggers—if you vote for it, you invite the nigger into your parlour—you invite him to ride in your carriage—you offer him one of your daughters in marriage, socially and politically." Woodruff of the *Gazette* stated the basic party position when he wrote, "We do not recognize that the negro has any political rights

16. Little Rock *Evening Republican*, January 14, 15, 17, 24, 1868.
17. *Ibid.*, February 1, 14, 15, 25, March 3, 4, 1868; John Stayton to Joe Stayton, March 13, 1868, quoted in Lady Elizabeth Luker, "Post Civil War Period in Jackson County," *Stream of History*, IV (1966), 36–37.

whatever, and his existence in the country is only tolerated by white men on the score of humanity."[18]

The Democrats also intimidated supporters of the constitution to keep them from voting, particularly trying to make voting as difficult as possible. Democratic spokesmen urged party clubs to watch the polls to note irregularities and count voters, but in practice the poll watchers' presence kept many Republican voters away and pressured others to vote Democratic. The party's leaders did not outwardly encourage violence, but their rhetoric and efforts overtly did. Woodruff was not explicit about how they should behave, but he urged Democrats to organize their own secret organizations to counter the Union League and to do what was necessary to render the latter harmless.[19]

Many whites unquestionably were open to manipulation on the racial issue. John W. Stayton, an attorney in Jackson County, expressed the fury of many when he wrote "the bare idea of being ruled by the miserable whelps that prowl around your kitchen at night and tamper with your private affairs on every occasion presented, is too bad, too bad." This concern was not enough, however, to create the political excitement the Democrats needed. The demands of economic survival pressed many Arkansans harder than a need to become involved in politics. Judge U. M. Rose complained that "it must be confessed that in some places our people have been hard to arouse and well nigh dead to every matter of public concern; tired of hunting for their rights, demanding rest, and willing to sell their liberties for something less than a mess of pottage."[20]

The election began on March 13. On April 1 the state board of election commissioners reported ratification of the Constitution, but the Democrats claimed intimidation and fraud and challenged the results. An investigation by military authorities concluded that although there had been ample fraud by both sides, it was unlikely that "any election for ratification of the constitution can be held in Arkansas where similar charges will not by some party be made." General Alvan C. Gillem decided that the election was

18. Little Rock *Daily Gazette*, February 28, 1868; Van Buren (Ark.) *Press*, February 28, 1868; *Debates and Proceedings of the Convention Which Assembled at Little Rock, January 7, 1868*, 665–66; John Stayton to Joe Stayton, March 13, 1868, in Luker, "Post Civil War Period in Jackson County," 36–37.

19. *Campaign Gazette*, March 6, 13, 1868; Little Rock *Evening Republican*, March 3, 31, April 13, 1868.

20. John Stayton to Joe Stayton, March 13, 1868, in Luker, "Post Civil War Period in Jackson County," 36–37; U. M. Rose to D. Walker, March 16, 1868, in *Pulaski County Historical Review*, VI (March, 1958), 7–8; M. N. Love to Father and Mother, March 8, 1868, in Mathew N. Love Papers, DU.

valid and reported on April 23 that the constitution had been ratified by a vote of 25,600 to 22,994. The newly elected General Assembly met on April 2, 1868, unanimously ratified the Fourteenth Amendment, elected United States senators, requested recognition, and then adjourned till Congress acted. Overriding a presidential veto, the United States House of Representatives passed a bill to readmit the state on June 20; the Senate followed on June 22. Arkansas was finally back in the Union.[21]

Full restoration was marked on July 3, 1868, by the inauguration of Governor Clayton. The Republicans implemented in the first session of the General Assembly as much of their promised legislation as they could. They created a public school system and inaugurated a state university. They submitted a bill to the electorate to allow state credit to be loaned to railroads. The General Assembly set up a program to encourage levee construction and created commissions to promote immigration, to develop natural resources, and to supervise public works and internal improvements. To support these measures the legislators raised taxes. The state general property tax levied in 1868 amounted to 1.425 percent of assessed value. Counties were allowed to raise a tax equal to the general state tax, and other municipalities could levy a maximum tax of 2 percent of assessed value. In addition, a one-dollar poll tax for schools was levied on all adult males. The state tax was three times that imposed by the previous General Assembly, county taxes one-and-a-half times that level, and the municipal tax new. The Republicans had quickly placed an economic pinch on the landed interests of the state.[22]

In the face of the tax threat, the Democrats desperately sought to rally for the elections in the fall of 1868. That election would select a president and new congressmen, fill legislative vacancies, and consider the railroad loan bill. Leading Democrats such as William E. Woodruff, Jr., urged opponents of the Republicans to register even if they had to perjure themselves when taking the constitutional oath. David Walker and others objected to this tactic, arguing that it accepted the principle of black suffrage, but the central committee and a majority of leaders reasoned that too much was at stake. In such circumstances action outweighed principle. Woodruff wrote to Walker on September 11: "I think we are justified in conducting the canvass on war principles, 'to destroy the enemy' being the first. . . . I do not believe there is any binding force in law or morals to an oath

21. George Watkins to D. Walker, March 29, 1868, in A. Howard Stebbins Collection, AHC; *House Executive Documents*, 40th Cong., 2d Sess., No. 278, pp. 4–5, 23 (quote); *House Journal*, 40th Cong., 2d Sess., 57, 65; *Congressional Globe*, 40th Cong., 2d Sess., 2375, 2399, 2438, 2440, 2487.

22. *Acts of Arkansas, 1868*, 148, 163, 166, 313, 327.

taken under duress." A month later Woodruff further defended those who decided to take the oath, writing that they "believe the voters' oath is not binding in conscience or law[;] that whatever obligation it has (if any) is during the excitement of the present government only."[23]

Woodruff's letter to Walker went on to make it apparent that Democratic party leaders worried about their ability to hold on to the electorate unless they acted decisively. Not only the party, but also the state's interests, were being threatened. "I am satisfied," Woodruff wrote, "that if the white people of Arkansas are not allowed an opportunity to vote as democrats, many thousands will do so as radicals, and you know what sort of radicals traitors make. The course we take is the only one that will save the democratic party." Judge George C. Watkins expressed the same concerns when he advocated political action: "Even if we do not succeed, we still have a party organization for our people to rally to."[24]

Whether there was a connection is not clear, but as the Democrats reorganized, a massive outbreak of violence occurred across the state. Its level intensified through the summer and autumn. In August blacks in Mississippi County fled to the woods for safety and the county's delegate to the Republican state convention, Dr. A. M. Johnson, was assassinated. The reign of terror hit the southern and eastern counties particularly hard, and individual blacks, bureau agents, state legislators, members of the board of registration, officers of the state guard, and even an assistant United States assessor were subject to assaults and attempted assassinations. The outbreak of violence reached its peak when Congressman James Hinds and state representative Joseph Brooks were assaulted by the secretary of the county Democratic committee in Monroe County. Hinds was killed and Brooks seriously wounded. The Republicans blamed the atrocities on the Ku Klux Klan, which they considered an arm of the Democratic party.[25]

Whether the secret Klan was ever fully organized in the state can never be known, nor can its possible connection with the Democratic party. Colonel Robert G. Shaver, who had commanded the 38th Arkansas Infantry, claimed to be the first wizard of the Klan, which he asserted had dens

23. Wm. E. Woodruff, Jr., to D. Walker, September 11, October 16, 1868, in Stebbins Collection.

24. Wm. E. Woodruff, Jr., to D. Walker, September 11, 1868, *ibid.;* G. C. Watkins to Walker, August 22, 1868, in David Walker Papers, UAF.

25. For examples of the violence see May–August, 1868, correspondence in Letters and Telegrams Received, Assistant Commissioner, Arkansas, BRFAL, RG 105, NA; Little Rock *Daily Gazette,* October 1, 6, 24, December 2, 1868; Little Rock *Morning Republican,* October 24, 1868; and Clayton, *Aftermath of the Civil War, in Arkansas,* 56–105. On the Klan, see Allen W. Trelease, *White Terror: The Ku Klux Klan Conspiracy and Southern Reconstruction* (New York, 1971), 98–103.

primarily in the southwest with 15,000 members, but he provided little information on its operations. Whether they intended to do so or not, however, the groups who carried out the violence did have a political impact and did strike at the Republicans. The objects of the attacks included bureau, military, and state officials—anyone, according to one bureau agent, who had "anything to do with the new order of affairs."[26]

Whether the violence of 1868 reflected a political conspiracy or simply the disruption of society, the Republicans had to respond to it and suppress it. Powell Clayton ordered the state militia to organize, and on November 4, 1868, he proclaimed martial law in Ashley, Bradley, Columbia, Lafayette, Mississippi, Woodruff, Craighead, Greene, Sevier, and Little River counties to end the attacks upon his supporters. State guard and militia units moved into those counties and crushed all resistance. The state troops' activities proved controversial when many engaged in plundering, but their defenders believed that many of the charges against them were partisan. Clayton was convinced that the problem justified the use of force no matter what crimes took place, and that the troops successfully pacified the state and ended the Klan threat.[27]

While state troops and Klansmen clashed, the state held its elections on November 3. The registrations in all of the counties under martial law had been overturned, so those counties did not vote at all. New registrations were ordered in Sharp, Jackson, Monroe, and Randolph counties, and their returns were not counted. Even so, the outcome gave little hope to the Republicans. Despite not having elections or not counting returns in fourteen counties, Republican candidates won easily only in the Third Congressional District, which included the northwest part of the state. There they elected Thomas Boles to Congress with 63 percent of the votes. In the First District, consisting primarily of eastern counties, Republican Logan M. Roots defeated C. S. Cameron by only 472 votes out of 13,829 cast, after no election was held in eight of the district's counties and 309 votes for Cameron in Crittenden County were disallowed. In the Second District, primarily the southwestern counties, Democrat Anthony A. C. Rogers of Pine Bluff defeated James T. Elliott even though five of the district's counties were under martial law. The Republican party could carry only one of the three congressional districts without tight control over registration and the voters. The Democrats had a potential statewide majority despite voting restrictions.[28]

26. Little Rock *Morning Republican*, April 3, 6, 1868; Little Rock *Daily Gazette*, August 11, 1911; Clayton, *Aftermath of the Civil War, in Arkansas*, 57; Eli H. Mix to C. H. Smith, July 27, 1868, in Letters and Telegrams Received, Assistant Commissioners, Arkansas, BRFAL, RG 105, NA.

27. Little Rock *Morning Republican*, November 6, 17, 1868; Staples, *Reconstruction in Arkansas*, 395; Trelease, *White Terror*, 149–74.

28. Little Rock *Daily Gazette*, January 9, 1869, returns for all three districts.

The cost to taxpayers of the Republican legislative program became an issue that eroded the party's strength even further in the months after the 1868 elections. The Republicans' development package unquestionably cost money, but leaders believed the expansion of the tax base that would take place would minimize the impact on individual taxpayers. Costs rose much faster than the resulting increase in the base, however. Within a year government expenditures reached $2 million per year, compared with $100,000 annually before the war. The state's bonded indebtedness passed $10 million, compared with an antebellum debt of less than $2 million. At the same time, the economy declined because of problems in cotton. Government had to raise more money while wealth in the state was decreasing.[29]

The state and local governments increased revenues first by raising tax rates. In 1868 the General Assembly imposed a state tax of 1.425 percent on the valuation, compared with .166 percent before the war. The new tax included .5 percent for general state expenses, .2 percent for the new school system, .25 percent to pay for the constitutional convention, .225 for the militia, and .25 for a sinking fund to pay for the public debt. After the convention and militia taxes expired in 1871, the rate dropped to .95. Increases also took place at the local level, where the county maximum was raised from 1.425 to 1.5 and municipalities were allowed a rate of 2 percent. Local authorities could raise other taxes to service bonds and to aid railroads. By 1871 county tax maximums were 2.0 percent for rural and 2.25 percent for urban areas; municipal tax rates were reduced to .75 percent.[30]

In addition, the General Assembly tried to solve its fiscal problem by reassessing real estate at market value. Assessed values of land had declined as a result of the war from $5.32 per acre in 1860 to $2.21 per acre in 1866. The reassessment program, implemented in 1868, increased the average assessment to $2.04 per acre that year, to $3.18 by 1870, and to $3.74 by 1873 (see Table 18). Assessors in many mountain counties were more diligent in their duties than in the plantation areas. Nonetheless, new assessments hit particularly hard at landowners already suffering because of the problems with cotton.[31]

Higher taxes and the reassessments furnished Democrats with an important issue. The increases were not as outrageous as the Republicans'

29. Staples, *Reconstruction in Arkansas*, 359, 363.

30. *Acts of Arkansas, 1868*, 177–79, 313; *Acts of Arkansas, 1873*, 367.

31. Little Rock *Daily Gazette*, June 20, 1869, March 28, 1871; *Biennial Report of the Auditor of Public Accounts of the State of Arkansas, for 1859 and 1860* (Little Rock, 1860), Table H; *Biennial Report of the Auditor of Public Accounts of the State of Arkansas for 1864, 1865, and 1866* (Little Rock, 1866), Table 9; *Biennial Report of the Auditor of Public Accounts of the State of Arkansas from October 1, 1872 to September 30, 1874* (Little Rock, 1874), 46–49.

TABLE 18

AVERAGE PER-ACRE REAL-PROPERTY ASSESSMENTS, 1860, 1865, 1868, 1870, 1871, 1873

| County | 1860 | 1865 | 1868 | 1870 | 1871 | 1873 |
|---|---|---|---|---|---|---|
| LOWLAND | | | | | | |
| Arkansas | 6.48 | 1.70 | 1.29 | 1.88 | 3.00 | 3.02 |
| Ashley | 4.43 | .79 | ★ | 2.27 | 3.40 | 2.72 |
| Bradley | 3.97 | .79 | .96 | 1.49 | 2.98 | 2.64 |
| Calhoun | 3.84 | .86 | ★ | 1.52 | 2.43 | 1.92 |
| Chicot | 22.83 | 2.22 | ★ | 4.27 | 5.98 | 4.37 |
| Clark | 5.38 | 1.65 | ★ | 3.18 | 3.81 | ★ |
| Columbia | 3.01 | ★ | ★ | 1.83 | 3.29 | 2.57 |
| Craighead | 3.32 | 1.06 | ★ | 4.29 | 3.44 | 2.10 |
| Crittenden | 10.64 | 2.96 | ★ | 3.60 | 4.32 | 5.84 |
| Cross | ★★ | 1.33 | ★ | 2.04 | 3.46 | 4.49 |
| Clayton | ★★ | ★★ | ★★ | ★★ | ★★ | 2.51 |
| Dallas | 4.16 | 1.10 | ★ | 1.26 | 2.89 | 2.18 |
| Desha | 5.45 | 2.55 | ★ | 4.43 | 4.43 | 2.66 |
| Drew | 4.02 | ★ | 1.12 | 2.60 | 3.40 | 3.14 |
| Dorsey | ★★ | ★★ | ★★ | ★★ | ★★ | 1.99 |
| Grant | ★★ | ★★ | ★★ | 1.19 | 1.90 | 1.12 |
| Hempstead | 3.89 | 1.02 | 1.51 | 3.16 | 3.48 | 3.89 |
| Independence | 3.67 | 2.07 | 2.61 | 2.32 | 2.55 | 4.04 |
| Jackson | 6.06 | 2.45 | 2.39 | 3.10 | 4.90 | 4.84 |
| Jefferson | 6.04 | 1.82 | 2.23 | 5.52 | 5.25 | 10.01 |
| Lafayette | 5.69 | ★ | 1.96 | 3.10 | 3.10 | 3.06 |
| Little River | ★★ | ★★ | ★★ | 3.24 | 3.24 | 3.08 |
| Lonoke | ★★ | ★★ | ★★ | ★★ | ★★ | 3.10 |
| Lincoln | ★★ | ★★ | ★★ | ★★ | ★★ | 3.56 |
| Lee | ★★ | ★★ | ★★ | ★★ | ★★ | 4.88 |
| Monroe | 6.92 | 1.95 | 1.65 | 1.98 | 3.36 | 5.38 |
| Mississippi | 5.10 | 1.81 | ★ | 1.64 | 3.69 | 4.10 |
| Nevada | ★★ | ★★ | ★★ | ★★ | ★★ | 2.51 |
| Ouachita | 4.75 | .86 | 1.02 | 1.85 | 3.33 | 3.03 |
| Phillips | 12.66 | 3.92 | 3.39 | 7.60 | 5.32 | 4.86 |
| Poinsett | 5.18 | ★ | .74 | .73 | 2.19 | 1.53 |
| Prairie | 4.69 | 2.15 | 1.35 | 2.41 | 3.03 | 2.58 |
| Pulaski | 7.49 | 4.63 | 5.43 | 6.03 | 5.43 | 6.53 |
| St. Francis | 6.15 | 2.06 | ★ | 3.93 | 3.93 | 2.89 |
| Union | 3.45 | .62 | ★ | 2.46 | 3.06 | 2.81 |
| White | 4.04 | 1.44 | 1.97 | 3.45 | 3.96 | 3.97 |
| Woodruff | ★★ | ★ | ★ | 5.14 | 4.63 | 5.47 |

TABLE 18

Average Per-Acre Real-Property Assessments, 1860, 1865, 1868, 1870, 1871, 1873 (continued)

| County | 1860 | 1865 | 1868 | 1870 | 1871 | 1873 |
|--------|------|------|------|------|------|------|
| UPLAND | | | | | | |
| Benton | 4.82 | 1.46 | * | 5.63 | 3.23 | 4.80 |
| Boone | ** | ** | ** | 6.00 | 3.60 | 4.39 |
| Baxter | ** | ** | ** | ** | ** | 3.38 |
| Carroll | 5.85 | 2.18 | 4.68 | 4.01 | 3.61 | 4.71 |
| Conway | ** | 2.94 | 2.00 | 2.46 | 3.44 | 6.62 |
| Crawford | 9.06 | * | 4.33 | 6.45 | 4.52 | 4.20 |
| Franklin | 5.18 | 2.38 | 2.80 | 5.86 | 4.64 | 3.93 |
| Fulton | 3.14 | .65 | * | 2.03 | 2.23 | 1.80 |
| Greene | 3.85 | * | * | 1.53 | 3.06 | 2.41 |
| Hot Springs | 3.87 | * | 3.34 | 3.31 | 2.65 | 5.94 |
| Howard | ** | ** | ** | ** | ** | 3.15 |
| Izard | 3.63 | .99 | * | 2.32 | 2.55 | 2.73 |
| Johnson | 4.89 | 2.77 | * | 5.00 | 4.50 | 4.52 |
| Lawrence | 4.31 | 1.47 | * | 2.55 | 2.55 | 2.82 |
| Madison | 5.65 | 2.89 | * | 3.03 | 3.03 | 3.74 |
| Marion | 4.92 | 1.85 | * | 3.40 | 2.72 | 3.08 |
| Montgomery | 6.44 | 1.73 | 3.87 | 4.07 | 2.45 | 2.57 |
| Newton | 6.12 | .56 | 4.63 | 5.48 | 2.74 | 5.12 |
| Perry | 4.83 | 2.18 | * | 4.44 | 3.33 | 3.52 |
| Pike | 4.31 | 1.53 | 1.94 | 2.45 | 2.45 | * |
| Polk | * | 1.85 | .68 | 2.33 | 2.33 | 2.41 |
| Pope | 6.17 | 4.28 | * | 5.52 | 3.32 | 3.72 |
| Randolph | 3.41 | 2.10 | 1.61 | 2.69 | 2.28 | 2.73 |
| Saline | 3.57 | 1.41 | 1.40 | 2.29 | 2.74 | 2.87 |
| Sarber | ** | ** | ** | ** | ** | 4.41 |
| Scott | 4.11 | 1.93 | * | 3.06 | 2.93 | 2.86 |
| Searcy | 5.41 | 2.28 | 3.04 | 4.23 | 2.54 | * |
| Sebastian | 4.70 | 3.43 | 3.24 | 5.48 | 4.39 | 4.36 |
| Sharp | ** | ** | ** | 3.05 | 2.28 | 2.98 |
| Van Buren | 3.66 | 1.12 | 1.66 | 1.67 | 2.17 | 3.10 |
| Washington | 4.60 | 3.73 | * | 3.92 | 4.31 | 4.28 |
| Yell | 4.76 | 2.19 | 3.16 | 7.19 | 4.02 | 5.02 |

*No report.
**Not yet a county.

opponents charged, and most of the money went to actual improvements, but Democratic leaders denounced Republican fiscal policy as unfair, and they believed that the reassessors dealt especially harshly with the old elite. William E. Woodruff, Sr., complained that "carpetbag & scallawag authorities appraise the property of all old citizens at most extravagant figures." Threatened, the elite counterattacked politically. They charged that taxes were oppressive and that the funds raised were unnecessary and wasted. The latter charge was particularly important because it undermined Republican justification of the increases as producing benefits for the state.[32]

In 1869 Republican and Democratic opponents of Governor Clayton united to create the Liberal Republican party. Lieutenant Governor Johnson and seventeen Republican legislators began the movement in April when they conferred on political issues and, as a result, charged the state government with extravagance, mismanagement, and corruption in administering the railroad program, funding of the state debt, and handling departmental expenses. The dissidents also criticized use of the militia and declarations of martial law. Seeking Democratic support, they declared that they thought the time had come to end disfranchisement. Although they contended they were loyal Republicans, they criticized Clayton and his followers as "selfish and corrupt men . . . who are determined to continue in power at all hazards and to the last extremity." The editor of the newspaper they started at Little Rock, the *Liberal*, proposed building a new party that was progressive, yet honest and fiscally conservative.[33]

The Liberals held a state convention on October 14, 1869, and organized the new party. The leadership consisted primarily of Republican scalawags, but Democrats also participated. The delegates at Little Rock included such odd allies as Democrat Thomas C. Peek, who had edited Hindman's *Old-Line Democrat*; Abraham H. Ryan, former commander of the 3d Arkansas Cavalry (Union); John Edwards, former commander of the 18th Iowa Infantry and a postwar settler at Fort Smith; and John Kirkwood, a prominent wartime Unionist. Former governor Isaac Murphy endorsed the party, saying that "some means of relief must be devised or the life of every great interest of the state will be crushed out." The party platform reaffirmed goals announced the previous April and declared its intention to unite all opponents of the Clayton administration.[34]

32. W. E. Woodruff to Vance and Vance, November 18, 1869, M. L. Bell to Woodruff, December 31, 1870, both in Woodruff Papers; Little Rock *Daily Gazette*, July 9, October 15, 1869.

33. Little Rock *Daily Gazette*, April 14, 1869; Little Rock *Liberal*, May 6, June 2, August 18, 1869.

34. Little Rock *Daily Gazette*, October 14, 15, 1869.

The appearance of the Liberal party pushed Clayton to modify his program, although other internal party problems also encouraged his move to the political center. A faction led by Joseph Brooks that urged more radical economic and social programs to aid blacks and lower-class whites had split with Clayton and threatened to take over the party. On October 15, Clayton promised a group that serenaded him at the state house that he would work to restore the ballot to the disfranchised. By promising concessions, he could attract moderates, but he did not have to actually cope with an expansion of the electorate immediately: changing the franchise required a constitutional amendment, and that had to wait for the 1871 General Assembly.[35]

The schisms among the Republicans created questions of strategy for the Democrats. David Walker and others concluded that in the congressional and legislative elections of 1870, an active Democratic campaign would reunify the Republicans, lead to more rigorous registration standards, and stimulate fraud. They opposed party organization and supported fusion with the Liberal Republicans to place sympathetic men into office. Despite some opposition, the party's leaders adopted this policy and the Democrats did not hold a state convention. In the congressional districts they supported fusion candidates such as James M. Hanks (a prominent Unionist from Helena), Anthony A. C. Rogers, and John Edwards. Candidates ran as Democrats only for the legislature.[36]

Fusion was successful. In the legislative elections the Democrats took eight state senate seats, six short of a majority. In the house of representatives, the Democrats and Liberals had thirty-eight seats, four short of controlling it. Fusion candidates carried two congressional districts: Hanks and Edwards were elected. Congress gave Edwards' seat to Thomas Boles as the result of an election contest, but the raw figures show that the fusion candidate did poll the majority of votes. Only in the Second District was a straight-out Republican successful: Oliver P. Snyder, a scalawag, defeated Rogers.[37]

Despite election gains, the results of a fusion policy were not clear and many Democrats were disgruntled. Clayton Republicans kept control of the General Assembly and elected the governor to the United States Senate. They prevented Liberal lieutenant governor Johnson from becoming governor by moving him to the position of secretary of state, allowing a Clayton

35. *Ibid.*, October 17, 1869.
36. *Ibid.*, September 17, 21, 24, 1870; John Harrell to D. Walker, July 12, 1870, Walker to S. F. Clark, August 21, 1870, in Walker Papers.
37. Little Rock *Daily Gazette*, November 12, 15, 18, 19, 1870, January 17, 1871; Fayetteville *Democrat*, November 12, 1870.

supporter to become the new governor. Rather than backing away, the Republican majority aggressively pursued their original program. They created the offices of state geologist and superintendent of the penitentiary, revised the 1868 levee law, and passed a new university act. Their new tax bill raised taxes further. Despite Clayton's promises, his supporters refused to end disfranchisement on their own and simply recommended an amendment to lift the disabilities. Of even further concern, fusion congressman John Edwards, before he was unseated, had voted for the Ku Klux Act of April, 1871, which gave the president the power to use the army to enforce voting-rights legislation passed in 1870 and to suspend the writ of habeas corpus where the law was resisted. Edwards' performance caused the editor of the Arkadelphia *Southern Standard* to call the results of fusion "shameless betrayal." Editors of the *Standard*, the Washington *Telegraph*, the Fayetteville *Democrat*, and the *Arkansas Gazette* urged party reorganization and abandonment of fusion.[38]

Democratic members of the General Assembly responded to demands at a meeting held on March 23, 1871, to prepare for the 1872 elections. They named a new state executive committee composed of many members of the 1868 committee. Although pressured to hold a state convention, the committee decided only to urge the formation of district and county committees to organize the party. The leaders did not like the results of fusion but were reluctant to commit themselves to any particular course. The editor of the *Arkansas Gazette* urged caution, pointing to the 1868 election as a case in which Democratic victory had been undone by fraud. He warned: "What has been done once will be done again, if we do not outgeneral our opposers." Democratic leaders played a wait-and-see game.[39]

As the 1872 elections came closer, the central committee finally called a convention of the Democratic-Conservative party for June 19. The late date offered the Democrats the advantage of seeing first the results of the national Liberal Republican convention, the state Republican convention, the state Liberal Republican convention, and the national Republican convention. The delay, however, did not make their course clearer. The regular Republicans, called the "minstrels," had met and not nominated a state ticket. The "brindletail" Republicans, led by Joseph Brooks and opposed to the regulars, had also met and endorsed the national Liberal Republican party and its candidate for president, Horace

38. *Acts of Arkansas, 1871*, 88, 177–79, 201, 341, 351; Staples, *Reconstruction in Arkansas*, 385–86; *Congressional Globe*, 41st Cong., 2d Sess., p. 3656; Arkadelphia (Ark.) *Southern Standard* in Fayetteville *Democrat*, May 31, 1871; Little Rock *Daily Gazette*, March 21, 26, 28, 1871.
39. Little Rock *Daily Gazette*, March 28, May 1, 31 (quotation), December 28, 1871.

Greeley. Organizing the Reform Republican party, the delegates nominated Brooks for governor on a platform that promised an end to disfranchisement, reduction of taxes, general government retrenchment, and limitation of the appointive powers of the governor. On June 18 the Liberal Republican party of Arkansas held its convention, endorsed the national Liberals, then left a decision on what local candidates to support to its executive committee.[40]

The Democratic central committee decided on fusion with the Liberals despite objections to their nomination of Brooks, who had a reputation for extreme radicalism—the editor of the *Arkansas Gazette* called Brooks "hardly the proper man for governor." The Democratic dilemma was expressed by that editor: "The hardest nut to crack is regarding the line of conduct to be followed in state policy. Shall we throw the conservative vote to the Brindle ticket already nominated, or to that of the Minstrels, yet to take the field—or shall we put forward a ticket that represents the popular heart, and, regardless of frauds and oppressions, take the chances?" The Democrats concluded that "it would be unwise and inexpedient for the Democratic party to nominate a state ticket," although they urged committees to run local candidates. Without openly supporting Brooks, the convention delegates that June did endorse the brindletail platform.[41]

Fusion had risks because it blurred distinctions between the political parties. Colonel Lucien C. Gause, for one, objected to it, saying that he had come to the Democratic convention "to save his party and his people" and that the position the delegates were taking would "bury both in oblivion." Leaders supported fusion, however, because they thought it was the quickest way to regain power. In 1871 they also thought that by endorsing the brindletail platform without the candidate, they could force concessions either from Brooks or from the minstrels. In August a committee of Reform Republicans, Liberal Republicans, and Democrats met to try to put together a unified state ticket. The brindletails refused to make concessions, and the Liberals bolted to nominate their own candidate for governor. When that candidate refused, Liberals returned reluctantly to their support of the Reform party.[42]

40. *Ibid.*, March 6, 9, May 19, 22, 23, 24, June 19, 1872; Little Rock *Morning Republican,* May 19, 1872, B. F. Askew to Harris Flanagin, March 25, 1872, A. H. Garland to Flanagin, June 6, 1872, U. M. Rose to Flanagin, May 31, 1872, all in Harris Flanagin Papers, AHC; A. H. Garland to Henry Rector, April 3, 1872, in Stebbins Collection.

41. Little Rock *Daily Gazette,* May 25, 28, June 20, 21, 22, 1872; A. H. Garland to Harris Flanagin, June 13, 1872, in Flanagin Papers.

42. Little Rock *Daily Gazette,* June 19, 22, July 24, August 9, 1872.

The minstrels responded to Brooks's nomination by nominating Elisha Baxter, a prewar resident of Independence County who had served in the General Assembly in 1854 and 1858 and had been elected to the United States Senate by the Murphy government in 1864. Although a supporter of Clayton, Baxter had a more conservative reputation than Brooks and potentially would attract more white voters. The minstrels also proposed a platform as liberal as that of the reformers in an effort to counter Brooks's concessions.[43]

The election ended in dispute. Both Brooks and Baxter claimed victory, but the official returns gave Baxter the edge, and the minstrel legislature would not favor Brooks in a contest. Brooks and his supporters threatened a confrontation but contented themselves with gathering evidence for a legal challenge. The Democrats initially sided with Brooks, but when Baxter promised to restore the vote to the disfranchised, their course was less clear. Despite their initial backing of the brindletails, party leaders decided in the circumstances to support Baxter. In the General Assembly the Democrats cooperated with Baxter in the election of Stephen W. Dorsey to the United States Senate, and Baxter in turn endorsed a legislative act submitting a constitutional amendment regarding the franchise to a popular vote. At the same time, the Democratic minority in the legislature moved closer to Baxter by helping block efforts by Brooks to hold hearings on the disputed election. The Democratic alliance with Baxter was strengthened further when John McClure and other Republican leaders split with the governor, leaving Baxter to search elsewhere for support.[44]

The franchise election was held on March 3, 1873. It attracted little publicity and only a third as many voters as had participated in the 1872 gubernatorial contest. The amendment passed by a ten-to-one margin. Despite the low turnout, the amendment's passage ensured that the Democrats would regain political power. Party leaders were divided over how to deal with the existing government until they could secure power on their own. At Little Rock leaders such as Augustus Garland, U. M. Rose, Samuel W. Williams, Freeman W. Compton, and Elbert H. English supported Baxter. David Walker, James Mitchell, Anson W. Hobson, Thomas Gunter, and other leaders in the countryside backed Brooks as he continued his efforts to have the 1872 election overturned. These

43. Little Rock *Morning Republican,* August 22, 1872.
44. Staples, *Reconstruction in Arkansas,* 397–401, 408–24; George H. Thompson, *Arkansas and Reconstruction: The Influence of Geography, Economics, and Personality* (Port Washington, N.Y., 1976), 104–110, 112–30.

rival leaders cooperated, however, in special elections ordered for November 4, 1873. In those elections the effect of the constitutional amendment was readily apparent: Democrats regained control of the General Assembly.[45]

Besides retaking control of the legislature, the Democrats, because of their role in the Brooks-Baxter conflict, also had virtual control over the governor's office. Brooks had taken his claim to the governor's office to the courts, which also heard proceedings against Baxter's right to the governorship initiated by supporters of John McClure. The courts rebuffed Brooks in 1873, but in April, 1874, the Pulaski County District Court issued a ruling stating that he was entitled to the office. Baxter refused to concede the issue, so Brooks's supporters forcibly seized the state capitol. Baxter moved his offices to a nearby hotel, where he continued to act as governor. In what became known as the "Brooks-Baxter War," each side prepared for an armed conflict while appealing for recognition by the federal government. After complex negotiations, a special session of the legislature, and presidential recognition, the "war" ended with Baxter, now a firm Democratic ally, holding the office and powers of the governorship.[46]

After the conclusion of the Brooks-Baxter episode, the Democratic legislature acted to consolidate its power by authorizing a constitutional convention. An election on June 30 approved the call and elected Democratic-Conservatives to seventy of the ninety-one convention seats. The Democratic victory ensured that the new constitution would reflect the interests of the party and its supporters. After writing the document, the delegates set October 4, 1874, as the date for an election to ratify it and to elect officials for the new government. On September 18 the Democrats held a state party convention at which they in effect announced an abandonment of fusion by naming Democratic candidates for all state offices despite pressure by some elements to nominate Baxter for the governorship. The Democrats no longer needed to make accommodations with enemies. Party leaders skillfully maneuvered Baxter into declining a nomination, then

45. Little Rock *Daily Gazette,* April 11, 1873; Van Buren (Ark.) *Press,* April 29, 1873; M. L. Bell to W. E. Woodruff, July 17, 1873, in Woodruff Papers; T. W. Gunter to David Walker, April 16, 1874, in Stebbins Collection; S. S. Griffith to W. W. Mansfield, April 30, 1874, in W. W. Mansfield Collection, AHC; J. R. Berry to Joseph Brooks, July 17, 1873, in Murphy-Berry Family Collection, AHC; James Mitchell to D. Walker, July 1, 1873, D. Walker to S. W. Williams, April 2, 1874, both in Walker Papers; Thompson, *Arkansas and Reconstruction,* 113, 124–26, 148–58.

46. Thompson, *Arkansas and Reconstruction,* 128–30; Staples, *Reconstruction in Arkansas,* 408–24.

selected Augustus H. Garland for governor on a straight-out party ticket.[47]

In October the constitution carried by a vote of 74,379 to 23,420, and Democratic candidates won every major state office. The legislative elections resulted in a senate composed of thirty-one Democrats and two Republicans and a house with eighty Democrats and ten Republicans. Many of the men prominent in politics before the war and during it returned to power. The new governor, Garland, had been a Whig and Unionist before the war, but had made his peace with secessionists and served in the Confederate Congress. The new state treasurer was Thomas J. Churchill, prewar postmaster at Little Rock, Democratic supporter of Robert W. Johnson, and Confederate general. Attorney General Simon P. Hughes had been sheriff of Monroe County and a lawyer before the war, then a lieutenant colonel in the Confederate army. State Auditor William Read Miller had held that same office before the war and then with the Confederate state government. Elbert English and Freeman Compton, both former Confederate judges, were elected to the supreme court. David Walker, another successful candidate for a position on the supreme court, had been an antebellum Whig and the pro-Union president of the state secession convention but had served as a military judge in the Confederate army. Only Secretary of State B. B. Beavers was a political unknown.[48]

The election of 1874 ended a decade and a half of political upheaval, including the war and the period of experimentation and conflict that followed. The men who had governed in the 1850s and who represented the principal interests of that period, who had taken the state out of the Union and presided over the Confederacy, were back in power. The vision of society held by Democratic-Conservative leaders was seen in the constitutional convention of 1874 and in subsequent legislatures that they dominated. The Democratic party existed to protect the landed interests of the state. To protect those interests, the party inaugurated a period of government penury. Offices were eliminated and salaries of public officials reduced by as much as 50 percent. The debt of the state was scaled down by fifteen million dollars in 1874, and six million dollars worth of bonds were repudiated in 1877. In 1884 a constitutional amendment prohibited the payment of disputed portions of the prewar debt, the Holford bonds

47. M. L. Bell to W. E. Woodruff, September 12, October 16, 1874, in Woodruff Papers; W. W. Mansfield to David Walker, August 5, 1874, Jordan E. Cravens to W. W. Mansfield, August 11, 1874, David Walker to Mansfield, July 24, August 18, 1874, all in Mansfield Collection; Staples, *Reconstruction in Arkansas*, 408–22.

48. Harper, comp., "Prominent Members of the Early Arkansas Bar," 116; *Historical Report of the Secretary of State, Arkansas* (Little Rock, 1978), 227; Thompson, *Arkansas and Reconstruction*, 4–5.

(issued by the Real Estate Bank before the war), or railroad and levee bonds. These actions reduced the state debt by two-thirds, which in turn allowed a sharp reduction in taxes. The state was now restricted to a maximum rate of 1.0 percent of assessed value, county taxes to 0.5 percent, and municipal taxes to 0.5 percent (although another 0.5 percent was allowed to pay existing obligations). School taxes were also limited. Assessment was placed in local hands. Land interests were thus relieved of the tax burden that had been imposed on them.[49]

Although fiscal policy was the primary concern of the Democrats, they also reestablished the power of landowners over local economies, particularly labor. The new constitution gave county courts jurisdiction over matters such as vagrancy and apprenticeship. Justices of the peace received exclusive jurisdiction in contract cases not exceeding one hundred dollars and concurrent jurisdiction in cases not exceeding three hundred dollars. These provisions placed most landlord-tenant disputes in local hands, ensuring the power of landed interests. Subsequent legislatures gave local authorities a greater threat over laborers by tightening trespass laws and designating the theft of items valued at two or more dollars as grand larceny punishable by imprisonment of up to five years. The General Assembly also gave landlords a primary lien, superior to that of a laborer, on farm produce. In the 1875–1876 session the legislature made it illegal for renters to contract to sell cotton before it had been harvested and registered with the landowner. These actions put landlords in a position of dominance over local economic activity.[50]

The return of the Democrats in 1874 for all practical purposes restored Arkansas to those who had dominated it before the war. Political triumph accomplished what the antebellum landed interests had been trying to do since the war's end. It signaled the reassertion of their control of the political institutions that provided the framework for their economic and social power. The desperation with which they fought to regain their political position indicates that for many of them the fight was one for actual survival.

49. Constitution of the State of Arkansas, 1874, Art. XIV, Sec. 3, Art. VII, Sec. 46, Art. XII, Sec. 4, Art. XIV, Sec. 3, Art. XVI, Secs. 8, 9, Amendment I; Clayton, *Aftermath of the Civil War, in Arkansas,* 353–56, 358–60; Thompson, *Arkansas and Reconstruction,* 233–39.

50. Constitution of the State of Arkansas, 1874, Art. VII, Secs. 28, 40, 65; *Acts of Arkansas, 1875–76,* 139–40; *Acts of Arkansas, 1874–75,* 72–73, 84–85, 90, 112, 128, 230–32.

# CONCLUSION
## Cotton, Landlords, and Democrats

THE LEGACY OF THE CIVIL WAR AND RECONSTRUCTION FOR
Arkansas was a somber one. Arkansas in 1874 was poorer relative to the
rest of the nation than it had been in 1860. The state's economy remained
primarily agricultural, while the rest of the nation industrialized and diversified. The census of 1900 showed the economic pattern that had developed
and that dominated into the 1950s. Manufacturing had become more important in that the value of manufactured goods now accounted for a larger
part of the value of all goods produced—about one-third in 1900—but this
difference reflected a decline in the value of agricultural goods more than
a real increase in industrial productivity. The population census showed
that 82 percent of workers in 1900 were engaged in agricultural or domestic
pursuits, roughly the same percentage as in 1860. The value of products
had changed, but not the jobs held by most Arkansans.[1]

The state's economy focused primarily on agriculture, and farms emphasized the cultivation of cotton. Existing statistics offer no firm basis for
comparison, but cotton may have dominated even more in 1900 than in
1860. In 1900 almost 40 percent of the state's farms derived their principal
income from cotton. Only livestock, the raising of which was the primary
endeavor of over 17 percent of farm units, challenged cotton for supremacy
as the state's leading cash product.[2]

Cotton was clearly king for landowners who used cash or share tenants,
the labor system that had developed after the Civil War, as the primary
means for cultivating their lands. Statewide by 1900, only 54.6 percent of
farms were operated by their actual owners. The rest were farmed by either
cash or share tenants. In the five counties with more than one-half of their
farm acreage devoted to cotton—Chicot, Crittenden, Jefferson, Lee, and
Phillips—tenants operated 78.2, 85.7, 77.5, 72.2, and 77.7 percent of the
farms. Black farmers particularly were caught in the tenant system. Across
the state 74.4 percent of black farmers were tenants in 1900. In the five
counties just listed, the respective percentages were 83.2, 91.7, 85.4, 79.6,
and 85.1.[3]

1. *Twelfth Census, 1900: Abstract*, Table 177, p. 383.
2. *Ibid.*, Table 119, p. 230.
3. *Ibid.*, Table 177, pp. 383–84; *Twelfth Census, 1900: Agriculture*, Pt. 1, Table 10, pp.
60–63.

The Democratic party dominated state government and provided the support that the landlords needed to maintain their system. Internal dissent and conflict characterized state Democratic politics, but as one historian has concluded, "the Delta region was a more powerful factor" and exercised greater muscle in party councils. The party supported the interests of the landlords by providing minimum government. They built no roads and few schools, and even expected the state penitentiary to be self-supporting. The inadequacy of public education was particularly obvious when compared with the rest of the nation. In 1900, 67.2 percent of Arkansas' school population enrolled in schools, compared with 68.9 percent nationally— but the Arkansas schools met for only 77.5 days per year as against a national average of 144.6. Only North Carolina had a shorter school year. The only states that spent less per capita for their schools were six other Deep South states.[4]

Tied to agriculture and controlled by a government that did nothing, Arkansas was doomed to economic depression. The 1900 census showed the state to be forty-fourth of forty-eight in the per capita value of its combined agricultural and manufacturing product: at $95.19 per person, it lagged far behind the national average of $233.34, not to mention the $300 and more of the industrialized northern states. Only New Mexico and three southern neighbors, Alabama, Georgia, and Mississippi, had smaller averages of production. Although twenty-second in agricultural productivity, Arkansas was forty-sixth in manufacturing with a $34-per-capita value that bettered only Mississippi's $26 and Idaho's $25.[5]

The social cost of economic depression was high, and Arkansas lagged behind the rest of the modernizing nation. Urbanization and the creation of a better-trained work force were part of the new patterns of modern life developing elsewhere. Arkansas' population remained primarily rural into the middle of the twentieth century. In 1900 only about 8.5 percent of the state's population lived in towns with more than 2,500 inhabitants. The increase over the 1-percent "urban" population of 1860 was slight. Without towns and changing values, with the continuing control of a Democratic party concerned with the state's landed interests and uninterested in education, the work force remained largely unskilled and immobile. In 1900

4. U.S. Department of the Interior, *Report of the Commissioner of Education* (Washington, D.C., 1901), Table 4, p. lxvi, Table 7, p. lxvix; Richard L. Niswonger, *Arkansas Democratic Politics, 1896–1920* (Fayetteville, 1990), 3 (quotation); Boyce Drummond, "Arkansas Politics: A Study of a One-Party System" (Ph.D. dissertation, University of Chicago, 1957); Joe T. Seagraves, "Arkansas Politics, 1874–1918" (Ph.D. dissertation, University of Kentucky, 1973).

5. *Twelfth Census, 1900: Abstract,* Table 177, pp. 383–84.

adult illiteracy was widespread. In that year 11.5 percent of whites could not read. The rate of illiteracy among blacks was 43 percent.[6]

That Arkansas faced problems after the war is unquestionable. The nature of the situation is open to debate. Arkansans blamed the war and Reconstruction and the losses that they suffered for their condition, but the problems were in many ways the product of their own decisions.

In 1860 Arkansas was a state with an expanding economy. Throughout the previous decade economic growth had been closely tied to high prices for cotton, the availability of slave labor, and the investments of outside businessmen and merchants in the system. Although facing the risks of agriculturalists everywhere, farmers had found it possible to make money in antebellum Arkansas, and they rushed to take advantage of it.

The economic conditions that existed in Arkansas in the 1850s, particularly growth and agrarianism, made possible its peculiar society. Whites lived in a relatively homogeneous community, linked by the belief that economic opportunities and limited government promised a chance for upward social mobility for each individual. The prewar experiences of many of them reinforced those ideas. The slaves, who constituted one-third of the state's total population and provided the bulk of the labor force in the cotton fields, existed outside that white community, sharing neither its belief in nor its potential for social mobility. Some few whites may have viewed blacks paternalistically, but the majority saw them as laborers whose work was essential to their owners' and the white community's economic success, and thus as a group whose continued enslavement was critical to the very survival of that community's way of life.

In the antebellum world of Arkansans, government and politics provided the legal framework within which the economy and society survived. The ultimate expression of government's role in protecting the existing system was exhibited when the state's political leaders seceded in 1861. Their decision was aimed ultimately at protecting slavery, the survival of which was essential in their minds not just to preserve a system of labor, but also to save the cotton economy and the society and beliefs that slaves and cotton made possible.

The war shook the roots of antebellum society. Individuals and their families suffered terribly, and poor whites particularly felt the pinch brought about by the destruction of material resources and the other burdens of the conflict. War challenged the unity of antebellum Arkansas and brought to the surface tensions submerged within the old system. The appearance of

---

6. *Ibid.*, Table 57, p. 74; Donald B. Dodd and Synelle S. Dodd, *Historical Statistics of the South, 1790–1970* (University, Ala., 1973), 6–7.

new attitudes and new leaders made it possible to move Arkansas in new directions during the war. The ambitions of wartime Unionists, as opposed to those of 1860 and 1861, reflected new ideas about the state's future. The Unionists found a vehicle in the Lincoln government created in occupied Arkansas in 1863, but their development as an alternative political force was frustrated by Union commanders who believed themselves in the state to conquer an enemy, not stage a political revolution. War also destroyed slavery, the underpinning for the old order, raising the ambitions and hopes of the freedmen, but those expectations were thwarted by a liberating army that had little interest in securing full freedom for these people.

The war ended leaving death and widespread destruction of property, but it did not destroy the relative position of whites within the antebellum social order. On the whole, the elite emerged from the conflict still the elite. Poorer classes hardly survived the war at all, but those who did remained economically beneath the wealthy planters and merchants who had dominated the state before secession. It was the survival of the latter class that eventually made it seem that the war had changed so little. Individuals suffered, but the war brought about no significant change in the means of production—the land—or in who owned it. The war may have caused some individuals to think differently about the state's future, but it did not change the basic interests of the people who had dominated society in 1860. In 1865 those people had to figure out a way to use their land to restore their fortunes and ensure their futures.

The path wealthy Arkansans saw to economic reconstruction was simple. They had to go back into cotton, which was bringing unparalleled prices in 1865 and offered a way to rapidly recoup any losses caused by the war. The only real problems they faced were the change in the labor force caused by emancipation and the existence of a government that they did not control. The labor force, even though free, was quickly reorganized to their needs, in part with the help of the Union army and the Freedmen's Bureau. The Unionist government created during the war offered little resistance to their resurgence either. Investing their all in growing cotton, they were undercut only by catastrophic weather and the collapsing price of their commodity through the postwar years. Their decisions placed them increasingly in the hands of their creditors, but even that did not destroy them. The new situation simply meant that they had to exercise tighter control over their land and their labor so as to extract the necessary profits.

The greatest potential for change caused by the war developed not during the conflict itself but in the postwar years. Congressional Reconstruction, brought about largely by the northern belief that the South had not fully accepted defeat, posed a real threat to the old system, bringing to power at the state and local levels individuals with little concern for the economic position of the elite. The state could have experienced revolutionary changes during the late 1860s and early 1870s under a Republican party that was willing to tax the landed interests in an effort to develop the transportation and educational systems, all with the hope of more diversified economic development. The taxes could have destroyed the power of the old landed elite and changed economic opportunities for the rest of the people of the state. National reconstruction policy and the skill of the old leaders prevented that from taking place. Regaining control over their labor force and, ultimately, over their government, the old leadership struggled successfully to protect themselves even in their reduced circumstances.

In the years following the collapse of Republican power, the postwar elite used the Democratic-Conservative party to impose on the state the institutions necessary to ensure that their position was not undermined. Rather than the New South envisioned by those who urged industrialization and diversification in other southern states, the legacy of Arkansas' leadership was a society that protected the interests of an elite whose power grew out of an economy too closely tied to the cultivation of a single crop. Unfortunately for this elite and for the state, this crop continued to decrease in economic importance into the next century. With the decline of cotton, political leaders were forced to impose even more stringent measures of the type developed in 1874. Control of labor and minimum government services became the cardinal principles of postbellum governmental policy. Redemption of Arkansas by the Democratic-Conservative party in 1874 worked very well for the landowners of the state. Not only were the large planters served well in subsequent years, but to a considerable degree the interests of all who owned their own farms were also protected. For the majority of the state's population, however, the legacy was a sober one. The power of the landed elite and their political spokesmen created a world that resisted modernization and one in which the lives of Arkansans in 1900 would not be dissimilar to those of their forebears in 1860.

When one looks at the history of Arkansas between 1850 and the end of Reconstruction, the evidence is there to make all sorts of conclusions concerning the continuity or discontinuity of antebellum society into the postbellum world. Individual experiences took place that suggest the antebellum world was absolutely destroyed, and looking at parts of the overall society may lead to the same conclusions. The war and postwar conditions impoverished the middle and the lower classes. Some individuals, however, were barely affected by the war. For the economic elite as a class, the war brought great material loss but little change in their local social and political power. The decline in the price of cotton reduced the wealth of the great planters as well as of the small farmers who grew the crop, but the basic economy with its single emphasis, the society dominated by those who controlled the land, and the government that served the interests of that elite had not changed at all. The same group—even the same individuals—who had been on top in 1860 remained to a large extent the masters in 1874. The Civil War unquestionably visited real suffering upon the people of Arkansas. The war ended slavery and changed the institutions connected with that particular labor system, but it did not alter other basic institutions of the antebellum world.

# BIBLIOGRAPHY

PRIMARY SOURCES

MANUSCRIPT COLLECTIONS

American History Center, University of Texas
    Brewster, J. D. Papers.
    Chambers, William W. Papers.
    Wright, George T. Papers.
Amistad Research Center, Tulane University
    American Missionary Association Papers.
University of Arkansas at Fayetteville
    Braly, Amanda M. F. M., Family Papers.
    McCollom, A. O. Papers.
    Reynolds, D. H. Papers.
    Turner, Jesse. Correspondence.
    Walker, David. Papers.
University of Arkansas at Little Rock
    Brownfield, Theron. Papers.
    Heiskell, J. N. Collection
      Dickinson, Everard B. Papers.
      Rust Family Papers.
    Ledger Collection.
    Moore, John Merrick. Papers.
    Sandford-Everett Family File.
    Scott, John R. H. Collection.
    Trulock Family Letters.
    Wilcox and Thompson Family Papers.
Arkansas History Commission
    Anderson Papers.
    Arkansas County Records
      MS Tax Rolls, 1850, 1860, 1866.
    Barksdale, William H. Journal.
    Bliss, Calvin C. Papers.
    Brown, John W. Diary.
    Caldwell, James E. Papers and Journal.
    Cook, Sue. Diary.
    Earle-Ward Family Papers.

Eno, Clara. Collection
   Williams, D. C. Papers.
Edmondson, Mary Sale. Diary.
Flanagin, Harris. Papers.
Fletcher, Elliott H. Papers.
Gillett, Orville. Papers.
Goodrich, Ralph L. Collection.
Gulley, L. C. Collection.
Haney, J. H. Diary.
Hanks, James M. Diary.
Kellam, Robert F. Diary.
Kie Oldham Collection.
Mansfield, W. W. Collection.
Martin Family Papers.
Martin, James E. Papers.
Martin, Jared. Papers.
Miller, Enoch K. Papers.
Montgomery Family Papers.
Morgan, Asa. Collection.
Murphy-Berry Family Collection
Pulaski County. Loose Probate Files.
Sims, Mary Owen. Journal.
Small Manuscripts Collection
   Campbell, John. Letters.
   Herring, Fred J. Collection.
   Hibbard, Alpha. Diary.
   Kerr, John. Letter.
   Lindsay Letter.
   McRae, Annie. Letter.
   Meek Letters.
   Nelson, Sarah A. Letter.
   Patrick, Mary S. Diary.
   Smith, E. Jane. Letter.
Stebbins, A. Howard. Collection.
Strong-McColloch Family Papers.
Washburn, Josiah W. Family Papers.
Wassell, Samuel Spotts. Family Collection.
Williams, Samuel W. Papers.
Woodruff, William E. Papers.
Young, William R. Papers.
Duke University

Benson, Burwell. Papers.
Carrigan, John W. Papers.
Chambers, James S. Papers.
Jones, Kimbrough. Papers.
Knight Collection.
Love, Mathew N. Papers.
Pickett, William J. Papers.
Pursley, Mary Frances Jane. Papers.
Sheppard, James. Papers.
Turner, Jesse. Papers.
Illinois State Historical Library
Smith, J. W. Letters.
Library of Congress
Johnson, Andrew. Papers.
Lincoln, Robert Todd. Papers.
Mann, Mary Tyler. Papers.
Louisiana State University at Baton Rouge
Golsen Brothers Papers.
Hilliard, Mrs. Isaac. Diary.
Pinson Papers.
Louisiana State University at Shreveport
Booker and Martin Family Papers.
Pendleton, George M. Family Letters.
National Archives
Records of the Bureau of Refugees, Freedmen, and Abandoned Lands,
Record Group 105.
Southern Collection, University of North Carolina
Armstrong Papers.
Wheat Family Papers.
Tennessee State Library and Archives
Brown, Campbell, and Richard Ewell. Papers.
Douglas–Maney Papers.
Knight Papers.
Wood Family Papers.

PUBLISHED DOCUMENTS

*Acts of Arkansas*. Various publication places and dates.
Adjutant General (Arkansas). *Report of the Adjutant General of Arkansas, for the Period of the Late Rebellion, and to November 1, 1866*. Washington, D.C., 1867.

*Arkansas House Journal.* Various publication places and dates.

*Arkansas Senate Journal.* Various publication places and dates.

Auditor, Office of the (Arkansas). *Biennial Report of the Auditor of Public Accounts of the State of Arkansas.* Various publication places and dates.

Constitutional Convention (Arkansas). *Debates and Proceedings of the Convention Which Assembled at Little Rock, January 7, 1868.* Little Rock, 1868.

————. *Journal of the Convention of Delegates of the People of Arkansas Assembled at the Capitol, January 4, 1864.* Little Rock, 1870.

————. *New Constitution with the Acts of the General Assembly of the State of Arkansas.* Little Rock, 1865.

Conway, Elias N. *Message of Elias N. Conway, Governor of Arkansas, to Both Houses of the General Assembly, November 6, 1860.* Little Rock, 1860.

*Report of the General Superintendent of Freedmen, Department of the Tennessee and the State of Arkansas for 1864.* Memphis, 1865.

*Report Relative to Leasing Abandoned Plantations and Affairs of the Freed People in the First Special Agency.* Washington, D.C., 1864.

U.S. Bureau of Refugees, Freedmen, and Abandoned Lands. *Report of the Commissioner of the Bureau of Refugees, Freedmen, and Abandoned Lands for the Year 1867.* Washington, D.C., 1867.

————. Alvord, John W. *Sixth Semi-Annual Report on Schools for Freedmen, July, 1868.* Washington, D.C., 1868.

U.S. Census Bureau. *Eighth Census, 1860: Agriculture.*

————. *Eighth Census, 1860: Manufactures.*

————. *Eighth Census, 1860: Population.*

————. *Eighth Census, 1860: Statistics.*

————. *Ninth Census, 1870: Compendium.*

————. *Ninth Census, 1870: Statistics.*

————. *Seventh Census, 1850: Compendium.*

————. *Seventh Census, 1850: Statistical View of Each of the States and Territories.*

————. *Tenth Census, 1880: Compendium.*

————. *Twelfth Census, 1900: Abstract.*

————. *Twelfth Census, 1900: Agriculture.*

————. Hilgard, Eugene W. *Report on Cotton Production in the United States.* Washington, D.C., 1884.

U.S. Congress. *Biographical Dictionary of the United States Congress, 1774–1989: Bicentennial Edition.* Washington, D.C., 1989.

————. 40th Cong., 1st Sess.

     *Senate Executive Documents,* No. 14 (Ser. 1308).

————. 39th Cong., 1st Sess.

*House Executive Documents*, No. 11 (Ser. 1255).
*House Executive Documents*, No. 70 (Ser. 1256).
*House Reports*, No. 30 (Ser. 1256).
*Senate Executive Documents*, No. 27 (Ser. 1238).
―――. 39th Cong., 2d Sess.
*House Miscellaneous Documents*, No. 15 (Ser. 1302).
*Senate Executive Documents*, No. 6 (Ser. 1276).
U.S. Department of the Interior. *Report of the Commissioner of Education.* Washington, D.C., 1901.
*The War of the Rebellion: A Compilation of the Official Records of the Union and Confederate Armies.* 128 vols. Washington, D.C., 1880–1901.
Warren, Joseph, comp. *Extracts from Reports of Superintendents of Freedmen. First series, May, 1864.* Vicksburg, 1864.
―――. *Extracts from Reports of Superintendents of Freedmen. Second Series, June 1864.* Vicksburg, 1864.
Yeatman, James E. *Report to the Western Sanitary Commission in Regard to Leasing Abandoned Plantations, with Rules and Regulations Governing the Same.* St. Louis, 1864.

NEWSPAPERS

*De Bow's Review* (New Orleans), 1851, 1857
Des Arc (Ark.) *Citizen*, 1861
Fayetteville *Arkansian*, 1859–61
Fayetteville *Democrat*, 1869, 1870, 1873
Fort Smith (Ark.) *Herald*, 1851, 1867–74.
Fort Smith (Ark.) *New Era*, 1863–74
Helena (Ark.) *Shield* and *Southern Shield*, 1850–62
Little Rock *Arkansas Banner*, 1850–51
Little Rock *Arkansas Gazette*, 1850–74
Little Rock *Arkansas Whig*, 1851–55
Little Rock *Daily Conservative*, 1866–67
Little Rock *Daily Pantograph*, 1865–66
Little Rock *Evening Republican* and *Morning Republican*, 1867–74
Little Rock *Liberal*, 1869
Little Rock *National Democrat*, 1864–65
Little Rock *Old-Line Democrat*, 1859–61
Little Rock *Patriot*, 1862
Little Rock *True Democrat*, 1852–62
Little Rock *Unconditional Union*, 1864–66
Memphis *Daily Argus*, 1866

Pine Bluff (Ark.) *Dispatch*, 1866–68
Van Buren (Ark.) *Press*, 1860–61, 1871–72
Washington (Ark.) *Telegraph*, 1850–65

PUBLISHED LETTERS, MEMOIRS, DIARIES, AND OTHER PRIMARY SOURCES

Baker, Russell P., ed. " 'This Old Book': The Civil War Diary of Mrs. Mary Sale Edmondson of Phillips County, Arkansas." *Phillips County Historical Quarterly*, X (March, 1972), 1–14, (September, 1972), 1–11, (December, 1972), 1–8, XI (March, 1973), 1–10, (June, 1973), 1–10, (September, 1973), 1–9, (December, 1973), 1–10, XII (March, 1974), 1–10, (June, 1974), 2–10.

Bearss, Edwin C., ed. *The Civil War Letters of Major William G. Thompson*. Fayetteville, 1966.

Blackburn, George M., ed. *"Dear Carrie . . .": The Civil War Letters of Thomas N. Stevens*. Mt. Pleasant, Mich., 1984.

Breckenridge, Mary E. "Adventures on a Hospital Boat on the Mississippi." *Phillips County Historical Quarterly*, I (December, 1962), 31–42.

Britten, Wiley. *Memoirs of the Rebellion on the Border, 1863*. Chicago, 1882.

"Cheatham Letter." *Clark County Historical Journal* (Winter, 1979–80), 107.

Chester, Samuel H. *Pioneer Days in Arkansas*. Richmond, Va., 1927.

Clayton Powell. *The Aftermath of the Civil War, in Arkansas*. New York, 1915.

*Confederate Women of Arkansas in the Civil War, 1861–65: Memorial Reminiscences*. Little Rock, 1907.

Cook, Sue. "Diary of Sue Cook." *Phillips County Historical Quarterly*, IV (December, 1965), 29–42, (March, 1966), 25–42, V (December, 1966), 32–40, VI (March, 1967), 33–41, (December, 1967), 30–40, (March, 1968), 20–33.

Cox, Florence Marie Ankeny, ed. *Kiss Josey for Me*. Santa Ana, Calif., 1974.

Cunningham, Carolyn R., ed. "The Legacy of Love: The Cotton Correspondence: Part I." *Phillips County Historical Quarterly*, VI (March, 1968), 34–37.

Davenport, Edward., ed. *History of the Ninth Regiment of Illinois Cavalry Volunteers* Chicago, 1888.

Dowell, Mrs. Walter A., ed. "The Job Neill Letters." *Independence County Chronicle*, VIII (1966), 27–37

Dyer, Gustavus W., and John Trotwood Moore, comps. *The Tennessee Civil War Veterans Questionnaires*. 5 vols. Easley, S.C., 1985.

Eison, James R., ed. "A Letter from Dardanelle to Jonesville, South Carolina." *Arkansas Historical Quarterly*, XXVIII (1969), 72–75.

Evans, Clarence, ed. "Memoirs, Letters and Diary Entries of German Settlers in Northwest Arkansas, 1853–1863." *Arkansas Historical Quarterly*, VI (1947), 225–49.

Ewing, Laura. "The Retreat from Little Rock in 1863." *Independence County Chronicle*, V (1963), 3–17.

Gaughan, Mrs. T. J., ed. *Letters of a Confederate Surgeon.* Little Rock, 1960.

Hackett, Otis. "Excerpts from the Diaries and Letters of Reverend Otis Hackett." *Phillips County Historical Quarterly*, I (1962), 23–48.

Hornor, Joseph M. "Some Recollections of Reminiscences of My Father." *Phillips County Historical Quarterly*, X (1971), 11–16.

Huckaby, Elizabeth Paisley, and Ethel C. Simpson, eds. *Tulip Evermore: Emma Butler and William Paisley, Their Lives in Letters, 1857–1887.* Fayetteville, 1985.

Hudson, James J., ed. "From Paraclifta to Marks' Mills: The Civil War Correspondence of Lieutenant Robert C. Gilliam." *Arkansas Historical Quarterly*, XVII (1958), 272–302.

"Indiana Troops at Helena." *Phillips County Historical Quarterly*, XVI (March, 1978), 20–31, (September, 1978), 1–8, XVII (March, 1979), 11–21, (June, 1979), 34–42, XVIII (June/September, 1980), 1–8, XIX (December/March, 1980), 1–7.

"Indigent Soldiers' Families." *Journal of the Hempstead County Historical Society*, XI (1987), 34–38.

Langsdorf, Edgar, ed. "The Letters of Joseph H. Trego, 1857–1864, Linn County Pioneer." *Kansas Historical Quarterly*, Pt. 2, XIX (August, 1951), 287–309, Pt. 3, XIX (November, 1951), 381–400.

Lemke, W. J., ed. "The Mecklin Letters Written in 1863–64 at Mt. Comfort by Robert W. Mecklin." *Washington County Historical Society Bulletin*, X (1955).

Longacre, Edward G., ed. "Letters from Little Rock of Captain James M. Bowler, 112th U.S. Colored Troops." *Arkansas Historical Quarterly*, XL (1981), 740.

McBrien, D. D., ed. "Letters of an Arkansas Confederate Soldier." *Arkansas Historical Quarterly*, II (March, 1943), 58–70, II (June, 1943), 171–84, II (September, 1943), 268–86.

McLean, William Edward. *The 43d Regiment of Indiana Volunteers.* Pine Bluff, Ark., 1981.

Moneyhon, Carl H., ed. "Life in Confederate Arkansas: The Diary of Virginia Davis Gray, 1863–1866." *Arkansas Historical Quarterly*, Pt. 1, XLII (Spring, 1983), pp. 47–85, Pt. 2, XLII (Summer, 1983), pp. 134–69.

Olsen, Louise P. "Some Reactions of Union Soldiers Stationed in the South During the Civil War." *Arkansas Historical Quarterly*, X (1951), 46–57.

Park, R. A. S., ed. *"Dear Parents:" The Civil War Letters of the Shibley Brothers of Van Buren.* Fayetteville, 1963.

Pearson, Benjamin F. "Benjamin F. Pearson's War Diary." *Annals of Iowa,* first installment, XV (1925), 83–129.

"Post Civil War Reminiscences of James Madison Hudson." *Jefferson County Historical Quarterly,* VII (1978), 5–11.

Powell, Wilson, ed. "Jacksonport's 'Arkansas Traveler' and the Civil War Letters of Thaddeus Rice." *Independence County Chronicle,* XIII (July, 1972), 2–15.

Quattelbaum, Amy, ed. "Letters from the Attic." *Jefferson County Historical Quarterly,* VII (1977), 17–21.

Rawick, George P., ed. *The American Slave: A Composite Autobiography.* 19 vols. Westport, Conn., 1972.

"Reminiscences of the Late Lon Slaughter as Told to Mrs. E. D. Wall, September 3, 1920." *Arkansas Historical Quarterly,* VIII (1949), 167–69.

Sperry, A. F. *History of the 33d Infantry.* Des Moines, 1866.

Stanley, Dorothy, ed. *The Autobiography of Sir Henry Morton Stanley.* New York, 1909.

Stillwell, Leander. *The Story of a Common Soldier of Army Life in the Civil War.* Erie, Kans., 1917.

Thompson, Tommy R., ed. "Searching for the American Dream in Arkansas: Letters of a Pioneer Family." *Arkansas Historical Quarterly,* XXXVIII (1979), 167–81.

Tilley, Nannie M., ed. *Federals on the Frontier: The Diary of Benjamin F. McIntyre.* Austin, 1953.

"The 28th Wisconsin Infantry at Helena." *Phillips County Historical Quarterly,* XII (March, 1974), 11–20, (June, 1974), 12–25, (September, 1974), 36–40, XIII (March, 1975), 23–33, (September, 1975), 7–17, (December, 1975), 7–16, XIV (March, 1976), 30–40, (June, 1976), 30–38.

Vining, George T. "An Early Settler Remembers." *Jefferson County Historical Quarterly,* VI (1975), 9–28.

Waterman, Robert E., and Thomas Rothrock. "The Earle-Buchanan Letters of 1861–1876." *Arkansas Historical Quarterly,* XXXIII (1974), 99–174.

Whitman, Clifford Dale, ed. "Private Journal of Mary Ann Owen Sims." *Arkansas Historical Quarterly,* XXXV (1976), 142–87.

Williams, Charles G., ed. "A Saline Guard: The Civil War Letters of Col. William Ayers Crawford, C.S.A., 1861–1865." *Arkansas Historical Quarterly,* Pt. 1, Vol. XXXI (1972), pp. 328–55, Pt. 2, Vol. XXXII (1973), pp. 71–93.

Worley, Ted R., ed. "Documents Relating to the Arkansas Peace Society of 1861." *Arkansas Historical Quarterly,* XVII (1958), 82–111.

———. "Diary of Lieutenant Orville Gillett, U.S.A., 1864–1865." *Arkansas Historical Quarterly,* XVII (1958), 164–204.

### A Note on Secondary Sources

The primary focus of this study is the overall impact of the Civil War on a society. The literature that it directly addresses is examined in the Introduction, and a reassessment of that literature here would be repetitious. There are many topics within the work that are touched upon tangentially, but a complete bibliography of all of the secondary work on those topics would be extensive and the reader would be served better by consulting specialized bibliographic guides to the period or topics than by my providing a simple listing of everything that has been consulted. Some works, however, have provided framework and focus for this study in addition to those addressed in the Introduction, and should be mentioned here.

There is no single modern study of the antebellum South that integrates the extensive literature written on the subject in the last thirty years; however, James Oakes, *The Ruling Race: A History of American Slaveholders* (New York, 1982) offers a good overview of southern society in assessing the slaveholding class in the South (particularly its ideology concerning slavery), its relationships with other members of society, and its importance in producing secession. Drew Gilpin Faust's *The Creation of Confederate Nationalism: Ideology and Identity in the Civil War South* (Baton Rouge, 1988), although focusing on the war years, adds to an understanding of the ideological structure holding together the prewar South and its role in producing secession.

There have been few efforts to analyze the dynamics of the lower classes in the South since Frank L. Owsley and his students in the 1940s; however, Donald L. Winters, " 'Plain Folk' of the Old South Reexamined: Economic Democracy in Tennessee," *Journal of Southern History,* LII (November, 1987), 565–86, provides an excellent assessment of the literature concerning these people. This study of mobility among the "plain folk" also shows the problems associated with any effort at characterizing their interests.

Emory M. Thomas' *The Confederate Nation, 1861–1865* (New York, 1979) and *The Confederacy as a Revolutionary Experience* (New York, 1971) are useful introductions to the wide variety of topics dealing with the Civil War experience in the South. The former is good particularly for its extensive bibliography, which covers much of the older material on economic and social change brought about by the war. The latter is particularly insightful in its examination of the variety of ways the war affected southern communities.

Thomas' books are somewhat dated, and some very good recent books have addressed issues dealt with by Thomas and have expanded questions raised by him. One issue of particular concern has been what happened within white society when it faced the problems of war. Wayne K. Durrill, *War of Another Kind: A Southern Community in the Great Rebellion* (New York, 1990), examines the breakdown of social order in Washington County, North Carolina, suggesting that the result was increasing class tension and local guerilla warfare. Michael Fellman, *Inside War: The Guerrilla Conflict in Missouri During the Civil War* (New York, 1989), also chronicles the collapse of society and relates domestic conditions in a western state to the outbreak of guerrilla warfare.

Another topic that has attracted recent attention is the war's effect on slavery. John Cimprich, *Slavery's End in Tennessee, 1861–1865* (University, Ala., 1985), and Clarence Mohr, *On the Threshold of Freedom: Masters and Slaves in Civil War Georgia* (Athens, Ga., 1986), show the extent of the changes that the war brought about—changes that would have altered slavery even in a postwar South that had won. James L. Roark, *Masters Without Slaves: Southern Planters in the Civil War and Reconstruction* (New York, 1977), shows how the changes in slavery and ultimate emancipation altered the general attitudes of slaveowners, but particularly their ideas regarding their former slaves.

George C. Rable, *Civil Wars: Women and the Crisis of Southern Nationalism* (Urbana, Ill., 1989), has broken new ground in his assessment of the impact of the war on southern women. This study concludes that short-term changes produced by the war ultimately gave way to resubordination of women in order to achieve other social goals.

Many of the works cited in the Introduction deal directly with Reconstruction; however, Eric Foner, *Reconstruction: America's Unfinished Revolution, 1863–1877* (New York, 1988), offers the best synthesis of recent work on this period and the revisionist scholarship that provides the background for my own attitudes toward the topic. Foner's bibliography, while selected, is close to comprehensive on studies done since the 1950s.

# INDEX